WINE BUYERS' GUIDE 2006

OVER 2,250 WORLD WINES
RATED BY QUALITY AND VALUE FOR MONEY

INTRODUCTION BY
ROBERT JOSEPH

MITCHELL BEAZLEY   NATIONAL

WINE BUYERS' GUIDE
by Robert Joseph

First published in Great Britain in 2005
by Mitchell Beazley, an imprint of Octopus
Publishing Group Ltd, 2–4 Heron Quays,
London E14 4JP

Revised edition 2006

ISBN: 1 84533 168 0

A CIP record for this book is available
from the British Library

Set in The Sans, Gill Sans, Giovanni
Printed and bound in Italy by Rotolito

Commissioning Editor Hilary Lumsden
Executive Art Editor Yasia Williams-
Leedham
Managing Editor Juanne Branquinho
Design Tim Pattinson
Typesetting Michael Florence
Production Gary Hayes

HOW THE BOOK WORKS

You would easily be forgiven for imagining that you are surrounded by a jungle of confusing bottles and labels in your local off-licence or supermarket wine section. It is hardly surprising that some people react by choosing a wine they already know, or grab one that's covered with special offer stickers. But, that's no way to be sure of carrying home the most interesting, tasty, and great value bottles. This is where the *Wine Buyers' Guide* comes in. It is the next best thing to having a team of wine experts in your pocket or handbag every time you go shopping.

The book is split into three sections. The first section features an introduction by Robert Joseph that covers all of the basics – from the best temperatures for particular wine styles and the ideal dishes to drink them with to advice on storage, vintages, and investment.

Then comes the listing of the 2,500 medal winners and best-value wines from the 2004 International Wine Challenge, the world's biggest wine competition. The wines are listed by country (and region), award, and price. Also featured are descriptions culled from the tasting panels' notes, guide prices, and codes of the stockists. Finally, there is a crucially useful key to all those stockist codes revealing where all of the wines can be bought.

KEY TO SYMBOLS USED

☆ particularly good value

★ truly great value

CONTENTS

INTRODUCTION

Quickly, bring me a beaker of wine, so that I may wet my mind and say something clever.

Aristophanes

Winemaking may be the second oldest profession in the world. According to research by Patrick McGovern of the University of Pennsylvania, it looks as though primitive man was crushing and fermenting grapes as long ago as 8,500 BC. Even more fascinatingly for those who like to take the Bible literally, McGovern and his fellow researchers' discoveries in Turkey's Taurus Mountains seem to add credibility to the story that Noah planted the first wine grapes close to Mount Ararat almost as soon as he had landed the ark.

Whenever the tide of wine began to flow, until quite recently, the business of selecting the red or white you were going to drink was as simple as picking a draught beer in your local today. If there was any choice on offer, all you had to remember was the names of half a dozen – mostly French – regions and, if you wanted to appear really sophisticated, a few of the better recent vintages. Now, however, as a glance at the 9,100 different bottles that were lined up for tasting at the 2005 International Wine Challenge will tell you, the picture is very different.

Wine is now being produced almost everywhere from Dorking in Surrey to Dalat in Vietnam, and top-quality wines are increasingly being made in unfamiliar parts of traditional countries. Serious vintage charts now have to take as much account of the weather in Chile's Casablanca Valley and Sicily, as Chablis and St-Emilion.

Australia, which was once the subject of a Monty Python joke, now sells more wine in Britain, and at a higher price per bottle, than France. Twenty-five years ago, grape names rarely appeared on wine labels; now they not only feature on most of them, but also include a bewildering and ever-growing number of newcomers such as Tannat, Tarango, and Touriga Nacional, of which few non-wine-buffs will ever have heard. And if that were not confusing enough, the shelves are punctuated by bottles with names like Fat Bastard, Old Git, and Yellow Tail, which seem to have nothing to do with wine at all.

Some people, quite reasonably, turn their backs on the jungle of bottles and make straight for the same wine they bought last week, one whose name they know, or that's on offer at the biggest discount. But doing that can be rather like restricting your diet to a tiny repertoire of recipes, or your television viewing to a single channel.

This book is for everyone who enjoys wine and would like to get the best out of it. Within the main section, you will find details and descriptions of 2,200 of the best and best-value wines from the 2005 International Wine Challenge, the world's biggest and toughest wine competition. If you are looking for a great classic burgundy or Bordeaux, a top example from the New World, or a cheap, tasty red or white to serve at a party, this is the place to look.

In this first section I endeavour to provide a concise survival guide to wine drinking at the beginning of the twenty-first century. From advice on matching wine and food to tips on storing, serving, investing – and even information on wine and health…

Tis pity wine should be so deleterious,
For tea and coffee leave us much more serious.

Lord Byron

BREAKING NEWS

You can't, they say, have too much of a good thing. But, as the world's winemakers proved in 2004, it is perfectly possible to produce 20 million hectolitres – enough to fill 2,660,000,000 bottles – more wine than the world wants to buy and drink. Readers of British newspapers were alerted to the current size of the wine lake by headlines describing plans to uproot vineyards in historic regions like Bordeaux, Muscadet, and Beaujolais, and by the decision by producers in southern France to give away 400,000 bottles as a protest against their economic plight. This kind of benificence came as a welcome contrast to 2005's series of demonstrations, riots, bombings of government buildings, and emptying of wine vats in southern France. At one point during the hot, dry summer, angry Languedoc winegrowers actually managed to set light to a Spanish wine tanker while the driver was asleep in his cab.

It was no coincidence that France's winemaking regions were the most stalwart supporters of the successful "Non" campaign against the European consitution; most embattled vignerons laid the blame for their problems firmly at the door of globalisation in general and the Anglo-Saxon, free-market notions of New World winemakers in particular. Ironically, however, there were plenty of English-speaking producers whose own survival seemed just as questionable. In Australia, grapes that might have been used to make 2005 vintage wine were left on the vines, because there were no buyers for them. California producers dealt with their excess stock by slashing prices, while reports published in early 2005 suggested that a third of South Africa's and nearly half of Australia's smaller wineries were trading at a loss.

Big is Beautiful

As classic economic theory would suggest, all this excess wine is good for bargain-hunting wine lovers. It has helped to fill the stores with buy-one-get-one-free offers and pegged the average cost of a bottle at just £3.79; incredibly, seven bottles out of every eight sell for less than a fiver. Unfortunately, however, far too many of those attractively priced bottles now bear identical labels. The sad truth is that in countries like Britain, we do our shopping in a shrinking number of chains which, in turn are reducing the numbers of wines they offer. Tesco, the UK's most successful grocer, cut its range by fifteen per cent this year and most of its competitors followed suit. Over thirty per cent of the wines we now buy come from ten Australian, California, and South African brands – and their share of the market grows with every year.

Sideways Glances

On the brighter side, 2005 saw the release of two full-length cinema films in which wine was the major focus. A lengthy, hopelessly one-sided but often highly watchable documentary called *Mondovino* attempted to do to vinous globalization what Michael Moore's *Farenheit 9/11* had tried to do to George W Bush (and to similar effect). Few people saw it in Britain, but it filled cinemas in France and is now available on video. Far more entertainingly, *Sideways* hilariously introduced outsiders to the kind of passion wine creates in California – as well as to the notion of Pinophilia. In America, the love of the principal character for the Pinot Noir, helped to raise sales of wines made from this variety by over a third. Just as remarkably, disdainful remarks in the film about the Merlot – currently California's most widely planted variety – drove would-be sophisticated New Yorkers to hesitate before pulling out $100 bottles which were once the pride of their cellar.

UNDERSTANDING THE TASTE

I rather like bad wine… one gets so bored with good wine.

Benjamin Disraeli

Buying wine today can often be like buying a gallon of paint. Just as the manufacturer's helpful chart can be daunting, with its endless shades of subtly different white, the number of bottles and the information available on the supermarket shelves can make you want to give up and reach for the one that is most familiar, or most favourably priced. If you're not a wine buff, why should you know the differences in flavour between wines made from the same grape in Meursault in France, Mendocino in California, and Maipo in Chile? Often, the retailer has provided descriptive terms to help you imagine the flavour of the stuff in the bottle. But these, too, can just add to the confusion. Do you want the one that tastes of strawberries or raspberries, the "refreshingly dry", or the "crisp, lemony white"? I can't promise to clear a motorway through this jungle, but, with luck, I will give you a path to follow when you are choosing a wine, and one from which you can confidently stray. Stated simply, the flavour you get out of any wine is the result of a combination of twelve factors.

1. THE GRAPE VARIETY (or varieties) from which it is made. This is the DNA of the wine. If your parents are tall and fair haired, you will probably inherit these characteristics, just as wines made from Cabernet Sauvignon will tend to taste of blackcurrant and those produced from Gewurztraminer will remind people of lychees.

2. THE CLIMATE If your blonde parents brought you up on a farm in Australia you'll probably look and behave differently to someone with a similar-looking mother and father living in an apartment block in Liverpool. Wines made from grapes grown in warm countries – or in unusually warm years like 2003 in Europe – will taste richer and riper than ones from cooler places and vintages.

3. SOIL Merlot grapes, like roses, like to be grown in clay; Chardonnay, like clematis, prefers chalk. Whatever the climate, the character of the soil will have an influence on the flavour of the wine.

4. WINEMAKING The vine-grower and winemaker (sometimes one and the same person) are like a gardener and a chef. The way the vines are grown, the yield per plant, harvesting date, and method of picking (by hand or machine) will all have a role to play; as will the way the grapes are handled in the winery. Also crucial are the temperature of fermentation (cooler = fresher wine; warmer = richer), the use of oak barrels, the blending of different grapes, and the period in barrel or tank before bottling.

5. LAWS, CUSTOMS, AND LOCAL FASHION In Europe, strict laws control the way wines can be made. Chardonnay is illegal in Bordeaux, for example, and Spanish Gran Reserva wines have to be aged for longer than Reservas. But in the New World, local fashion is important too. It's a rare Californian who doesn't age his Chardonnay in oak barrels.

6. AGE As humans age they become more or less attractive. Some grow wiser, others go senile. Some do both. As wine ages it also changes, losing its initial fruitiness and taking on other, "winier", characteristics. Grape varieties age differently (Chardonnay is generally better older than Sauvignon Blanc) but the climate, soil, and winemaking are important. Some wines – most inexpensive reds and whites of any price – are simply not built to last.

7. HEALTH Some wines are ill before they are bottled (because of faulty winemaking); some – around five per cent – are spoiled by mouldy corks that can make the wine taste musty or simply a little flat. Others that have escaped these fates can be spoiled by being stored in places that are too hot or dry. Corks can then leak and the wine will age prematurely and become like sherry or downright vinegary.

8. THE WAY IT IS SERVED If our first impressions of people are affected by the way they are dressed, our reaction to a wine is bound to reflect the smartness of the label, the use of a decanter, and shape and thinness of the glass. But temperature will be important too. Just compare warm and cool orange juice.

9. THE SETTING Meeting someone at a bus stop is very different from being interviewed by them or encountering them on a blind date. The same wine will taste quite different at a cocktail party, a barbecue, and a smart dinner.

10. FOOD Just try eating a Mars Bar with a glass of Coke. They don't go well together, but a cup of tea can go down a treat with fish and chips. A spicy dish can apparently strip all the flavour from a wine that was quite tasty with plainly roasted chicken.

11. PRECONCEPTION If you have been told that the person you are about to meet is a supermodel or a convicted rapist, the information given to you will probably influence your reaction to them. It is hard to ignore the label on a bottle of Dom Pérignon Champagne or Château Latour – or a sticker saying "Bulgarian Bargain – Buy One Get Two Free".

12 PERSONAL TASTE If you don't have a sweet tooth, you probably won't enjoy a £200 bottle of Château d'Yquem any more than the best pudding Gordon Ramsay can invent. There's no law to say you have to like Champagne.

TASTING VS DRINKING

The English language offers some useful pairs of terms. You can simply see something happen, or you can watch it; you can hear a sound, or you can listen to it; you can drink a wine, or you can taste it. A recent survey revealed that over half the people questioned could not remember the nationality of the wine they last drank in a restaurant, its grape variety, or producer. Reading this, I wondered if they might have had stronger memories of the dishes they ate, or the waiter, or the decor. And I bet they would have had almost perfect recall of every goal and save in the most recent football match they watched. Our capacity to remember anything depends on how much attention we pay to it. And with even local bistros charging £75 for dinner with a bottle of house red, I reckon that, however delightful the company, it may be worth focusing a little more closely on the flavours in the glass.

Tasting

Wine tasting is surrounded by mystery and mystique. But it shouldn't be – because all it really consists of is asking yourself two questions: do you like the wine? And does it taste the way you expect it to? Champagne costs a lot more than basic Spanish cava, so it should taste recognizably different. Some do, some don't.

SEE The look of a wine can tell you a lot. Assuming it isn't cloudy (send it back if it is), it will reveal its age and hint at the grape and origin. Some grapes, like Burgundy's Pinot Noir, make naturally paler wines than, say, Bordeaux's Cabernet Sauvignon; wines from warmer regions have deeper colours. Tilt the glass away from you over a piece of white paper and look at the rim of the liquid. The more watery and brown it is, the older the wine (Beaujolais Nouveau will be pure violet).

SWIRL Vigorously swirl the wine around the glass for a moment or so to release any reluctant and characteristic smells.

SNIFF You sniff a wine before tasting it for the same reason you sniff a carton of milk before drinking it. The smell can tell you more about a wine than anything else. If you don't believe me, try tasting anything while holding your nose. When sniffing, take one long sniff or a few brief ones. Concentrate on whether the wine seems fresh and clean, and on any smells that indicate how it is likely to taste.

What are your first impressions? Is the wine fruity, and, if so, which fruit does it remind you of? Does it have the vanilla smell of a wine that has been fermented or matured in new oak barrels? Is it spicy? Or herbaceous? Sweet or dry? Rich or lean?

SIP Take a small mouthful and (this takes practice) suck air between your teeth and through the liquid. Look in a mirror while you're doing this: if your mouth looks like a cat's bottom and sounds like a child trying to suck the last few drops of Coke through a straw, then you're doing it right. Hold the wine in your mouth for a little longer to release as much of its flavour as possible. Focus on the flavour. Ask yourself whether it tastes sweet, dry, fruity, spicy, herbaceous. Is there just one flavour, or do several contribute to a "complex" overall effect? Now concentrate on the texture of the wine. Some – like Chardonnay – are mouth-coatingly buttery, while others – like Gewurztraminer – are almost oily. Muscadet is a wine with a texture that is closer to that of water.

Reds, too, vary in texture; some seem tough and tannic enough to make the inside of one cheek want to kiss the inside of the other. Traditionalists rightly claim that tannin is necessary for a wine's longevity, but modern winemakers distinguish between the harsh tannin and the "fine" (non-aggressive) tannin to be found in wine carefully made from ripe grapes. A modern Bordeaux often has as much tannin as old-fashioned examples – but is far easier to taste and drink.

SPIT The only reason to spit a wine out – unless it is actively repellent – is simply to remain upright at the end of a lengthy tasting. I have notes I took during a banquet in Burgundy at which there were dozens of great wines and not even the remotest chance to do anything but swallow. The descriptions of the first few are perfectly legible; the thirtieth apparently tasted "very xgblorefjy". If all you are interested in is the taste, not spitting is an indulgence; you should have had ninety per cent of the flavour while the wine was in your mouth. Pause for a moment or two after spitting the wine out. Is the flavour still there? How does what you are experiencing now compare with the taste you had in your mouth? Some wines have an unpleasant aftertaste; others have flavours that linger deliciously in the mouth.

A Way with Words

Before going any further, I'm afraid there's no alternative but returning to the thorny question of the language you are going to use to describe your impressions.

When Washington Irving visited Bordeaux 170 years ago, he noted that Château Margaux was "a wine of fine flavour – but not of equal body". Lafite on the other hand had "less flavour than the former but more body – an equality of flavour and body". Latour, well, that had "more body than flavour". He may have been a great writer, but he was evidently not the ideal person to describe the individual flavours of great Bordeaux. Michelangelo was more poetic, writing that the wine of San Gimignano "kisses, licks, bites, thrusts, and stings…". Modern pundits say wines have "gobs of fruit" and taste of "kumquats and suede". Each country and generation comes up with its own vocabulary. Some descriptions, such as the likening to gooseberry of wines made from Sauvignon Blanc, can be justified by scientific analysis, which confirms that the same aromatic chemical compound is found in the fruit and wine. Then there are straightforward descriptions. Wines can be fresh or stale, clean or dirty. If they are acidic, or overly full of tannin, they will be "hard"; a "soft" wine, by contrast, might be easier to drink, but boring. There are other less evocative terms. While a watery wine is "dilute" or "thin", a subtle one is "elegant". A red or white whose flavour is hard to discern is described as "dumb". Whatever the style of a wine, it should have "balance". A sweet white, for example, needs enough acidity to keep it from cloying. No one will enjoy a wine that is too fruity, too dry, too oaky, or too anything for long. The flavour that lingers in your mouth long after you have swallowed or spat it out is known as the "finish". Wines whose flavour – pleasant or unpleasant – hangs around, are described as "long"; those whose flavour disappears quickly are "short". Finally, there is "complex", the word that is used to justify why one wine costs ten times more than another. A complex wine is like a well-scored symphony, while a simpler one could be compared to a melody picked out on a single instrument.

Should I Send it Back?

Wines are subject to all kinds of faults, though far fewer than they were as recently as a decade ago.

ACID All wines, like all fruit and vegetables, contain a certain amount of acidity. Without it they would taste dull and go very stale very quickly. Wines made from unripe grapes will, however, taste like unripe apples or plums – or like chewing stalky leaves or grass.

BITTER Bitterness is quite different. On occasion, especially in Italy, a touch of bitterness may even be an integral part of a wine's character, as in the case of Amarone.

CLOUDY Wine should be transparent. The only excuse for cloudiness is in a wine like an old burgundy whose deposit has been shaken up.

CORKED Ignore any cork crumbs you may find floating on the surface of a wine. Genuinely corked wines have a musty smell and flavour that comes from mouldy corks. Some corks are mouldier, and wines mustier, than others, but all corked wines become nastier with exposure to air. Around five per cent of wines – irrespective of their price – are corked.

CRYSTALS Unless someone is trying to kill you with powdered glass, ignore fine white crystals at the bottom of the bottle. These are just tartrates that occur naturally.

FIZZY Don't.

MADERIZED/OXIDIZED Madeira is fortified wine that has been intentionally exposed to the air and heated in a special oven. Maderized wine is stale, unfortified stuff that has been accidentally subjected to warmth and air. Oxidized is a broader term, referring to wine that has been exposed to the air – or made from grapes that have cooked in the sun. The taste is reminiscent of poor sherry or vinegar – or both.

SULPHUR (SO_2/H_2S) Sulphur dioxide is routinely used as a protection against bacteria that would oxidize (q.v.) a wine. In excess, sulphur dioxide may make you cough or sneeze. Worse, though, is hydrogen sulphide and mercaptans, its associated sulphur compounds, which are created when sulphur dioxide combines with wine. Wines with hydrogen sulphide smell of rotten eggs, while mercaptans may reek of rancid garlic or burning rubber. Aeration or popping a copper coin in your glass may clean up these characteristics.

VINEGARY/VOLATILE Volatile acidity is present in all wines. In excess, however – usually the result of careless winemaking – what can be a pleasant component (like a touch of balsamic vinegar in a sauce) tastes downright vinegary.

STORING

No man also having drunk old wine straightway desireth new: for he saith, The old is better.

Luke 5:39

Wine improves with age. The older I get, the better I like it.

Anon

According to a widely touted statistic, the average bottle of wine is drunk within twelve hours of its purchase. This is, of course, nonsense; the correct figure is probably closer to a week. But in either case, most people have little need for anything more than a rack in the kitchen with sufficient space to accommodate the contents of your Teswaybury bag. But, sooner or later, most of us discover that it can be worthwhile buying in larger quantities – on a shopping trip to Calais, or by mail, or from a wine warehouse that only offers its wine by the dozen.

Keeping that wine for a while reveals another truth that is often forgotten nowadays: some wines do benefit from being left to themselves for a few years, and finding older wines on the high street isn't easy. Before you know it, you're well on your way to thinking about having a cellar – or at least some kind of storage area – where your bottles are not going to be spoiled by the central heating.

Perfect Conditions

Wine is a living liquid containing no preservatives. Its life cycle comprises youth, maturity, old age, and death. When not treated with reasonable respect it will sicken and die.

Julia Child

While many of us live in homes that are ill-suited for storing wine, one can often find an unused grate or a space beneath the stairs that offers wine what it wants: a constant temperature of around 7–10°C/45–50°F (never lower than 5°C/41°F nor more than 25°C/77°F), reasonable humidity (install a cheap humidifier or leave a sponge in a bowl of water), sufficient ventilation to avoid a musty atmosphere, and, ideally, an absence of vibration (wines stored beneath train tracks – or beds – age faster). Alternatively, invest in a fridge-like Eurocave that guarantees perfect conditions – or even adapt an old freezer. Beware of cellars that are too damp, however. The humidity in mine has been sufficient to destroy a fair few of my labels.

Racks and Cellar Books

Custom-built racks can be bought "by the hole" and cut to fit. Square chimney stacks can be used too. If you have plenty of space, simply allocate particular racks to specific styles of wine. Unfortunately, even the best-laid cellar plans tend to fall apart when two cases of Australian Shiraz have to be squeezed into a space big enough just for one.

If the size of the cellar warrants it, give each hole in the rack a cross-referenced identity, from A1 at the top left to, say, Z100 at the bottom right. As bottles arrive, they can then be put in any available hole and their address noted in a cellar book, in which you can record when and where you obtained it, what it cost, and how each bottle tasted (is it improving or drying out?). Some people, like me, prefer to use a computer program (a database or spreadsheet).

To Drink or Keep?

Bad news isn't wine. It doesn't improve with age.

Colin Powell

But it is not every wine that will repay you for tucking it away. There are plenty of wonderful examples that never improve beyond the first few years after the harvest, and are none the worse for that. There are plenty of actors and singers who never manage to match the successes of their youth. On the other hand, like children who turn out to be late developers in their last years at school, some wines take a very long time to live up to their potential. So, what follows is a guide to which corks to pop soon and which bottles to treasure for a few years in the rack. But before letting you loose on it, I must give you an essential couple of words of warning. The longevity of any wine – even from the best addresses – depends on the vintage. Château Margaux from the ordinary 1997 harvest, for example, will be dead and gone long before the far better 1996. On the other hand, the likely lifespan will also be influenced by the quality of the vineyard and the way the wine is made. So, that Château Margaux 1997 will enjoy a much longer life than most of the other Bordeaux produced in that year.

DRINK AS SOON AS POSSIBLE Most wine at under £7.50, particularly basic whites such as Chardonnay and Sauvignon Blanc, and reds such as Merlot, Cabernet, and Zinfandel. French *vins de pays* and all but the best white Bordeaux; cheap red Bordeaux and most Beaujolais. Nouveau/Novello/Joven reds, Bardolino, Valpolicella, light Italian whites, almost all "blush" and rosé.

LESS THAN FIVE YEARS Most moderately priced (£5–10) California, Chilean, Argentine, South African, and Australian reds and whites. Petit-Château Bordeaux and Cru Bourgeois, and lesser Cru Classé reds from poorer vintages (such as 1997); basic Alsace, red and white burgundy, and better Beaujolais; Chianti, Barbera, basic Spanish reds; good mid-quality Germans. All but the very best Sauvignon from anywhere, Albariño from Spain, and Australian Verdelho.

FIVE TO TEN YEARS Most Cru Bourgeois Bordeaux from good years; better châteaux from lesser vintages; all but the finest red and white burgundy, and Pinot Noir and Chardonnay from elsewhere; middle-quality Rhônes; southern French higher flyers; good German, Alsace, dry Loire, Austrian Grüner Veltliner, and finer white Bordeaux; most mid-priced Italian and Portuguese reds; most Australian, California, and Washington State; South African, Chilean, and New Zealand Merlots and Cabernets on sale at under £15. Late harvest wines from the New World and medium-quality Sauternes.

OVER TEN YEARS Top-class Bordeaux, Rhône, burgundy, and sweet Loire from ripe years; top-notch German and Bordeaux late harvest, Italian IGT, Barolo, and the finest wines from Tuscany; best Australian Shiraz, Cabernet, Rieslings, and Semillon; and California Cabernet, and finest Merlot and Zinfandel.

SERVING

*The art in using wine is to produce the greatest possible
quantity of present gladness, without any future depression.*

The Gentleman's Table Guide, 1873

The Romans used to add salt to their wine to preserve it, while the Greeks favoured pine resin. Burgundians often refer to Napoleon's taste for Chambertin, but rarely mention that he diluted his red wine with water. A century ago, the English used to add ice to claret – and in winter, skiers drink hot "mulled" wine, adding sugar, fruit, and spices. Today, snobs sneer at Chinese wine drinkers who apparently prefer their Mouton Cadet with a dash of Sprite, but they conveniently forget about the sangria they probably enjoyed drinking in Spain. It's well worth questioning accepted rules – especially when they vary between cultures. The following advice is based on common sense and experience – to help you to enjoy serving and drinking wine. Ultimately, the best way to serve a wine is the way you and your guests are going to enjoy it. If a dash of Sprite makes a meanly acidic red Bordeaux easier to swallow, it certainly gets my vote.

Some Like it Hot

Some styles of wine taste better at particular temperatures. White and sparkling wines are more often served too cold than too hot. Paradoxically, it is the reds that suffer most from being drunk too warm. Few who serve wines at "room temperature" recall that the term was coined long before the invention of central heating. Be ready to chill a fruity red in a bucket of ice and water for five to ten minutes before serving.

Red Wine

When serving red, focus on the wine's flavour. Tough wines are best slightly warmer. The temperatures given are a rule-of-thumb guide:

1   *Beaujolais and other fruity reds: 10–13°C (50–55°F) – an hour in the fridge*
2   *Younger red burgundy and Rhônes and older Bordeaux, Chianti, younger Rioja, New World Grenache, and Pinotage: 14–16°C (57–61°F).*
3   *Older burgundy, tannic young Bordeaux, Rhônes, Zinfandel, bigger Cabernet Sauvignon, Merlot, Shiraz, Barolo, and other bigger Italian and Spanish reds: 16–18°C (61–64°F).*

Rosé

Rosé should be chilled at 10–15°C (50–59°F), or five to ten minutes in a bucket of ice and water.

White Wine

The cooler the wine, the less it will smell or taste. Subtler, richer wines deserve to be drunk a little warmer.

1   *Lighter, sweeter wines and everyday sparklers: 4–8°C (two or three hours in the fridge or 10–15 minutes in ice and water).*
2   *Fuller-bodied, aromatic, drier, semi-dry, lusciously sweet whites; Champagne; simpler Sauvignons; and Chardonnays: 8–11°C.*
3   *Richer, dry wines – burgundy, California Chardonnay: 12–13°C.*

The Perfect Outcome

The patented Screwpull is still the most reliable way to get a cork out of a bottle. The "waiter's friend" is the next best thing, especially the modern versions with a hinged section designed to prevent corks from breaking. Whatever corkscrew you choose, avoid the models that look like a large screw. These often simply pull through old corks. These fragile stoppers are often most easily removed using a two-pronged "Ah So" cork remover. But, these are tiresome for younger wines and useless for synthetic corks.

Which Glasses?

On occasions when no other glass was available I have enjoyed great wine from the glass in my hotel bathroom. I suspect, though, I'd have gotten more out of the experience if something a bit more stylish had come to hand. Glasses should be narrower across the rim than the bowl. Red ones should be bigger than white, because whites are best kept chilled in the bottle rather than warming in the glass. If you like bubbles in your sparkling wine, serve it in a flute rather than a saucer from which they will swiftly escape. Schott, Spiegelau, and Riedel are among a number of companies that now produce attractive glasses that are specially designed to bring out the best in particular styles of wine.

To Breathe or Not to Breathe?

After what may well have been a fairly lengthy period of imprisonment in its bottle, many a wine can be a bit sulky when it is first poured. Giving it a breath of air may help to banish the sulkiness and bring out the flavour and richness, which is why many people tend to remove the cork a few hours before the wine is to be served. This well-intentioned action, however, is almost a complete waste of time (the contact with oxygen offered by the neck of the bottle is far too limited). If you want to aerate a wine, you'd be far better off simply pouring it into a jug and back into the bottle just before you want to drink it. Broad-based, so-called "ship's decanters" not only look good, but also facilitate airing wine as it flows down the inside of the glass in a fine film. Alternatively, small devices are now available that bubble air into wine to mimic the effect of decanting.

As a rule, young red and – surprisingly perhaps – white wines often benefit from exposure to air, especially when the flavour of a white has been temporarily flattened by a heavy dose of sulphur dioxide. Older red wines, however, may be tired out by the experience and may rapidly lose some of their immediate appeal. Mature red Bordeaux, Rhône, and port, for example, may need to be decanted in order to remove the unwelcome mudlike deposit that has dropped to the bottom of the bottle. This initially daunting task is far easier than it seems. Simply stand the bottle up for a day before decanting it. Pour it very slowly, in front of a flashlight or candle, watching for the first signs of the deposit. Coffee filters suit those with less steady hands.

Order of Service

The rules say that white wines and youth, respectively, precede red wines and age; dry goes before sweet (most of us prefer our main course before the dessert); the lighter the wine, the earlier. These rules are often impossible to follow. What are you to do, for example, if the red Loire is lighter-bodied than the white burgundy? Can the red Bordeaux follow the Sauternes that you are offering with the foie gras? Ignore the absolutes but bear in mind the common sense that lies behind them. Work gently up the scale of fullness, "flavoursomeness", and quality, rather than swinging wildly between styles.

THE LABEL

Labels are an essential part of the business of wine nowadays, but even a century ago they barely existed. Wine was sold by the barrel and served by the jug or decanter. Indeed, the original "labels" were silver tags that hung on a chain around the neck of a decanter and were engraved with the word "claret", "hock", "port", or whatever.

Today, printed labels are required to tell you the amount of liquid in the bottle, its strength, where it was made, and the name of the producer or importer. Confusingly, though, labelling rules vary between countries and between regions. Labels may also reveal a wine's style: the grape variety, oakiness, or sweetness, for example. And, lastly, they are part of the packaging that helps to persuade you to buy one wine rather than another. When buying, bear in mind the following:

1   *Official terms such as* appellation contrôlée, grand *or* premier cru, qualitätswein *and* reserva *are as reliable in quality terms as official statements by politicians.*

2   *Unofficial terms such as "Réserve Personnelle" and "Vintner's Selection" are either a genuine reflection of the winemaker's pride in the wine, or a device to increase sales.*

3   *Knowing where a wine comes from is often like knowing where a person was born; it provides no guarantee of how good the wine will be. Nor how it will have been made (though there are often local rules). There will be nothing to tell you, for instance, whether a Chablis is oaky, nor whether an Alsace or Vouvray is sweet.*

4   *But, do look out for terms like "Oak Aged", "Fût de Chêne", "Barrel Select", and "Show Reserve" which indicate woodiness and expressions, while "Tradition" often refers to a less oaky French wine. "Moëlleux", "Doux", "Vendange Tardive", "Grains Nobles", "Amabile", and "Late" or "Noble Harvest", all refer to sweetness.*

5   *"Old Vines" or "Vieilles Vignes" may indicate better wine.*

6   *"Big name" regions don't always make better wine than supposedly lesser ones. Cheap Bordeaux is far worse than similarly priced wine from Bulgaria.*

7   *Don't expect wines from the same grape variety to taste the same: a South African Chardonnay may taste drier than one from California. The flavour and style will depend on the climate, soil, and producer.*

8   *Just because a producer makes a good wine in one place, don't trust him, or her, to make other good wines, either there or elsewhere. The team at Lafite Rothschild produces less classy Los Vascos wines in Chile; Robert Mondavi's inexpensive Woodbridge wines bear no relation to the quality of his Reserve wines from Napa.*

9   *The fact that there is a château on a wine label has no bearing on the quality of the contents.*

10 *Nor does the boast that the wine is bottled at that château.*

11 *Nineteenth-century medals look pretty on a label; they say nothing about the quality of the twentieth- or twenty-first century stuff in the bottle.*

12 *Price provides some guidance to a wine's quality: a very expensive bottle may be appalling, but it's unlikely that a very cheap one will be better than basic.*

Germany

- Village
- Grape variety
- Official quality – higher than qualitätswein
- Estate-bottled
- Producer
- Alcoholic strength
- Official quality approval code
- Estate
- Village, region, and country
- Vintage
- Vineyard
- Region
- Ripeness. Spätlese and Auslese are riper – and sweeter – unless "Trocken" (dry) appears on the label

Champagne

- Region
- Village
- The village where the producer is based
- Vintage
- The Champagne house – one of the best in the region
- White wine from white grapes: here, this means Chardonnay

NM means this is made by a merchant rather than a grower (RM) or cooperative (CM). And that it's not a secondary brand (MA).

Burgundy

- Region
- Village
- Premier cru – one of the best vineyards
- Vintage
- Estate-bottled
- Vineyard
- Appellation
- Producer – an estate rather than a merchant

GRAPE VARIETIES

Chardonnay, a character in the TV drama "Footballers' Wives", was the name given to 52 girls [in England] in 2002, with 14 others being called Chardonay. In 2003, the number of babies named Chardonnay rose to 91.
The Office for National Statistics

After tasting 120 bottles, Tim Atkin decides he'll drink "Anything But Chardonnay"
The Observer, *Sunday May 30, 2004*

Believe it or not, the first wines that described themselves as Chardonnay only began to arrive from Australia and California as recently as the beginning of the 1980s. Before that we drank plenty of Chardonnay, of course, but it came in bottles labelled as Chablis, white burgundy, or Mâcon Blanc. Merlot, once an unheralded ingredient in red Bordeaux, is now one of Britain's most popular styles, while in America, a wine called Marilyn Merlot (carrying a portrait of America's most famous actress and presidential mistress) enjoys cult status and sells for £50 per bottle. "Varietals" – made from single varieties of grape – are now officially the spice of wine.

Today, as the French authorities belatedly wrestle with the question of whether to allow regions like Burgundy and Bordeaux to benefit from this trend, producers and wine drinkers are acknowledging that shelves full of subtly varying versions of the same grape are getting rather boring. So, there is a growing move towards "new" varieties, such as Pinot Grigio and Malbec, that are already well known in Europe, and more obscure efforts like Grüner Veltliner, Carmenère, and Tannat. If the broadening of the range on offer has to be welcome – Chile's Carmenère is a particularly exciting recent arrival – there is plenty of evidence of wines chosen for the sake of novelty rather than flavour. Watch out for watery, flavourless Pinot Grigio.

When choosing wines from the New or Old World, it is worth bearing in mind the following thoughts. Some wines are made from single grape varieties – e.g. red or white burgundy, Sancerre, German Riesling, most Alsace wines, and Barolo – while others, such as red or white Bordeaux, California "Meritage" wines, port, and Châteauneuf-du-Pape, are blends of two or more types of grape. Champagne can fall into either camp, as can New World "varietal" wines, which, though generally labelled as "Chardonnay", "Merlot", "Shiraz", etc., can often – depending on local laws – contain up to twenty-five per cent of other grape varieties. Blends are not, per se, superior to single varietals – or vice versa.

White Grapes

The quest for alternative white grapes is arguably more fierce than the hunt for reds to replace Merlot and Cabernet Sauvignon. Heavy bets are being placed on Pinot Grigio – especially in the USA – but Sauvignon Blanc is enjoying a wave of popularity, Riesling is enjoying a revival, and there is a buzz of excitement surrounding Austria's Grüner Veltliners.

ALBARIÑO/ALVARINHO A rapidly rising star, producing fresh, dry, floral wines, generally in cool Rías Baixas in the Northern Spanish region of Galicia close to Bilbao. Occasionally oaked, it is at its best within a couple of years of the harvest. Not unlike Australia's Verdelho. Also grown in Portugal, where it is called Alvarinho and used – often in blends – for Vinho Verde.

CHARDONNAY The world's most popular and widely planted premium white grape variety, and the one whose name has become almost a synonym for dry white wine, is surprisingly hard to define. The flavour of any example will depend enormously on the climate, soil, and the particular type of clone. Burgundy, and the best California examples (Kistler, Peter Michael, Sonoma Cutrer), taste of butter and hazelnuts; lesser New World efforts are often sweet and simple, and often very melony (a flavour that comes from the clone). Australians range from subtle, buttery pineapple to oaky, tropical fruit juice. Petaluma, Giaconda, Coldstream Hills, and Leeuwin show how it can be done. New Zealand's efforts are tropical too, but lighter and fresher (Te Mata, Cloudy Bay). Elsewhere, Chile is beginning to hit the mark, as is South Africa (Jordan). In Europe, look around southern France (various *vins de pays*), Italy (Gaja), Spain, and Eastern Europe, but beware of watery cheaper versions.

CHENIN BLANC Loire variety with naturally high acidity that makes it ideal for fresh sparkling, dry, and luscious honeyed wines; also raw stuff like unripe apples and, when over-sulphured, old socks. Most California Chenins are semi-sweet and ordinary. South Africans once called it the Steen, and now use it for both dry and luscious sweet wines (the Forrester-Meinert is a great dry example). There are few good Australians (but try Moondah Brook) or New Zealanders (Millton).

GEWURZTRAMINER Outrageous, oily-textured stuff that smells of parma violets and tastes of lychee fruit. At its best in Alsace (Zind Humbrecht, Schlumberger, Faller), where identically labelled bottles can vary greatly in their level of sweetness. Wines that guarantee luscious sweetness will be labelled as either Vendange Tardive or – the intensely sweet – Sélection de Grains Nobles. Try examples from Germany, Chile, New Zealand, and Italy, too.

MARSANNE A classic, flowery, lemony variety used in the Rhône in wines like Hermitage (from producers like Guigal); in Australia – especially in Goulburn in Victoria (Tahbilk and Mitchelton); in southern France (in blends from Mas de Daumas Gassac); in Switzerland (late harvest efforts from Provins); and in innovative wines from California. At its best young or after five or six years.

MUSCAT The only variety whose wines actually taste as though they are made of grapes, rather than some other kind of fruit or vegetable. In Alsace, southern France, and northeast Italy it is used to make dry wines. Generally, though, it performs best as sparkling wine (Moscatos and Asti Spumantes from Italy, and Clairette de Die Tradition from France) and as sweet, fortified wine. Look out for Beaumes de Venise and Rivesaltes in southern France, Moscatel de Setúbal in Portugal, Moscatel de Valencia in Spain, and Liqueur Muscat in Australia (Morris, Chambers, Yalumba).

PINOT BLANC/PINOT BIANCO As rich as Chardonnay, but with less fruit, and far less often oaked. At its worst – when over-cropped – it makes neutral wine. At its best, however (usually in Alsace, where it is called Pinot Blanc), it can develop a lovely cashew-nut flavour. When well handled it can also do well in Italy, where it is known as Pinot Bianco (Jermann), and in Germany (especially in Baden), where it is called Weissburgunder.

PINOT GRIS/PINOT GRIGIO In 2003, Italy's winemakers shamelessly exported more Pinot Grigio to the USA (where it is now seen as a popular unoaked, easy-drinking alternative to woody, buttery Chardonnay) than they actually produced. Which was not bad going, when you consider just how many bottles bearing Pinot Grigio labels were still on offer in Italy and in pizza bars in the UK. The explanation for this particular loaves-and-fishes trick lies in the neutral flavour of most commercial Pinot Grigio; it was all too easy to use other grapes to produce wine that tasted just like it. It is also an Alsace variety known as Tokay but unrelated to any other Tokay. Wines can be spicy, and sweet or dry. The perfumed, aromatic qualities are associated with later-harvest examples. In Germany it is called Rülander and Grauerburgunder. Look for examples from Oregon (Eyrie), California, and New Zealand.

RIESLING The king of white grapes. Misunderstood, mispronounced – as Rice-ling rather than Rees-ling – and mistaken – for cheap German wine made from quite different grapes. At its best, it makes dry and sweet, grapey, appley, limey wines, which develop a spicy, "petrolly" character with age. Quality and character depend on soil – ideally slate – more than climate, and while the best examples come from Germany, in the Mosel (Loosen, Maximin Grünhaus) and Rhine (Schloss Johannisberg), and Alsace (Zind-Humbrecht, Faller), this variety can perform well in such different environments as Washington State, Australia's Clare Valley (Grosset, Tim Adams) and Western Australia, and New Zealand (Villa Maria). Not to be confused with unrelated varieties such as Lazki, Lutomer, Welsch, Emerald, or White Riesling. Particularly successful under screwcap.

SAUVIGNON BLANC The grape of Loire wines, such as Sancerre and Pouilly-Fumé, and white Bordeaux, where it is often blended with Sémillon. This gooseberryish variety performs wonderfully in Marlborough in New Zealand (where the flavours can include asparagus and pea pods), in South Africa (Thelema), and in Australia (Shaw & Smith, Cullen). Chile has good examples (from Casablanca) and Washington State can get it right, as can California (Cakebread, Frog's Leap), but many examples are sweet or overburdened by oak. Oaked US versions, wherever they are produced, are usually labelled Fumé Blanc, a term first coined by Robert Mondavi. Only the best of these improve after the first couple of years.

SÉMILLON In Bordeaux – in blends with Sauvignon – this produces sublime dry Graves and sweet Sauternes. In Australia (with no é), there are great, long-lived dry, pure (often unoaked) Semillons from the Hunter Valley (especially from Tyrrell and McWilliams) and (more usually oaked) Barossa Valley. Good "noble" late harvest examples have also been produced (by de Bortoli) in Riverina. Elsewhere in Australia the grape is sometimes blended with Chardonnay. Progress is being made in Washington State and South Africa (Boekenhoutskloof), but most examples from California, New Zealand, and Chile are disappointing.

VIOGNIER A cult grape, the Viognier was once only found in Condrieu and Château Grillet in the Rhône, where small numbers of good examples showed off its extraordinary perfumed, peach-blossomy, gingery character, albeit at a high price. Today, however, it has been widely introduced to the Ardèche, Languedoc-Roussillon, and California (where it is sometimes confused with the Roussanne), and made with loving care (though often over-oaked) in Eastern Europe, Argentina, and particularly Australia (especially Yalumba)

Red Grapes

The first red varietal to become a star was the Cabernet Sauvignon. Then the softer, Merlot claimed the spotlight, and now the featured artists range from Burgundy's Pinot Noir to Spain's Tempranillo, Italy's Sangiovese, and Portugal's Touriga Nacional.

BARBERA A widely planted, wild-berryish Italian variety at its best in Piedmont, where it is increasingly successful in blends with Nebbiolo and Cabernet (look out for Elio Altare, Bava, and Roberto Voerzio). Good in Argentina; making inroads into California and Australia (Crittenden "I"; Brown Bros).

BONARDA A juicy, berryish Italian variety that is doing well in Argentina, both by itself and in blends with grapes like Malbec and Syrah (try Zuccardi).

CABERNET FRANC Cabernet Sauvignon's "kid brother", this grape is usually a supporting actor in Bordeaux (though taking the lead at Cheval Blanc). In the Loire, it is used neat to make wines like Chinon and Bourgueil, and in Italy it produces often quite ordinary stuff in the northeast. At its best, the wine should be brightly blackcurranty.

CABERNET SAUVIGNON Usually associated with the great reds of the Médoc and Graves (in blends with Merlot), and top New World reds, especially from California, Chile, and Australia. Bulgaria has good-value examples, as do southern France (*vin de pays*), Spain (in the Penedés, Navarra, and – though this is kept quiet – Rioja). The hallmark to look for is blackcurrant, though unripe versions taste like a blend of weeds and capsicum. There are some great Cabernets in Italy, too. Good New World Cabernets can smell and taste of fresh mint, but, with time, like Bordeaux, they develop a rich "cigar box" character.

CARMENÈRE A recently rediscovered grape that was once widely grown in Bordeaux but is now only found in Chile (where it was mistaken for Merlot) and Italy (where the confusion is with Cabernet Franc). The flavour is like a cross between peppery Grenache and Merlot.

GAMAY The juicy, "boiled sweet" grape of Beaujolais and, to a lesser extent, the Loire and Gaillac. Needs the right soil and careful handling if it is not to make light, weedy wine.

GRENACHE/GARNACHA Freshly ground black pepper is the distinguishing flavour here, sometimes with the fruity tang of sweets. At home in Côtes du Rhône and Châteauneuf-du-Pape, it is also used in Spain (as the Garnacha) in blends with Tempranillo. There are good "bush vine" examples from Australia.

MALBEC Another refugee from Bordeaux, this lightly peppery variety is used in southwest France (for Cahors), the Loire, and Italy, where it generally produces dull stuff. It shines, however, in Argentina (Zuccardi, Catena), and is now also at home in both Chile and Australia.

MERLOT The most widely planted variety in Bordeaux and the subject of over-planting in California. In Bordeaux, where, in some vintages it performs better than Cabernet Sauvignon, it is at its best in Pomerol, where wines can taste of ripe plums and spice, and in St-Emilion, where the least successful wines show the Merlot's less lovable dull and earthy character. Wherever it is made, the naturally thin-skinned Merlot should produce softer, less tannic wines than Cabernet Sauvignon.

NEBBIOLO/SPANNA The red wine grape of Barolo and Barbaresco in Piedmont now, thanks to modern winemaking, increasingly reveals a lovely cherry and rose-petal character, often with the sweet vanilla of new oak casks. Lesser examples for earlier drinking tend to be labelled as Spanna.

PINOT NOIR The wild-raspberryish, plummy, and liquoricey grape of red burgundy is also a major component of white and pink Champagne. It makes red and pink Sancerre, as well as light reds in Alsace and Germany (where it is called Spätburgunder). Italy makes a few good examples, but for the best modern efforts look to California, Oregon, Australia, Chile, South Africa, and especially New Zealand (Martinborough, Felton Road).

PINOTAGE Almost restricted to South Africa, this cross between Pinot Noir and Cinsaut can, in the right hands, make berryish young wines that may develop rich, gamey-spicy flavours. Poorer examples can be dull and "muddy"-tasting. Try Beyerskloof, Kanonkop, Grangehurst, Spier, and Vriesenhof. Watch out also for "Cape Blends" made by adding Pinotage to other varieties such as Cabernet Sauvignon.

SANGIOVESE The grape of Chianti, Brunello di Montalcino, and a host of popular IGT wines in Italy, not to mention "new wave" Italian-style wines in California and Argentina. The recognizable flavour is of sweet tobacco, wild herbs, and berries.

SYRAH/SHIRAZ The spicy, brambly grape of the Northern Rhône (Hermitage, Cornas, etc.) and the best reds of Australia (Henschke Hill of Grace and Penfolds Grange), where it is also blended with Cabernet Sauvignon (just as it once was in Bordeaux). Marqués de Griñon has a great Spanish example, and Isole e Olena makes a fine one in Tuscany. Increasingly successful in California and Washington State and, finally, in South Africa. Surprisingly good, too, in both Switzerland and New Zealand.

TANNAT At home in Madiran in southwest France, this grape is now showing what it can do in Uruguay where its wines are less tough and more mulberryish than in Europe.

TEMPRANILLO Known under all kinds of names around Spain, including Cencibel (in Navarra), and Tinto del Pais (in Ribera del Duero) and Tinta Roriz in Portugal, the grape gives Spanish reds their recognizable strawberry character. Often blended with Garnacha, it works well with Cabernet Sauvignon. So far, little used in the New World, but watch out for examples from Argentina and Australia (Nepenthe).

ZINFANDEL/PRIMITIVO Until recently thought of as California's "own" variety, but now proved (by DNA tests) to be the same variety as the Primitivo in southern Italy. In California it makes rich, spicy, blueberryish reds (Turley and Ridge Vineyards), "ports", and (often with a little help from sweet Muscat) sweet pink "White Zinfandel". Outside California, Cape Mentelle makes a good example in Western Australia.

Other Varieties

Still members of the chorus rather than globally recognised stars in their own right, all of the following varieties can produce good wines when grown in the appropriate places and treated carefully. Watch out for them.

WHITE

Aligoté Lean burgundy grape, well used by Leroy.

Arneis Perfumed variety in Piedmont.

Bouvier Dull variety, used for late harvest wines in Austria.

Chasselas Usually bland variety that comes into its own in Switzerland.

Colombard Appley, basic; grown in southwest France, USA, and Australia.

Furmint Limey variety, traditionally used for Tokaj.

Godello Ancient aromatic Spanish grapegrown in the north west.

Kerner Dull German grape. Can taste leafy.

Müller-Thurgau/Rivaner An occasionally impressive grape; grown in both Germany and England.

Roussanne Fascinating Rhône variety that deserves more attention.

Scheurebe/Samling Grapefruity grape grown in Germany and Austria.

Silvaner/Sylvaner Often earthy variety of Alsace and Germany. Can shine in the Franken region of Germany.

Torrontés Grapey, Muscat-like variety of Argentina.

Ugni Blanc/Trebbiano Basic grape of southwest France and Italy.

Verdejo Lightly spicy Spanish grape that is not related to the Verdelho.

Verdelho Limey grape found in Madeira and Australian table wine.

Viura Widely planted, so-so Spanish variety.

Welschriesling Basic. Best in late harvest Austrians. Like Lutomer and Laszki and Italico "Rieslings", not related to the genuine Riesling.

RED

Baga Portuguese variety used for Bairrada. Rhymes with Rugger.

Blaufrankisch Blueberryish variety used primarily in Austria.

Bonarda Light, juicy Italian variety that is now at home in Argentina.

Bracchetto Strawberryish Italian variety used to make off-dry sparkling red.

Cinsaut/Cinsault Spicy Rhône variety; best in blends.

Carignan Toffeeish, non-aromatic variety widely used in southern France.

Dolcetto Cherryish Piedmont grape, now being used in Australia. Drink young.

Dornfelder Successful, juicy variety grown in Germany.

Freisa Interesting, light, fruity Italian variety. Rare.

Gamay Beaujolais/Valdiguié Pinot Noir cousin, unrelated to Gamay.

Mourvèdre/Mataro Spicy Rhône grape; good in California and Australia, but can be hard and "metallic".

Petit Verdot Spicy ingredient of Bordeaux. It is now being used on its own in Spain and Australia.

Petite-Sirah Spicy; thrives in California and Mexico. Known as Durif in Australia.

Ruby Cabernet Basic Carignan/Cabernet Sauvignon cross.

St. Laurent Austrian variety that is very similar to Pinot Noir.

Touriga Nacional Plummy variety used for port and Portuguese table wine, especially new wave efforts from the Douro.

Zweigelt Berryish variety used in Austria.

WINE STYLES

People who like this sort of thing will find this the sort of thing they like.

Abraham Lincoln

General de Gaulle was famously quoted as saying that France was almost impossible to run as a country because of the number of cheeses it produces. But the Gallic cheeseboard pales by comparison with the bewildering array of French wines. Bordeaux alone boasts over fifty different appellations and some 12,000 separate estates. And the picture is no different elsewhere: in the New World, a new winery opens every day. Whether you shop at a supermarket or from a traditional merchant, the expression "spoiled for choice" is likely to spring to mind. How, without hours of study, is anyone to find their way through this jungle? The answer lies, as it does in choosing books or music, in breaking the incomprehensible mass into understandable sections.

Any Colour But Black

Wine can be separated into easily recognizable styles: red, white, and pink; still and sparkling; sweet and dry; light and fortified. To say that a wine is red and dry says little, however, about the way it tastes. It could be a tough young Bordeaux, a mature Rioja, or a blueberryish Zinfandel.

Knowing the grape and origin of a wine can give a clearer idea of what it is like, but it won't tell you everything. The human touch is as important in wine as it is in the kitchen. Winemakers vary as much as chefs. Some focus on obvious fruit flavours, while others – in France, for example – go for the *goût de terroir* – the character of the vineyard. In a world that is increasingly given to instant sensations, it is perhaps unsurprising that it is the fruit-lovers rather than the friends of the earthy flavour who are currently in the ascendent.

New World/Old World

Until recently, these two philosophies broadly belonged to the New and Old Worlds. Places like California and Australia made wine that was approachably delicious when compared with the more serious wine being produced in Europe, which demanded time and food. Today, however, there are Bordeaux châteaux with a New World approach and South Africans who take a pride in making wine as resolutely tough and old-fashioned as a Bordeaux of a hundred years ago.

Gurus, Flying Winemakers, and Consultants

These changes owe much to the influence of gurus like Robert Parker, the US critic whose word is nearly law on the other side of the Atlantic and among more impressionable wine buyers elsewhere. But supermarkets must take as much of the blame or credit. It is hard to say whether we buy balsamic vinegar and snow-peas nowadays because they are available on the high street, or if it's the other way round. But there is no question that the tradition of simply making wine the way one's father did and offering it for sale has been steadily replaced by a more tailored approach. And, if you can't ring the right bells with the critics, supermarkets, and their customers, you can simply call in a consultant – such as Michel Rolland – who helps to produce wine all over the world. Today, you can choose between a Chilean white made by a Frenchman – or a claret bearing the fruity fingerprint of a winemaker who learned his craft in the Barossa Valley.

Fruit of Knowledge

European old-timers like to claim that the Australians use alchemy to obtain those fruity flavours. In fact, their secret lies in a combination of a nearly ideal climate and the winemaking process. Picking the grapes when they are ripe (rather than too early); preventing the picked grapes from cooking beneath the midday sun (as often happens in Europe while work stops for lunch); pumping the juice through pipes that have been cleaned daily rather than at the end of the harvest; fermenting at a cool temperature (overheated vats can cost a wine its freshness); and storing and bottling it carefully will all help a wine made from even the dullest grape variety to taste fruitier.

Come Hither

If the New Worlders want their wines to taste of fruit, they are – apart from some reactionary South Africans and Californians – just as eager to make wine that can be drunk young. They take care not to squeeze the red grapes too hard, so as not to extract bitter, hard tannins, and they try to avoid their white wines being too acidic.

Traditionalists claim these wines do not age well. It is too early to say whether this is true, but there is no question that the newer wave red Bordeaux of, say 1985, have given more people more pleasure since they were released than the supposedly greater 1970 vintage, whose wines often remained dauntingly hard throughout their lifetime. A wine does not have to be undrinkable in its youth to be good later on; indeed, wines that start out tasting unbalanced go on tasting that way.

Strength of Purpose

One of the biggest changes in wine over the last two decades has been the rise in its average alcoholic strength. in the early 1980s, European reds and whites would have weighed in at eleven to thirteen per cent with the latter being an exception to the rule. Today, 12.5 per cent is the lowest you are likely to see (apart from off-dry and sweeter German whites which still come in at under nine per cent). This trend was the inevitable consequence of the desire to make riper, fruitier wine. The richer you want your wine to be, the later you pick. the later the harvest, the sweeter the grapes. More sugar makes for sweeter and/or more alcoholic wine. In California, where reds at over 15.5 per cent are too strong to be imported into Europe, water is now being legally added to vats. Even so, bear in mind that US labelling law allows a one per cent leeway, so a fifteen per cent Cabernet may actually pack a sixteen per cent punch.

Roll Out the Barrel

Another thing that sets many new wave wines apart has nothing to do with grapes. Wines have been matured in oak barrels since Roman times, but traditionally new barrels were only bought to replace ones that were worn out and were falling apart. Old casks have little flavour, but for the first two years or so of their lives, the way the staves are bent over flames gives new ones a recognizable vanilla and caramel character.

Winemakers once used to rinse out their new casks with dilute ammonia to remove this flavour. Today, however, they are more likely to devote almost as much effort to the choice of forest, cooper, and charring (light, medium, or heavy "toast") as to the quality of their grapes. Winemakers who want to impress their critics take pride in using one hundred per cent – or more – new oak to ferment and mature their wine. Some pricey, limited-production red Bordeaux actually goes through two sets of new oak barrels to ensure that it gets double helpings of rich vanilla flavour.

Oak-mania began when Bordeaux châteaux began to spend the income from the great vintages of the 1940s on replacements for their old barrels – and when New World winemakers noticed the contribution the oak was making to these wines. Ever since, producers internationally have introduced new barrels, while even the makers of cheaper wine have found that dunking giant "teabags" filled with small oak chips into wine vats could add some of that vanilla flavour too. In France, the use of oak chips is considered to be little better than adding flavourings, and the procedure is rigorously forbidden for *appellation contrôlée* wines. In the New World, oak chips are rarely, if ever, used for premium wines.

If you like oak, you'll find it in top-notch Bordeaux and burgundy (red and white), Spanish Crianza, Reserva, or Gran Reserva, and Italians whose labels use the French term "barrique". The words "Elévé en fût de Chêne" on a French wine could, confusingly, refer to new or old casks. Australian "Show Reserve" will be oaky, as will Fumé Blanc and "Barrel Select" wines.

Red Wines – Fruits, Spice, and Cold Tea

Red wines vary far more than many people suppose. Colours range from the dark pinky-violet of the Gamay to the near-black of some Zinfandel. Some grapes, such as the Pinot Noir, are good at producing silky-soft wines, while others like the Nebbiolo and Cabernet Sauvignon are far more macho in style.

SUMMER FRUITS If you enjoy your red wines soft and juicily fruity, the styles to look for are Beaujolais; burgundy and other youthful wines made from the Pinot Noir; Côtes du Rhône; Rioja and reds from Spain; inexpensive Australians; young St-Emilion and Merlots from almost anywhere. Look too for Barbera and Dolcetto from Italy, and *nouveau*, *novello*, and *joven* (young) wines.

THE BERRY BROTHERS Cabernet Sauvignon takes the prize for the most blackcurranty grape, but Pinot Noir is raspberryish, and the Tempranillo of Spain can taste of strawberries. Shiraz – when it is not strongly smoky and spicy – is blackberryish, while Merlot can be like mulberry.

THE KITCHEN CUPBOARD Italy's Sangiovese is not so much fruity as herby, while the Syrah/Shiraz of the Rhône and Australia, the peppery Grenache, and – sometimes – the Zinfandel and Pinotage can all be surprisingly spicy. Other peppery grapes include Malbec and Chile's greatest contribution to the wine world, the Carmenère.

SOME LIKE IT TOUGH Most basic Bordeaux and more traditional Bordeaux is fairly light and tannic, as are older-style wines from Piedmont and Portugal, and old-fashioned South African reds. Italy's Nebbiolo will almost always make tougher wines than, say, Merlot.

White Wines – Honey and Lemon

If dry wines with unashamedly fruity flavours are what you want, try the Muscat, the Torrontés in Argentina, Australian Riesling, and New World and Southern French Chardonnay and Sauvignon Blanc. Beware though the growing trend in the New World of leaving a bit of sweetness in examples of these grapes.

NON-FRUIT For more neutral styles, go for Italian Soave, Pinot Bianco, Pinot Grigio, or Frascati; Grenache Blanc; Muscadet; German or Alsace Silvaner; and most traditional wines from Spain and southern France.

MINERAL WEALTH One of the characteristics treasured by European traditionalists – and rarely found in the New World – is a stony, "mineral" flavour that has nothing to do with tannin or acidity and is derived from the soil in which the grapes were grown. To taste this at its best in white wines, try top-class Chablis, Sancerre, or Pouilly-Fumé. Another Loire white – Savennières – can show off this character very well too, as will the best drier Rieslings from Germany.

RICHES GALORE The combination of richness and fruit is to be found in white burgundy; better dry white Bordeaux; and in Chardonnays, Semillons, and oaked Sauvignon (Fumé) wines from the New World.

AROMATHERAPY Some perfumed, spicy grapes, like the Gewurztraminer, are frankly aromatic. Also try late harvest Tokay-Pinot Gris – also from Alsace. Other aromatic varieties include Viognier, Arneis, Albariño, Scheurebe, and Grüner Veltliner.

MIDDLE OF THE ROAD Today, people want wine that is – or says it is – either dry or positively sweet. The Loire can get honeyed *demi-sec* – semi-sweet – wine right. Otherwise, head for Germany and Kabinett and Spätlese wines.

Sweet – Pure Hedonism

Sweet wine is making a comeback at last. The places to look for good examples are Bordeaux, the Loire (Moelleux), Alsace (Vendange Tardive or Sélection des Grains Nobles), Germany (Auslese, Beerenauslese, Trockenbeerenauslese), Austria (Ausbruch), the New World (late-harvest and noble late-harvest), and Hungary (Tokaj 6 Puttonyos). All of these wines should have enough fresh acidity to prevent them from being cloying. Also, they should have the characteristic dried-apricot flavour that comes from grapes that have been allowed to be affected by a benevolent fungus known as "botrytis" or "noble rot".

Other sweet wines such as Muscat de Beaumes de Venise are fortified with brandy to raise their strength to fifteen degrees of alcohol or so. These wines can be luscious, too, but, like the sweet Muscats of Valencia in Spain and Samos in Greece, they never have the complex flavours of "noble rot".

Pink – The Perfect Compromise?

Pink is, as the fashion cliché-mongers might like to say, the "new black". Rosé wine is definitely making a comeback. But tread carefully when shopping. Provence and the Rhône should offer peppery-dry rosé, just as the Loire and Bordeaux should have wines that taste deliciously of blackcurrant. Sadly, many taste dull and stale. Still, they are a better bet than California's dire sweet "white" or "blush" rosé (Fetzer's sparkling Syrah and Bonny Doon's Cigare Volant are honorable exceptions). Australia and New Zealand have some good examples of Grenache and Cabernet. Whatever the origin, look for the most recent vintage and the most vibrant colour.

Sparkling – From Basic to Brilliant

If you find Champagne too dry, but don't want a frankly sweet grapey fizz like Asti, try a fruity New World sparkling wine from California or Australia, or a sparkling Riesling (but not a cheap Sekt) from Germany. If you don't like that fruitiness, try traditional Spanish Cava, Italian Prosecco, or French Blanquette de Limoux. Even within Champagne, styles vary widely. Some are always fuller in flavour than others (Bollinger is heftier than Pol Roger for example). Brut, is sweeter than Brut Sauvage (which can be downright acidic), but drier than Extra Dry. And to confuse matters further, one producer's Brut may be much sweeter than another's.

A WORLD OF WINE

Whatever the grape variety, climate, and traditions, and despite the popularity of "global brands" with flavours almost as "international" as that of Coca Cola, the local tastes of the place where a wine is made still largely dictate its style. Let's take a whirlwind tour of the most significant winemaking nations.

FRANCE

Still the benchmark, or set of benchmarks, against which winemakers in other countries test themselves. This is the place to find the Chardonnay in its finest oaked (white burgundy) and unoaked (traditional Chablis) styles; the Sauvignon (from Sancerre and Pouilly-Fumé in the Loire, and in blends with the Sémillon in Bordeaux); the Cabernet Sauvignon and Merlot (red Bordeaux); the Pinot Noir (red burgundy and Champagne); the Riesling, Gewurztraminer, and Pinots Blanc and Gris (Alsace). The Chenin Blanc still fares better in the Loire than anywhere else, and despite their successes in Australia, the Syrah (aka Shiraz) and Grenache are still at their finest in the Rhône.

France is handicapped by the unpredictability of the climate in most of its best regions; by the unreliability of winemakers, too many of whom are still happy to coast along on the reputation of their region; and by *appellation contrôlée* laws that allow them to get away with selling poor-quality wine and prevent them from innovating and blending across regions, as is commonplace in the New World.

Alsace

Often underrated, and confused with German wines from the other side of the Rhine, Alsace deserves to be more popular. Its odd assortment of grapes makes wonderfully rich, spicy, dry, off-dry, and late harvest styles. There is also sparkling wine and a little red Pinot Noir. One word of warning: while there are two categories for luscious late harvest wines – Vendange Tardive and Sélection de Grains Nobles – many wines you might expect to taste dry are actually quite sweet.

Bordeaux

For all but the most avid wine buff, Bordeaux is one big region (producing half as much wine as Australia) with a few dozen châteaux that have become internationally famous for their wine. Visit the region, or take a look at the map, however, and you will find that this is essentially a collection of quite diverse sub-regions, many of which are separated by farmland, forest, or water.

Heading north from the city of Bordeaux, the Médoc is the region that includes the great communes of St-Estèphe, Pauillac, St-Julien, and Margaux, where some of the finest red wines are made. The largely gravel soil suits the Cabernet Sauvignon, though lesser Médoc wines, of which there are more than enough, tend to have a higher proportion of the Merlot. For the best examples of wines made principally from this variety, though, you have to head eastward to St-Emilion and Pomerol, Fronsac and the Côtes de Castillon, and to the regions of Bourg and Blaye, where the Merlot is usually blended with the Cabernet Franc.

To the south of Bordeaux lie Pessac-Léognan and the Graves, which produce some of Bordeaux's lighter, more delicate reds. This is also dry white country, where the Sémillon and Sauvignon Blanc hold sway. A little farther to the southeast, the often misty climate provides the conditions required for the great sweet whites of Sauternes and Barsac.

Each of these regions produces its own individual style of wine. In some years, the climate suits one region and/or grape variety more than others. The year 2000, for example, was better for the Médoc than for St-Emilion. So beware of vintage charts that seek to define the quality of an entire vintage across the whole of Bordeaux. Beware too of cheap, basic Bordeaux of either colour, and of supposedly slightly better basic Médoc, St-Emilion, and Sauternes. As even the grandees of Bordelais are now admitting, these are rarely a good buy.

Burgundy

The heartland of the Pinot Noir and the Chardonnay and Chablis, Nuits-St-Georges, Gevrey-Chambertin, Beaune, Meursault, Puligny-Montrachet, Mâcon-Villages, Pouilly-Fuissé, and Beaujolais. The best wines theoretically come from the Grands Crus vineyards; next are the Premiers Crus, followed by plain village wines and, last of all, basic Bourgogne Rouge or Blanc. The region's individual producers make their wines with varying luck and expertise, often selling in bulk to merchants who are just as variable in their skills and honesty. So, one producer's supposedly humble wine can be finer than another's pricier Premier or Grand Cru. The most important name on any label is that of the producer rather than the village or vineyard.

Champagne

Top-class Champagne has toasty richness and subtle fruit. Beware of cheap examples, though, and big-name producers who should know better. Among the big names, style is all: Pol Roger is light and crisp, while Bollinger and Krug are much richer and deeper in flavour. Choosing the brand of Champagne whose style you like, is a little like selecting a perfume (it is no accident that the many of the fizz and scent makers belong to the same companies).

The Loire Valley

The heartland of fresh, dry Sauvignons and honeyed, sweet Quarts de Chaume, Coteaux de Layon, and Bonnezeaux, and dry, sweet, and sparkling Vouvray, all of which, like dry Savennières, display the Chenin Blanc at its best. The Chinon and Bourgueil reds do the same for the Cabernet Franc. As in Alsace, beware of Vouvrays that are sweeter than you expect.

The Rhône Valley

Every year, the popularity of this region continues to grow, helped in part by the success of the local Syrah grape in its incarnation as Shiraz in the New World. Today, the world wants the ripe, spicy flavours of this grape and of the Grenache and Viognier, the value for money of Côtes du Rhône, and the excitement of great good Condrieu. Bear in mind that this is a big region and years that are good in the north (Côte Rôtie, St-Joseph, Cornas, Crozes Hermitage, and Hermitage) are not always as fine in the south (Châteauneuf-du-Pape, Gigondas, etc.), and vice versa.

The Southwest

Despite their fame among French wine buffs, these were often pretty old-fashioned. Today, a new wave of winemakers is learning how to extract fruit flavours from grapes like the Gros and Petit Manseng, the Tannat, Mauzac, and Malbec. Wines like Cahors, Madiran, Gaillac, and Jurançon are worth the detour for anyone bored with the ubiquitous Cabernet and Chardonnay, and dissatisfied with poor claret.

The Midi

Southern France in general, and Languedoc-Roussillon in particular, offers modern *vins de pays*, and improving Corbières, Fitou, Minervois, Coteaux de Languedoc (especially Pic St-Loup), and Limoux (where Mouton Rothschild has a venture). Increasingly dynamic winemaking is also raising the quality in Provence, where classics such as Cassis and Bandol now attract as much attention as rosé.

Eastern France

Savoie's zingy wines are often only thought of as skiing fare, but, like Arbois' nutty, sherry-style whites, they are characterfully different, and made from grape varieties that are grown nowhere else. Look out for rich Vin de Paille, made from grapes dried on mats.

GERMANY

Led by younger producers like Ernst Loosen, Rainer Lingenfelder, and Phillipp Wittmann, a quiet revolution is taking place. Expect to find rich, dry, and fruitily off-dry whites (ideally, but not necessarily, made from Riesling), classic later harvest styles, and a growing number of good reds (especially Pinot Noir). The Pfalz, Mosel, and Baden are regions to watch.

ITALY

The most exciting and confusing wine country in the world. Bar none. While classics like Barolo and Chianti are still made the way they used to be, producers often do their own, frequently delicious, thing, using indigenous and imported grape varieties and designer bottles and labels in ways that leave legislators – and humble wine drinkers – exhilarated and exasperated in equal measure. The fast-improving south (especially Puglia) and Sicily are worth watching out for.

SPAIN

As elsewhere, the vinous revolution has been most fruitful in regions that were previously overlooked. So, while traditionalists focused their attention on regions like Rioja, Navarra, and Ribera del Duero, and early modernists such as Miguel Torres looked to the Penedés, some of the most exciting fireworks have been seen in Galicia (source of lovely, aromatic white Albariño) and Priorat, an area that used to make thick red wine in which a spoon could stand unaided. Now, producers like Alvaro Palacios are making deliciously stylish wines there that sell easily for $100 in New York (but are, perhaps for this very reason, rather harder to find in London).

Elsewhere, Rioja is improving fast (thanks often to the addition of a little Cabernet to the red blend) and increasingly good wines are coming out of Navarra, Somontano, Toro, and Rueda. Ribera del Duero offers some great reds (Vega Sicilia, Pesquera, and Pingus) but prices are high here too.

PORTUGAL

The sleeping beauty has awoken. Afer spendng far too long in the shadow of Spain, Italy, and France, Portugal's winemakers are now making world-class wines. The key to Portugal's growing success lies in grapes like the Touriga Nacional that are grown nowhere else, and innovative winemakers like Luis Pato, Jose Neiva, J. Portugal Ramos, J.M. da Fonseca, and Sogrape, with a little help from Australians Peter Bright and David Baverstock, the ubiquitous Michel Rolland and Daniel Lioze, winemaker of

Château Lynch-Bages in Bordeaux. Regions of interest are Douro Palmella, Estremadura, and Alentejo, as well as historically better-known Dão and Bairrada.

AUSTRIA

The source of wonderful late harvest wines from producers like Kracher and Opitz, dry whites (especially Grüner Veltliner) from Willi Brundlmayer, Rudi and FX Pichler, and Emmerich Knoll, as well as increasingly impressive reds (St-Laurent). The word Smaragd – which means emerald – on a label should be a mark of quality.

SWITZERLAND

Switzerland is the only place in the world where the Chasselas produces anything even remotely memorable – and sensibly uses screwcaps for many of its wines. Other worthwhile grapes are the white (Petite) Arvigne and Amigne (de Vétroz), but Syrah can be good too and there are some curious white Merlots.

BULGARIA

The pioneer of good Iron Curtain reds, Bulgaria remains a source of inexpensive Cabernet Sauvignon and Merlot, as well as the earthy local Mavrud. Efforts to produce premium wines have yet to pay off.

HUNGARY

Hungary's strongest hand lies in the Tokajs, the best of which are being made by foreign investors. Reds are improving, as are affordable Sauvignons and Chardonnays.

ROMANIA, MOLDOVA, AND FORMER YUGOSLAVIA

Still struggling to make their mark beyond their own borders with better than basic fare. Romania has inexpensive Pinot Noir, Moldova produces aromatic white, and Croatia can offer interesting reds from local varieties.

ENGLAND AND WALES

Thanks to global warming, the vineyards of England and Wales are using recently developed German grape varieties to make Loire-style whites; high-quality late harvest wines; quirky reds produced under plastic polytunnels; and – particularly – sparkling wines that are now winning well-earned medals at the International Wine Challenge.

GREECE

In the year of the Olympics, outsiders are beginning to take some notice of Greece's new wave wines. The best producers use either "international" grapes or highly characterful indigenous varieties – or blends of both. Prices are high (so is demand in chic Athens restaurants), but worth it from producers like Tsantali, Château Lazaridi, Gentilini, Gaia, and Hatzimichali.

CYPRUS

Still associated with cheap sherry-substitute and dull wine, but things are changing. Look out for the traditional rich Commandaria.

TURKEY

Lurching out of the vinous dark ages, Turkey has yet to offer the world red or white wines that non-Turks are likely to relish.

LEBANON

Once the lone exemplar of Lebanese wines overseas, Château Musar is now joined by the similarly impressive Château Ksara, Château Kefraya, and Massaya (a joint venture with the co-owners of Le Vieux Telegraphe in Châteauneuf-du-Pape.

ISRAEL

Some of Israel's best Cabernet and Muscat are produced at the Yarden winery in the Golan Heights – which raises interesting questions as boundaries are drawn and redrawn in this region. Labels to look out for include Yarden, Askalon, and Mt. Tabor.

AUSTRALIA

The country whose wines were once the butt of a Monty Python joke astonishingly now not only outsells France in Britain, but commands higher prices per bottle. The combination of cooperation, competitiveness, and open-mindedness of its producers has been crucial. Where else would almost a complete region like the Clare Valley decide, for quality reasons, to switch from natural corks to screwcaps in a single vintage? Just as important has been the readiness to explore and exploit new regions – areas like the Barossa and Hunter valleys have now been joined by Orange, Robe, Mount Benson, Young, and Pemberton – and styles – such as Semillon-Chardonnay and Cabernet-Shiraz blends.

A more controversial factor has to be the dynamism and power of a quartet of giant companies – BRL Hardy, Mildara Blass, Orlando, and Southcorp – that collectively control over seventy-five per cent of the country's wines and approach winemaking in a way that is very reminiscent of the Japanese motor industry.

NEW ZEALAND

This New World country has one of the most unpredictable climates, but produces some of the most intensely flavoured wines. There are gooseberryish Sauvignon Blancs, Chardonnays, and innovative Rieslings and Gewurztraminers, and arguably even more impressive Pinot Noirs. Hawke's Bay seems to be the most consistent region for Cabernets and Merlots (and the occasional Shiraz), while Central Otago and Martinborough compete over Pinot Noir. Gisborne, Marlborough, Auckland, and Martinborough all share the honours for white wine.

NORTH AFRICA

Once the plentiful source of blending wine for French regions such as Burgundy, North Africa's vineyards have been hampered in recent years by Islamic fundamentalism. New investment is, however, now beginning to arrive from Italy and France (including a new venture in Morocco that is partly financed by French actor Gérard Dépardieu).

SOUTH AFRICA

The fastest-improving country in the New World? No longer the source of "green" wines made from over-cropped and underripe grapes grown on virused vines, the Cape is now making terrific lean but ripe Rieslings and Sauvignons, and delicious reds made from Cabernet, Merlot, and the local Pinotage. Thelema, Boekenhoutskloof, Saxenburg, Plaisir de Merle, Rust en Vrede, Rustenberg, Naledi/Sejana, Zandvliet, Vergelegen, Fairview, Grangehurst, Kanonkop, and Vriesenhof are names to watch – as are the up-and-coming regions of Malmesbury and Robertson.

THE USA

While California produces most of the wine in the US, it would be a mistake to ignore the often impressive efforts of wineries in other states.

California

Despite a glut of grapes that led to the selling of a lot of wine at ludicrously low prices, the best-known winemaking state of the Union is still on a roll at the moment. The Napa Valley now faces serious competition from Sonoma (where the giant E.&J. Gallo is making some serious reds and whites), and southern regions such as Santa Cruz and Santa Barbara. The Merlot grape has now overtaken the Cabernet Sauvignon to become the most widely planted red wine grape, but there is a growing trend towards making wines from the Pinot Noir (especially in Carneros and Russian River) and from varieties more traditionally associated with the Rhône and Italy. Amid all this excitement, however, one problem remains. California may produce some of the very finest wines in the world, but its daily-drinking efforts still offer some remarkably poor value.

The Pacific Northwest

Outside California, head north to Oregon for some of the best Pinot Noirs in the USA (at a hefty price) and improving, but rarely earth-shattering, Chardonnays, Rieslings, and Pinot Gris. Washington State has some Pinot too, on the cooler, rainy, west side of the Cascade Mountains. While on the east, irrigated vineyards produce great Sauvignon and Riesling, as well as top-notch Chardonnay, Cabernet Sauvignon, and some impressive Syrah and Merlot.

New York and Other States

Once the source of dire "Chablis" and "Champagne", New York State is now producing worthwhile wines, particularly in the micro-climate of Long Island, where the Merlot thrives. The Finger Lakes are patchier but worth visiting, especially for the Rieslings and cool-climate Chardonnays. Elsewhere Virginia, Missouri, Texas, Maryland, and even Arizona are all producing wines to compete with Calfornia, and indeed some of the best that Europe can offer.

CANADA

Icewines, made from grapes picked when frozen on the vine, are the stars here, though Chardonnays and Cabernet Francs are improving fast. Okanagan in British Columbia seems to be the region to watch.

CHILE

One of the most exciting wine-producing countries in the world, thanks to ideal conditions, skilled local winemaking, and plentiful investment. The most successful grapes at present are the Cabernet, Merlot, and – especially – the local Carmenère, but the Chardonnay, Pinot Noir, Sauvignon, and Riesling can all display ripe fruit and subtlety often absent in the New World.

ARGENTINA

As it chases Chile, this is a country to watch. The wines to look for now are the peppery reds made from the Malbec, a variety once widely grown in Bordeaux and still used in the Loire. Cabernets, Sangioveses, and Tempranillos can be good too, as can the juicy Bonarda and grapey but dry white Torrontes.

BUYING

I wonder what the vintners buy one half so precious as the stuff they sell?

Omar Khayyam

If Rip Van Winkle were to wake up after dozing for twenty-five years and pop down to the shops to buy a bottle of wine with which to celebrate, he'd be in for a shock. Most of the off-licence chains he'd have known – Peter Dominic, Fullers, Augustus Barnett et al. – have disappeared, and the Anjou Rosé, Bulls Blood, and Lutomer Riesling he'd have been used to drinking have been firmly elbowed into the shadows by Australian Chardonnay, Chilean Merlot, and California White Zinfandel. Prices have gone up of course, but less than Rip might have expected. Back in the 1970s, you'd have been lucky to be offered discounts of ten per cent; today Threshers offers three bottles for the price of two on all its wines, and elsewhere, Buy-One-Get-One-Free offers are common. If "BOGOF's" are a novelty, so, of course, is the idea of doing your shopping over the internet. But which of these options offers the best wines and the best value?

Supermarket/High Street

Supermarkets are performing the same magic trick on independent wine shops as they have on butchers, bakers, and greengrocers: they've made them disappear. Today, four out of five bottles of wine we buy pass through a checkout along with the soap powder and dog food. And, in the case of over one bottle in four, that checkout is in a Tesco store. Just as supermarkets have broadened the range of foods we eat, so they have introduced us to wines we might never otherwise have tried – and generally at prices we can afford. But there is a downside; while most of the better chains offer some smart wines – especially online – the focus is increasingly on branded efforts and discounts. And things aren't getting better. In 2005 Tesco cut its range by fifteen per cent, while Morrisons imposed its limited wine selection on its new acquisition Safeway.

Specialist Merchant

Buying from a specialist wine merchant is like going to an independent bookshop or boutique. The range on offer might not be bigger or better than in the high street, but it is likely to be more characterful and you are much more likely to deal with a person who actually knows something about the wines on offer. So you can, for example, ask about whether a particular wine is worth leaving to mature – and for how long. Some specialists, such as Berry Bros & Rudd and Lay & Wheeler offer hundreds of different wines from all over the world; others specialize in one country or area. Most sell by mail, but not all print lists. Go to **robertjoseph-onwine.com** for contact details.

By Mail/Internet

There are few UK-based companies that only exist online (though the French-based wineandco.com and chateauonline are both geared up to supply UK customers). Some wine retailers, however, including Waitrose and Tesco, propose wines over the Net that are not available in their shops. The Net is also a worthwhile option when browsing traditional merchants' sales and *en primeur* offers.

Wine Clubs

If you are happy to leave other people to choose your wines for you, firms such as the Sunday Times Wine Club may suit you down to the ground. Another advantage of these monthly selections, of course, is that they may introduce you to styles of wine you might never otherwise have encountered. But, inevitably, for all the unexpected delights, there are bound to be occasional disappointments, and, once you have got beyond the ludicrously cheap case that attracted you to join the club in the first place, you may well find that the wine is costing rather more than it might elsewhere.

En Primeur

Once upon a time, the only wines that could be bought while still in the barrel were top clarets, but now producers everywhere have got in on the act. There are two reasons for buying in this way, usually through a traditional merchant. You should – though this is far from certain – save money. The price of top Bordeaux in a good vintage can shoot up after it is first released, but there are years when it is cheaper in bottle than in the cask. The second reason applies to wines such as burgundy that are produced in tiny quantities. If you don't buy a case now, you may never see it again.

Under the Hammer

Auctions offer two advantages to wine lovers. Now that traditional merchants rarely offer really old bottles, bidding against others may be your only option. But firms like Christie's and Sotheby's are also a good source of bargains. When restaurants and wine merchants go bust, their stock, whch may include the humblest house wine and cases of half-bottles of Champagne, is offered in the same sale rooms as the two-million-pound collections of wine buffs, although not usually on the same occasions. Bargain hunters make sure they are on the mailing lists of these auction houses, or follow the auction pages of magazines like *Wine International* and *Decanter*. As a rule, the humbler fare is to be found at sales not described as offering "fine wine". It is also worth looking out for auctions by regional houses such as Straker Chadwick (01873 852 624), Bigwood (bigwoodauctioneers.co.uk), and Lithgow (lithgows.auctions@onyxnet.com), and online sales by winebid.com and uvine.com. When bidding, remember other costs, such as VAT, the buyer's premium, and duty that would have to be paid on wine sold "in bond".

Cross Channel

Fifteen per cent of our wine now comes from across the Channel. For anyone in southern England, there's every reason to take advantage of cheap crossings and savings of at least £20 per case on wine. You can legally import as much as you like for your own and your guests' consumption, so buying this way is perfect for weddings. At French branches of a UK chain, you can save money on familiar wines, but there are more interesting French wines in locally owned shops. Beware of apparent bargains in French supermarkets – try one bottle before risking a dozen – but take advantage of seasonal "Foires à Vins", when big-name Bordeaux are sold at genuinely low prices.

From the Producer

Surprisingly perhaps, given all the wine we bring home from Calais, we have been very slow to catch on to the idea of buying directly from French producers. Drive through any village in France's major wine regions during the weekend and you are almost sure to see Belgians, Germans, and Swiss struggling to shoehorn an extra case or two into their already-overloaded cars. Seeing where a wine was born and brought up, and meeting the man or woman whose name appears on the label, can, at its best, be like spending a few moments with a favourite author. Prices are often lower than in French shops, and you might well find wines that would otherwise never reach these shores.

VINTAGES

On one occasion someone put a very little wine into a [glass], and said that it was sixteen years old. "It is very small for its age," said Gnathaena.

Athenaeus, "The Deipnosophists", XIII, 47 (c. AD200)

Thirty years or so ago, good wine was only produced when the climate was just right. Man had yet to develop ways – physical, chemical, and organic – of combating pests and diseases. Really disastrous years are a rarity now, however, but some places are naturally more prone to tricky vintages than others.

Northern Europe, for example, suffers more from unreliable sun and untimely rain than more southerly regions, let alone the warm, irrigated vineyards of Australia and the Americas. A dependable climate does not necessarily make for better wine; grapes develop more interesting flavours in what is known as a "marginal" climate – which is why New World producers are busily seeking out cooler, higher-altitude sites in which to plant their vines.

It's an Ill Wind

Some producers can buck the trend of a climatically poor year – by luckily picking before the rainstorms, carefully discarding rotten grapes, or even using equipment to concentrate the flavour of a rain-diluted crop. In years like these, well-situated areas within larger regions can, in any case, make better wines than their neighbours. France's top vineyards, for example, owe their prestige partly to the way their grapes ripen. The difference in quality between regions can, however, also be attributed to the types of grape that are grown. Bordeaux had a fair-to-good vintage for red wine in 1997, but a great one for Sauternes. Similarly, there are vintages where, for example, the St-Emilion and Pomerol châteaux have already picked their Merlot grapes in perfect conditions before rainstorms arrive to ruin the prospects of their counterparts' later-ripening Cabernet Sauvignon in the Médoc, only a few miles away.

The following pages suggest regions and wines for the most significant vintages of this and the past century.

I remember the taste of the vintage wine
From '63 through to '69
And I'm proud of the things we believed in then
If I had the chance I'd go around again

The Moody Blues, Vintage Wine

2005 (SOUTHERN HEMISPHERE) Early reports show Argentina, Chile, and New Zealand making exceptional wines. Quality might be more variable in Australia and South Africa, wheare the hot summer led to super-ripe, possibly early-evolving, reds.
2004 A classic vintage for Germany, and a good (more typical than 2003) one in Bordeaux, the Northern Rhône, and for white burgundy. Portugal did well too, but California's quality was mixed. Australia and New Zealand had fine, harvests and both Chile and Argentina did well. South Africa had a good, rather than great year.
2003 Extraordinarily hot year with sometimes good, if atypical – and probably short-lived – Bordeaux (including Sauternes), the Loire, Germany, Champagne, Alsace, and Burgundy, but the Northern Rhône was disappointing. Good for South Africa and Marlborough Sauvignon Blanc.

2002 A mixed – and currently unrewarding – year in Bordeaux. Good examples should soften well. Great for red burgundy, Loire, Alsace, Champagne, Germany, and Austria. The New World did well, especially Australia and Argentina.

2001 Good red Bordeaux but great sweet and dry whites. Whites are better than reds in Burgundy and the Northern Rhône and most good Loires were sweet. Piedmont and Tuscany produced great wines, as did Tokaj and Germany. Spanish wines were not outstanding, but there was some high-quality port. Chile, South Africa, and New Zealand did well, and there were signs of brilliance in California.

2000 Great Bordeaux (Médoc). Red burgundy, Sauternes, and most of Northern France fared less well. Spain saw one of its largest harvests ever; and Portugal produced fine table wines and vintage port. Italy saw its best results in the south and also in the whites of the northeast, and there were good efforts from Germany. Tokaj was great. Australia's best wines were from Western Australia and the Hunter Valley.

1999 A patchy year, with great red and white burgundies and Sauternes, but variable red Bordeaux. Worthwhile Rhône, Loire, and Alsace. Look out for top Italian – especially Chianti – Tokaj, and German wines from the Mosel-Saar-Ruwer. Spain was good rather than great. Australia's stars were from Coonawarra and Victoria. New Zealand, Chile, and Argentina did well.

1998 A mixed, rainy, vintage throughout the northern hemisphere. There were some great red Bordeaux (St-Emilion, Pomerol, and top Médoc and Graves), lovely Sauternes and Alsace, and fine white burgundies (especially Chablis) and ports. Red burgundies were initially tough but have softened. California reds were varied.

1997 Bordeaux produced light reds and brilliant sweet whites, and Burgundy had great whites and variable reds. Alsace, Germany, and Austria made terrific wines, as did the port houses of the Douro and producers in the USA, Australia, and New Zealand. Italy had a truly great year.

1996 Classic Bordeaux (especially Médoc, Graves, and Sauternes), white burgundy, and Loire. Patchy Alsace, Rhône, and Germany, and fair in Italy, Spain, and Portugal. California, New Zealand, and Australia produced top-class red and white wines.

1995 Classy red Bordeaux and white burgundy. Italian and Loire reds, Rhône, Alsace, German, Rioja, and Ribera del Duero are all good, as are Australia, New Zealand, South Africa, and North and South America.

1994 Unripe red Bordeaux, fine northern Rhône reds, fading red burgundy, and great vintage port. Average-to-good Italian reds and German; California had a great vintage, and Australian were good to very good.

1993 Red Bordeaux is tiring now. There are excellent Tokaj, Alsace, and Loire (red and white), good red burgundy, and top-class whites. Wines were better in South Africa and New Zealand than in Australia.

1992 Poor Bordeaux but good white burgundy. Fading red burgundy. Taylor's and Fonseca produced great vintage port. Fine California Cabernet.

1991 Maturing Bordeaux and good Northern Rhône reds. Fine port and good wines from Spain, South Africa, California, New Zealand, and Australia.

1990 Great Bordeaux, Champagne, Germans, Alsace, Loire whites, red Rhône, burgundy, Australia, California, Barolo, and Spanish reds.

1985–9 1989 Great red and good white Bordeaux and Champagne. Stunning Germans and red Loire; excellent Alsace. Good red and superb white Rhône, good red burgundy. **1988** Evolving red Bordeaux and Italian reds, fine Sauternes and Champagne, Tokaj, German, Alsace, Loire reds and sweet whites, good Rhône, and red burgundy which is now ready for drinking.

We may lay in a stock of pleasures, as we would lay in a stock of wine; but if we defer tasting them too long, we shall find that both are soured by age.

Charles Caleb Colton (1780–1832)

1987 Fading red Bordeaux and burgundy. **1986** Fine red and white Bordeaux, Australian reds, white burgundy. **1985** Reds from Bordeaux, Rhône, burgundy, Spain, Italy, Champagne; port, Champagne, Alsace, sweet Loire.
1980–4 1984 South African and Australian reds, Riesling. **1983** Red Bordeaux, red Rhône, Portuguese reds, Sauternes, madeira, vintage port, Tokaj, Alsace. **1982** Red Bordeaux, Australian, Portuguese and Spanish reds, Italian reds, burgundy, Rhône. **1981** Alsace. **1980** Madeira, port.
1970–9 1979 Sassicaia. **1978** Rhône, Portuguese reds, Bordeaux, burgundy, Barolo, Tuscan and Loire reds. **1977** Port, sweet Austrian. **1976** Champagne, Loire reds and sweet whites, sweet German, Alsace, Sauternes. **1975** Top red Bordeaux and port, Sauternes. **1974** California and Portuguese reds. **1973** Napa Cabernet, sweet Austrian. **1972** Tokaj. **1971** Bordeaux, burgundy, Champagne, Barolo, Tuscan reds, sweet Germans, red Rhône, Penfolds Grange. **1970** Port, Napa Cabernet, red Bordeaux, Rioja.
1960–9 1969 Red Rhône, burgundy. **1968** Madeira, Rioja, Tokaj. **1967** Sauternes, Châteauneuf-du-Pape, German TBA. **1966** Port, burgundy, red Bordeaux, Australian Shiraz. **1965** Barca Velha. **1964** Red Bordeaux, Tokaj, Vega Sicilia, Rioja, sweet Loire, red Rhône. **1963** Vintage port, Tokaj. **1962** Top Bordeaux and burgundy, Rioja, Australian Cabernet and Shiraz. **1961** Red Bordeaux, Sauternes, Champagne, Brunello, Barolo, Alsace, red Rhône. **1960** Port, top red Bordeaux.
1950–9 1959 Red Bordeaux, Sauternes, Tokaj, Germans, Loire, Alsace, Rhône, burgundy. **1958** Barolo. **1957** Madeira, Vega Sicilia, Tokaj. **1956** Yquem. **1955** Red Bordeaux, Sauternes, port, Champagne. **1954** Madeira. **1953** Red Bordeaux, Tokaj, Champagne, sweet German, Côte Rôtie, burgundy. **1952** Red Bordeaux, madeira, Champagne, Barolo, Tokaj, Rhône, burgundy. **1951** Terrible. **1950** Madeira.
1940–9 1949 Bordeaux, Tokaj, sweet Germans, red Rhône, burgundy. **1948** Port, Vega Sicilia. **1947** Bordeaux, burgundy, port, Champagne, Tokaj, sweet Loire. **1946** Armagnac. **1945** Port, Bordeaux, Champagne, Chianti, sweet Germans, Alsace, red Rhône, burgundy. **1944** Madeira, port. **1943** Champagne, red burgundy. **1942** Port, Rioja, Vega Sicilia. **1941** Madeira, Sauternes. **1940** Madeira.

ANNIVERSARY WINES 1906 red burgundy and Sauternes. **1916** Yquem. **1926** red Bordeaux and burgundy, Sauternes. **1936** Madeira.

INVESTMENT

Wine can bring an annual return of fifteen per cent. But as with other investments, this depends on choosing well and following the market. Bear in mind, that the actual quality – drinkability – of the wine will rise and fall, often irrespective of its market value.

Youth Before Age

Once, the only wines worth investing in came from "blue chip" estates such as Châteaux Latour, Cheval Blanc, and Haut-Brion; top burgundies and port with a proven ability to age and improve over ten to twenty years – or that had already done so. Today, auctions are full of newcomers, both among the wines and the bidders. There are Bordeaux from small estates (e.g. Clinet) and recently launched "garage" wines produced from tiny quantities, such as Le Pin and Valandraud, and New World "cult" efforts from Napa and Barossa. The common quality of these wines is a rich, seductive, fruity, oaky character rarely encountered in traditional Bordeaux that required years to lose the tannic character of its youth. Their capacity to age – and retain their early value – is increasingly being questioned, and 2005 saw the first major downturn in the prices paid for Bordeaux "garage" wines *en primeur* – as futures.

The Rules

1) Wines fetch different prices in different countries. 2) No wine lasts forever. 3) Be wary of unproven potential. 4) Only buy *en primeur* from financially solid merchants. 5) Only buy wines that have been carefully cellared. 6) Store wines carefully – and insure them. 7) Follow their progress – read the critics and watch the auctions. 8) Beware of falling reputations for wines and vintages. 9) At auction, take note of possible extra costs. 10) It is easier to turn a gold ring into cash than a prize Bordeaux.

France

BORDEAUX Châteaux Angélus, Ausone, Cheval Blanc, Cos d'Estournel, Ducru-Beaucaillou, Eglise-Clinet, Figeac, Grand-Puy-Lacoste, Gruaud-Larose, Haut-Brion, Lafite, Lafleur, Latour, Léoville Barton, Léoville Las Cases, Lynch-Bages, Margaux, la Mission-Haut-Brion, Montrose, Mouton-Rothschild, Palmer, Pétrus, Pichon Lalande, Pichon Longueville, le Pin, Rauzan-Ségla, Valandraud. Vintages: 1982, 1983 (Margaux), 1988, 1989, 1990, 1995, 1996, 1998, 2000. 1999 and 2001 2002 (top properties only) and well-rated 2003's.

BURGUNDY Drouhin Marquis de Laguiche, Gros Frères, Hospices de Beaune (from Drouhin, Jadot, etc.), Méo-Camuzet, Romanée-Conti (la Tâche, Romanée-Conti), Gouges, Lafon, Leflaive, Leroy, Denis Mortet, Roumier, de Vogüé.
RHONE Chapoutier, Chave, Guigal (top wines), Jaboulet Aîné "La Chapelle."

Other Countries

PORTUGAL (port) Cockburn's, Dow's, Fonseca, Graham's, Noval, Taylor's, Warre's.
CALIFORNIA Beaulieu Georges de Latour, Diamond Creek, Dominus, Duckhorn, Dunn, Harlan Estate, Howell Mountain, Grace Family, Matanzas Creek, Robert Mondavi Reserve, Opus One, Ridge, Spottswoode, Stag's Leap.
AUSTRALIA Armagh, Clarendon Hills, Tahbilk 1860 Vines Shiraz, Henschke Hill of Grace, Cyril Henschke, Mount Edelstone, Penfolds Grange and Bin 707, Petaluma Cabernet, "John Riddoch", Virgin Hills, Yarra Yering.

WINE ON THE WEB

I have a laptop which worke3 perfectl6 until I spille3 red wine 1 on the ke6boar3. I switched the power off and 1 moppe3 up what I coul3, then left it overnight. In the morning I foun3 that ever6thing worke3 fine but some ke6s 3on't work on the keyboard. Not onl6 that but the 1 computer sometimes thinks that the '1' ke6 is pressed down, so I get 1's t6pe3 ever6where! is there an6thing I can 3o to solve these problems?

Enquiry to an online forum

Somewhere lurking in the furthest reaches of the Net, there is probably a statistic revealing just how many people do irreparable damage to their computers every year while browsing for wine. When I typed "wine" "spill" and "keyboard" into Google, it came up "about 625,000 sites" that might have offered the answer, but sadly I did not have time to stray beyond the first few pages.

Wine and the Web have been having a relationship for quite some time now. It began like love at first sight. Even when the expression "going online" was still the preserve of men with strange glasses who didn't get out very much, there were those who believed that the new medium and the wine industry were made for each other. Wine merchants and online publishers raised ludicrous sums and launched websites galore, filling their pages with informative words from writers who began to imagine that an electronic fortune was there for the taking.

But financial reality bit hard into those dreams. First to disappear from the newcomers was those words about wine, but it did not take long for the entire sites to bite the electronic dust. The last surviver of those heady days was Virginwines.com, and in 2005, that firm too was swallowed up by Direct Wines, the giant behind Laithwaites and the Sunday Times Wine Club. Today, the merchant offering the best online vinous information is, ironically, Berry Bros & Rudd (bbr.com) a company born in the days when orders were taken down by quill pen.

News and Views

As flakier efforts have come and gone, it is interesting to see that the most informative sites have survived. The grandaddy of these is the US-based Robin Garr's Wine Lovers Page (www.wineloverspage.com) which combines first-class contributions from professional writers such as Sue Courtney and Natalie MacLean with quirky contributions from readers. There are wine recommendations and enough forums to keep the most eclectic wine lover engrossed.

On the other side of the Pacific, despite rumours of its demise, James Halliday's winepros.com is still very much alive. There are fewer bells and whistles than there were – this was once intended to be a global one-stop shop for wine information – and you need to subscribe to get the best stuff, but it remains essential reading for anyone wanting in-depth insight into the Antipodes.

Jamie Goode's wineanorak.com claims to be one of the most interesting and comprehensive wine resources on the Web, and it doesn't disappoint. Apart from reliable recommendations, book reviews, and thoughtful, well-researched features, it also offers a great little gallery of vinous photographs. Another similarly fine site with links to all the UK forums is Tom Cannavan's wine-pages.com.

Among the magazines that boast a good online presence, I'd particularly recommend the US-based *Wine Spectator* (winespectator.com) and *Decanter*

(decanter.com) for their news coverage. The former magazine has a huge range of wine reviews, as does *Wine International* (wineint.com), which offers the results of the annual International Wine Challenge and some wide ranging advice of food-and-wine matchingdrawn from its International Sommelier Challenge. Another US magazine whose online version is worth visiting for its archive of feaures is the *Wine Enthusiast* (winemag.com), while the site of the recently launched *World of Fine Wine* (finewinemag.com) also shows potential at the more intellectual end of the scale. All of these sites rely on advertising and sponsorship to survive. Subscription-based sites that stand apart from the herd include Jancis Robinson's first class Purple Pages (jancisrobinson.com), Steve Tanzer's International Wine Cellar (wineaccess.com) and Robert Parker's erobertparker.com, which is worth visiting, if only for the quality of its forum discussions. Also of note for anyone fascinated by Burgundy and interested in keeping track of what is happening there, is Allen Meadows' excellent Burghound.com.

Local Knowledge

One of the hazards of being a writer of any kind lies in the accumulation of books and other written material that one keeps because it may come in handy one day – despite the fact that the information is losing its accuracy by the week. Thanks to the Net, most of that material can be given away or shredded. If I want to know how many hectares of Pinot Noir there are in Sonoma, or the year that Arbois became an appellation, I can simply go onto Google and look it up. And so can you. Alternatively, you might speed up the search – or be happily distracted – by visiting a few sites that offer links to other sites. Try bestwinesites.com, wineinfonet.com (very US-focused), or winetitles.com (similarly Antipodean). My own robertjoseph-onwine.com also has a long list of links.

The Labtec spill-resistant keyboard is an excellent choice for those who require a simple, yet stylish product. This reliable keyboard will last for years thanks to its sturdiness and durability. Buy now for £5.80.

Offer on www.comparestoreprices.co.uk

Buying Online

It is a rare and peculiarly Luddite terrestrial firm that has not yet set out its wares online. Among the recently arrived latecomers to the party are the Wine Society (www.thewinesociety.com), which can be joined at the click of a mouse, and Justerini & Brooks (www.justerinis.com), which only turned electronic after closing its earthly shops in London and Edinburgh. Berry Bros makes no secret of the fact that this old firm's UK base partly exists to further its ambitions as global traders. pages are offered in both Chinese and Japanese.

If these sites are looking for wine buyers beyond the shores of the UK, two firms based on the other side of the Channel are equally keen to sell wine here. Wineandco.com and chateauonline.com should both be of interest to anyone frustrated by the paucity of the Gallic range available here, though both performed surprisingly poorly when I went looking for wines from more obscure areas. Indeed I might have done as well or better at smaller UK-based companies like les Caves de Pyrène (www.lescaves.co.uk).

Finally, there is one site that all true wine lovers discover sooner or later. wine-searcher.com does what it says on the tin: it helps you find specific wines by browsing countless retailers' lists across the world. It is, in other words, a wine buyer's Google.

WINE AND HEALTH

It sloweth age, it strengtheneth youth, it helpeth digestion, it abandoneth melancholie, it relisheth the heart, it lighteneth the mind, it quickenth the spirits, it keepeth and preserveth the head from whirling, the eyes from dazzling, the tongue from lisping, the mouth from snaffling, the teeth from chattering and the throat from rattling; it keepeth the stomach from wambling, the heart from swelling, the hands from shivering, the sinews from shrinking, the veins from crumbling, the bones from aching, and the marrow from soaking.

Robert Noecker

This wonderful endorsement for wine which was written in the sixteenth century, copied by Joseph Lyons and published by Robin Garr on wineloverspage.com, is sadly incomplete. According to modern research, wine may, in moderation, also be effective against a range of other ailments – from Alzheimers to heart disease. Which is just as well, really, when one considers the damage alcohol of any kind can do when taken in excess.

For the sake of balance, let's look at the negative side first.

Why Wine is Bad for You

HANGOVERS All alcohol is hangover fare and port is worse than most. Try to drink plenty of water before going to bed. Take Vitamin B on the Morning After, or Marmite. Otherwise, go for protein and refreshing orange juice diluted with sparkling mineral water.

PREGNANCY Taken in excess, wine, like all alcohol, is dangerous for mothers-to-be. Less well-known is the fact that drinking soon after conception may actually impair the chances of becoming pregnant in the first place. Once the test proves positive, however, women who fancy the occasional glass of red or white will be pleased to hear that in 1997, the UK Royal College of Obstetricians and Gynaecologists reported that up to fifteen units per week should do no harm to a foetus.

CALORIES AND CARBS All wine is fattening. Muscadet and red Bordeaux with the same 12.5 degrees of alcohol strength, have the same number of calories (around 110 per glass). Stronger wines with, say, fourteen more, while sweeter, but less alcoholic German wines that weigh in at nine have fewer than eighty calories.

A Stanford University survey suggests the action of the wine on the metabolism may make its calories less fattening. According to the US Department of Agriculture, a five-ounce glass of wine has about 0.8 to 1.8 grams of carbohydrates. A number of Californian Chardonnay however might have three grams of carbs, because of their sweetness.

WINE, MIGRAINE, AND ALLERGIES Red wine, like chocolate, can inhibit a useful little enzyme called phenosulfotransferase-P, or PST-P, which detoxifies bacteria in the gut. An absence of PST-P is linked to migraine, which is why some people complain of headaches after drinking a glass or two of wine. Other people have found that red wine is also associated with episodic skin allergies.

Fortunately, some of these conditions can apparently come and go over time. Interestingly, there also seems to be differences in the effects of particular styles of wine. Chianti, for example, seems to have fewer histamines than red wines from other regions.

WINE AND ASTHMA Wines that are heavily dosed with sulphur dioxide (used to combat bacteria in most dried, bottled, and canned foods) may induce asthma attacks among those who are susceptible to this condition. Red wines in general, and New World and organic wines in particular, have lower sulphur levels. The highest levels of sulphur will be in sweet white wines and wines with low alcohol levels.

Why Wine Might be Good for You

Of all the alcoholic drinks we enjoy, red wine gets the strongest support from the medical researchers, but there are studies that suggest that white wine and beer (though rarely spirits) and even grape juice also may help to extend your life.

HEARTY GOOD WISHES Scarcely a month seems to pass without the publication of yet another report showing the beneficial properties of an anti-fungal compound called resveratrol that is found in high concentration in grape skins, as well as in peanuts. and some other foods. The magic property of the compound lies in helping blood to flow better. A glass or three of red per day (Resveratrol is not as present in whites) seems, like aspirin, to prevent blood clots and is now being prescribed to heart surgery patients.

PROTECTION AGAINST CANCER, STROKES, AND DEMENTIA? Wine may actually help to cause mouth and throat tumours (it may, but only in the case of heavy smokers), but resveratrol may be similarly effective against various forms of cancer. These could, according to some researchers, include cancers of the bowel, breast, and ovaries, as well as melanomas. One theory is that the resveratrol inhibits the proliferation of human intestinal cancerous cells and the formation of tumours in mice predisposed to intestinal tumours. Prof. Djavad Mossalayi of the Victor Segalen University has proved that it is also toxic to cancerous cells in humans. Red wine is also rich in gallic acid, an acknowledged anticarcinogenic, and wine's role in reducing stress has also been associated with a lower incidence of certain forms of cancer.

Wine may also be effective against dementia and Alzheimers in the over-sixty-fives and there is some evidence that two to three glasses per day could reduce the risk of strokes by almost thirty per cent.

OTHER POSSIBLE BENEFITS Wine and beer both seem to combat a bacteria that causes peptic ulcers, and red wine in particular may be helpful against pneumonia and bronchitis, though the former drink is less likely to cause gout than the latter. Red wine may also be used to augment the treatment of Aids, according to Dr. Marvin Edeas of the Hôpital Antoine Béclère in Clamart in France, who is studying the way the polyphenols rejuvenate blood. It may also be effective against diseases such as sickle cell anaemia and thalassaemia. Another theory suggests that red wine may be beneficial in maintaining bone density in post-menopausal women, and this reducing the risk of fractures. A 2002 study in New York uncovered that anti oxidants in the wine appear to prevent the creation of free radicals; harmful molecules that damage lung tissues. Wine of both colours also counters both constipation and diarrhoea, while white wine in particular stimulates the urinary functions. Wine also kills cholera bacteria and combats typhoid and trichinella, the poisonous compound in "bad" pork.

Young women who drink a glass or two of red per day may reduce the risk of getting Type 2 Diabetes, and Canadian studies suggest that the polyphenols in red wines may be effective against cold sores and even genital Herpes.

For more information, visit thewinedoctor.com; red-wine-and-health.com; healthydrinkingscience.com and http://www.winepros.org/wine101/wine-health.htm.

WINE AND FOOD

What is the best wine with a Grilled Buffalo Burger with Blue Cheese?
Sent to the erobertparker.com online forum by Jason G,
Senior Executive Oenophile Member # 1765

Buffalo meat tastes like a cross between beef and ham. I'd try a German Spätlese.
Reply from Paul H, Executive Oenophile Member # 2694

It requires a certain type of mind to see beauty in a hamburger.
Ray Kroc, Chairman of McDonalds

Have no Fear

One of the most daunting aspects of wine has always been the traditional obsession with serving precisely the right wine with any particular dish – of only ever drinking red with meat and white with fish or shellfish. It may be reassuring to learn that some of these time-honoured rules are just plain wrong. In Portugal, for example, fishermen love to wash down their sardines and salt cod with a glass or two of harsh red wine. In Burgundy, they even poach fish in their local red.

On the other hand, the idea that a platter of cheese needs a bottle of red wine can be thrown away right now. Just take a mouthful of red Bordeaux immediately after eating a little goat's cheese or Brie. The wine will taste metallic and unpleasant because the creaminess of the cheese reacts badly with the tannin – the toughness – in the wine. A dry white would be far more successful (its acidity would cut through the fat), while the Bordeaux would be shown at its best alongside a harder, stronger cheese. If you don't want to offer a range of wines, try sticking to one or two cheeses that really will complement the stuff in the glass.

Don't take anything for granted. Rare beef and red Bordeaux surprisingly fails the test of an objective tasting. The protein of the meat somehow makes all but the fruitiest wines taste tougher. If you're looking for a perfect partner for beef, uncork a burgundy. However, if it's the Bordeaux that takes precedence, you'd be far better off with lamb.

The difference beteen an ideal and a passable food-and-wine combination can be very subtle. Most of us have, after all, happily quaffed red Bordeaux with our steak, but just as an avid cook will tinker with a recipe until it is just right, there's a lot to be said for making the occasional effort to find a pairing of dish and wine that really works. Like people who are happier as a couple than separately, some foods and wines simply seem to bring out the best in each other.

A Sense of Balance

There is no real mystery about the business of matching food and wine. Like classic food combinations, some flavours and textures are compatible, and some are not. Strawberry mousse is not really delicious with chicken casserole, but apple sauce can do wonders for roast pork.

The key to spotting which relationships are marriages made in heaven, and which have the fickleness of Hollywood romances, lies in identifying the dominant characteristics of the contents of both the plate and the glass. Then, learn by experience which are likely to complement each other, either through their similarities or through their differences.

Likely Combinations

Without question, the greatest invention in the history of mankind is wine. Oh, I grant you that the wheel was also a fine invention, but the wheel does not go nearly as well with pizza.

Dave Barry

Some foods and their characteristics, though, make life difficult for almost any drink. Sweetness, for example, in a fruity sauce served with a savoury dish seems to strip some of the fruitier flavours out of a wine. This may not matter if the stuff in your glass is a blackcurranty New World Cabernet Sauvignon, but it's bad news if it is a bone-dry white or a tough red with little fruit to spare. Try fresh strawberries with Champagne – delicious; now add a little whipped cream to the equation and you'll spoil the flavour. Creamy and buttery sauces can have the same effect on a wine and call for a similarly creamy white – or a fresh, zippy one to cut through the fattiness.

Spices are very problematic for wine – largely due to the physical sensation of eating them rather than any particular flavour. A wine may not seem nasty after a mouthful of chilli sauce, it will simply lose its fruity flavour and taste of nothing at all – which, in the case of a fine red, seems a pity. The way a tannic red dries out the mouth will also accentuate the heat of the spice. The ideal wine for most Westerners to drink with any spicy dish would be a light, possibly slightly sweet, white or a light, juicy red.

Always Worth a Try

Some condiments actually bring out the best in wines. A little freshly ground pepper on your meat or pasta can accentuate the flavour of a wine, just as it can with a sauce. Squeezing fresh lemon onto your fish will reduce the apparent acidity of a white wine – a useful tip if you have inadvertently bought a case of tooth-strippingly dry Muscadet. And, just as lemon can help to liven up a dull sauce, it will do the same for a dull white wine, such as a basic burgundy or a Soave, by neutralizing the acidity and allowing other flavours to make themselves apparent. Mustard performs a similar miracle when it is eaten with beef, somehow nullifying the effect of the meat protein on the wine.

Cooking with Wine

I cook with wine, sometimes I even add it to the food.

W.C. Fields

Finally, a word or two about how best to use wine in the kitchen (apart from its role as refreshment, and as a tranquilizer for the moments when sauces curdle). Wine that's not good enough to drink is probably not good enough to pour into the frying pan or casserole. On the other hand, despite the advice of classic French recipes, your "coq au vin" won't be spoiled by your unwillingness to make it with a pricey bottle of *grand cru* burgundy. A decent, humbler red will do perfectly well, though it is worth trying to use a similar style to the one suggested.

Second – and just as important – remember that, with the exception of a few dishes such as sherry trifle or zabaglione, in which wine is enjoyed in its natural state, wine used as an ingredient needs to be cooked in order to remove the alcohol. So, add it early enough for the necessary evaporation to take place.

THE INTERNATIONAL WINE CHALLENGE

From tiny acorns... Way back in 1984, wine writer and broadcaster Charles Metcalfe and I thought it might be interesting to compare a few English white wines with examples from other countries for a feature in a magazine we had launched a few months earlier that would later become *Wine International*. So, we set out a representative collection of some fifty carefully camouflaged bottles, in the basement of a London restaurant, and invited a group of experts to mark them out of twenty. We never imagined that the home team would surprise everyone by beating well-known bottles from Burgundy, the Loire, and Germany – or that the modest enterprise we had immodestly called "The International Wine Challenge" would develop into the world's biggest, most respected wine competition.

The following year's Challenge attracted around 200 entries, while the third and fourth competitions saw numbers rise to 500 and 1,000 respectively. This annual doubling thankfully slowed down eventually, but by the end of the century the competition was, by a substantial margin, the largest in the world, attracting entries from countries ranging from France and Australia to Thailand and Uruguay. In April 2005, there were over 9,100 wines.

Origins in London

It is no accident that the International Wine Challenge was born in London. For centuries, British wine drinkers have enjoyed the luxury of being able to enjoy wines from a wide variety of countries. Samuel Pepys may have been a fan of Château Haut-Brion from Bordeaux, but plenty of other eighteenth-century sophisticates in London (and elsewhere in Britain) were just as excited about the sweet, late-harvest whites that were being produced at that time by early settlers in South Africa.

More recently, as wine became steadily more popular, wines from California, Australia, New Zealand, and South America all found their way to these shores. Other arrivals were wines from regions, like the Languedoc-Roussillon in France and Southern Italy, that had often been overlooked. As the twenty-first century dawned, Britain's biggest supermarket chains boasted daunting ranges of 700 to 800 different wines. A well-run, truly impartial competition provided an invaluable means of sorting the best and most interesting of these bottles from the rest. Publishing their descriptions and information on where to buy them provided unequalled guidance for anyone wanting to broaden their drinking experience.

The Tasting Panels

If the diversity of the wines on offer in Britain created a need for the International Wine Challenge, the calibre of this country's wine experts provided the means with which to run the competition. The nation that spawned the Institute of Masters of Wine – the trade body whose members have to pass the world's toughest wine exam – is also home to some of the most respected wine critics and merchants on the planet.

These are the men and women – some 420 of them – who, along with winemakers and experts from overseas, make up the tasting panels for the Challenge. So, a set of wines might well have been judged by a group that included a traditional merchant, the buyer from a supermarket chain, an Australian winemaker, a French sommelier, and a Portuguese wine critic. Argument between these diverse palates is surprisingly rare; when agreement is impossible, one of my co-chairmen Charles Metcalfe and Derek Smedley MW, or myself, is called in to adjudicate.

Two-round Format

During the first of the two rounds of the competition, wines are assessed to decide whether or not they are worthy of an award – be it a medal or a seal of approval. At this stage, typicality is taken into account, and tasters are informed that they are dealing, for example, with Chablis, Chianti, or South African Chenin Blanc. Around thirty-six per cent of the wines will leave the competition with no award. A further thirty per cent will receive seals of approval; the remainder will be given gold, silver, or bronze medals. The entries that have been thought medal-worthy in the first round, and the "seeded" entries that won recognition in the previous year's competition, then pass directly to the second round. Now, the judges face the task of deciding on the specific award each wine should receive – if any (they can still demote or throw wines out completely). At this stage, the wines are still grouped by grape and region, but a team of tasters might be confronted with sets of similar wines from, say, Chile, Australia, and California.

Super-jurors

As a final check, after it has been open for a while, every wine goes before a team of "super-jurors". These are mostly Masters of Wine, winemakers, and professional buyers from leading merchants and retailers whose daily work involves the accurate assessment of hundreds of wines. The vital role of the super-jurors is both to ensure that tasters have not been overly harsh on wines that were reticent when first poured, or on ones with subtle cork taint that was initially unnoticed – and to watch out for entries that may have been over-estimated because of the immediate attraction of oakiness, for example. If two super-jurors agree, they can jointly up- or down-grade a wine.

Trophies and Great Value Awards

The super-jurors also decide which gold medal winners deserve the additional recognition of a trophy. These supreme awards can be given for any style, region, or nationality of wine. The judges are free to withhold trophies and to create them as they see appropriate (this year's several German trophies are a good example). The trophies, like all of the wines in the competition are judged irrespective of their price. Wines that are particularly fairly priced for their award get Good Value Awards and a set of widely available, most highly marked wines are named Great Value Wines of the Year after a tasting by the super-jurors. The International Wine Challenge 2005 Trophy winners are listed on pages 46–8.

In this book you will find the medal winners and seals of approval that represent particularly good value.

Grading of Awards and Key to Symbols Used in the Book

Gold medals have scored the equivalent of at least 18.5/20 (or 95/100) and are exceptional. Silver has scored over 17/20 (or 90/100), bronze over 15.5/20 (or 85/100), and seals of approval over 14/20 (or 80/100).

☆ particularly good value

★ truly great value

WINES OF THE YEAR AND TROPHIES

Winemakers of the Year

Sparkling	*Champagne Ruinart*
White	*Dr Loosen*
Red	*Abadía Retuerta*
Fortified	*Emilio Lustau*

Great Value Trophies

Sparkling	*Paul Langier Champagne Rosé NV*
	Tesco Premier Cru Champagne NV
	Somerfield Prince William Champagne NV
White	*Canti Chardonnay Pinot Grigio Veneto 2004*
	TriVento Viognier 2004
	Calvet Limited Release Bordeaux 2004
	Tierra Antica Sauvignon Blanc 2004
	Domaine des Hautes Noëlles, Muscadet de Sèvre-et-Maine Sur Lie 2004
	Sileni, Cellar Selection Sauvignon Blanc 2004
Red	*Berberana Dragon VDT Castilla-la-Mancha 2003*
	Sainsbury Reserve Selection Chilean Cabernet Sauvignon 2003
	Caves St Pierre, Préférence Côtes du Rhône 2004
	Palandri Boundary Road Shiraz 2002
	Cantine Due Palme, Primitivo Salento 2003
	Errazuriz Merlot 2004
Late Harvest	*T Noble Late Harvest 2001*
Fortified	*Croft Distinction Port*
	Dow's LBV Port
	Waitrose Solera Jerezana Fino del Puerto Sherry
	Manzanilla La Gitana
	Marsala Superiore Garibaldi Dolce

Supreme Trophies

Daniel Thibault Trophy (for the finest sparkling wine) *Dom Ruinart 1996*
The White Wine Trophy *O'Leary Walker, Watervale Riesling 2004*
The Red Wine Trophy *Abadía Retuerta, Selecci'on Especial 2001*
The Sweet Wine Trophy *Dr Loosen, Erdener Prälat Riesling Auslese 2004*
The Fortified Trophy *Lustau Emperatriz Eugena Very Rare Oloroso*
James Rogers Trophy (for the finest wine in its first year of production)
Malhadinha 2003
Len Evans Trophy (for consistency over the past 5 years) *Emilio Lustau*
Edmund Penning-Rowsell Trophy (for the finest red Bordeaux)
Château Magrez-Tivoli 2002

National and Regional Trophies

ARGENTINA
Argentine Cabernet Sauvignon *Finca Flichman Reserva Cabernet Sauvignon 2004*

Argentine Red Trophy   *Trapiche, Malbec Single Vineyard La Consulta 2003*

AUSTRALIA
Australian Chardonnay   *Eileen Hardy Chardonnay 2001*
Australian Riesling   *O'Leary Walker, Watervale Riesling 2004*
Australian Cabernet Sauvignon *Houghton, Jack Mann Cabernet Sauvignon 1999*
Australian Shiraz   *Yaldara Farms Shiraz 2002*
Australian White Trophy   *O'Leary Walker, Watervale Riesling 2004*
Australian Red Trophy   *Houghton, Jack Mann Cabernet Sauvignon 1999*

AUSTRIA
Austrian White Trophy   *Hans Tschida, Sämling TBA 2002*
Austrian Red Trophy   *Weinlaubenhof Kracher, Illmitz Zweigelt 2003*

CHILE
Chilean Red Trophy   *Errazuriz Merlot 2004*

FRANCE
Champagne NV   *Tesco Premier Cru Champagne*
Champagne Blanc de Blancs *Dom Ruinart 1996*
Vintage Champagne   *Gauthien Brut Millésimé 1998*
Mature Champagne   *Charles Heidsieck Blanc des Millénaires 1983*
Rosé Champagne   *Laurent-Perrier Grand Siècle Alexandra Rosé 1997*
Alsace   *Barmès-Buecher, Gewurztraminer Rosenberg 2003*
Chablis   *Jean-Marc Brocard, Chablis Vieilles Vignes 2003*
White Burgundy   *Louis Jadot Meursault 2002 Louis Jadot*
Red Burgundy   *Jean-Claude Boisset, Beaune 1er Cru Les Grèves 2003*
Jurançon   *Domaine Cauhapé, Chant des Vignes 2003*
Southern French   *Domaine Massamier La Mignarde, Domus Maximus 2000*
Rhône   *Delas Frères, Hermitage Marquis de la Tourette 2000*
French White Trophy   *Barmès-Buecher, Gewürztraminer Rosenberg 2003*
French Red Trophy   *Domaine Massamier La Mignarde, Domus Maximus 2000*

GERMANY
German Dry Riesling   *Domdechant Werner Riesling Classic 2003*
German Sweet Riesling   *Dr Loosen, Erdener Prälat Riesling Auslese 2004*
German Trophy   *Dr Loosen, Erdener Prälat Riesling Auslese 2004*

ITALY
Piemonte   *Cascina Morassino, Barbaresco Morassino 2001*
Veneto   *Cantina Valpolicella Negrar, Vigneti di Jago Amarone Valpolicella Domini Veneti 2000*
Tuscany   *Villa Cafaggio San Martino 2001*
Italian White Trophy   *Moncaro, Le Vele Verdicchio dei Castelli di Jesi Classico 2004*

Italan Red Trophy   *Cantina Valpolicella Negrar, Vigneti di Jago*
                                        Amarone Valpolicella Domini Veneti 2000
New Zealand White Trophy *Sileni Cellar Selection Sauvignon Blanc 2004*
New Zealand Red Trophy   *Saint Clair, Doctors Creek Pinot Noir 2003*

PORTUGAL
Douro   *Quinta do Vallado Reserva 2003*
Touriga   *Cortes de Cima, Touriga Nacional 2003*
Alentejo   *Herdade da Malhadinha Nova, Malhadinha 2003*
Madeira   *Cossart Colheita Malmsey 1998*
Tawny Port   *Graham's 30 Year Old Tawny Port*
Single Quinta   *Quinta de Roriz Vintage 2000*
LBV   *Smith Woodhouse Bottle Matured LBV 1994*
Vintage Port   *Offley Vintage Port 2003*
Port Trophy   *Offley Vintage Port 2003*
Portuguese Red Trophy *Herdade da Malhadinha Nova, Malhadinha 2003*

SPAIN
Priorat   *Bodegas de Cal Grau, Les Ones 2002*
Somontano   *Viñas del Vero, Secastilla Somontano 2003*
Bierzo   *Descendientes de J.Palacios, Petalos del Bierzo 2003*
Manzanilla   *Bodegas Hidalgo, Manzanilla La Gitana*   -
                         Lustau Emperatriz Eugenia Very Rare Oloroso
Spanish Red Trophy   *Abadía Retuerta, Seleccion Especial 2001*

SOUTH AFRICA
South Red African Trophy *Diemersfontein Carpe Diem Pinotage 2003*

USA
Red Trophy   *Hahn Estates Cabernet Sauvignon 2003*

International Trophies
Sauvignon Blanc   *Sileni Cellar Selection Sauvignon Blanc 2004*
Gewurztraminer   *Barmès-Buecher, Gewurztraminer Rosenberg 2003*
Riesling   *O'Leary Walker, Watervale Riesling 2004*
Chardonnay   *Louis Jadot Meursault 2002 Louis Jadot*
Pinot Noir   *Saint Clair, Doctors Creek Pinot Noir 2003*
Zinfandel   *Lowe Zinfandel 2003*
Cabernet Sauvignon / Merlot *Château Magrez Tivoli 2002*
Syrah / Grenache / Mourvedre *Domaine Massamier La Mignarde, Domus Maximus 2000*
Fortified Muscat   *Sanchez Romate Hermanos Moscatel Ambrosia*

ARGENTINA

Chasing its western neighbour Chile hard, Argentina is winning friends – and awards at the International Wine Challenge – with a variety of styles, many of which are hard to find elsewhere. Among these, it is worth particularly picking out the Torrontes – a curious Muscat-like variety that is almost unique to this country and, of course, the Malbec whose peppery Argentine reds are forcing the French to reconsider the way they handle these grapes. Look out, too, for the characterfull berryish Bonarda which seems to achieve more here than it usually does in Italy. Undeniably a country to watch for flavour and value.

SILVER
ARGENTINIAN WHITE

★ TRIVENTO VIOGNIER 2004, TRIVENTO Mᴇɴᴅᴏᴢᴀ – *Bright gold. White blossom, apricot, and white pepper etch the nose. Powerful, warming palate of lush peach fruit.*	£4.90 CNL/RAV TAN/WRW
☆ ELEMENTOS CHARDONNAY VIOGNIER 2004, PEÑAFLOR Sᴀɴ Jᴜᴀɴ – *Exotic, vigorous, youthful nose of lychees, satsumas, pineapples, and limes. This wine displays admirable equilibrium with length.*	£5.00 EHL
☆ FINCA DE ALTURA TORRONTES 2004, VIÑAS DE ALTURA Sᴀʟᴛᴀ – *Youthfully aromatic with zippy lemon sherbet on the nose. The palate is intense with lychee and crisp acidity.*	£5.00 VNO
☆ ALAMOS CHARDONNAY 2004, BODEGA CATENA ZAPATA Mᴇɴᴅᴏᴢᴀ – *This luscious beauty is a full-bodied yet graceful wine, with a big palate of lychees, passion-fruit, and mangosteen.*	£6.50 MWW/FLY
CANDELA VIOGNIER 2004, ESCORIHEULA GASCON Mᴇɴᴅᴏᴢᴀ – *Fresh stone fruits explode from the vivid nose. Round, vibrant, and weighty, with firm cleansing acidity.*	£7.60 FLY/PLB

B R O N Z E
ARGENTINIAN WHITE

☆ TRIVENTO CHARDONNAY TORRONTES 2004, TRIVENTO Mendoza – *A tropical Chardonnay with lychees, passion-fruit and mangoes on the nose and palate, balanced by a crisp acidity.*	£4.10 POR/RAV TAN/FLA WRW
☆ CARANCHO CHARDONNAY 2004, MENDOZA VINEYARDS Mendoza – *Pale and star bright, with a perfume of night-blooming jasmine and a palate of soft pear fruit.*	£5.00 WST
☆ LA CIMA TORRONTES 2004, LA RIOJANA La Rioja – *A young light aromatic wine with a crisp bite and good varietal character on the palate.*	£5.00 VGN
☆ SANTA JULIA VIOGNIER 2005, FAMILIA ZUCCARDI Mendoza – *Layers of juicy apricot and lush floral fruit matched with a citrus edge. The finish round and mouthwatering.*	£5.00 THI/JSM
TERRAZAS RESERVA CHARDONNAY 2004, TERRAZAS DE LOS ANDES Mendoza – *Tinged with green, this golden wonder has a handful of spices and racy acidity buttressing its smoky lemon flesh.*	£9.50 FHM/FLA WDI/HAC

S E A L   O F   A P P R O V A L
ARGENTINIAN WHITE

☆ SANTA LUCIA SÉMILLON CHARDONNAY 2004, LES GRANDS CHAIS DE FRANCE Mendoza – *Textured lemons, apples, and hints of nutmeg.*	£3.00 ALD
☆ LA FINCA SAUVIGNON BLANC 2004, FINCA LA CELIA Mendoza – *Fresh, sweetly ripe gooseberry fruit.*	£4.00 CWS
☆ SIGNOS CHARDONNAY CHENIN BLANC 2004, BODEGAS CALLIA San Juan – *Fresh golden apples and waxy lemons.*	£4.00 D&D

☆ SOMERFIELD ARGENTINE CHARDONNAY 2004, PEÑAFLOR Mendoza – *Freshly squeezed lemon and juicy peach flavours.*	**£4.00** SMF

TROPHY
ARGENTINIAN RED

MALBEC SINGLE VINEYARD LA CONSULTA 2003, BODEGAS TRAPICHE Mendoza – *Youthful nose of earth and dark fruit. Juicy raspberry flavours, cherries and prunes line the softly spiced palate.*	**£.00** NOT AVAILABLE IN THE UK
FINCA FLICHMAN RESERVA CABERNET SAUVIGNON 2004, FINCA FLICHMAN Mendoza – *Classic cassis, cedar, and cigar aromas. Lush fruit married to ripe tannins and precise new oak. Deep and complex.*	**£6.00** STG/MSW

GOLD
ARGENTINIAN RED

☆ BASTIANA 1561 SYRAH 2004, TRIVENTO Mendoza – *Scents of coaldust, flowers, and red plums. Crammed with damsons, raspberries, and hints of grilled meats.*	**£6.00** LAI
☆ LAS MORAS CABERNET SAUVIGNON SHIRAZ RESERVA 2003, FINCA LAS MORAS San Juan – *Notes of blackcurrant and mulberry. Rich black fruit on a framework of supple tannins and creamy new oak.*	**£7.00** CRI
☆ ANTIS CABERNET SAUVIGNON 2003, ANDEAN WINERIES Mendoza – *Ripe cassis, plum, and fruitcake aromas. Fabulous fruit purity, sensual tannic structure, and creamed oak.*	**£7.50** WPR/OCM
☆ CLOS DE LOS SIETE 2003, CLOS DE LOS SIETE Mendoza – *Michel Rolland's Argentinian masterwork is a whirl of silky blueberry, vanilla, coffee, and capsicum. Excellent.*	**£10.50** DOU

SILVER
ARGENTINIAN RED

☆ LA CIMA MALBEC 2004, LA RIOJANA FAMATINA VALLEY – *Rich, fruity aromas of redcurrants and blackberries. The palate is tinged with vanilla and coconut, supporting firm tannins.*	£5.00 VGN
FAMIGLIA MALBEC 2003, VALENTIN BIANCHI MENDOZA – *Concentrated, richly fruited and contemporary. Integrated, perfumed, and soft, it's full of blackberry flavours and coffee scents.*	£8.00 CHN
MALBEC LUIGI BOSCA 2002, LUIGI BOSCA MENDOZA – *A muscular, dark-fleshed offering, bramble fruits and scents of undergrowth on the nose, with a long balanced finish.*	£8.00 H&H
WEINERT MALBEC 2000, BODEGA Y CAVAS DE WEINERT MENDOZA – *Tobacco-scented black cherry and Victoria plum flavours. Scents of bonfire, asphalt, and toast. A round, powerful, integrated wine.*	£9.30 TAN/JSM WDI/HAC WRW
SAURUS PATAGONIA SELECT MALBEC 2003, FAMILIA SCHROEDER NEUQÉN – *Notes of mulberry, leather, and spice. Ripe fruit on a solid tannic frame with a good lick of vanilla oak.*	£10.00 MOR
CANALE BLACK RIVER RESERVE MALBEC 2004, HUMBERTO CANALE RIO NEGRO – *Deep, dark, and herb-strewn, with a smooth chocolatey texture and black plum flavours.*	£10.50 HWL
B CRUX 2002, BODEGAS O FOURNIER MENDOZA – *Big and chocolatey, with deep, intense crunchy blackcurrants, caramel, and dark plums. Spicy and ripe, with smooth texture.*	£11.20 BNK/SCK CCS/FLA
ALTIMUS 2002, MICHEL TORINO SALTA – *Deep, black fruit is liberally spiced with powerful oak flavours. Mint and liquorice curls from this inviting wine.*	£18.00 JSM
TRAPICHE ISCAY 2002, TRAPICHE MENDOZA – *Powerfully oaked, yet with good balance of fruit. Tight blueberry and blackberry flavours sprinkled with flakes of coconut.*	£20.00 HBJ

B R O N Z E
ARGENTINIAN RED

☆ GAUCHO BONARDA MALBEC 2004, VALENTIN BIANCHI **Mendoza** – *Smoky burning leaf aromas mingle with loganberries and mulberries on the brooding, structured palate.*	£4.00 CHN
☆ LA PUERTA MALBEC 2004, VALLE DE LA PUERTA **La Rioja** – *Round, robust and packed with fruit. Vivid acidity and structured tannins. Fresh, flavourful and long.*	£4.00 PAT
☆ SANTA JULIA FUZION SHIRAZ CABERNET SAUVIGNON 2004, FAMILIA ZUCCARDI **Mendoza** – *Fresh strawberry flavours meld with moist prunes, blueberries, and sweet little wildflowers. Full-bodied and structured.*	£4.00 THI
☆ TRIVENTO MALBEC 2004, TRIVENTO **Mendoza** – *Red plums, cherries, earth, and mixed spices tumble together in this flavourful wine. Vivid acidity freshens the fruit.*	£4.50 THS
☆ RESERVE MALBEC 2004, TRIVENTO **Mendoza** – *Wild raspberries, blackcurrants, and scents of garrigue emanate from this wine. Effortlessly fruity and very attractive.*	£4.90 RAV
☆ BALBI MALBEC 2004, BALBI **Mendoza** – *Freshly lit cigarillos, blackberries, leather, and allspice scent this robust, balanced, full-bodied, youthful Malbec.*	£5.00 AD1
☆ CASA MIRIAM RESERVE MALBEC 2004, CASA MIRIAM **Mendoza** – *Deep and filled with flavour, this wine has powerful blackberry and leather characteristics.*	£5.00 HPF
☆ ELEMENTOS SHIRAZ MALBEC 2003, PEÑAFLOR **San Juan** – *Little ripe sloes, hedgerow flowers, tobacco, Victoria plums, and chocolate flavour this robust, deeply coloured wine.*	£5.00 JSM
☆ MALBEC PIRCAS NEGRAS 2004, **La Rioja** – *This organically produced wine has leather, spicebox, damson, and blackcurrant flavours and scents. Young and clear.*	£5.00 VER

PASCUAL TOSO MALBEC 2004, PASCUAL TOSO **MENDOZA** – *Blackcurrants, spicebox, tobacco leaf, and tarmac elements combine in this mid-weight, balanced tipple.*	**£5.30** TNG/RAV WRW
TRAPICHE MALBEC 2004, TRAPICHE **MENDOZA** – *Blueberries, mulberries, raspberries, and hedgerow flowers scent and flavour this wine. Dense and dark.*	**£5.40** HBJ
RESERVE SHIRAZ MALBEC 2004, TRIVENTO **MENDOZA** – *Open, well-defined black and red vine fruit nose. The plum palate has caramel, peppers, and spice undertones.*	**£5.50** THS
TRAPICHE MERLOT 2004, BODEGAS TRAPICHE **MENDOZA** – *A hint of leafiness accents the sweet plum fruit nose. The finish is smoky and lingering.*	**£5.70** HBJ/CTC
CRIOS DE SUSANA BALBO SYRAH BONARDA 2003, DOMINIO DEL PLATA **MENDOZA** – *Tobacco, pepper, toast, rubber and cough syrup scent the nose. The palate is of creamy blackcurrants.*	**£5.90** ABY
RESERVA NIETO SENETINER 2003, BODEGAS NIETO SENETINER **MENDOZA** – *Ripe loganberry, prune and exotic cumin and coriander elements entwine in this characterful, full, powerful wine.*	**£6.00** CPR
RESERVA NIETO SENETINER 2003, BODEGAS NIETO SENETINER **MENDOZA** – *Glinting garnet colour. A touch of earthiness on the nose and a lengthy palate of plum jam.*	**£6.20** TRO/CPR RSV
BANDERAS SHIRAZ MALBEC RESERVE 2004, PEÑAFLOR **SAN JUAN** – *Black cassis, Havana cigars, crushed oregano, lilac, vanilla, and dessicated coconut flow from this concentrated wine.*	**£7.00** JSM
MALBEC BARREL SELECT 2003, BODEGA NORTON **MENDOZA** – *Powerful flavours of ripe, soft, chewy prunes. Rich, its opulent flesh is lifted and balanced.*	**£7.00** BWC
SANTA JULIA RESERVA CABERNET SAUVIGNON 2003, FAMILIA ZUCCARDI **MENDOZA** – *Currants, flowers, and minerals scent and flavour this mouthwatering Cabernet.*	**£7.00** THI

SANTA JULIA RESERVA MALBEC 2003, FAMILIA ZUCCARDI MENDOZA – *Clear, star-bright and packed with brooding dark plums, crisp redcurrants, star anise and vanilla beans.*	£7.00 THI
SANTA JULIA RESERVA TEMPRANILLO 2003, FAMILIA ZUCCARDI MENDOZA – *Crushed redcurrant, kirsch, coffee, earth, and wild herb palate. Sweet vanilla bean and toasted nut nose.*	£7.00 THI
ALTOS LAS HORMIGAS MALBEC 2004, ALTOS LAS HORMIGAS MENDOZA – *Clear, fragrant red and black hedgerow fruit flavours are laced with aromatic saddle leather nuances. Full-bodied.*	£7.30 V&C/RSV FLY
PASCUAL TOSO RESERVE MALBEC 2003, PASCUAL TOSO MENDOZA – *Perfumed with Havana cigars, violets, tree bark, and black cherries. Displaying restrained signs of evolution.*	£7.90 TPE/TNG
CANALE ESTATE RESERVE MERLOT 2003, CANALE RÍO NEGRO – *Plum fruit mingles with smoke and herbs; red plums and blackcurrants entwine.*	£8.00 M&S
CHAKANA CABERNET SAUVIGNON RESERVE 2003, CHAKANA WINES MENDOZA – *Very expressive, with a slightly chewy palate of warm velvety black cherry flavour. Balanced and dense.*	£8.00 L&T
CHAKANA MALBEC RESERVE 2003, CHAKANA WINES MENDOZA – *Dark cherries, blackberries, and spicebox aromas. Full-bodied, densely fruited, and balanced.*	£8.00 L&T
BENMARCO MALBEC 2003, DOMINIO DEL PLATA MENDOZA – *Robust yet refined, sultry prune and sloe flavours with a bouquet of smoke and crushed clove buds.*	£8.10 ABY
CABERNET SAUVIGNON RESERVA 2003, BODEGA NORTON MENDOZA – *Blackcurrant and cherry pie flavours. Full-bodied, with a tight-knit, very firm tannic structure.*	£9.00 BWC
PASSO DOBLE 2004, VIGNETI LA ARBOLEDA MASI MENDOZA – *Pretty, bright plum and sweet herb aromas. Mouthwatering, spicy, balanced and fresh. Medium-weight and youthful.*	£9.00 BWC

SANTA JULIA MAGNA RED 2002, FAMILIA ZUCCARDI **MENDOZA** – *Red cherries, coconut, vanilla pod, and toast intermingle on the nose and palate. Finely balanced with some evolution.*	£9.00 THI
TERRAZAS RESERVA CABERNET SAUVIGNON 2003, TERRAZAS DE LOS ANDES **MENDOZA** – *Freshly picked currants, capsicum, ground pepper, and tobacco. Aromatic and big.*	£9.60 FHM/MHU FLA/WDI HAC
Q TEMPRANILLO 2002, FAMILIA ZUCCARDI **MENDOZA** – *Powerful yet bright, its rich blackberry flesh riven by fresh acidity. Hints of bonfire, wildflowers, and toast perfume the bouquet.*	£10.00 TOS
PAISAJE DE BARRANCAS 2002, FINCA FLICHMAN **MENDOZA** – *Full, heady and forward, with powerful, lifted cassis and black plum fruit. Floral hints and very firm tannins.*	£10.50 FLY
PAISAJE DE TUPUNGATO 2002, FINCA FLICHMAN **MENDOZA** – *Highly coloured, with a palate of fresh redcurrants and a stylish hint of eucalyptus. Youthful.*	£10.50 FLY
ZUCCARDI Q TEMPRANILLO 2002, FAMILIA ZUCCARDI **MENDOZA** – *Smooth as silk. This bright, textured wine has red cherry flavours, tobacco leaf tannins, and a long finish.*	£11.40 TNG/THI
SUSANA BALBO MALBEC 2003, DOMINIO DEL PLATA **MENDOZA** – *Fine, linear ripe black cherry, cedar, smoke, leather and moist earth aromas and flavours spill from this brooding beauty.*	£12.00 WSO
TRAPICHE MEDALLA 2002, BODEGAS TRAPICHE **MENDOZA** – *Entering middle age with grace and style. Saddle, menthol, and redcurrant characteristics.*	£13.60 HBJ
A CRUX MALBEC 2002, BODEGAS O FOURNIER **MENDOZA** – *Saddle leather, liquorice, juicy plum fruit, and whiffs of lilac reel from this complex, layered, persistent wine.*	£18.40 BNK/SCK CCS/FLA
QUIMERA 2002, ACHAVAL FERRER **MENDOZA** – *Cool climate elegance. Very perfumed and floral, with delicate, complex fresh redcurrant flavours.*	£20.00 C&B

SEAL OF APPROVAL
ARGENTINIAN RED

☆ SANTA LUCIA SHIRAZ CABERNET 2004, LES GRANDS CHAIS DE FRANCE **Mendoza** – *Bright blueberry and plum flavours coalesce.*	£3.00 ALD
☆ SAINSBURY'S ARGENTINIAN BONARDA NV, SAINSBURY'S **La Rioja** – *Clear, ripe, lifted red berry fruit.*	£3.50 JSM
☆ TRIVENTO SHIRAZ MALBEC 2004, TRIVENTO **Mendoza** – *Deep blueberry and prune flavours. Robust.*	£3.90 NTT/POR RAV/TAN FLA/WRW
☆ CHE SYRAH 2003, PEÑAFLOR **San Juan** – *Floral notes hover over the palate of blueberries.*	£4.00 WXC
☆ LA FINCA CABERNET SAUVIGNON 2004, FINCA LA CELIA **Mendoza** – *Ripe blackcurrant flavours explode in the mouth.*	£4.00 CWS
☆ LA PUERTA SYRAH 2004, VALLE DE LA PUERTA **La Rioja** – *Lifted and intense. Vivid strawberry fruit.*	£4.00 PAT
☆ ORIGIN MALBEC MERLOT 2003, TRIVENTO **Mendoza** – *Robust prune and tar aromas. Plummy.*	£4.00 THS
☆ RIO DE PLATA MERLOT 2004, BODEGAS ETCHART **Mendoza** – *Clear damson flesh is lifted by bright acidity.*	£4.00 CAX
☆ SANTA JULIA FUZION SHIRAZ MALBEC 2004, FAMILIA ZUCCARDI **Mendoza** – *Juicy Victoria plum flavours. Boot polish nuances.*	£4.00 THI

☆ SIGNOS SHIRAZ CABERNET 2004, BODEGAS CALLIA **SAN JUAN** – *Smoke, leather, and ripe black berries.*	£4.00 D&D
☆ TESCO ARGENTINIAN BONARDA NV, TESCO **MENDOZA** – *Intense flavours of blackberries and leather.*	£4.00 TOS
☆ TRAPICHE MERLOT MALBEC 2004, BODEGAS TRAPICHE **MENDOZA** – *Blue-black plums, raspberries, and prunes.*	£4.00 HBJ

B R O N Z E
ARGENTINIAN ROSÉ

SANTA JULIA SYRAH ROSÉ 2005, FAMILIA ZUCCARDI **MENDOZA** – *Fairly streaming with juicy raspberries, dusky plums, notes of undergrowth, and a sweet little nosegay of flowers.*	£5.20 TNG/THI JSM

B R O N Z E
ARGENTINIAN SWEET

TORRONTES TARDIO 2004, BODEGAS ETCHART **SALTA** – *Pefumed with a bouquet of flowers. Flavours of limes, green apples, and fresh white peaches.*	£8.00 WTS

FOR STOCKIST CODES turn to page 317. For regularly updated information about stockists and the International Wine Challenge, visit wineint.com. For a full glossary of wine terms and a complete free wine course, visit robertjoseph-onwine.com

AUSTRALIA

Anyone who has taken even a passing interest in wine will have become aware of the way that Australia's winemakers have supplanted their French counterparts in the affection of British consumers. Today, more people are familiar with the flavour of Australian Shiraz and Chardonnay than with such Gallic classics as Burgundy and Bordeaux. And the trend is continuing in the Aussies' favour, as we discover great Aussie wines made from other varieties such as Semillon, Riesling, Malbec, Mourvèdre, and even Zinfandel. When we came to look at value for money – comparing medals to price – Australia did slightly less well than in the past, but we still found nearly 500 bargains...

TROPHY
AUSTRALIAN WHITE

EILEEN HARDY CHARDONNAY 2001, HARDY WINE COMPANY TASMANIA – *A superb nose of honey, resin, butter and white pear fruit. The citrus-laden palate is bright, fresh, and long.*	**£.00** NOT AVAILABLE IN THE UK
O'LEARY WALKER WATERVALE RIESLING 2004, O'LEARY WALKER SOUTH AUSTRALIA – *Lime blossom and citrus. The palate is fresh, with flavours of pineapples and lychees, caramel, and flint.*	**£.00** NOT AVAILABLE IN THE UK

GOLD
AUSTRALIAN WHITE

☆ **MCGUIGAN BIN 9000 SEMILLON 1999, MCGUIGAN SIMEON WINES** NEW SOUTH WALES – *Aromas of smoke, citrus, and honeysuckle. Rich, waxy lime and citrus fruit is checked by fine-boned acidity.*	**£6.50** VNO
☆ **THOMAS HYLAND CHARDONNAY 2003, PENFOLDS WINES** SOUTH AUSTRALIA – *Peach blossom, honeysuckle, toasted almonds, and lemons perfume the bouquet. Flavours of butterscotch, smoke, oranges, and marzipan.*	**£9.00** MWW/JSM

☆ ADAMS ROAD CHARDONNAY 2004, VASSE FELIX **Western Australia** – *Lush peach flesh is balanced by a fresh seam of acidity, and the sophisticated oak adds texture and richness.*	**£10.00** AWO/MW W FLA
☆ HRS CHARDONNAY 2004, HASELGROVE WINES **South Australia** – *Nutmeg, ginger, and honeysuckle nose. Flavours of nectarine, dill, peach, newly mown hay, and butterscotch line the palate.*	**£10.00** D&D
CAPE MENTELLE CHARDONNAY 2003, CAPE MENTELLE **Western Australia** – *Oatmeal and an edge of vanilla add interest to the aromatic tropical palate of starfruit, grapefruit, and melons.*	**£13.70** FHM/BNK JNW/WDI HAC
HOUGHTON PEMBERTON CHARDONNAY 2003, HOUGHTON **Western Australia** – *This is a nutty, generous wine with plenty of honeyed flavours and generous, mouthwatering lemon and mandarin orange flesh.*	**£14.00** CNT
ST ANDREWS RIESLING 2000, WAKEFIELD WINES **South Australia** – *Fine, poised petrol and citrus aromas. Crunchy and crisp, on a wealth of white peach, mineral, mango flavours.*	**£16.50** TNG
VAT 1 SEMILLON 1998, TYRRELL'S **New South Wales** – *Complex lime, quince, and floral aromas, balanced by ripe waxy citrus fruit and refreshing mineral acidity.*	**£19.00** FHM

SILVER
AUSTRALIAN WHITE

☆ ROSEMOUNT SEMILLON CHARDONNAY 2004, ROSEMOUNT ESTATE **Southeastern Australia** – *A youthful waxy, lemon nose. Sweet white blossom piquancy and a viscous mouthfeel.*	**£6.00** BGN/JSM HAC
☆ ANNIES LANE SEMILLON 2004, ANNIES LANE **South Australia** – *Fresh lemons and limes coupled with lively acidity, a creamy mouthfeel, good length, and a juicy, spicy finish.*	**£7.00** WFB
☆ BANWELL FARM SEMILLON 2003, ST HALLETT **South Australia** – *Beeswax and lemon perfumes continue on to the palate, cut through with crisp acidity and a viscous mouthfeel.*	**£7.00** M&S

☆ JAMIESONS RUN CHARDONNAY 2003, JAMIESONS RUN **South Australia** – *Intensely tropical, buttery ripe pineapple nose. Honeydew melon and grapefruit flavours and a creamy, dreamy texture.*	£7.00 WFB
☆ NEXT CHAPTER CHARDONNAY 2004, SALTRAM **South Australia** – *Opulent lemon, tropical guava, butter, and banana cream pie flavours and scents. Fresh acidity and good balance.*	£7.00 WFB
☆ ANNIES LANE RIESLING 2004, ANNIES LANE **South Australia** – *Greengages, lemons, and honey on the nose. Peaches, tea, kerosene, lime juice, and minerals flavour the palate.*	£7.50 WFB
JOT CHARDONNAY 2004, ARROWFIELD ESTATE **New South Wales** – *Clear, bright, and youthful. A wine of elegance and understatement, its fresh, poised lemony flavours are focused and very appealing.*	£8.00 ARF
WAKEFIELD RIESLING 2004, WAKEFIELD WINES **South Australia** – *Clear, crisp, light-bodied, and refreshing, this sports plenty of lemon zest flavours and aromas of minerals and flowers.*	£8.10 WIDELY AVAILABLE
KATNOOK FOUNDER'S BLOCK SAUVIGNON BLANC 2004, WINGARA WINE GROUP **South Australia** – *Intense leafy nose with crisp gooseberry fruit on the palate, uplifted by some delicate floral notes.*	£8.30 FLY
HEARTLAND VIOGNIER PINOT GRIS 2004, HEARTLAND WINES **South Australia** – *Whitecurrant, ripe pear, Granny Smith apple, lemon, lime, dried apricot, and bright satsuma flavours and scents.*	£8.50 NFW/TAN
TERRA BAROSSA PINOT GRIS 2004, THORN-CLARKE **South Australia** – *A spiced apricot cake nose and a palate that is sweet and full, with round ripe honeyed fruit.*	£8.50 NFW
TIM ADAMS CLARE VALLEY RIESLING 2004, TIM ADAMS WINES **South Australia** – *Pleasing petrol aromas. The attack of well-knit pear, apple, and ripe lemon fruit is crisp, clean, and fresh.*	£8.90 AUC/NFW TOS/OZW
CAPEL VALE RIESLING 2004, CAPEL VALE WINES **Western Australia** – *Bright lemon and pineapple scents. The palate displays some evolution, with toast, ruby grapefruit, and green apple flavours.*	£9.00 D&D

THE LAST DITCH VIOGNIER 2004, D'ARENBERG **SOUTH AUSTRALIA** – *Lavish peach and vivid lemon peel flavours spill from the palate. A delicate herbal edge enlivens the rich fruit.*	**£9.40** POR/V&C NFW/CCS FLY
PETER LEHMANN RESERVE SEMILLON 1999, PETER LEHMANN WINES SOUTH AUSTRALIA – *Kerosene, honey, and floral aromas. Crisp and well-balanced like elderflower sorbet, with a lovely fresh, uplifting quality.*	**£9.70** POR/NFW
ASHBROOK SEMILLON 2004, ASHBROOK ESTATE **WESTERN AUSTRALIA** – *Fresh green fruit on the nose. The palate has crisp, bright flavours with plenty of exotic Asian spices.*	**£10.00** CCS
WOLF BLASS PRESIDENT'S SELECTION CHARDONNAY 2003, WOLF BLASS WINES SOUTH AUSTRALIA – *Buttery crumbled biscuits and toasted walnut flavours integrate with banana, satsuma, and Bramley apples on the palate.*	**£10.00** BGN/TOS JSM
NEPENTHE CHARDONNAY 2003, NEPENTHE **SOUTH AUSTRALIA** – *Mineral shards sear the smooth, textured palate of Poire William and grapefruit. The nose displays muted signs of development.*	**£10.10** TNG/EDC FLA
EDEN VALLEY VIOGNIER 2004, YALUMBA **SOUTH AUSTRALIA** – *Exotic aromas of lychee and perfumed white peaches. Flavours of apricot and pineapple saturate the palate.*	**£10.20** CEB/NFW AWO/FLA
PENLEY ESTATE CHARDONNAY 2003, PENLEY ESTATE **SOUTH AUSTRALIA** – *Flowers, honey, ghee, peaches, and yeast aromas. The palate is round and concentrated, with spicy melon flavours.*	**£12.00** NFW
STONIER CHARDONNAY 2004, STONIER VICTORIA – *Nuts, toast, and flowers make an appearance on the nose. The palate shows an intensity of freshly squeezed lime flavours.*	**£14.00** WDI/HAC
STEINGARTEN RIESLING 2002, JACOB'S CREEK **SOUTH AUSTRALIA** – *Intense limeade, red apple, white stone fruit, and fresh hay aromas. The palate is packed with citrus fruit.*	**£15.00** CAX
BASTARD HILL CHARDONNAY , YARRA BURN VICTORIA – *Nuts, toast, and honey aromas, with flavours of lemon sherbet, pine needle, orange marmalade, and hay.*	**£20.00** CNT

MCWILLIAM'S MOUNT PLEASANT LOVEDALE SEMILLON 1999, MCWILLIAM'S New South Wales – *Bright gold with a mature nose of honey and beeswax. The palate is soft and toasty with citrus fruit notes.*	**£20.00** E&J
BROOKLAND VALLEY RESERVE CHARDONNAY 2003, BROOKLAND VALLEY Western Australia – *Ripe apples and melted butter, and a palate richly decorated with white peach, grapefuit, and honeydew melon flavours.*	**£25.00** CNT

B R O N Z E
AUSTRALIAN WHITE

☆ COLDRIDGE CHARDONNNAY 2004, COLDRIDGE ESTATE Southeastern Australia – *Pleasantly nutty, with spices and smoke whirling above the palate of balanced, integrated citrus fruit.*	**£3.70** MWW
☆ KELLY'S REVENGE RIESLING 2004, CONSTELLATION Southeastern Australia – *Green apples, honeysuckle, nectarines, and bright lime flavours. Dry and focused.*	**£4.40** MCT
☆ CO-OP AUSTRALIAN LIME TREE CHARDONNAY 2004, ANGOVE'S South Australia – *Lemons, limes, and fresh apple flavours. Aromas of flowers. Zingy acidity. Youthful.*	**£4.50** CWS
☆ TORTOISESHELL BAY SEMILLON SAUVIGNON BLANC 2004, CASELLA WINES New South Wales – *A lovely sherbet and herb nose. The palate has good concentration and balanced acidity. A pretty, lively, attractive wine.*	**£4.60** RAV
☆ BEAR CROSSING UNWOODED CHARDONNAY 2004, D&D WINES South Australia – *Ripe and lifted, with nutty orange and lemon fruit flavours. Pale gold. Dreamy and creamy.*	**£5.00** D&D
☆ MOONDARRA RESERVE CHARDONNAY 2004, KINGSTON Southeastern Australia – *Full-bodied flavours of nectarines, mandarin oranges, and freshly picked lemons.*	**£5.00** WAV
☆ WILDCARD CHARDONNAY 2004, PETER LEHMANN WINES South Australia – *Lemon yellow, with pear drop, Bramley apple, and mandarin orange flavours. Rich spice and fresh green pepper aromas.*	**£5.00** BGN

SHORT MILE BAY RIESLING 2004, CONSTELLATION SOUTHEASTERN AUSTRALIA – *Flowers and fresh citrus rise from the nose. The palate is off-sweet, rich, powerful, and balanced.*	**£5.20** MCT
BROWN BROTHERS DRY MUSCAT 2004, BROWN BROTHERS VICTORIA – *Unctuously sweet, round, aromatic, and honeyed. No wonder Pliny dubbed Muscat the "grape of the bees".*	**£5.30** BGN/TOS CNL/TAN JSM
MAKERS TABLE UNWOODED CHARDONNAY 2004, SALTRAM VICTORIA – *Pear and apple dominate the nose and palate of this fresh, balanced wine of good finesse.*	**£6.00** WFB
BROKEN EARTH VIOGNIER 2003, TANDOU WINES SOUTHEASTERN AUSTRALIA – *Enticing elderflower blossom aromas. Ripe orange peach flavours and a hint of peppery ginger.*	**£7.00** PLB
BROWN BROTHERS RIESLING 2004, BROWN BROTHERS VICTORIA – *A sweet and crisp gooseberry-style palate. Very appealing balance and a long and gentle finish.*	**£7.00** MAC
CV UNWOODED CHARDONNAY 2004, CAPEL VALE WINES WESTERN AUSTRALIA – *Pale and clear, with lemon fruit, smoke, and toast on the nose. Ripe yet cool and elegant, with some complexity.*	**£7.00** D&D
RUTHERGLEN MARSANNE 2004, RUTHERGLEN ESTATES VICTORIA – *Pungent ginger spice on the nose. Stone fruit palate. Good definition, fresh acidity, and nice weight.*	**£7.00** JSM
Y SERIES RIESLING 2004, YALUMBA SOUTH AUSTRALIA – *A key-lime nose and a fruit salad palate. Good acidity balances the fuller body. A more delicate floral finish.*	**£7.00** NFW/FLA
PROMISED LAND UNWOODED CHARDONNAY 2004, WAKEFIELD WINES SOUTH AUSTRALIA – *Pineapples and lime juice flavours. Aromas of grapefruit and acacia blossom. Vibrant and fresh.*	**£7.10** WPR/TPE NFW/TNG OZW/RAV
Y SERIES VIOGNIER 2004, YALUMBA SOUTH AUSTRALIA – *Enticing honeysuckle aromas and luscious, juicy tropical fruit. Hints of ginger and vanilla on the finish.*	**£7.10** WIDELY AVAILABLE

Y SERIES VIOGNIER 2004, YALUMBA SOUTH AUSTRALIA – *Enticing honeysuckle aromas and luscious, juicy tropical fruit flavours. Hints of vanilla on the finish.*	**£7.10** NFW/AWO TOS/MWW FLA/CTC
SYNERGY COONAWARRA CHARDONNAY 2004, LECONFIELD WINES SOUTH AUSTRALIA – *Toast, apricot, and pear scents. Tangy freshly picked lemon and green apple skin flavours. Minerally finish.*	**£7.20** NFW/TNG
YELLOW LABEL SOUTH AUSTRALIA CHARDONNAY 2004, WOLF BLASS WINES SOUTH AUSTRALIA – *Fruit cocktail scents. The palate is warm and honeyed, its sunny apple flavours graced with a hint of nettle.*	**£7.20** BGN/TOS MWW/JSM
MADFISH RIESLING 2004, HOWARD PARK WINES WESTERN AUSTRALIA – *A plucky, zesty Riesling with herbs on the aromatic nose and palate. Characterful and different.*	**£7.60** V&C/JNW
BRIGHTVIEW CHARDONNAY 2004, SIMON HACKETT SOUTH AUSTRALIA – *Lemon meringue pie, pear drop, and acacia bouquet. Lemon yellow with green glints.*	**£7.70** FHM/NFW CNL/WRW
BROWN BROTHERS SAUVIGNON BLANC 2004, BROWN BROTHERS WINES (MILAWA) PTY LTD VICTORIA – *Vivid gooseberry aromas and flavours. Bright, fresh, and grassy. Medium-bodied.*	**£7.80** CNL
TAHBILK MARSANNE 2002, TAHBILK VICTORIA – *Ripe nectarine fruit on the nose and dried apricots on the palate. Characterful nutty finish.*	**£7.80** ADN/FLA
CHAPEL HILL UNWOODED CHARDONNAY 2004, CHAPEL HILL SOUTH AUSTRALIA – *Ripe tropical pineapples, yellow apples, and perfume of powdery white flowers. Fresh and approachable.*	**£7.90** AUC/NFW OZW/FLA
HOPE ESTATE CHARDONNAY 2003, HOPE ESTATE NEW SOUTH WALES – *Linden flowers and honey scent the nose. The palate has plenty of lemon meringue flavours.*	**£7.90** WPR/TNG RAV
BIN 7 RIESLING 2004, LEASINGHAM SOUTH AUSTRALIA – *A light-bodied Riesling with apple and pear flavours and aromas. Refreshingly crisp finish.*	**£8.00** CNT

EDEN VALLEY RIESLING 2004, PETER LEHMANN SOUTH AUSTRALIA – *Quintessential petrol aromas. The palate is rich and round and lifted by lively acidity.*	**£8.00** PLE
MAMRE BROOK CHARDONNAY 2003, SALTRAM SOUTH AUSTRALIA – *Whiffs of smoke and toast scent the nose. The palate is ripe, warm, and firm, with hints of flint and crunchy apple flavours.*	**£8.00** WFB
PEMBERTON CHARDONNAY 2003, SWINGS AND ROUNDABOUTS WESTERN AUSTRALIA – *Butter and mango scents grace the bouquet. The palate has a creamy texture and zingy acidity.*	**£8.00** FLY
SMITHBROOK SAUVIGNON BLANC 2004, SMITHBROOK WESTERN AUSTRALIA – *A very light wine with appealing apple and pear fruit on the nose and a palate offset by delicate citrus acidity.*	**£8.00** BWL
ORGANIC CHARDONNAY 2004, PENFOLDS SOUTH AUSTRALIA – *Green-gold colour. The peachy palate has tropical overtones and floral notes. Crisp and balanced.*	**£8.20** BNK/VER WDI/HAC
THE OLIVE GROVE CHARDONNAY 2004, D'ARENBERG SOUTH AUSTRALIA – *Fresh citron married to sweet aromatic oak on nose and palate. Refreshing, youthful, and very pungent.*	**£8.20** NFW/CCS FLY
THE HERMIT CRAB VIOGNIER MARSANNE 2004, D'ARENBERG SOUTH AUSTRALIA – *Fleshy, round, and warming, this powerful wine has intense apricot kernel flavours and a toasty nose.*	**£8.60** WIDELY AVAILABLE
CAPEL VALE VERDELHO 2004, CAPEL VALE WINES WESTERN AUSTRALIA – *Green-tinged, with herbs on the nose and a crisp apple palate. Viscous and oily with a long refreshing finish.*	**£9.00** D&D
EDEN VALLEY RIESLING 2004, PEWSEY VALE SOUTH AUSTRALIA – *Aromas of lemon and marzipan follow through to the palate. Long, zesty finish.*	**£9.00** NFW/AWO RSV/FLA
HUNTER VALLEY SEMILLON 2004, BROKENWOOD NEW SOUTH WALES – *A clean and attractive wine with taut Granny Smith apple fruit, a fair zip of acidity, and a crisp finish.*	**£9.00** AWO/CCS FLY

KIRRIHILL RIESLING 2004, KIRRIHILL ESTATES	£9.00
SOUTH AUSTRALIA – *A mixture of tea leaves, melon, and orange peel. The passion-fruit palate has mature petrolly flavours.*	THI
MOUNT BARKER RIESLING 2004, PLANTAGENET	£9.00
WESTERN AUSTRALIA – *Elderflower perfume. Very elegant and refined, with bags of tart apples and good balance.*	NEC/RSV OZW/CCS BEN/FLY
PURPLE PATCH RIESLING 2004, CHAIN OF PONDS	£9.00
WINES SOUTH AUSTRALIA – *Mineral and kerosene notes on the nose. The palate is crisp and lemony with fresh acidity on the finish.*	AWO/D&D
TIM ADAMS SEMILLON 2003, TIM ADAMS WINES	£9.00
SOUTH AUSTRALIA – *An oaky nose and a creamy, soft palate. Forward fruit, yet overall, a subtle and restrained wine.*	AUC/POR TOS/OZW
YARRA BURN SAUVIGNON BLANC SEMILLON 2004,	£9.00
YARRA BURN VICTORIA – *Very light tropical mango and honeydew melon aromas. Crisp, steely, and tight kiwi fruit palate.*	CNT
NINTH ISLAND SAUVIGNON BLANC 2004, PIPERS	£9.10
BROOK VINEYARD TASMANIA – *A tart but sweet gooseberry nose, with a rich, ripe core of grapefruit and passionfruit. Good intensity.*	FHM/CPR WRK
CLARE VALLEY SEMILLON 2003, TIM ADAMS WINES	£9.30
SOUTH AUSTRALIA – *Ripe, round, and lush, this buttery Semillon has warm flavours of roast lemons and cloves with new-mown hay on the nose.*	AUC/NFW TOS
MCPHERSON RESERVE CHARDONNAY 2001,	£9.50
MCPHERSON VICTORIA – *Aniseed, butter, and clotted cream elements on the nose. The palate is long, with a zesty lime oil finish.*	TNG/NZH
EDEN VALLEY VIOGNIER 2003, YALUMBA	£9.80
SOUTH AUSTRALIA – *Expressive white peach and nectarine aromas and a balanced palate with honeysuckle on the finish.*	NFW/AWO TAN/FLA
GOLD LABEL RIESLING 2003, WOLF BLASS	£10.00
SOUTH AUSTRALIA – *Fresh acidity, crisp golden apples, ripe pears and peaches, and pretty floral scents. Lusciously ripe.*	WFB

HRS VIOGNIER 2004, HASELGROVE WINES SOUTH AUSTRALIA – *Pure apricot with a hint of musk. Round flavours of tropical lychee and stone fruit with crisp acidity and a lengthy finish.*	**£10.00** D&D
JARAMAN CHARDONNAY 2003, WAKEFIELD WINES SOUTH AUSTRALIA – *Richly oaked, with notes of artichoke and smoke. Vinous, textured, and packed with mature citrus flavours. Ripe and long.*	**£10.00** SWS
SHOW RESERVE CHARDONNAY 2002, WYNDHAM ESTATE SOUTHEASTERN AUSTRALIA – *Alluring brass-gold. The nose and palate have a dollop of warming, silky oak married to compliant lemon fruit.*	**£10.00** FHM
TAMAR RIDGE RIESLING 2004, TAMAR RIDGE WINES TASMANIA – *Zesty nose. A tangy citrus palate packed with flavour and scored by fresh acidity. Long and lively.*	**£10.00** OZW
TAMAR RIDGE SAUVIGNON BLANC 2004, TAMAR RIDGE WINES TASMANIA – *A zippy cut grass and asparagus nose. Bright, fresh, and tart, with good structure and a long finish.*	**£10.00** OZW
TESCO FINEST BAROSSA OLD VINES SEMILLON 2003, TESCO SOUTH AUSTRALIA – *A very attractive floral nose with a subtle mineral character. The palate is rich, with weight and elegance.*	**£10.00** TOS
COLDSTREAM HILLS CHARDONNAY 2003, COLDSTREAM HILLS VICTORIA – *The rich tropical nose has alluring lemon meringue and guava aromas. Vanilla essence and lychee flavours abound.*	**£10.30** SWP
EDEN VALLEY RESERVE RIESLING 2004, PENFOLDS SOUTH AUSTRALIA – *This wine has crisp acidity, aromatic purity, lovely balance, and a complex citrus palate.*	**£10.30** SWP
MOUNT BARKER CHARDONNAY 2004, PLANTAGENET WESTERN AUSTRALIA – *Orange zest and tangerine aromas. Pretty bruised apple flavours. Touches of melted butter and cardamom pod.*	**£10.40** NEC/V&C CCS/BEN FLY
SANDALFORD CHARDONNAY 2003, SANDALFORD WINES WESTERN AUSTRALIA – *Pale, buttery, and creamy, with lush tangerine fruit, lively acidity, and good weight. Spicy notes.*	**£10.50** AWO

THE CONTOURS EDEN VALLEY RIESLING 2000, PEWSEY VALE **SOUTH AUSTRALIA** – *A very petrolly nose. The palate is robust and citrusy with good length and balance.*	£11.00 NFW/AWO
ULEYBURY SEMILLON 2001, ULEYBURY **SOUTH AUSTRALIA** – *From the Northern Adelaide Hills facing the gulf of St Vincent. Sweetly ripe, linear, and packed with satiny lemon fruit.*	£11.00 AVD
KATNOOK ESTATE SAUVIGNON BLANC 2004, WINGARA WINE GROUP **SOUTH AUSTRALIA** – *A bright candied fruit nose and generous zesty citron palate. Robust acidity is off-set by an oily, weighty texture.*	£11.50 FLY
TAMAR RIDGE CHARDONNAY 2003, TAMAR RIDGE WINES **TASMANIA** – *Spicewood and melon bouquet. Light-bodied, approachable, and elegant, with apple fruit flavours.*	£12.00 OZW
CLARE VALLEY RIESLING 2004, MOUNT HORROCKS **SOUTH AUSTRALIA** – *A pale wine with a light, fruity body. Some bitter lemon zest flavours on the finish.*	£12.30 POR/AWO RSV/BEN FLY
PORT PHILLIP ESTATE CHARDONNAY 2003, PORT PHILLIP ESTATE **VICTORIA** – *Fresh pear, grapefruit, and mangosteen aromas. A thirst-quenching, vibrant Chardonnay.*	£13.00 P&S
YARRA VALLEY CHARDONNAY 2003, OAKRIDGE VINEYARD **VICTORIA** – *Seductive apricot compôte nose. Vanilla flavours complement the ripe juicy pineapple palate.*	£13.00 TOS
PATRICIA CHARDONNAY 2002, BROWN BROTHERS **VICTORIA** – *Intensely nutty, with smoke and butter on the nose. The palate drips with mangoes and melons. Golden green.*	£13.10 CPW
GATHERING SAUVIGNON BLANC 2003, STARVEDOG LANE **SOUTH AUSTRALIA** – *A mélange of gooseberries, Golden Delicious apples, elderflowers, and mace. Rich, velvety, and mouthwatering.*	£13.70 CPR/NFW
PICARDY CHARDONNAY 2003, PICARDY WINERY **WESTERN AUSTRALIA** – *Bright golden yellow, with a nose of creamy white fruit and a lush palate of ripe pears.*	£14.00 LAY

YARRA BURN CHARDONNAY 2003, YARRA BURN **Victoria** – *Noisette and figs compete with guava and peaches on the nose and palate. Clean, crisp, and beautiful.*	**£14.00** TNG
YABBY LAKE CHARDONNAY 2003, YABBY LAKE VINEYARD **Victoria** – *Red mango and white guava nose. Dreamy oak overtones soften the long, spicy palate of crisp lemon fruit.*	**£14.50** C&B
BROOKLAND VALLEY CHARDONNAY 2002, BROOKLAND VALLEY **Western Australia** – *Pale straw yellow. Toast and vanilla essence meld with candlewax, ghee, and green plums on the bouquet and in the mouth.*	**£15.00** CNT
PERSONAL RESERVE CHARDONNAY 2003, MCGUIGAN SIMEON WINES **New South Wales** – *Ripe, broad, and full. A touch of honey enriches the palate of textured green apple fruit.*	**£15.00** VNO
PERSONAL RESERVE CHARDONNAY 2004, MCGUIGAN SIMEON WINES **New South Wales** – *Clean, open, round, ripe, and balanced, with pretty oak and lime and lemon fruit.*	**£15.00** VNO
RESERVE CHARDONNAY 2003, COLDSTREAM HILLS **Victoria** – *Green gold. Impressive orange oil and roast nut nose. Big yet pretty, and saturated with cool climate fruit flavour.*	**£15.30** SWP
HOWARD PARK CHARDONNAY 2003, HOWARD PARK WINES **Western Australia** – *Round, luxuriant, and packed with melons and pears. Creamy yet fresh, with a spicy finish.*	**£15.40** V&C/JNW WRK
M3 VINEYARD CHARDONNAY 2003, SHAW AND SMITH **South Australia** – *Pineapple fruit maintains its dominance over the oak. A wine of contrasts, its pleasingly light body possessing a touch of earthiness.*	**£16.00** NEC/NFW RSV/CCS BEN/FLY
ST ANDREWS CHARDONNAY 2000, WAKEFIELD WINES **South Australia** – *Attractive and evolved, this wine is smooth and round with a textured mouthfeel and crisp lemon tart flavours.*	**£16.30** WIDELY AVAILABLE
BEGINNING CHARDONNAY 2001, STARVEDOG LANE **South Australia** – *Rich lemon, lime, mandarin orange, and ripe pear flavours. Warm, buttery toast scents linger on the nose.*	**£17.20** CPR/NFW

SAINT ANDREWS CHARDONNAY 2001, WAKEFIELD WINES **South Australia** – *Interesting aromas of tar and melon. The palate is evolved and soft, with butterscotch, vanilla, and fruit salad flavours.*	£17.20 FHM/TPE TNG/OZW
THE VIRGILIUS EDEN VALLEY VIOGNIER 2004, YALUMBA **South Australia** – *White peach and apricot aromas with a delicate ginger spice. Minerality and stone fruit on the palate.*	£19.00 CEB/NFW
RESERVE BIN CHARDONNAY 2000, PENFOLDS **New South Wales** – *Tropical fruit aromas. Lime zest flavours and scents. The oak lends honey and butter notes to the peach kernel flesh.*	£20.00 WDI/HAC
VAT 47 CHARDONNAY 2002, TYRRELL'S **New South Wales** – *Lively and fresh, with herbal nuances, elegant lemony fruit, toasty oak, and a buttery texture.*	£20.30 WDI/HAC WRW

SEAL OF APPROVAL
AUSTRALIAN WHITE

☆ SOMERFIELD FIRST FLIGHT DRY WHITE N/V, RIVERINA ESTATE **New South Wales** – *Luxuriant white and yellow tropical fruit.*	£3.00 SMF
☆ VINTNERS COLLECTION SEMILLON CHARDONNAY 2003, CONSTELLATION **Southeastern Australia** – *Smoothly textured, rich, and lemony.*	£3.50 LCC
☆ CO-OP JACARANDA HILL SEMILLON 2004, ANGOVE'S **Southeastern Australia** – *Bright yellow and white tropical fruit flavours.*	£4.00 D&D

TROPHY
AUSTRALIAN RED

☆ LOWE ZINFANDEL 2003, LOWE FAMILY WINE COMPANY **New South Wales** – *Intense spice and plum cake aromas. The palate is big, with soft tannins and well-integrated creamy oak.*	£12.30 SFW

YALDARA FARMS SHIRAZ 2002, MCGUIGAN SIMEON WINES SOUTH AUSTRALIA – *Scents of cigars, bittersweet chocolate, red peppers, and coconut milk. Long, luxuriant flavours of mulberries and black cherries.*	£19.00 TOS/VNO
JACK MANN CABERNET SAUVIGNON 1999, HOUGHTON WESTERN AUSTRALIA – *Powdered minerals, wildflowers, freshly mown hay, and vanilla beans. Layers of satiny French oak and vivid morello cherry fruit.*	£42.50 CNT

GOLD
AUSTRALIAN RED

☆ BETHANY BAROSSA SHIRAZ 2002, BETHANY WINES SOUTH AUSTRALIA – *A firm, savoury array of cherry pie, saddle leather, and blackberries. Sweetly ripe and densely packed.*	£8.00 D&D
☆ BASILISK SHIRAZ MOURVÈDRE 2002, MCPHERSON VICTORIA – *Rich and spicy with blackberry and cracked pepper. The tarry palate has ripe fruit, lush tannins, and sweet oak.*	£9.00 TNG
☆ JIP JIP ROCKS SHIRAZ 2004, JIP JIP ROCKS SOUTH AUSTRALIA – *Eucalyptus, cloves, smoke, and mouthwatering red cherry flavours. Youthful, round, and very elegant.*	£9.00 ORB
☆ KANGARILLA ROAD SHIRAZ 2003, KANGARILLA ROAD SOUTH AUSTRALIA – *Baked bramble, sweet currant, and wood smoke aromas. Lush and rich with supple tannins and a scoop of vanilla oak.*	£10.00 MWW
☆ JESTER MCLAREN VALE SHIRAZ 2004, MITOLO SOUTH AUSTRALIA – *Sweet vanilla and coconut aromas. Raspberry and black damson fruits with cooling touches of chocolate and mint.*	£10.10 NEC/NFW AWO/RSV CCS/FLY
☆ PERTARINGA UNDERCOVER SHIRAZ 2003, PERTARINGA SOUTH AUSTRALIA – *Blueberry, blackberry, and damson aromas. Dark fruit layered on a framework of ripe tannins and creamy vanilla oak.*	£10.10 NFW/TNG EDC/OZW RAV
☆ STELLA BELLA CABERNET MERLOT 2001, STELLA BELLA WINES WESTERN AUSTRALIA – *Elegant, restrained cocoa powder, moist prune, and black plum flavours are underpinned by fine dusty tannins.*	£10.90 TNG/OZW CCS/JSM

☆ **WILLOWS VINEYARD CABERNET SAUVIGNON 2001, SCHOLZ VINTNERS** Sᴏᴜᴛʜ Aᴜꜱᴛʀᴀʟɪᴀ – *Sweet blackberry, mint, and eucalyptus. The palate has lush berry fruit, harmonious tannins, and creamy oak.*	**£11.00** AUC
☆ **YAKKA SHIRAZ VIOGNIER 2003, LONGVIEW VINEYARD** Sᴏᴜᴛʜ Aᴜꜱᴛʀᴀʟɪᴀ – *Ripe blackcurrant fruit dusted with cinnamon, nutmeg, and clove spice. Herbs, black cherries, and sweaty saddle scents and flavours.*	**£11.00** FLY
BATTLE OF BOSWORTH SHIRAZ 2002, BATTLE OF BOSWORTH Sᴏᴜᴛʜ Aᴜꜱᴛʀᴀʟɪᴀ – *Pungent blackberry, tar, and smoke aromas. Succulent spicy fruit married to supple tannins and creamy new vanilla oak.*	**£12.60** NFW/TNG OZW/RAV FLA/VER
PERTARINGA OVER THE TOP SHIRAZ 2002, PERTARINGA Sᴏᴜᴛʜ Aᴜꜱᴛʀᴀʟɪᴀ – *Rich blackberry, vanilla, and leather aromas on the nose. The palate is round with lots of ripe black fruit, friendly tannins, and lashings of creamy oak.*	**£12.60** NFW/TNG EDC/OZW RAV
D'ARENBERG THE LAUGHING MAGPIE SHIRAZ VIOGNIER 2003, D'ARENBERG Sᴏᴜᴛʜ Aᴜꜱᴛʀᴀʟɪᴀ – *Opulent blackberry, spice, and vanilla aromas. Lashings of black fruit, friendly tannins, and well-integrated toasty oak.*	**£12.70** WIDELY AVAILABLE
ANGELS SHARE 2003, TWO HANDS WINES Sᴏᴜᴛʜ Aᴜꜱᴛʀᴀʟɪᴀ – *The palate is rich with juicy ripe blackberry fruit balanced by solid tannins and well-integrated vanilla oak.*	**£13.70** NFW/AWO TNG/CCS JSM
MAJELLA CABERNET SAUVIGNON 2002, MAJELLA WINES Sᴏᴜᴛʜ Aᴜꜱᴛʀᴀʟɪᴀ – *Crammed with finest chocolate and choicest blackcurrants. Exceptionally ripe, with a vivid peppermint streak lifting its richness.*	**£13.70** WIDELY AVAILABLE
BLACKWELL BAROSSA SHIRAZ 2002, ST HALLETT Sᴏᴜᴛʜ Aᴜꜱᴛʀᴀʟɪᴀ – *A heady mix of dark cherry, coffee, and plums, with gamey hints. Raspberry fruit with a sprinkle of vanilla.*	**£14.00** POR/NFW JSM
PORT PHILLIP PINOT NOIR 2003, PORT PHILLIP ESTATE Vɪᴄᴛᴏʀɪᴀ – *Full-bodied red stone fruit flesh. Pine nut, wild strawberry undertones, and aromas on the nose.*	**£14.00** P&S
SHOW RESERVE MCLAREN VALE SHIRAZ 2001, ROSEMOUNT ESTATE Sᴏᴜᴛʜ Aᴜꜱᴛʀᴀʟɪᴀ – *Pungent leather and bramble aromas. Lush black fruit with integrated tannins and lashings of oak.*	**£14.00** WDI/HAC

KATNOOK ESTATE CABERNET SAUVIGNON 2002, WINGARA WINE GROUP SOUTH AUSTRALIA – *Its layers of spice, blackberries, and blueberries fill the mouth with a textured attack and a lasting finish.*	£14.50 FLY
THE MCRAE WOOD CLARE VALLEY SHIRAZ 2001, JIM BARRY SOUTH AUSTRALIA – *Sweet blackberry, eucalyptus, and wood smoke aromas. Tightly packed with super-ripe berries, lush creamy oak, and fine grained tannins.*	£15.10 NFW/AWO TAN/FLA
WOLF BLASS GREY LABEL SHIRAZ 2002, WOLF BLASS WINES SOUTH AUSTRALIA – *Pungent blackberry, smoke, and tar notes. Layered sweet fruit, excellent tannic structure, and a dollop of new oak.*	£18.00 WFB
YABBY LAKE PINOT NOIR 2003, YABBY LAKE VINEYARD VICTORIA – *Clear, intense black cherry and mulberry flavours. Generously spiced with ground cumin, crushed tomato leaves, and cinnamon bark.*	£19.50 C&B

SILVER
AUSTRALIAN RED

★ BOUNDARY ROAD SHIRAZ 2002, PALANDRI WINES WESTERN AUSTRALIA – *Weighty, ripe berry fruit flavours. Rich, round, and full, with complex aromas of cloves and dusty autumn leaves.*	£6.00 CWS
☆ KISS CHASEY CABERNET SHIRAZ MERLOT 2004, SWINGS AND ROUNDABOUTS WESTERN AUSTRALIA – *Earthy notes of freshly turned earth mingle with raspberries and currants on the nose. Elegant peppery fruit.*	£6.30 FLY
☆ BIN 999 MERLOT 2003, WYNDHAM ESTATE SOUTHEASTERN AUSTRALIA – *Powerful sugar plum aromas. The palate is a lively, exciting affair, packed with sun-warmed fruit and soft tannins.*	£7.00 FHM
☆ PALANDRI ESTATE SHIRAZ 2002, PALANDRI WINES WESTERN AUSTRALIA – *Notes of mint and eucalyptus scent the nose. Flavours of damsons, mulberries, and herbs permeate the palate.*	£7.50 EDC
HEARTLAND WIRREGA SHIRAZ 2002, HEARTLAND SOUTH AUSTRALIA – *Bright and youthful, blackberry compôte with tingling eucalyptus aromas. Rich, concentrated fruit character balanced with delicate warm spice.*	£8.00 ODD

MARGARET RIVER SHIRAZ 2004, SWINGS AND ROUNDABOUTS WESTERN AUSTRALIA – *Hints of pepper and mocha on the nose and a palate of big soft crushed blackberries.*	£8.00 FLY
WAKEFIELD CABERNET SAUVIGNON 2003, WAKEFIELD WINES SOUTH AUSTRALIA – *Intense blackcurrant, raspberry, and blueberry flavours. The nose has plenty of flowers, leather, and hints of spice.*	£8.10 WIDELY AVAILABLE
FAITH SHIRAZ 2003, ST HALLETT SOUTH AUSTRALIA – *The palate is packed with dark berries; its sweetly ripe flavours flooded with fresh acidity and supported by supple tannins.*	£8.20 BNK/NFW JSM
PETER LEHMANN CABERNET SAUVIGNON 2002, PETER LEHMANN WINES SOUTH AUSTRALIA – *Laden with vanilla bean aromas. Vivid, muscular tannins are subsumed into the many layers of sumptuous fruit.*	£8.50 NFW
PETER LEHMANN MERLOT 2003, PETER LEHMANN WINES SOUTH AUSTRALIA – *Deep yet bright, with rosemary, coffee, and chocolate. Prune and plum flavours with the merest hint of sundried tomato.*	£8.50 NFW
BANWELL FARM SHIRAZ 2002, ST HALLETT SOUTH AUSTRALIA – *Plums, capsicum, leather, and flowers scent the bouquet. Integrated oak, scarlet, and dusky black damson flavours.*	£9.00 M&S
MCLAREN VALE SHIRAZ 2003, ANGOVES SOUTH AUSTRALIA – *Sweetly herbaceous nose with warm earth and coffee undertones. The palate is loaded with ripe cherries and blackberries.*	£9.00 D&D
STICKS YARRA VALLEY CABERNET 2003, STICKS YARRA VALLEY WINERY VICTORIA – *A deep purple palate of game, cassis, and coal smoke. Ripe and ready to drink.*	£9.00 MWW
TAHBILK RESERVE CABERNET SAUVIGNON 1998, TAHBILK VICTORIA – *This structured wine has an attack of red and black berries underpinned by a taut, integrated tannic structure.*	£9.00 CTL
KATNOOK FOUNDER'S BLOCK CABERNET SAUVIGNON 2002, WINGARA WINE GROUP SOUTH AUSTRALIA – *Pretty violet, rosemary, and mint notes. A full complement of ripe berries, walnuts, roast herbs, and savoury grilled meat.*	£9.30 FLY

NINTH ISLAND PINOT NOIR 2004, PIPER'S BROOK VINEYARD **Tasmania** – *Richly coloured and intriguing. A nose of mace, allspice, and green peppercorns and a palate of vibrant red cherries.*	**£9.30** FHM/CPR RSV/CNL WRK/JSM
TWO GENTLEMEN'S GRENACHE 2003, PERTARINGA **South Australia** – *Refined petal, pepper, spicebox, and strawberry scents. Supple, juicy fruit, grippy tannins and a long, floral finish.*	**£9.80** NFW/TNG EDC/OZW RAV
JARAMAN SHIRAZ 2002, WAKEFIELD **South Australia** – *Aromas of sweetly ripened fruits. The palate exudes elegance with supple blackberries, chocolate truffle, and fine cigar.*	**£10.00** SWS
KIES MONKEY NUT TREE MERLOT 2002, KIES FAMILY WINES **South Australia** – *Toast, spices and cigar aromas. The palate is spicy and sweetly fruited, with mellow yet balanced tannins.*	**£10.00** NFW
KIRRIHILL ESTATES SHIRAZ 2002, KIRRIHILL ESTATES **South Australia** – *Black pepper and mulberry on the nose. Concentrated fruits are well integrated with warming spice and long peppery finish.*	**£10.00** THI
MAMRE BROOK CABERNET SAUVIGNON 2002, SALTRAM **South Australia** – *Lively violet and blackberry aromas and flavours pervade this stylish offering. Explosive flavours, strong tannins, and a long finish.*	**£10.00** WFB
THE FERGUS 2002, TIM ADAMS WINES **South Australia** – *Sweet aromas of freshly baked currant and blackberry tart. Brambles and blueberries populate the leathery, savoury palate.*	**£10.00** AUC/TOS
RICHARD HAMILTON HUT BLOCK CABERNET SAUVIGNON 2002, LECONFIELD WINES **South Australia** – *Scents of asphalt, leaves, and flowers. The palate is a rich array of tight-knit blue and black berries.*	**£10.70** NFW/TNG
HOWARD PARK SCOTSDALE 2002, HOWARD PARK WINES **Western Australia** – *Plenty of fresh crushed mint aromas and lively acidity. Velvet black fruit flavours and silky tannins.*	**£10.80** JNW
VALLEY FLOOR BAROSSA SHIRAZ 2003, LANGMEIL WINERY **South Australia** – *Soft squashed raspberries, cream, toffee, and earth aromas. Opulent and lingering, its blackberry fruit laced with herbs.*	**£11.00** ADN

MCLAREN VALE GRENACHE 2003, WIRRA WIRRA VINEYARDS SOUTH AUSTRALIA – *Delicate notes of smoke, roast herbs, and toasted almonds. Coffee and chocolate nuances and spicy red cherry flavours.*	**£11.50** HBJ
PHOENIX CABERNET SAUVIGNON 2003, PENLEY ESTATE SOUTH AUSTRALIA – *Aromas of menthol, eucalyptus, and violets. The palate is densely fruited with blackberries and blueberries.*	**£12.20** POR/NFW CCS
RUFUS STONE HEATHCOTE SHIRAZ 2003, TYRRELL'S VICTORIA – *Vivid flavours of raspberries, stone, and coffee, and aromas of violets, candied cherries, and blackberries.*	**£12.70** TYR /FLA HAC
WILSON GUNN RESERVE MCLAREN VALE SHIRAZ 2003, HJH BARREL WINES SOUTH AUSTRALIA – *Sweet flowers, eucalyptus, and pepper. The palate is herbal, intense, well-structured, and saturated with mulberry fruit.*	**£12.90** LAI
LEDGE SHIRAZ 2002, CHAIN OF PONDS WINES SOUTH AUSTRALIA – *Green apple, currant, and chocolate aromas. The palate is balanced, and packed with vibrant blackcurrant flavours.*	**£13.00** AWO/D&D
MORAMBRO CREEK 2003, C&E BRYSON SOUTH AUSTRALIA – *Inky and intense, with ground nutmeg, toast, and sweet coconut. Very long, with dense, smoky red fruit flavours.*	**£13.00** WOZ
PENNY'S HILL SPECIALIZED SHIRAZ CABERNET MERLOT 2003, PENNY'S HILL SOUTH AUSTRALIA – *Opulently rich blackberry and cherry flavours. Herbal notes, mint, and flowers add lift to the clear, saturated palate.*	**£13.00** NFW
PONDALOWIE VINEYARDS SHIRAZ 2003, PONDALOWIE VINEYARDS VICTORIA – *Blueberries, spice, loganberries, and leather assail the senses. A densely constructed, richly fruited effort from Pondalowie.*	**£13.00** AUC/OZW
WOLF BLASS PRESIDENTS SELECTION CABERNET 2002, WOLF BLASS WINES SOUTH AUSTRALIA – *A sprinkling of mint, raspberry leaves, smoke, and thyme. Flavours of creamy oak, smoke, dusky cherries, and chocolate.*	**£13.00** MWW
SPEAR GULLY SHIRAZ 2003, SPEAR GULLY VICTORIA – *Milk chocolate, cracked pepper, raspberries, and tobacco leaves. Full-bodied and deeply coloured, with a long finish.*	**£13.70** AUC/POR OZW

PICARDY PINOT NOIR 2003, PICARDY WINERY **WESTERN AUSTRALIA** – *A warm concoction of figs and cherry compôte. Firm and complex, with hints of bay leaf and nutmeg-dusted strawberries.*	**£14.00** LAY
HAND PICKED BAROSSA SHIRAZ VIOGNIER 2002, YALUMBA **SOUTH AUSTRALIA** – *Minty and deep, with blackberry, plum, vanilla, and undergrowth scents. The textured palate boasts chewy cherry fruit flavours.*	**£15.00** NFW/FLA
HEYSEN 2002, ROLF BINDER WINES **SOUTH AUSTRALIA** – *Sweet cassis and redcurrant nose. The fine mouthcoating texture buoys the palate of plums and spice.*	**£15.00** NFW/SCK CCS
MCGUIGAN PERSONAL RESERVE CABERNET SAUVIGNON 1998, MCGUIGAN SIMEON WINES **SOUTH AUSTRALIA** – *A nose redolent of menthol and scents of earth, its palate a dense wall of blackcurrants, minerals, and tree bark.*	**£15.00** VNO
MCLAREN VALE GSM 2001, ROSEMOUNT ESTATE **SOUTH AUSTRALIA** – *Fresh black plums and greengages. Vanilla bean smoothness and integrated tannins ensconce the cinnamon, blackberry, and asphalt palate.*	**£15.00** WDI/HAC
SHIRAZ VIOGNIER 2001, LADBROKE GROVE **SOUTH AUSTRALIA** – *Warm nose of bonfire smoke, baked black plums, and menthol. Ripe juicy cherries and toasty oak flavour the palate.*	**£16.00** AVD/WOZ
BALNAVES CABERNET SAUVIGNON 2001, BALNAVES OF COONAWARRA **SOUTH AUSTRALIA** – *Fragrances of vanilla pod, blackcurrant leaves, and cinnamon bark. Powerfully ripe, mature berries, and robust integrated tannins.*	**£16.20** CCS/BEN FLY
BRAVE FACES 2003, TWO HANDS WINES **SOUTH AUSTRALIA** – *Peppery, raspberry nose. Balanced, with supple tannins, silky vanilla, and stylish juicy blackberry flavours.*	**£17.40** NFW/AWO TNG/OZW CCS
GREY LABEL CABERNET SAUVIGNON 2002, WOLF BLASS WINES **SOUTH AUSTRALIA** – *Rich blackberry and mulberry flavours. Spicebox, teapot, and currant leaf aromas add another dimension.*	**£18.00** WFB
WILGHA SHIRAZ 2002, HOLLICK **SOUTH AUSTRALIA** – *Bramble fruits, balanced tannins, redcurrants, and undertones of oak. Fine, rich, mouthcoating, and long. Hints of mint and eucalyptus.*	**£18.00** SCK/CCS FLA

WILLIAM RANDELL SHIRAZ 2001, THORN CLARKE SOUTH AUSTRALIA – *Aromas of sun-drenched berries and baked earth, the palate displaying ripe fruit wrapped in warm coffee and chocolate.*	£18.00 NFW
PATRICIA SHIRAZ 2002, BROWN BROTHERS VICTORIA – *Rich, juicy, and powerful, with hints of flowers and leather. A polished palate of cassis, prunes, and mocha.*	£18.50 CPW
THE ABERFELDY 2002, TIM ADAMS WINES SOUTH AUSTRALIA – *Full bodied and elegantly rich, cool with minty blackberry, crisp acidity, and plenty of toasted vanilla oak.*	£19.30 AUC/POR OZW
WIRRA WIRRA RSW SHIRAZ 2002, WIRRA WIRRA VINEYARDS SOUTH AUSTRALIA – *Densely layered with cocoa, liquorice, black cherries, and earth. A powerful and complex wine.*	£19.40 HBJ
THE MENZIES COONAWARRA CABERNET SAUVIGNON 2001, YALUMBA SOUTH AUSTRALIA – *Leather, smoke, and blackberry compôte aromas and flavours. Lushly fruited yet buoyed by uncompromising tannins.*	£19.50 NFW/RSV
PENLEY ESTATE 2002, PENLEY ESTATE SOUTH AUSTRALIA – *Morello cherry, bramble pie, and mulberry flavours provide a ravishing feast. Bright, with opulent vanilla oak elements.*	£20.00 MOR
ST ANDREWS MERLOT 2002, WAKEFIELD WINES SOUTH AUSTRALIA – *Tight little blue-black hedgerow fruit flavours. Fresh, mouthcoating, and tightly knit, with fine, grainy tannins and a long finish.*	£20.00 SWS
THE SIGNATURE BAROSSA CABERNET SAUVIGNON SHIRAZ 2001, YALUMBA SOUTH AUSTRALIA – *Hints of menthol and pine cones scent the nose. Toasty red stone fruit flavours, vanilla, coconut, and coffee.*	£20.00 NFW
THE IRONSTONE PRESSINGS GRENACHE SHIRAZ MOURVÈDRE 2002, D'ARENBERG SOUTH AUSTRALIA – *The powerful prune, Victoria plum, and strawberry nose flavours are dotted with cinnamon spice. Muscular and dense.*	£21.30 POR/NFW OZW/CCS FLY
THE IRONSTONE PRESSINGS GRENACHE SHIRAZ MOURVÈDRE 2003, D'ARENBERG SOUTH AUSTRALIA – *Cedar bark, vanilla, and dark damson fruit. Ripe cherry and currant fruit sprinkled with cracked pepper.*	£21.40 POR/NFW OZW/CCS DAR/FLY

RAVENSWOOD CABERNET SAUVIGNON 2000, HOLLICK SOUTH AUSTRALIA – *Fresh gum tree and menthol notes scent the nose. The palate is full of currants. Structured and dense.*	**£21.50** BNK/SCK CCS
LEASINGHAM CLASSIC CLARE CABERNET SAUVIGNON 2001, LEASINGHAM SOUTH AUSTRALIA – *Black fruits, sweet spice, and dried herbs. The palate is warm and dense, with chocolate, smoke, liquorice, and toffee.*	**£22.00** CNT
PENLEY ESTATE RESERVE CABERNET SAUVIGNON 2002, PENLEY ESTATE SOUTH AUSTRALIA – *Spearmint, earthy minerals, mouthwatering Victoria plums, and blackcurrants. Juicy fruit, sweet herbs, and spices on the nose.*	**£23.00** CEB/NFW CCS
BROOKLAND VALLEY RESERVE CABERNET SAUVIGNON 2001 WESTERN AUSTRALIA – *Intensely perfumed with flowers, herbs, and redcurrants. Flavours of mulberries and blackberries pour from the structured, sophisticated palate.*	**£25.00** CNT
NEST EGG MERLOT 2002, BIRD IN HAND SOUTH AUSTRALIA – *Crème de cassis, prune, and earth flavours line the velvety palate. Full-bodied, with a layered, structured quality.*	**£25.00** AVD
KING LOUIS CABERNET 2003, FOX GORDON SOUTH AUSTRALIA – *Blackcurrant essence and lifted spearmint and eucalyptus aromas. Sweet juicy fruit with a firm tannic backbone.*	**£26.00** ODD
HANNAH'S SWING SHIRAZ 2003, FOX GORDON SOUTH AUSTRALIA – *Plum and earthy mushroom aromas, delicate French oak, and fine chalky tannins. An elegant wine that needs time to evolve.*	**£27.00** ODD
THE TALLY 2001, BALNAVES OF COONAWARRA SOUTH AUSTRALIA – *Leather and spice play with menthol on the nose. Harmonious and deep, with layers of blackcurrant fruit flavours.*	**£29.60** CCS/FLY
BLACK LABEL SHIRAZ CABERNET SAUVIGNON 2001, WOLF BLASS WINES SOUTH AUSTRALIA – *Black fruit flavours scented with toast and coconut milk. Admirably balanced tannin and acidity. Spice and herb nuances.*	**£30.00** WFB
COONAWARRA ESTATE FIRST GROWTH 2000, PARKER ESTATE SOUTH AUSTRALIA – *Spices, currant leaves, and roast herbs. The palate is packed with blackberries, summer wildflowers, and savoury hints of game.*	**£30.00** C&B

COMMAND SINGLE VINEYARD SHIRAZ 2001, ELDERTON WINES SOUTH AUSTRALIA – *Blueberry compôte and cream bouquet. Lively yet soft, with warm black fruit flavours and bright cleansing acidity.*	£31.50 FLY

B R O N Z E
AUSTRALIAN RED

☆ JINDALEE MERLOT 2003, JINDALEE SOUTHEASTERN AUSTRALIA – *Big, clear, and chocolatey, with hints of green pepper, vanilla, and game, this is an enchanting wine.*	£5.00 EHL
SHORT MILE BAY MERLOT 2004, SHORT MILE BAY SOUTHEASTERN AUSTRALIA – *Menthol, black fruits, and spice. With its juicy flavours, firm tannins, and medicinal hints, this one's a winner.*	£5.20 MCT
SHORT MILE BAY SHIRAZ 2004, CONSTELLATION SOUTHEASTERN AUSTRALIA – *Blackberries, stony minerals, earth, and pepper. Fresh and leathery. Balanced and fresh.*	£5.20 MCT
MIGHTY MURRAY ESTATE MALBEC 2004, ANDREW PEACE WINES SOUTHEASTERN AUSTRALIA – *Vivid red plum fruit, loganberries, black cherries, and hints of tomato flavour. Aromas of saddle leather and cloves.*	£5.50 ASD
OXFORD LANDING SHIRAZ 2003, YALUMBA SOUTH AUSTRALIA – *Cassis and mulberry fruit on the nose, with spicy oak and full rich vanilla flavours on the mid-palate.*	£5.50 NFW/TOS
PETER LEHMANN GRENACHE 2002, PETER LEHMANN SOUTH AUSTRALIA – *Earthy, with bitter chocolate, currants, saddle leather, and minerals on the nose, and a structured strawberry fruit palate.*	£5.70 POR/BGN NFW/TOS FLA
JACOBS CREEK CABERNET SAUVIGNON 2003, JACOBS CREEK SOUTHEASTERN AUSTRALIA – *Roast coffee bean and eucalyptus nose. Flavours of crunchy cassis and creamy oak. Supple tannins.*	£5.80 BGN/TOS JSM
MOORE'S CREEK SHIRAZ 2004, TYRRELLS VINEYARDS NEW SOUTH WALES – *Firm, structured, and filled with plum fruit. Aromatic mineral and earth tones.*	£5.80 FLA/ICL HAC

HARDYS NOTTAGE HILL SHIRAZ 2003, HARDYS SOUTHEASTERN AUSTRALIA – *Soft and straightforward. The nose is subtle and gives way to a round palate that includes light fruit and floral notes.*	£6.00 BGN
HOUGHTON CYGNET CABERNET SHIRAZ 2002, HOUGHTON WESTERN AUSTRALIA – *Capsicum and lavender aromas. Flavours of blackcurrant jam.*	£6.00 CNT
MIGHTY MURRAY RESERVE SHIRAZ 2004, ANDREW PEACE WINES SOUTHEASTERN AUSTRALIA – *Sultry black and purple colour. An intriguing Shiraz with mocha-laced fruit. Firm tannins and enjoyable length.*	£6.00 ASD
STICKLEBACK RED 2003, HEARTLAND WINES SOUTH AUSTRALIA – *Brambly nose. Red spiced fruit palate. Long and understated, with hints of coal and cedar.*	£6.00 NFW
THE DELVER PETIT VERDOT 2004, MCGUIGAN SIMEON SOUTHEASTERN AUSTRALIA – *Aromas of violets and spice. Mouthwatering attack of bramble fruit. Round and bursting with blackberries and cherries.*	£6.00 LAI
HANWOOD ESTATE CABERNET SAUVIGNON 2004, MCWILLIAMS SOUTHEASTERN AUSTRALIA – *Opaque purple. Redcurrant fruit, minerals, and creamy vanilla on the nose. Intense and warming.*	£6.50 TOS/E&J
TRIMBOLI'S FAMILY RESERVE SHIRAZ 2004, RIVERINA ESTATE NEW SOUTH WALES – *Ripe and round, with generous spice, soft tannins, and mint notes. Rich prune and raisin flavours.*	£6.50 LAI
WATERSTONE BRIDGE RESERVE SHIRAZ 2003, YALDARA SOUTH AUSTRALIA – *Juicy, with floral notes. A refreshing wine with soft tannins and quaffable creamy fruit.*	£6.60 TPE/RAV
BIN 555 SHIRAZ 2002, WYNDHAM ESTATE SOUTHEASTERN AUSTRALIA – *Elegant, intense, and well balanced. Ripe rich cherry scents. The palate is caressed by chocolate cream.*	£7.00 FHM/MW W JSM
BROWN BROTHERS BARBERA 2002, BROWN BROTHERS VICTORIA – *Earthy, deep, and evolved. Rich sweet blackberry fruit. Good balance and a lasting finish.*	£7.00 ASD

MONTY'S HILL OAK AGED SHIRAZ CABERNET 2002, WINGARA WINES **Victoria** – *Rich dark fruit laced with lifted eucalyptus and prevalent oak. Lingering finish.*	£7.00 LAI
NEXT CHAPTER CABERNET MERLOT 2003, SALTRAM **South Australia** – *Ripe blackcurrants, spices, and prunes; eucalyptus, mint, and vanilla. A satisfyingly layered wine.*	£7.00 WFB
RESERVE SOUTH AUSTRALIAN SHIRAZ 2000, LINDEMANS **Southeastern Australia** – *Clear, bright juicy cherry and raspberry flavours. This well-made wine is full and powerful yet has great subtlety.*	£7.00 SWP
SAINSBURY'S CLASSIC SELECTION WESTERN AUSTRALIA CABERNET SAUVIGNON MERLOT 2003, FOREST HILL **Western Australia** – *Medium-full, with floral notes and star anise on the nose. Mouthwatering and round.*	£7.00 JSM
SAINSBURYS CLASSIC SELECTION BAROSSA SHIRAZ 2003, ST HALLETT **South Australia** – *Flowers, cranberries, and sundried red peppers on the nose. The palate has spiced Victoria plums and touches of mint.*	£7.00 JSM
SKUTTLEBUTT CABERNET SAUVIGNON SHIRAZ MERLOT 2003, STELLA BELLA WINES **Western Australia** – *This structured wine has loads of ripe blackberry flavours and is veering gracefully towards mid-life.*	£7.00 ALL
STONEHAVEN STEPPING STONE CABERNET SAUVIGNON 2002, STONEHAVEN **South Australia** – *Aromas of capsicum, tea, mint, and stone. Fresh red berries flavour the firm palate.*	£7.00 CNT
THE MILL SANGIOVESE 2002, WINDOWRIE WINES **New South Wales** – *Blackcurrant fruit and mint leaf nose and palate lifted by fresh acidity and firm tannins.*	£7.00 RSV
Y SERIES SHIRAZ 2003, YALUMBA **South Australia** – *Intense, with pepper and blueberry fruit on the nose, soft structure with rich, creamy vanilla and spice.*	£7.00 BGN/NFW AWO/FLA CTC
PROMISED LAND CABERNET MERLOT 2004, TAYLORS **South Australia** – *Well-integrated oak, ripe cassis fruit, and a streak of roast herb flavour. Soft, spicy, and balanced.*	£7.10 WPR/NFW TNG/OZW RAV

PALANDRI CABERNET MERLOT 2002, PALANDRI WINES **Western Australia** – *Coarsely cracked black pepper and cedary oak on the nose. Alpine strawberry palate.*	£7.20 BGN/EDC
PROMISED LAND SHIRAZ CABERNET 2003, WAKEFIELD WINES **South Australia** – *Ripe, sultry blackcurrant fruit flavours. Accents of toast and tobacco. A full-bodied blend with pretty floral notes.*	£7.20 TPE/NFW TNG/OZW RAV
STEP ROAD SHIRAZ 2003, STEP ROAD WINES **South Australia** – *White chocolate nose. Very nice leg streaks, and a long vanilla, coffee, and blackberry palate.*	£7.20 NFW/PLB
HOUGHTON CABERNET SAUVIGNON 2002, HOUGHTON **Western Australia** – *Rich, firm, and tightly knit, with excellent overall balance and spicy, minted cassis fruit.*	£7.30 BNK
HOUGHTON SHIRAZ 2002, HOUGHTON **Western Australia** – *Green peppers, gum tree, and white pepper nose. Flavours of red apple, strawberry, and pipe tobacco. Stirring stuff.*	£7.30 BNK
MARGARET RIVER CABERNET SAUVIGNON 2001, HOUGHTON **Western Australia** – *Dark red, its developed nose and cassis palate scored by spearmint and eucalyptus.*	£7.30 BNK
PALANDRI ESTATE MERLOT 2002, PALANDRI WINES **Western Australia** – *Mint chocolate ice cream aromas. The medium-full body has spiced plums and a clean, firm finish.*	£7.50 EDC
YARRA GLEN SHIRAZ 2003, YARRA GLEN **Victoria** – *Deep purple in colour with a scents and flavours of crushed black fruits, liquorice, and chocolate.*	£7.50 LAI
BIMBADGEN ESTATE SHIRAZ 2003, BIMBADGEN ESTATE **New Southwales** – *Almost opaque purple-black. Strawberries and spice dance on the nose. Juicy fruit supported by chewy tannins.*	£7.70 HBJ
BREMERVIEW SHIRAZ 2002, BLEASDALE **South Australia** – *Deep purple-red with a nose of red fruit and liquorice. Rich and inviting with long-lasting jammy fruit finish.*	£7.80 FHM/POR NFW/JEF RAV

HILLTOPS CABERNET 2002, CHALKERS CROSSING **NEW SOUTHWALES** – *This Cabernet has plenty of blackberry character. Try it with game and roast vegetables.*	**£7.90** ABY
HILLTOPS SHIRAZ 2002, CHALKERS CROSSING **NEW SOUTH WALES** – *Chocolate and black fruit on the nose. The palate is creamy and mature, with herb and blackcurrant flavours.*	**£7.90** ABY
TRYST CABERNET SAUVIGNON ZINFANDEL TEMPRANILLO 2003, NEPENTHE SOUTH AUSTRALIA – *Polished, juicy, integrated and fresh. This wine is packed to the gunnels with blackberries, liquorice, and tree bark.*	**£7.90** OZW/FLA
BAROSSA VALLEY ESTATE SHIRAZ 2002, BAROSSA VALLEY ESTATES SOUTH AUSTRALIA – *Green peppers, game, cassis, and charred wood scents and flavours. Long, balanced, and creamy.*	**£8.00** CNT
BUCKINGHAM ESTATE RESERVE SHIRAZ 2003, HARVEY RIVER BRIDGE WESTERN AUSTRALIA – *Cedar and cherry fragrance. Ripe juicy black berries and oak. Clean, firm, and medium-long.*	**£8.00** BUC
BUSH VIEW SHIRAZ 2002, EVANS & TATE **WESTERN AUSTRALIA** – *Elegant, rich, and full, with subtle oak flavours and intense spice all wrapped up in velvety tannins.*	**£8.00** M&S
CERAVOLO SAGIOVESE 2004, CERAVOLO WINES **SOUTH AUSTRALIA** – *Spices and mineral notes rise from the nose. The palate is ripe, young, and ruby red, with plenty of cherry fruit.*	**£8.00** ADN
CV SHIRAZ 2003, CAPEL VALE WINES **WESTERN AUSTRALIA** – *Young and subtle with a green nose. Cherries and raspberries flavour the palate, which has chewy tannins and a clean finish.*	**£8.00** D&D
MAGNUS SHIRAZ CABERNET 2002, LEASINGHAM **SOUTH AUSTRALIA** – *Fresh, balanced, integrated, and clear, this star-bright blend has powerful dark plum flavours and hints of earth on the nose.*	**£8.00** CNT
MVS SHIRAZ 2003, HASELGROVE WINES **SOUTH AUSTRALIA** – *Saddle leather, smoke, and lilacs. Blackcurrants and kirsch. Would accompany roast lamb perfectly.*	**£8.00** D&D

YELLOW TAIL RESERVE SHIRAZ 2003, CASELLA WINES New South Wales – *Deep, brooding dark fruits inlaid with mulling spices and sweet vanilla oak. Long mocha-infused finish.*	£8.00 SWS
SYNERGY COONAWARRA SHIRAZ 2003, LECONFIELD WINES South Australia – *Lifted menthol and earth scents mark the nose. Flavours of ripe red cherries, chocolate, and coffee fill the palate. Clear and poised.*	£8.10 NFW/TNG
WAKEFIELD SHIRAZ 2004, WAKEFIELD WINES South Australia – *Immense bags of lush berry fruit and warm spice on the palate. Powerful and lingering.*	£8.10 WIDELY AVAILABLE
BAROSSA BUSH VINE GRENACHE 2003, YALUMBA South Australia – *Gently maturing, with velvety plum jam flesh, soft, sweet oak, cinnamon bark tannins, and a long chocolatey finish.*	£8.20 NFW/AWO FLA/CTC
BAROSSA SHIRAZ 2002, YALUMBA South Australia – *Flowers, PVC, and fruitcake nose. Elegant and restrained, its long, creamy palate fresh, and meaty.*	£8.20 CEB/NFW AWO/TAN FLA
WAKEFIELD MERLOT 2004, WAKEFIELD WINES South Australia – *Bright purple. Youthful, its plentiful soft summer fruit flavours suspended in a web of firm tannins.*	£8.20 WPR/NFW TNG/OZW RAV
MARGARET RIVER CABERNET SAUVIGNON 2003, RINGBOLT South Australia – *Ruby-purple, its redcurrant fruit spiked with Turkish coffee. The finish is long and spicy.*	£8.30 AWO/TOS RSV
SNAKE CREEK SHIRAZ 2001, ODDBINS South Australia – *Vibrant red cherry flavours. Bonfire aromas. Leather hints. Medium-bodied. A cracker.*	£8.50 ODD
WILSON GUNN MCLAREN VALE SHIRAZ 2002, HJH BARREL WINES South Australia – *Rich and ripe, its blueberry flavours buoyed by a clear streak of acidity.*	£8.50 LAI
BMW CABERNET SAUVIGNON 2001, GEOFF MERRILL Southeastern Australia – *Red cherries and herbs flavour this Cabernet. Aromas of mint and hints of earth scent the nose.*	£9.00 SMF

MILLERS GROVE PRIVATE RESERVE SHIRAZ 2003, WINDOWRIE ESTATE Southeastern Australia – *Fresh, rich, comforting cherry pie flavours. The nose is interestingly nutty. Clean, smooth, and juicy.*	£9.00 VGN
PALANDRI SHIRAZ 2002, PALANDRI WINES Western Australia – *Purple plum nose. Soft palate of berries and hints of spice. The finish is long and polished.*	£9.00 PAN
STICKS YARRA VALLEY SHIRAZ 2003, STICKS YARRA VALLEY Victoria – *A smoky nose complements flavours of tobacco and earth. Well-knit, with a structured, juicy palate.*	£9.00 MWW
THOMAS HYLAND CABERNET SAUVIGNON 2002, PENFOLDS Southeastern Australia – *Deep violet with tawny hints, deep young blackcurrant flavours, and firm tannins. Well-crafted.*	£9.00 SWP
THOMAS HYLAND SHIRAZ 2003, PENFOLDS Southeastern Australia – *Balanced blackberries, cassis, and eucalyptus nose. The tannins are ripe. Smoky red and black berry flavours.*	£9.00 MWW/JSM
THREE GARDENS BAROSSA SHIRAZ GRENACHE MOURVÈDRE 2003, LANGMEIL WINERY South Australia – *Lots of coconut oak and kirsch aromas. The palate is filled with prunes, coffee, plums, and currants.*	£9.00 ADN
WOOP WOOP SHIRAZ 2004, WOOP WOOP South Australia – *Lively and youthful, the palate is laden with bright blackberries and warm mocha. The finish is soft with subtle hints of spice.*	£9.00 JSM
BROWN BROTHERS SHIRAZ 2002, BROWN BROTHERS Victoria – *Ruby in colour with a pleasing fruity nose, this wine releases hints of licorice and spice amongst its firm tannins and echoes of chocolate.*	£9.10 ESL/CNL TAN
CHALAMBAR SHIRAZ 2003, SEPPELT Southeastern Australia – *Mint and eucalyptus aromas. Big, with a satiny mouthfeel and soft ripe tannins. Medicinal loganberry flavours.*	£9.30 SWP
HILL OF GOLD MUDGEE CHARDONNAY 2004, ROSEMOUNT ESTATE New South Wales – *Pea green and gold hue. The nose has plenty of tropical fruit salad scents, and the palate is laden with apples and pears.*	£9.30 SWP

PENFOLDS ORGANIC CLARE VALLEY CABERNET MERLOT SHIRAZ 2002, PENFOLDS SOUTH AUSTRALIA – *Youthful, yet showing development. We applaud this characterful, cassis-laden, organic beauty.*	**£9.40** BGN/BNK CTC
PYRAMID HILL MERLOT 2003, PYRAMID HILL SOUTH AUSTRALIA – *Firm and intense, with supple tannins and warm, clear, soft, juicy, black fruit. Mint notes.*	**£9.40** C&B
BERESFORD MCLAREN VALE SHIRAZ 2003, STEP WINES SOUTH AUSTRALIA – *Lifted, rich, dark, and smooth, with grippy tannins and a mouthful of cherries, minerals, wildflowers, mint, and coffee.*	**£9.50** NFW
TIM ADAMS SHIRAZ 2003, TIM ADAMS WINES SOUTH AUSTRALIA – *Beautiful earthy liquorice and ripe fruit flavour. Deep, lasting, and very well balanced.*	**£9.50** AUC/CEB TOS
BLEWITT SPRINGS SHIRAZ 2001, BLEWITT SPRINGS SOUTH AUSTRALIA – *Huge, spicy cassis, and fruitcake nose. Rich, sweetly ripe blackberry palate supported by supple tannins.*	**£9.70** TNG/OZW
MCLAREN VALE PETIT VERDOT 2002, PIRRAMIMMA SOUTH AUSTRALIA – *Sweet lilacs, rich chocolate, redcurrants and red pepper flakes spin from the nose. The palate is deep, dark, and most original.*	**£9.70** TNG/MW W
MITCHELTON SHIRAZ 2003, MITCHELTON VICTORIA – *Dark as night; thick inky black colour and alluring pungent blackberry scent. Soft cedar and smoke notes. Intriguing…*	**£9.90** FLY
ADAMS ROAD CABERNET SAUVIGNON MERLOT 2003, VASSE FELIX WESTERN AUSTRALIA – *Sweet red peppers, cassis and smoke on the nose; herb and fresh damson palate.*	**£10.00** NFW/AWO MWW/FLA
ADAMS ROAD SHIRAZ 2003, VASSE FELIX WESTERN AUSTRALIA – *Medium weight. Intense, super-ripe aromas. A strong oak and spice palate buttressed by firm tannins.*	**£10.00** NFW/AWO FLA
ANGOVES COONAWARRA CABERNET SAUVIGNON 2003, ANGOVES SOUTH AUSTRALIA – *Rich currants flavour the robust palate. Earthy, yet lifted and perfumed.*	**£10.00** D&D

ASHMEAD FAMILY TANTALUS SHIRAZ CABERNET SAUVIGNON 2003, ELDERTON WINES South Australia – *Crunchy cassis, lively acidity, sinewy tannins, and scents of leaves. Hints of fig on the finish.*	£10.00 FLY
BETHANY CABERNET MERLOT 2002, BETHANY WINES South Australia – *Intense fruit gum aromas on the nose give way to a palate of blackberry preserves.*	£10.00 D&D
BIN 128 COONAWARRA SHIRAZ 2001, PENFOLDS South Australia – *Summer rain, smoke, mulberries, hedgerow flowers, and tobacco flavour this powerful, full-bodied Coonawarra Shiraz.*	£10.00 JSM
BIN 138 OLD VINE GRENACHE SHIRAZ MOURVEDRE 2003, PENFOLDS South Australia – *Brooding, soft, and full-flavoured, its bright summer fruit flavours scattered with pulverised peppercorns.*	£10.00 WDI/HAC
CAPEL VALE SHIRAZ 2001, CAPEL VALE WINES Western Australia – *Creamy soft berry and green pepper flavours. The nose is bold, with plum and oak scents. Firm and direct.*	£10.00 D&D
ELDREDGE VINEYARDS CABERNET SAUVIGNON 2002, ELDREDGE VINEYARDS South Australia – *The berry nose is restrained, and the firm, smoky palate has cedar and dark fruit flavours.*	£10.00 AUC
HARDYS TINTARA SHIRAZ 2000, HARDYS South Australia – *Ripe strawberries and kirsch, hints of game, and well-rounded velvety tannins.*	£10.00 BNK
KIRRIHILL CABERNET SAUVIGNON 2001, KIRRIHILL ESTATES South Australia – *The brick-red colour hints at maturity, and the nose of creamy blackcurrants fruit is smooth and sultry. Well made.*	£10.00 THI
LIMESTONE COAST SHIRAZ 2001, STONEHAVEN South Australia – *Light berry, mocha, and mint flavours. The tannins are smoothing out. Long and balanced.*	£10.00 CNT
MAMRE BROOK SHIRAZ 2002, SALTRAM South Australia – *Inky colour and scents of pepper. The plum and vanilla pod flavours possess an edge of smoke.*	£10.00 WFB

MCLAREN VALE CABERNET SAUVIGNON 2001, PIRRAMIMMA SOUTH AUSTRALIA – *Richly ripe, with smooth-as-silk tannins, aromatic herbs, and sundried red stone fruit flavours. Long.*	£10.00 MWW
MCLAREN VALE CABERNET SAUVIGNON 2002, PIRRAMIMMA SOUTH AUSTRALIA – *Hints of eucalyptus peek through the wall of rich blueberry and mulberry fruit. Purple-black. Warming.*	£10.00 MWW
MCLAREN VALE SHIRAZ 2001, PIRRAMIMMA SOUTH AUSTRALIA – *Blackberry compôte with hints of vanilla and cream, perfumed flowers, and subtle spices.*	£10.00 MWW
MCLAREN VALE SHIRAZ 2002, PIRRAMIMMA SOUTH AUSTRALIA – *Sweetly ripe yet quite dry, with fine tannins and complex notes of cassis, menthol, and mocha.*	£10.00 MWW
MOONDAH BROOK SHIRAZ 2001, MOONDAH BROOK WESTERN AUSTRALIA – *Wild black summer berries, raspberry leaves, flowers, wet stones, and loam scent and flavour this Shiraz.*	£10.00 CNT
ORIGIN RESERVE SHIRAZ 2002, GRANT BURGE SOUTH AUSTRALIA – *Vibrant cassis and red berry fruit on the nose, with a ripe yet savoury palate and lingering finish.*	£10.00 THS
POINT LEO PINOT NOIR 2004, STONIER VICTORIA – *Soft, ripe strawberry fruit sits prettily amongst firm, integrated tannins. Herbal notes and lingering finish.*	£10.00 M&S
REDSTONE 2002, CORIOLE SOUTH AUSTRALIA – *Bright and focused, its rich flavours rent by enervating acidity. Long and balanced.*	£10.00 ESL/NFW SCK/CCS
SCARPANTONI ESTATE SCHOOL BLOCK 2003, SCARPANTONI ESTATE SOUTH AUSTRALIA – *Soft and animated. With ripe tannins and supple dark fruits, this wine's perfectly suited to drinking now.*	£10.00 LAI
SERAFINO RESERVE SHIRAZ 2002, SERAFINO WINES SOUTH AUSTRALIA – *Liquorice, clove, honeysuckle, and blackberry flavours and aromas. Concentrated and round.*	£10.00 PLB

STARVEDOG LANE SHIRAZ VIOGNIER 2003, STARVEDOG LANE SOUTH AUSTRALIA – *Big, spicy, and chocolatey, with a firm, long, fruit-packed palate of currants, cranberries, and apricots.*	£10.00 CPR/NFW
THE FERGUS 2003, TIM ADAMS WINES SOUTH AUSTRALIA – *Soft young strawberry fruit accented with leather scents. The round flesh is supported by a backbone of thrusting herbs.*	£10.00 AUC/TOS
TIM ADAMS CABERNET 2002, TIM ADAMS WINES SOUTH AUSTRALIA – *Fresh red and green bruschetta nose. Herbs and fresh currant on the palate. Long finish.*	£10.00 AUC
TINTARA CABERNET SAUVIGNON 2001, HARDYS SOUTH AUSTRALIA – *Sweet toasty oak on nose and palate. The bright currant palate has evolving tannins.*	£10.00 BGN/BNK
WIRRA WIRRA CHURCH BLOCK CABERNET SHIRAZ MERLOT TBC, WIRRA WIRRA SOUTH AUSTRALIA – *Deeply flavoured, with rich capsicum, ripe plum, and sweet black fruits.*	£10.00 JSM
WYNNS COONAWARRA ESTATE CABERNET SAUVIGON 2001, WYNNS SOUTH AUSTRALIA – *Menthol refreshes the concentrated cassis and chocolate palate. Lifted.*	£10.00 MWW/WDI HAC
HEINRICH 2003, ROLF BINDER WINES SOUTH AUSTRALIA – *Port-like, ripe, and lifted, with floral notes on the nose. The palate is juicy, herbal, and filled with round strawberry flavours.*	£10.20 NFW/SCK CCS
SELKIRK SHIRAZ 2002, BREMERTON SOUTH AUSTRALIA – *Bonfire smoke, leather, star anise, and blackberry aromas and flavours. Menthol hints.*	£10.20 NFW/SCK CCS/FLA
STELLA BELLA SHIRAZ 2003, STELLA BELLA WINES WESTERN AUSTRALIA – *The berry palate is well-balanced, with meaty notes and spice. Firm rustic tannins and a crisp lift to the finish.*	£10.30 TNG/OCM CCS
ALKOOMI SHIRAZ VIOGNIER 2003, ALKOOMI WINES WESTERN AUSTRALIA – *Concentrated berry and green leaf nose maturing into a balanced and jammy black and raspberry fruit palate. A medium-long finish.*	£10.40 BNK/LAY

CHAPEL HILL CABERNET SAUVIGNON 2001, CHAPEL HILL **South Australia** – *Old world charm. The cassis fruit has graceful oak treatment which complements rather than dominates.*	**£10.40** AUC/TOS OZW/FLA
CHAPEL HILL CABERNET SAUVIGNON 2002, CHAPEL HILL **South Australia** – *Menthol, herbs, pepper, and blackberries to the fore. This winner is chewy, elegant, and full.*	**£10.40** AUC/TOS OZW/FLA
CHAPEL HILL CABERNET SAUVIGNON 2001, CHAPEL HILL **South Australia** – *Glowing blackcurrant flavours shine from the round palate. Generously fruited. Toast, hawthorn, and leather scents.*	**£10.50** AUC/OZW FLA
MCLEAN'S FARM RESERVE 2003, BARR-EDEN WINES **South Australia** – *Redcurrants, Victoria plums, loganberries, and hints of loam blend harmoniously together on nose and palate. Lifted tarry notes.*	**£10.50** POR/TOS
THE WALLACE 2003, GLAETZER WINES **South Australia** – *Deep purple-ruby, with inviting fruit character and spicy overtones. Sweet vanilla oak and grippy tannins round out the palate.*	**£10.50** NFW/OZW
DEVILS ELBOW CABERNET SAUVIGNON 2002, LONGVIEW VINEYARD **South Australia** – *Stewed fruit and creamy vanilla aromas rise from the nose. The palate has hints of herbs and lots of sweet cassis.*	**£11.00** FLY
MCLEAN'S FARM TRINITY CORNER SHIRAZ 2002, BARR-EDEN WINES **South Australia** – *Medicinal notes, tar, earth, and classy, integrated oak on the nose. A wine of finesse, charm, and good balance.*	**£11.00** AUC
SANDALFORD WINES CABERNET SAUVIGNON 2003, SANDALFORD WINES **Western Australia** – *The port-like nose and purple colour complement the palate of red and black fruit cocktail.*	**£11.00** NEC/HAC
WILLOWS VINEYARD SHIRAZ 2002, SCHOLZ VINTNERS **South Australia** – *Inviting nose of stewed fruits, dusty tannins, and creamy vanilla. Long finish. Mature.*	**£11.00** AUC
YERING STATION SHIRAZ VIOGNIER 2002, YERING STATION **Victoria** – *Crushed mint leaf and raspberry aromas and flavours. The sensual pillow of fruit is has edgy, structured tannins.*	**£11.00** NFW/MW W JSM

LALLA ROOKH 2002, CORIOLE SOUTH AUSTRALIA – *Mature, taut, and lifted, with dried cherry and chocolate aromas and flavours. Intense.*	**£11.30** NFW/SCK CCS
SHIRAZ 2003, VOYAGER ESTATE WESTERN AUSTRALIA – *Rich and sweet fruit-forward palate with floral and honey hints. Long finish with chewy tannins.*	**£11.30** TNG
BAROSSA CABERNET SAUVIGNON 2003, HERITAGE WINES SOUTH AUSTRALIA – *Dark as ink. Scents and flavours of wood, peppers, and spice. Fabulous intensity.*	**£11.50** AUC
BAROSSA SHIRAZ 2003, HERITAGE WINES SOUTH AUSTRALIA – *Inky, intense, and leafy, with coffee bean oak, ripe bright raspberry flavours, and scents of earth.*	**£11.50** AUC
BLEASDALE FRANK POTTS 2003, BLEASDALE SOUTH AUSTRALIA – *Charred wood, blackcurrant jam, and smoke, earth, and spices. Long and balanced, with sinewy tannins.*	**£11.50** FHM/POR NFW/JEF RAV
HOLLICK CABERNET SAUVIGNON 2002, HOLLICK SOUTH AUSTRALIA – *Minty and focused, with notes of pepper and leathery cassis flavours.*	**£11.50** ESL/SCK TNI/CCS
MCLAREN VALE SHIRAZ 2001, CHAPEL HILL SOUTH AUSTRALIA – *Ruby red in colour, with rich aromas of ripe plums and black pepper spice and a lifted floral finish.*	**£11.50** AUC/OZW FLA
SHOTFIRE RIDGE SHIRAZ 2002, THORN-CLARKE SOUTH AUSTRALIA – *Intense black olive, leather, and forest fruit nose. Savoury notes emanate from the youthful, restrained palate of peppers and cherries.*	**£11.50** NFW
SIGNATURE SHIRAZ 2003, BIMBADGEN ESTATE NEW SOUTH WALES – *Restrained and inky. Notes of mint lift the dark fruit flavours, which are supported on a web of firm tannins.*	**£11.50** HBJ
GREEN POINT SHIRAZ 2003, GREEN POINT VICTORIA – *Subtle roses, citrus, and forward blueberries dance on nose and palate. Sweetly ripe and round.*	**£11.60** FHM/CEB BNK/MHU

CAPE MENTELLE CABERNET MERLOT TRINDERS 2002, CAPE MENTELLE WESTERN AUSTRALIA – *Juicy damson fruit radiates from the nose and palate of this soft, seductive wine.*	**£11.70** WIDELY AVAILABLE
HYLAND SHIRAZ 2003, PENLEY ESTATE SOUTH AUSTRALIA – *Blackberry pie and hickory smoke characteristics. This wine is vibrant and inviting. Drink this holiday season.*	**£11.70** NFW/CCS
SMITH & HOOPER LIMITED EDITION WRATTONBULLY MERLOT 2002, SMITH & HOOPER (YALUMBA) SOUTH AUSTRALIA – *Bouquet garni, blackberry, raspberry, and cherry flavours. Powerful and medium-full.*	**£11.70** NFW/RSV
JUNIPER ESTATE CABERNET SAUVIGNON 2001, JUNIPER ESTATE WESTERN AUSTRALIA – *Soft black cherry and blackberry flavours and scents. Very ripe, yet rather elegant.*	**£12.00** ADN
Nº 6 SHIRAZ CABERNET 2003, BROTHERS IN ARMS SOUTH AUSTRALIA – *Generous and round, with masses, cherry and blackberry fruit and a characterful, lifted minty nose.*	**£12.00** NFW/OZW
RUFUS STONE MCLAREN VALE SHIRAZ 2003, TYRRELL'S NEW SOUTH WALES – *Enormous amount of dark plum and black cherry fruit. Grippy, long, and creamy. Very approachable.*	**£12.00** HAC
TAMAR RIDGE PINOT NOIR 2003, TAMAR RIDGE WINES TASMANIA – *Big and ripe, with savoury notes of tamarind and grilled meats. Strawberry and raspberry fruit melts into finely honed tannins.*	**£12.00** OZW
CORIOLE SHIRAZ 2002, CORIOLE SOUTH AUSTRALIA – *Rich cherry, sweet plum, and vanilla bean aromas with dark chocolate, spearmint, and violets on the palate.*	**£12.20** NFW/SCK CCS/TAN FLA
LOWE MERLOT 2003, LOWE FAMILY WINE COMPANY NEW SOUTH WALES – *Ripest sloes, undergrowth notes, and scents of parsley. Fresh acidity balances the fruit.*	**£12.30** SFW
PRESIDENT'S SELECTION SHIRAZ 2002, WOLF BLASS WINES SOUTH AUSTRALIA – *Bright, forward blackcurrant fruit and smoky oak nose. Long, savoury finish.*	**£12.30** TOS/MWW JSM

THE DERELICT VINEYARD GRENACHE 2003, **D'ARENBERG S**OUTH **A**USTRALIA – *Considerable tannins support the capsicum, crushed pepper, and blackcurrant flavours. Spicy, fresh, and long.*	**£12.40** POR/NFW OZW/CCS DAR/FLY
BALGOWNIE CABERNET SAUVIGNON 2000, **BALGOWNIE ESTATE V**ICTORIA – *Ripe, soft, and long, with an open-knit, ephemeral nose and palate of sun-warmed blackcurrant fruit.*	**£12.50** CPR/RSV WRK
BALGOWNIE ESTATE SHIRAZ 2001, BALGOWNIE ESTATE VICTORIA – *Rosemary, spice, and peach kernel nose; blueberry fruit palate. Fresh acidity, pretty spice, and mineral undertones.*	**£12.50** CPR/RSV WRK
MT TEMPRANILLO 2004, PONDALOWIE VINEYARDS VICTORIA – *Soft, sensual red cherry fruit is buttressed by firm tobacco leaf tannins. Mocha, smoke, and liquorice notes.*	**£12.50** AUC/OZW
SHOW RESERVE CABERNET MERLOT 1998, **WYNDHAM ESTATE S**OUTHEASTERN **A**USTRALIA – *Mature, harmonious, and laden with cassis, this blend is soft and attractive.*	**£12.50** FHM
BATTLE OF BOSWORTH CABERNET SAUVIGNON 2002, **BATTLE OF BOSWORTH S**OUTH **A**USTRALIA – *Savoury notes hint at evolution on the nose. The palate is balanced, mouthwatering, and packed with currants.*	**£12.60** NFW/TNG OZW/RAV FLA/VER
MITCHELTON CRESCENT 2002, MITCHELTON VICTORIA – *Aromatic, softly peppered nose. Deeply coloured. Firm, soft, and clean. A very attractive wine.*	**£12.70** FHM/FLY
BIN 407 CABERNET SAUVIGNON 2002, PENFOLDS SOUTHEASTERN **A**USTRALIA – *Eucalyptus, blackcurrant, and spicebox elements. This young wine would benefit from another year or two.*	**£13.00** MWW/WDI HAC
COONAWARRA SHIRAZ 2001, BOWEN ESTATE SOUTH **A**USTRALIA – *Menthol notes dance on the ripe blue plum fruit bouquet. Leather, smoke, and hints of clove cosset the flavours.*	**£13.00** AUC/OZW TAN
PONDALOWIE BLEND 2003, PONDALOWIE VINEYARDS VICTORIA – *Leather, liquorice, mint leaves, and crushed strawberries scent the nose. The palate has summer pudding flavours.*	**£13.00** AUC/OZW

YERING STATION PINOT NOIR 2003, YERING STATION **VICTORIA** – *Bright, sweet raspberry fruit and mineral notes with a smooth, rich, structured palate. Very well made.*	**£13.00** NFW
CAPE MENTELLE SHIRAZ 2002, CAPE MENTELLE **WESTERN AUSTRALIA** – *A well knit, ripe, and fruity full red, with cherries and chocolate on the palate. Well balanced. Medium-long finish.*	**£13.10** WIDELY AVAILABLE
RIFLE & HUNT CABERNET SAUVIGNON 2002, PERTARINGA SOUTH AUSTRALIA – *Juicy and well balanced, with a ripe minty blackcurrant nose and palate. Hints of rubber. Long.*	**£13.20** NFW/TNG EDC/OZW
DIRECTOR'S CUT SHIRAZ 2003, HEARTLAND WINES **SOUTH AUSTRALIA** – *Black purple colour. Violets, white pepper, and chocolate stud the palate. Lingering finish of blackberries.*	**£13.50** NFW/OZW
PENNY'S HILL SHIRAZ 2003, PENNY'S HILL **SOUTH AUSTRALIA** – *Fresh red fruit is supported by firm tannins. Long, deep, and creamy, with applewood scents.*	**£13.50** NFW
GRANT BURGE FILSELL SHIRAZ 2003, GRANT BURGE **WINES SOUTH AUSTRALIA** – *Lush and juicy with ripe berry and subtle vanilla flavours. Minty eucalyptus lingers on the long finish.*	**£13.60** NFW/FLY WDI/HAC WRW
JACOB'S CREEK RESERVE SHIRAZ 2002, JACOB'S **CREEK SOUTH AUSTRALIA** – *Ripe jammy plum fruit with spicy notes and background of chocolate and toasty oak nuances.*	**£13.70** FHM/BGN JSM
SPEAR GULLY SHIRAZ 2002, SPEAR GULLY VICTORIA – *Firm, grippy tobacco, sweet pepper, and cherry characteristics. The tannis are integrated and the finish clean.*	**£13.70** AUC/POR OZW/FLA
MAJELLA SHIRAZ 2002, MAJELLA WINES **SOUTH AUSTRALIA** – *Blackberries, cigars, eucalyptus, and stony minerals crowd the nose and palate. Long, dense, and concentrated.*	**£14.00** NFW/TNG OZW/CCS
SHOW RESERVE COONAWARRA CABERNET **SAUVIGNON 2001, ROSEMOUNT ESTATE** **SOUTH AUSTRALIA** – *Ripe plums, spicebox, cocoa, and mint. Admirable complexity, round flavours, and a long finish.*	**£14.00** WDI/HAC

THE STICKS AND STONES TEMPRANILLO GRENACHE SAOZAO 2003, D'ARENBERG SOUTH AUSTRALIA – *Powerful red pepper, vanilla, cherry compôte, and cedar elements litter this intense, concentrated wine.*	**£14.00** NFW/CCS DAR/FLY
VASSE FELIX CABERNET SAUVIGNON 2002, VASSE FELIX WESTERN AUSTRALIA – *Dark, inky, complex, and spicy. Bittersweet chocolate and crushed bramble fruit flavours.*	**£14.00** NFW/AWO
MOUNT BARKER CABERNET SAUVIGNON 2002, PLANTAGENET WESTERN AUSTRALIA – *Blackcurrant and eucalyptus and green pepper aromas. The palate has chalky tannins and fresh acidity.*	**£14.20** WIDELY AVAILABLE
STRATHBOGIE RANGES RESERVE SHIRAZ 2002, PLUNKETT WINE VICTORIA – *A gently spicy nose. The palate is packed full of rich cherry jam yet ends briskly and cleanly.*	**£14.30** AWO/CCS
BLUE PYRENEES ESTATE RESERVE RED 2000, BLUE PYRENEES ESTATE VICTORIA – *Hedgerow fruits, leather, and tobacco aromas. Evolved and ready to drink this holiday season.*	**£14.40** TNG
CHARLESTON PINOT NOIR 2003, NEPENTHE SOUTH AUSTRALIA – *Divine bouquet of mint, eucalyptus, and game. Lively acidity freshens the chewy palate of black cherry fruit.*	**£14.40** NFW/FLA
201 SHIRAZ CABERNET SAUVIGNON 2001, PENLEY ESTATE SOUTH AUSTRALIA – *Concentrated, integrated, and mouthcoating, this blackcurrant beauty offers hints of undergrowth on its long finish.*	**£14.50** NFW/CCS
CINNIBAR 2003, GEMTREE SOUTH AUSTRALIA – *Red cherry flesh is scored with sensuous vanilla bean flavours. Smoothly textured, with delicious hints of raspberry leaves.*	**£14.50** AVD/WOZ
KATNOOK ESTATE MERLOT 2002, WINGARA WINE GROUP SOUTH AUSTRALIA – *Cracked pepper, olive, and blackberry aromas. Juicy savoury spiced meat, medjool date, and prune palate.*	**£14.50** FLY
ANTHONYS RESERVE SHIRAZ 2001, SIMON HACKETT SOUTH AUSTRALIA – *A thrust of black pepper is accompanied by eucalyptus and mint notes. Long and complex.*	**£14.80** FHM/HPW NFW/CNL WRW

PARKER ESTATE CABERNET SAUVIGNON 2001, PARKER ESTATE South Australia – *Plenty of oak and dashes of mint infuse the nose and palate of this cherry-flavoured wonder.*	£14.80 C&B
BIN 389 CABERNET SAUVIGNON SHIRAZ 2001, PENFOLDS South Australia – *Satin-textured, mouthwatering, and polished, this vivid wine has plenty of menthol, white pepper, and sweet cassis.*	£15.00 TOS/MWW JSM
FRANKLAND RIVER SHIRAZ GI 2002, HOUGHTON Western Australia – *Concentrated hedgerow fruit flavours on the palate. Simple and youthful, with soft tannins and a plum tart finish.*	£15.00 CNT
GENUS 4 FARMS SHIRAZ 2003, MCGUIGAN SIMEON WINES South Australia – *Smoky blueberry fruit nose. The palate is packed with brambles, pepper, and vanilla bean flavours.*	£15.00 VNO
GOLD LABEL SHIRAZ VIOGNIER 2003, WOLF BLASS WINES South Australia – *Ripe, heavy, chewy blackberry and redcurrant fruit flavours. A sturdy wine with sweet floral aromas.*	£15.00 WFB
HAND PICKED BAROSSA MOURVÈDRE GRENACHE SHIRAZ 2003, YALUMBA South Australia – *Black plum and red cherry nose. The tannic structure sustains the creamy, peppery fruit on the long finish.*	£15.00 NFW
HAND PICKED TRICENTENARY VINES BAROSSA GRENACHE 2003, YALUMBA South Australia – *Lifted, youthful aromas of Victoria plums, prunes, leather, smoke, and cherries. The savoury currant palate has chewy tannins.*	£15.00 NFW
MCGUIGAN PERSONAL RESERVE CABERNET SAUVIGNON 2000, MCGUIGAN SIMEON WINES New South Wales – *Robust and firm yet luxuriant, with cassis and fine fresh herbs on nose and palate.*	£15.00 VNO
MCWILLIAMS CABERNET SAUVIGNON 2001, MCWILLIAMS Southeastern Australia – *Roses, redcurrants, and whortleberries on the nose. Developed, with integrated oak, this wine is complete.*	£15.00 E&J
MERUM SHIRAZ 2002, MERUM WINES Western Australia – *Bursting with big sweet fruit on the palate. Savoury tannins and a long finish reveal layers of this wine's sophistication.*	£15.00 ROG

MERUM SHIRAZ 2003, MERUM WINES **WESTERN AUSTRALIA** – *Delightful floral scents perfume the fruit. Hints of smoke. Farmyard characteristics.*	**£15.00** ROG
PAUL CONTI MARIGINIUP SHIRAZ 2002, PAUL CONTI **WESTERN AUSTRALIA** – *Red berry and violet nose with hints of eucalyptus and licorice. Hints of cocoa and spice.*	**£15.00** VRS
PEMBERTON REGIONAL RANGE MERLOT 2001, HOUGHTON **SOUTH AUSTRALIA** – *Young, structured, and leafy, with mouthwatering flavours of oven-fresh cherry pie.*	**£15.00** CNT
VASSE FELIX SHIRAZ 2002, VASSE FELIX **WESTERN AUSTRALIA** – *Treacle and raspberry compôte compete with chocolate and liquorice on the nose. Beautiful and intriguing, with persistence and poise.*	**£15.00** NFW/AWO
WOLF BLASS GOLD LABEL CABERNET SAUVIGNON 2001, WOLF BLASS WINES **SOUTH AUSTRALIA** – *Crunchy cassis crouches on firmly interwoven tannins. Tobacco and anise elements.*	**£15.00** MWW
WOLF BLASS GOLD LABEL CABERNET SAUVIGNON CABERNET FRANC 2001, WOLF BLASS **SOUTH AUSTRALIA** – *Powerful and dark. Warming and toasty, with a lifted attack of leather, graphite, and fruit.*	**£15.00** JSM
ROSEMOUNT TRADITIONAL MCLAREN VALE 2002, ROSEMOUNT ESTATE **SOUTH AUSTRALIA** – *Heady dark blackcurrant fruit buttressed by firm tannins. Chewy, serious, long, and dense.*	**£15.50** WDI/HAC
ADELAIDE HILLS SHIRAZ 2003, SHAW AND SMITH **SOUTH AUSTRALIA** – *Meat juice and Bourbon vanilla bouquet. The full-bodied palate has juicy black plums and spice.*	**£15.80** AWO/RSV CCS/BEN FLY
KATNOOK ESTATE SHIRAZ 2003, WINGARA WINE GROUP **SOUTH AUSTRALIA** – *Fine dark fruits and baked earth aromas. Herbaceous hints and ripe round tannins.*	**£16.00** ESL/FLY
ULEYBURY SANGIOVESE 2001, ULEYBURY **SOUTH AUSTRALIA** – *Blackcurrants, plums, and peppers galore. Hints of mint, tobacco, and tomato ketchup.*	**£16.00** AVD

FOGGO ROAD CABERNET SAUVIGNON 2001, SIMON HACKETT South Australia – *Displaying some maturity, its lively kirsch flavours smoothed out with savoury barnyard tones.*	**£16.10** FHM/HPW NFW/CNL WRW
ASHMEAD FAMILY BAROSSA SHIRAZ 2003, ELDERTON WINES South Australia – *Fresh blueberries, crème fraîche, and powdered vanilla scents. Rich plum tart and tobacco flavours.*	**£16.70** FLY
ELMOR'S EBENEZER OLD VINE SHIRAZ 1998, ROEHR WINES South Australia – *Earthy yet light-handed, this powerful Shiraz has loam, tayberry and flower characteristics.*	**£16.90** ROG
ST GEORGE CABERNET SAUVIGNON 2001, LINDEMANS South Australia – *Mouthwatering red fruit flavours. Smooth, round, and polished. Eucalyptus notes.*	**£17.00** WDI/HAC
SUCKFIZZLE CABERNET SAUVIGNON 2001, STELLA BELLA WINES Western Australia – *Attractive and ripe, this spicy wine envelops the taster, demanding to be enjoyed.*	**£17.00** OCM/OZW CCS
YERING STATION SHIRAZ VIOGNIER 2003, YERING STATION Victoria – *Subtle violets and soft tangy fruits are the key to this effortlessly smooth, mouthwatering wine.*	**£17.00** FLA/JSM
OLD BLOCK SHIRAZ 2002, ST HALLETT South Australia – *Toasty, clear, and medium-bodied, this is a soft, balanced, and spicy wine packed with plum fruit.*	**£17.50** POR/BNK NFW/JSM
EIGHT UNCLES SHIRAZ 2003, FOX GORDON South Australia – *Peppers, blackberries, and spice on the nose. The palate is luscious, full-bodied, and warming.*	**£18.00** ODD
PETER LEHMANN MENTOR 2000, PETER LEHMANN WINES South Australia – *Blackish colour. Displays maturity; its evolved ripe blackcurrant coulis flavours begging to be enjoyed now.*	**£18.00** POR/NFW
MOUNT BARKER SHIRAZ 2002, PLANTAGENET Western Australia – *Red fruit nose. The sweetly ripe blueberry and clove palate finishes in a long, crisp fashion.*	**£18.50** V&C/AWO CCS/BEN FLY

PATRICIA CABERNET SAUVIGNON 2002, BROWN BROTHERS Victoria – *Dry, deep, and young. Leather elements and blackfruit jam sit solidly on the chewy, structured palate.*	£18.50 CPW
JOSEPH CABERNET MERLOT MODA 2001, PRIMO ESTATE South Australia – *Beautifully ripe, with a linear herbaceousness cutting through the richness of the red fruit.*	£19.00 AUC/OZW
THE STOCKS MCLAREN VALE SHIRAZ 2002, WOODSTOCK WINES South Australia – *Inky purple colour. Restrained nose of ripe berries and savoury spices. Firm tannins support the fruit on the long balanced finish.*	£19.00 TNG
THE VICAR 2001, CHAPEL HILL South Australia – *Juicy plums, black pepper, eucalyptus, smoke, and mint all tumble together on nose and palate. Complex and long.*	£19.00 AUC/OZW FLA
19TH MEETING CABERNET SAUVIGNON 2004, STARVEDOG LANE South Australia – *Elegant cool mint green elements on the nose and a rather enticing blackcurrant fruit palate.*	£20.00 CPR
REUNION SHIRAZ 2001, STARVEDOG LANE South Australia – *Medicinal notes and herb scents on the nose. The palate is taut and packed with black cherry fruit.*	£20.00 CPR/NFW
THE ANVIL HEATHCOTE SHIRAZ 2001, REDBANK Victoria – *A creamy and varied palate with savoury black fruit, leather, tobacco, red peppers, butter, and floral notes. Complex and balanced.*	£20.00 BWC
VAT 9 HUNTER SHIRAZ 2001, TYRRELL'S New South Wales – *Bark, pepper, pine needles and blueberries. The palate is an unctuous, full, youthful, mouthful of bramble fruit. Will continue to develop.*	£20.00 CPW
WYNNS HAROLD CABERNET SAUVIGNON 2001, WYNNS South Australia – *Poised, with evolved flavours of cherry and blackcurrant and tobacco leaf tannins.*	£20.00 SWP
ST ANDREWS CABERNET SAUVIGNON 2000, WAKEFIELD WINES South Australia – *Ruby red. Developed, its mature cassis flavours spiked with eucalyptus and cosseted in soft tannins.*	£20.70 FHM/TNG RAV

CHARLES MELTON NINE POPES 2002, CHARLES MELTON SOUTH AUSTRALIA – *Enticing nose of white pepper, cranberries, and earth. Leather accents the blueberry flavours.*	£20.80 WIDELY AVAILABLE
CHARLES MELTON SHIRAZ 2002, CHARLES MELTON SOUTH AUSTRALIA – *This wine is restrained and elegant, its mulberry and roast nut flavours unfurling slowly and persisting on the finish.*	£21.00 WIDELY AVAILABLE
MCLAREN VALE SHIRAZ 2002, PAXTON WINES SOUTH AUSTRALIA – *Deep ruby purple, with nose of brambles and hints of eucalyptus. A full rich palate of creamy red fruits and toasty vanilla.*	£21.00 WOZ
ST ANDREWS CABERNET SAUVIGNON 2001, WAKEFIELD WINES SOUTH AUSTRALIA – *Nicely quirky, its fresh acidity married to an unexpected density, richness, and length. Blackcurrant-tastic.*	£21.50 FHM/TNG OZW
THE COPPERMINE ROAD CABERNET SAUVIGNON 2002, D'ARENBERG SOUTH AUSTRALIA – *Minty and bright, with plums, currants, and a plentiful dollop of sweet oak.*	£21.90 NFW/CCS DAR/FLY
BULL AND BEAR 2002, TWO HANDS WINES SOUTH AUSTRALIA – *Fine, tight little blueberries and sensual raspberries mingle with spearmint and redcurrants on the nose and palate.*	£22.40 NFW/TNG OZW/CCS
THE DEAD ARM SHIRAZ 2003, D'ARENBERG SOUTH AUSTRALIA – *Sweet red tasty fruit with a delectable minty flavour. A wine that achieves good balance with its varied elements and long finish.*	£23.60 FHM/V&C DAR/FLY
EIGHT SONGS SHIRAZ 2000, PETER LEHMANN SOUTH AUSTRALIA – *Roasted almonds, sundried tomatoes, and dark plum fruit. Displays signs of maturity. Drinking well now.*	£25.00 POR
GLAETZER SHIRAZ 2002, GLAETZER WINES SOUTH AUSTRALIA – *Elegant, chewy, and laden with strawberry fruit. Earthy, with firm tannins and a very long finish.*	£27.50 NFW
RAYNER VINEYARD SHIRAZ 2003, BROKENWOOD SOUTH AUSTRALIA – *Blueberry and raspberry flavours blend with a whisper of vanilla and spearmint nuances.*	£27.90 CCS/FLY

SAVITAR MCLAREN VALE SHIRAZ 2003, MITOLO **SOUTH AUSTRALIA** – *Deep red plum colour that matches the beautiful intensity of the nose. Bushels of fruit. Good balance and great finish.*	£28.10 NFW/AWO CCS/FLY
CONAWARRA STENTIFORDS OLD VINE SHIRAZ 2000, MCWILLIAM'S **SOUTH AUSTRALIA** – *An elegant, full-bodied red, almost port-like, with spice and black fruits, and hints of tobacco and eucalyptus.*	£30.00 E&J
STONEWELL SHIRAZ 1999, PETER LEHMANN **SOUTH AUSTRALIA** – *Clear, sweetly ripe, and soft, with rich mulberry fruit and hints of espresso. Big and spicy.*	£30.00 POR/NFW
BLUE MUDGEE SHIRAZ CABERNET 2000, ROSEMOUNT ESTATE **NEW SOUTH WALES** – *Concentrated, powerful, and very intense, this wine boasts ripe cassis, kirsch, vanilla, currant leaves, and bonfire smoke.*	£35.30 SWP
KATNOOK ESTATE ODYSSEY 2000, WINGARA WINE GROUP **SOUTH AUSTRALIA** – *Ripe cassis and well-integrated oak. Brisk tannins support the forward fruit flavours.*	£35.50 FLY
BIN 707 CABERNET SAUVIGNON 2002, PENFOLDS **SOUTHEASTERN AUSTRALIA** – *Rich, heavy, and full, this powerful wine has plenty of soft plum fruit and herbal hints.*	£38.00 MWW/WD I HAC
RWT BAROSSA VALLEY SHIRAZ 2002, PENFOLDS **SOUTH AUSTRALIA** – *Elegant, with refreshing ripe fruit aromas. Soft but chewy with a creamy vanilla finish.*	£38.00 MWW/WD I HAC
GRAVEYARD SHIRAZ 2003, BROKENWOOD **NEW SOUTH WALES** – *Powerful yet controlled, this textured, balanced wine has smoky notes and lush currant fruit.*	£40.00 CCS/FLY
MCWILLIAMS 1877 2001, MCWILLIAMS **SOUTHEASTERN AUSTRALIA** – *This perfumed blend has violets, loam, peppermint, leather, liquorice, cherry compôte, and vanilla pod aromas and flavours.*	£40.00 E&J
THE OCTAVIUS OLD VINE BAROSSA SHIRAZ 2001, YALUMBA **SOUTH AUSTRALIA** – *Concentrated plummy fruits, well-structured tannins, and lingering sweet fruit on the finish.*	£40.00 NFW

EMIGRÉ 2002, THE COLONIAL WINE COMPANY SOUTH AUSTRALIA – *Christmas spice, with ripe red fruits beneath. The palate is rich and warming with well-rounded berry fruit and spice.*	**£47.50** BBR
E&E BLACK PEPPER SHIRAZ 2000, BAROSSA VALLEY ESTATE SOUTH AUSTRALIA – *Fine, tight-knit, and very long, this powerhouse has not only pepper but also strawberries, saddle leather, mint, cigars, and minerals on its layered palate.*	**£48.30** BNK/EDC

SEAL OF APPROVAL
AUSTRALIAN RED

☆ **BADGERS CREEK AUSTRALIAN RED WINE NV, LES GRANDS CHAIS DE FRANCE** SOUTHEASTERN AUSTRALIA – *Fresh red cherries, cranberries, and herbs. Flavourful.*	**£3.00** ALD
☆ **COLDRIDGE SHIRAZ CABERNET 2003, COLDRIDGE ESTATE** SOUTHEASTERN AUSTRALIA – *Fleshy and robust. Hedgerow fruit flavours.*	**£3.70** MWW
☆ **TESCO AUSTRALIAN SHIRAZ CABERNET NV, TESCO** SOUTH AUSTRALIA – *Bright red berries glow on the weighty palate.*	**£3.80** TOS
☆ **FOOTSTEPS SHIRAZ NV, CONSTELLATION** SOUTHEASTERN AUSTRALIA – *Vivid mulberry flavours with menthol notes.*	**£4.00** MCT
☆ **JACARANDA HILL SHIRAZ 2004, ANGOVES** SOUTH AUSTRALIA – *Fragrant with violets, smoke, and saddle leather.*	**£4.00** D&D
☆ **MOONDARRA SHIRAZ CABERNET 2004, CRANSWICK** SOUTHEASTERN AUSTRALIA – *A flavourful blend packed with red fruit.*	**£4.00** WAV
☆ **RANSOMES VALE SHIRAZ PETIT VERDOT NV, CALIFORNIA DIRECT** SOUTHEASTERN AUSTRALIA – *Ripe blackberries and dates. Hints of pepper.*	**£4.00** ALD

☆ STONERIDGE SHIRAZ CABERNET SAUVIGNON 2003, ANGOVES SOUTHEASTERN AUSTRALIA – *Flavourful cassis, mulberries, and undergrowth.*	£4.00 D&D
☆ TESCO AUSTRALIAN CABERNET MERLOT NV, MCGUIGAN SIMEON WINES SOUTHEASTERN AUSTRALIA – *A balanced, food-friendly, soft, round blend.*	£4.00 TOS
☆ TESCO AUSTRALIAN MERLOT NV, MCGUIGAN SIMEON WINES SOUTH AUSTRALIA – *Peppery notes rise from fresh redcurrant fruit.*	£4.00 TOS

SILVER
AUSTRALIAN SPARKLING

☆ BAY OF FIRES PINOT NOIR CHARDONNAY 2001, BAY OF FIRES TASMANIA – *Saturated with mouthwatering cranberry and lemon flavours, this sparkler sports ebullient mousse, floral notes, and very fresh acidity.*	£12.00 CNT
☆ STARVEDOG LANE SPARKLING 2000, STARVEDOG LANE SOUTH AUSTRALIA – *Fine, creamy mousse buoys the palate of apples, fresh bread, pear, and biscuits. Rich, dry, deep, and balanced.*	£14.00 CPR/NFW RSV
ARRAS CHARDONNAY PINOT NOIR 1999, ARRAS TASMANIA – *Fresh lemon zest, crushed redcurrants and hazelnuts. The palate is mature yet zingy, with notes of toast.*	£28.00 CNT

BRONZE
AUSTRALIAN SPARKLING

PREMIUM CUVÉE NV, JANSZ TASMANIA – *Rich redcurrant, flavours meld with juicy starfuit and tangerines on the palate. Fine, frothy mousse, and zesty acidity.*	£10.40 AWO/RSV OZW/CCS FLA/CTC
PREMIUM VINTAGE CUVÉE 2000, JANSZ TASMANIA – *Focused, ripe and sultry, this guava and apple flavoured fizz is lifted by invigorating mousse. Nutty notes.*	£12.60 OZW/TAN FLA

GREEN POINT VINTAGE BRUT 2001, GREEN POINT **VICTORIA** – *Tasty flavours of apples and pears softened by a creamy texture. Tartness dominates the full-bodied, clean finish.*	**£13.40** TPE/MHU
SPARKLING SHIRAZ 2003, MAJELLA WINES **SOUTH AUSTRALIA** – *Robust plum and blueberry flavours are buoyed by fresh acidity and ebullient mousse. Hints of leather and liquorice.*	**£14.10** NFW/TNG OZW/CCS FLA

SEAL OF APPROVAL
AUSTRALIAN SPARKLING

☆ THE LAKES SPARKLING BRUT NV, MCGUIGAN SIMEON WINES **SOUTHEASTERN AUSTRALIA** – *Sultry white fruit flavours. Hints of nutmeg.*	**£5.00** TOS/VNO
☆ HARDYS STAMP SPARKLING WINE NV, HARDYS **SOUTHEASTERN AUSTRALIA** – *Ripe flavours of apple, currant, and strawberry.*	**£6.50** BGN/TOS JSM
☆ BANROCK STATION SPARKLING SHIRAZ NV, HARDYS **SOUTHEASTERN AUSTRALIA** – *Deep plum flavours. Intense refreshment.*	**£7.00** BNK/TOS JSM
☆ DEAKIN ESTATE BRUT CHARDONNAY PINOT NOIR NV, DEAKIN ESTATE **VICTORIA** – *Big, bouncy bubbles lift the ripe flavours.*	**£7.50** FLY

GOLD
AUSTRALIAN SWEET

☆ MOUNT HORROCKS CLARE VALLEY CORDON CUT RIESLING 2004, MOUNT HORROCKS **SOUTH AUSTRALIA** – *Pungent lemon zest, candied orange peel, and petrol. Elegant, oily, and viscous, with round, fat, spiced citrus flavours.*	**£13.90** POR/RSV BEN/FLY

SILVER
AUSTRALIAN SWEET

BROWN BROTHERS FAMILY RESERVE NOBLE RIESLING 1999, BROWN BROTHERS Victoria – *Round yet delicate, with toffee, cooked orange, pineapple, and lemon. Ripe, firm, and balanced, with pine kernel notes.*	**£11.50** CPW

BRONZE
AUSTRALIAN SWEET

☆ **NOBLE TAMINGA 2001, TRENTHAM ESTATE** South Australia – *Floral, yeast, and lychee notes. Attractive and unusual, with pretty sundried stone fruit flavours.*	**£6.40** ESL/SCK CCS/FLA

GOLD
AUSTRALIAN FORTIFIED

☆ **BROWN BROTHERS LIQUEUR MUSCAT NV, BROWN BROTHERS** Victoria – *Barley sugar, treacle, coffee bean, and fig preserve. Medicinal notes give lift to the palate of marmalade and walnuts.*	**£12.70** V&C/CNL

BRONZE
AUSTRALIAN FORTIFIED

RUTHERGLEN MUSCAT NV, STANTON & KILLEEN Victoria – *Refined white chocolate, caramel, satsuma, lilac and honey flavours and scents. Rich, mouthcoating, and long.*	**£10.40** BNK/NFW RSV/CCS TAN/FLY
CLASSIC RUTHERGLEN MUSCAT NV, STANTON & KILLEEN Victoria – *Fresh yet staggeringly luscious. Vivid raisin, toffee, honey, and candied grapefruit flavours are scored by bright acidity.*	**£16.70** NFW/CCS

AUSTRIA

Steadily distancing itself from the brief scandal of nearly a generation ago, and – stylistically – from its German neighbours, Austria is now one of the world's most interesting wine producing countries. Initially, most of the spotlight has been hogged by examples of the spicy-rich local Grüner Veltliner and by the extraordinary late harvest wines. But the Austrians are proving that theirs is a pony with several more tricks. Rieslings are very successful, as are some very characterful reds, such as this year's award-winning Zweigelt.

SILVER
AUSTRIAN WHITE

GRÜNER VELTLINER SANDGRUBE PRIVATFÜLLUNG 2004, WOLFGANG AIGNER NIEDERÖSTERREICH – *A light sparkle tickles the tongue, with off-dry flavours and fresh acidity. Ripe apple fruits and long cleansing finish.*	**£10.20** HAM
RIESLING LOIBENBERG 2003, RAINER WESS NIEDERÖSTERREICH – *Soft, green plum and whitecurrant fruit fills the palate. The nose has delicate herbal notes with white flower scents.*	**£16.50** CEL
RIESLING PRIVAT 2003, WEINGUT NIGL NIEDERÖSTERREICH – *Hints of peppermint and flowering rosemary on the nose, the palate is laden with crisp red apple fruit.*	**£21.90** GON
RIESLING ZÖBINGER HEILIGENSTEIN 2002, WILLI BRÜNDLMAYER NIEDERÖSTERREICH – *Balanced and fresh, with piercing pear, flower, lemon, grass, green apple, and mineral flavours.*	**£26.00** RWD

B R O N Z E
AUSTRIAN WHITE

PINOT GRIS GOLA 2004, GERHARD WOHLMUTH STYRIA – *Crisp elderflower notes on the nose. Light fruit and refreshing acidity on the palate. A thirst quencher.*	**£9.30** HAM
SAUVIGNON BLANC ERNTE 2004, GERHARD WOHLMUTH STYRIA – *Full and lemony, this crisp and juicy wine would be an ideal match for seafood.*	**£11.00** HAM
GRÜNER VELTLINER ALTE REBEN 2002, WILLI BRÜNDLMAYER NIEDERÖSTERREICH – *An attractive fruity nose with an aromatic undertone. The palate is well-balanced with citrus acidity and long length.*	**£19.00** RWD
GRÜNER VELTLINER SPIEGEL RESERVE 2003, WEINGUT JURTSCHITSCH SONNHOFF NIEDERÖSTERREICH – *Grass, pepper, ripe silky pear, and fresh lychee flavours entwine in this pretty, layered wine. Notes of cinnamon spice.*	**£20.00** ODD
SPIEGEL GRÜNER VELTLINER 2003, WEINGUT LOIMER NIEDEROSTERREICH – *A minerally nose with a ripe attack of sweet spice on the palate, creamy texture, and clean finish.*	**£20.30** CCS/FLY
RIESLING HEILIGENSTEIN LYRA 2002, WEINGUT BRÜNDLMAYER NIEDERÖSTERREICH – *Smoky, pungent, peppery Urgestein minerality, with well-integrated sweetness that is balanced with sweet herbs, peachs, and blossoms.*	**£24.00** RWD

T R O P H Y
AUSTRIAN RED

☆ ILLMITZ ZWEIGELT 2003, WEINLAUBENHOF KRACHER BURGENLAND – *Toffee and candied cherry, crammed with damsons, blueberries, and toast, its richness mitigated by bright acidity.*	**£9.00** NYW

TROPHY
AUSTRIAN SWEET

SÄMLING 88 TBA 2002, HAUS TSCHIDA Burgenland – *Candied lemon peel, burnt orange, and barley sugar. Fine, persistent grapefruit acidity cuts through all that velvety flesh.*	£.00 NOT AVAILABLE IN THE UK

GOLD
AUSTRIAN SWEET

KRACHER TBA NO 4 2002, WEINLAUBENHOF KRACHER Burgenland – *Fragrant lychee and barley sugar with Seville orange marmalade and apricots. Round, luscious, and fragrant.*	£24.50 LEA

SILVER
AUSTRIAN SWEET

TBA NO 7 GRANDE CUVÉE 2002, WEINLAUBENHOF KRACHER Burgenland – *Lush marmalade flavours pour from the palate. Long, intensely sweet richness lifted by a spritz of lemon zest freshness.*	£27.00 NYW
TBA NO 8 2002, WEINLAUBENHOF KRACHER Burgenland – *Steely fresh orange and mineral nose. Palate has lots of Tuscan honey, lime blossom, melon, and toast flavours.*	£28.50 NYW
WELSCHRIESLING SCHEUREBE NO 12 2002, WEINLAUBENHOF KRACHER Burgenland – *Intense lemon, honey, and orange liqueur flavours.The powerful palate is balanced with delicate tea leaf and blossom hints.*	£38.00 NYW

BRONZE
AUSTRIAN SWEET

LENZ MOSER PRESTIGE BEERENAUSLESE 2001, WINKELLEREI LENZ MOSER Burgenland – *Brilliant, clear yellow tones, harmonious balance of acidity and sweetness, pure cantaloup with honey, and long lasting finish.*	£8.00 FTH

BOUVIER TBA 1999, ALFRED FISCHER BURGENLAND – *Elegant, fresh, and full, with lusciously sweet, compelling burnt coconut, and white apple flavours.*	**£8.80** TNG/CCS RAV
TRAMINER AUSLESE 2003, WEINLAUBENHOF KRACHER BURGENLAND – *Lush peach, apricot, cinnamon, and Turkish Delight flavours and aromas characterise this heady nectar.*	**£9.00** NYW
LENZ MOSER PRESTIGE TBA 2002, WEINKELLEREI LENZ MOSER BURGENLAND – *Complex nose of nuts and honey. Balanced with perfect mingling of acidity and sweet fruit, great maturing potential.*	**£11.00** FTH
WEISBURGUNDER BEERENAUSLESE 2002, WEINGUT SEPP MOSER NIEDERÖSTERREICH – *Notes of damp earth and black coffee. Very good acidity with long rustic finish.*	**£12.90** FHM/MDN
HÖPLER TBA 2001, HÖPLER BURGENLAND – *Aromas of toast and walnuts. Good acidity on the palate with honey, coconut, and tangy orange peel on the finish.*	**£17.80** HOE
HÖPLER EISWEIN 2002, HÖPLER BURGENLAND – *Intense little green plum, grass, white pepper, mineral, and apple flavours and aromas. Textured, vivid, and long.*	**£19.50** HOE
TBA NO 3 2002, WEINLAUBENHOF KRACHER BURGENLAND – *Luxurious peach, passion fruit, and mineral aromas with elegant flavours and long lasting length.*	**£23.00** NYW
TBA NO 5 2002, WEINLAUBENHOF KRACHER BURGENLAND – *Pungent nose of lemon curd and overripe fruits. Mouth-filling and viscous with crisp acidity and lingering length.*	**£24.00** NYW
TBA NO 6 2002, WEINLAUBENHOF KRACHER BURGENLAND – *Deep honeyed nose with notes of pineapple and peach. The palate is well-balanced with subtle, understated sweet fruits.*	**£26.00** NYW

CHILE

The country whose winemakers are breathing hardest down the Australians' necks is undoubtedly Chile. It is revealing that, while the Aussies picked up more medals this year, the Chileans came within a whisker of matching their tally of value for money awards. Reds still predominate, with particularly interesting efforts being made from the Cabernet Sauvignon, Merlot, and Chile's "own" grape, the peppery Carmenère which was once an essential ingredient of claret. Among whites, it is interesting to see how many successful Sauvignon Blancs are now being made here, including a rare – and very delicious – example of a late harvest version.

GOLD
CHILEAN WHITE

☆ **RESERVA ESPECIAL CHARDONNAY 2004, VIÑA TABALI** Pisco – *Passion fruit, mangosteen, jackfruit, and pineapple. Mandarin oranges, sweet juicy pears, bananas, and vanilla pods. Technicolour and widescreen.*	£10.00 ASD

SILVER
CHILEAN WHITE

☆ **CHARDONNAY SANTIAGO 1541 2004, VIÑA UNDURRAGA** Lontue Valley – *Fine, fresh candied lemon and apple blossom aromas. Vibrant flavours of fresh orange juice and crushed almonds.*	£3.00 NTT
☆ **MARAVILLA SAUVIGNON BLANC 2004, VISTAMAR WINES** Central Valley – *An unusual nose of green olives and blackcurrant leaves. Pretty elderflower notes. A characterful wine.*	£4.50 VNO
★ **TIERRA ANTICA SAUVIGNON BLANC 2004, TAMARA WINES** Limari Valley – *Asparagus nose. Subtle white fruits and minerals on the palate. Honeysuckle tones and vibrant gooseberry fruit finish.*	£5.00 CAB

☆ LA TIERRA Y EL HOMBRE SAUVIGNON BLANC 2004, INDOMITA REGIONAL BLEND – *Gooseberry aromas and flavours are offset by fresh acidity and a viscous mouthfeel. Juicy and satisfying.*	**£5.60** ABY
☆ SANTA ISABEL SAUVIGNON BLANC 2004, VIÑA CASABLANCA ACONCAGUA REGION – *Elegant, with a subtle grass and elderflower nose. Particularly fragant, floral, and elegant. A very individual wine.*	**£7.00** MOR
RESERVE CHARDONNAY 2004, VIÑA CONO SUR ACONCAGUA REGION – *Citrus notes on the nose, with ripe stone fruit and tropical tones. A buttery edge with a hint of spice.*	**£8.00** NZH
VISION CHARDONNAY 2003, CONO SUR ACONCAGUA REGION – *Big, classic, opulent, and velvety, with a delightful waft of tobacco smoke and lemon curd flavour. Deep yet bright.*	**£9.00** WST
GRAN ARAUCANO SAUVIGNON BLANC 2002, LURTON ACONCAGUA REGION – *Rich nose with gooseberry and lychee notes. The palate has a backbone of acidity and mineral steeliness.*	**£9.50** POR/JSM

BRONZE
CHILEAN WHITE

☆ SANTA CAROLINA WHITE NV, SANTA CAROLINA CENTRAL VALLEY – *Juicy peaches and nectarines on the nose and palate alongside a seasalt tang. Idiosyncratic.*	**£4.00** PFC
☆ SAN ANDRES CHILEAN SAUVIGNON CHARDONNAY 2004/5, SAN PEDRO CENTRAL VALLEY – *Honeyed notes on the nose and a stewed apple, whitecurrant, and cream palate. Soft and approachable.*	**£4.30** MHV
☆ CALITERRA CHARDONNAY 2004, CALITERRA CENTRAL VALLEY – *Soft orchard fruits on nose and palate. Pale and green-hued, with a streak of dried herbs.*	**£5.00** HMA
☆ PKNT CHARDONNAY 2004, TERRAUSTRAL CENTRAL VALLEY – *Fresh tropical flavours: limes, pineapple, guava, and mango. Youthful and medium-bodied.*	**£5.00** ASD

MONOS LOCOS SAUVIGNON BLANC 2004, VIÑA CONCHA Y TORO CENTRAL VALLEY – *Fresh acidity is balanced by sweet lemon and lime fruit. A crisp, invigorating finish.*	£5.50 VGN
EXPLORER SAUVIGNON BLANC 2004, VIÑA CONCHA Y TORO CENTRAL VALLEY – *A potpourri nose and smoky, grassy character gooseberry palate. Good intensity of fruit.*	£5.70 RAV/FLA WRW
SAUVIGNON BLANC ELQUI VALLEY 2004, VIÑA FALERINA PISCO – *Ripe gooseberries, cut grass, lime cordial, and sliced pears spring from this lively, sunny wine. Bright and balanced.*	£6.00 LAI
CARMEN CHARDONNAY 2004, VIÑA CARMEN MAIPO VALLEY – *Round, soft, and full, with generous citrus and ripe pear flavour. Characterful.*	£6.40 NEC/FLY WRW
CHARDONNAY VIOGNIER EL DELIRIO RESERVE 2004, VIÑA BOTALCURA MAULE VALLEY – *Grass and pineapple aromas. Perfumed and tropical, with freshly baked apple pie flavours.*	£6.70 TNG/CCS
ANAKENA SINGLE VINEYARD VIOGNIER 2004, ANAKENA RAPEL VALLEY – *Intense citrus and apricot aromas. Pineapple and melon tropical fruit flavours with a crisp balanced finish.*	£7.20 HPW/TPE RSV/WRK WRW
RESERVE SAUVIGNON BLANC 2004, VIÑA CARMEN CASABLANCA VALLEY – *A classic, confident Sauvignon, with plenty of green gooseberry aromas and flavours. Well balanced.*	£7.70 FLY
TERRACED GRAN RESERVA CHARDONNAY 2004, LUIS FELIPE EDWARDS COLCHAGUA VALLEY – *Toasty, full, round, and persistent, with a peach and apple palate of some complexity.*	£8.00 D&D
TESCO FINEST CHILEAN SAUVIGNON BLANC 2004, TESCO REGIONAL BLEND – *A more reserved nose with sweet peardrop aromas. The palate is pretty, light, fresh, and floral.*	£8.00 TOS
VISION GEWÜRZTRAMINER 2004, CONO SUR ACONCAGUA REGION – *Bright pineapples, rose petals, juicy peaches, and ruby grapefruit bound from the flavour-packed palate. Lusciously rich.*	£8.00 WST

VISION RIESLING 2003, CONO SUR **Bío-Bío** – *Deep golden yellow. Rich ripe fruit on the nose and palate. Flowers and green apples. Balanced and long.*	£8.00 WST
VISION VIOGNIER 2004, CONO SUR **Rapel Valley** – *Deep gold, with apricots, peach, and warm ginger on the nose. Ripe, with a spicy mouthfeel. Long.*	£8.00 WST
WINEMAKERS RIESLING LOT 20 2004, VIÑA CONCHA Y TORO **Bío-Bío** – *Dense flavours of ripe lemons, Rose's lime cordial, pear juice, and minerals all wrapped up in zingy acidity.*	£8.00 ODD
CHARDONNAY BOTALCURA LA PORFIA GRAND RESERVE 2003, VIÑA BOTALCURA **Maule Valley** – *Round, soft, exotic and creamy, this wine offers an unctuous texture and generous spice. Long lemon flavours.*	£8.20 TNG/CCS
ANAKENA ONA VIOGNIER CHARDONNAY SAUVIGNON BLANC 2004, ANAKENA **Rapel Valley** – *Pronounced citrus, orange peel, and cream nose is matched by a creamy fruit palate with a long finish.*	£10.00 SWS
FLORESTA LEYDA SAUVIGNON BLANC 2004, SANTA RITA **Maipo Valley** – *Fresh, focused, and ripe, this Sauvignon Blanc is saturated with flavour and lifted by fresh acidity.*	£10.00 WTS
GRAN ARAUCANO CHARDONNAY 2002, LURTON **Aconcagua Region** – *Very rich and forward, with juicy pineapple and ripe orange melon flavours. Sweet oak. Deeply coloured.*	£10.00 JSM
WILD FERMENT CHARDONNAY 2002, VIÑA ERRÁZURIZ **Casablanca Valley** – *More restrained and discreet than some of its contemporaries, with its delicate pears, herbs, and minerals.*	£10.10 EDC/JSM
TERRUNYO SAUVIGNON BLANC 2004, VIÑA CONCHA Y TORO **Aconcagua** – *A fresh crisp and nutty style with almond notes on the palate and layers of fruit and acidity.*	£10.20 RAV/FLA WRW/WSO
AMAYNA SAUVIGNON BLANC 2003, VIÑA GARCES SILVA **Leyda Valley** – *An attractive nose with asparagus hints. Round and redolent of tropical fruit, with a crisp finish.*	£13.50 HAR

AMAYNA CHARDONNAY 2003, VIÑA GARCES SILVA **LEYDA VALLEY** – *Banana and whipped cream nose. The palate is packed with mouthwatering fruit salad and mango flavours. Evolved.*	**£14.50** HVN
AMELIA CHARDONNAY 2003, VIÑA CONCHA Y TORO **ACONCAGUA REGION** – *Lemon yellow colour. Tropical, with touches of nutmeg and mace on the nose. Balanced and integrated.*	**£17.00** POR/RAV FLA/WRW

SEAL OF APPROVAL
CHILEAN WHITE

☆ SANTA LUCIA SAUVIGNON CHARDONNAY NV, LES GRANDS CHAIS DE FRANCE **CENTRAL VALLEY** – *Green tropical berries and pineapples.*	**£3.00** ALD
☆ 35 SOUTH CHARDONNAY SAUVIGNON BLANC 2004, SAN PEDRO **CENTRAL VALLEY** – *Fresh apples, gooseberries, and nettles.*	**£3.50** TOS
☆ SINGLE VINEYARD SAUVIGNON BLANC SANTIAGO 1541 2004, VIÑA UNDURRAGA **CURICÓ VALLEY** – *Gooseberries, apples, and lemons galore.*	**£3.80** NTT
☆ VALLE ANDINO CHARDONNAY 2004, TERRANOBLE **MAULE VALLEY** – *Fresh citrus mingles with lychee and passionfruit.*	**£3.90** MCT
☆ CHILEAN CHARDONNAY 2004, VIÑA MORANDÉ **CENTRAL VALLEY** – *Flowers, pineapples, pears, and peaches.*	**£4.00** SMF
☆ CO-OP CHILEAN CHARDONNAY 2004, AGRÍCOLA CANTALEJOS **CENTRAL VALLEY** – *Fresh pineapple and banana aromas and flavours.*	**£4.00** CWS
☆ LOS CAMACHOS SAUVIGNON BLANC 2004, VIÑA SAN PEDRO **CENTRAL VALLEY** – *Bananas and gooseberries flavour this wine.*	**£4.00** WRT

TROPHY
CHILEAN RED

★ **ERRÁZURIZ MERLOT 2004, VIÑA ERRÁZURIZ** **CURICÓ VALLEY**– *Very ripe and peppery, with a full palate of firm blackcurrant fruit. Meaty and savoury, with hints of the barnyard.*	**£6.40** BGN/EDC TOS/FLA JSM

GOLD
CHILEAN RED

☆ **RESERVE SELECTION CHILEAN CARMENÈRE 2003, SAINSBURY'S** **RAPEL VALLEY** – *Tar and roast almond nose. Soft acidity and integrated tannins. Cranberry fruit and hints of mint and black pepper.*	**£4.50** JSM
FAMILY COLLECTION CABERNET SAUVIGNON 2000, ARESTI **CURICÓ VALLEY** – *Savoury, farmy notes, rich spices, and black cherry fruit. Warm, supple, and savoury, with smoke and toast.*	**£14.00** EUW

SILVER
CHILEAN RED

★ **RESERVE SELECTION CHILEAN CABERNET SAUVIGNON 2003, SAINSBURY'S** **RAPEL VALLEY** – *Clear, mouthwatering flavours of raspberries, red apples, and tar. The nose has aromas of earth and flowers.*	**£4.50** JSM
☆ **VALLE ANDINO RESERVA CABERNET SAUVIGNON 2003, TERRANOBLE** **MAULE VALLEY** – *Very attractive, ripe, and juicy, with blackberry jam, spicebox, and roast herbs on nose and palate.*	**£4.50** MCT
☆ **VENTISQUERO CLASICO MERLOT 2004, VIÑA VENTISQUERO** **COLCHAGUA** – *This is a deep, youthful red, with lifted grassy aromas, juicy cherry fruit flavours, and mint hints.*	**£5.00** PLB
☆ **BOUCHON MERLOT 2004, J BOUCHON** **MAULE VALLEY** – *Darkest violet. Lively acidity and warm damson fruit flavours underpinned by a firm tannic structure. Roast coffee nuances.*	**£5.30** H&H

☆ ANAKENA CARMENÈRE 2003, ANAKENA **RAPEL VALLEY** – *Full, smooth, and tarry, its dark soft mulberry fruit caught in a web of firm walnut-skin tannins.*	**£5.70** TNG/WRK WRW
☆ DOÑA DOMINGA SINGLE VINEYARD MERLOT 2003, VIÑA CASA SILVA **RAPEL VALLEY** – *Freshly ground coffee, kirsch liqueur, and coal aromas. The palate is pure and toasty, soft but firm.*	**£6.00** L&T
☆ ORGANIC CABERNET CARMENÈRE 2003, CONO SUR **RAPEL VALLEY** – *Blackberries and roasted herbs. The palate is awash with intense black fruit flavours, anise, and liquorice. Earthy.*	**£6.00** WST
☆ SERAPHIM 2003, VIÑA LEYDA **RAPEL VALLEY** – *Menthol, cardamom, and cinnamon scents. The palate is a big, powerful agglomeration of earth, cassis, and truffle oil.*	**£6.00** VGN
☆ YALI RESERVE CARMENÈRE 2003, VIÑA VENTISQUERO **MAIPO VALLEY** – *Dark red and ripe, this is intensely concentrated, deep wine with chocolate notes and fresh strawberry flavours.*	**£6.00** PLB
☆ CONO SUR RESERVE CABERNET SAUVIGNON 2003, VIÑA CONO SUR **MAIPO VALLEY** – *Blackberries, spearmint, peppercorn, and smoke. Intense and round, its plum and mulberry fruits ripe and soft.*	**£7.00** WST
☆ DOÑA DOMINGA RESERVE CABERNET SAUVIGNON 2003, VIÑA CASA SILVA **RAPEL VALLEY** – *Intense layers of blackberries, mocha, thyme, cinnamon, and charcoal. Deep, lush, and vivid, with a long finish.*	**£7.00** L&T
☆ TERRAMATER RESERVA 2003, TERRAMATER **MAIPO VALLEY** – *The nose is sweetly perfumed with coffee, nutmeg, and allspice. Weighty bramble fruit and vanilla bean palate.*	**£7.10** YOB
☆ RESERVA CARMENÈRE 2004, VIÑA CASA SILVA **RAPEL VALLEY** – *Forest fruit flavours and scents. Deep and dripping with bitter cherry juice for the duration of the long finish.*	**£7.40** BBO/TNI
FUNDACION SYRAH CARMENÈRE 2004, LAITHWAITES **PISCO** – *Redcurrants, capsicum, and spring flowers scent the nose. Plenty of black and blue berries and tobacco leaf tannins.*	**£8.00** LAI

GRAND RESERVE MERLOT 2003, VIÑA VENTISQUERO **MAIPO VALLEY** – *Crunchy cranberries and raspberries. Scents of summer rain, tar, blueberries, and flowers. Focused and long.*	£8.00 PLB
TABALI CABERNET SAUVIGNON RESERVA 2002, TABALI **PISCO** – *Firmly structured and well-knit, this wine offers spiced plum fruit and delicate crunchy green pepper overtones. Very pretty.*	£8.00 JSM
VIU MANENT CABERNET SAUVIGNON RESERVE 2003, VIU MANENT **RAPEL VALLEY** – *Violets, blackcurrants, and notes of undergrowth. Red and black vine fruits, smoke, coal dust, and spice. Glossy.*	£8.00 TNG
WILLIAM COLE ALTO VUELO 2003, WILLIAM COLE VINEYARDS **ACONCAGUA REGION** – *Blackberry pie aromas and flavours. Densely coloured and intensely flavoured, with chocolate nuances and hints of violets.*	£8.00 HPW
ANAKENA ONA CABERNET MERLOT CARMENÈRE 2003, ANAKENA **RAPEL VALLEY** – *Mouthwatering black cherry aromas and flavours. Plenty of cinnamon spice and delightful hints of sweet vanilla.*	£8.50 HPW/RSV WRK
COLUMBINE CABERNET SAUVIGNON RESERVE 2003, WILLIAM COLE VINEYARDS **ACONCAGUA REGION** – *Rich, ripe berry aromas and seductive black berry fruit. Fine tannins and an intricate thread of acidity.*	£9.00 HPW
TERRUNYO CARMENÈRE 2003, CONCHA Y TORO **RAPEL VALLEY** – *Cassis, smoke, mint, and chocolate. Firm, with creamy dark fruit. Spices, smoke, and green peppers add complexity.*	£10.70 FLA/WRW
1865 CABERNET SAUVIGNON 2001, SAN PEDRO **MAIPO VALLEY** – *Aromas of sun-warmed redcurrants, toast, vanilla, and hedgerow flowers scent the nose. Full-bodied and long.*	£13.00 RWM
CABERNET SAUVIGNON LOS LINGUES GRAN RESERVA 2003, VIÑA CASA SILVA **RAPEL VALLEY** – *Grassy notes hover over vanilla seeds and blackberries. Cedar, cassis, spearmint, warm cherries, and cocoa.*	£14.50 BBO/TNI
CONO SUR 20 BARRELS MERLOT 2003, CONO SUR **COLCHAGUA VALLEY** – *Dark and concentrated with blackberry and spice. Cassis and eucalyptus with a seductive softness.*	£15.00 WST

CUVÉE ALEXANDRE SYRAH 2003, CASA LAPOSTOLLE **RAPEL VALLEY** – *Inky purple with roast coffee, chocolate, vanilla bean, and juicy blackberries. Balanced, textured, and long. Aristocratic and stylish.*	**£15.20** FHM/POR BBO
LA CUMBRE SHIRAZ 2003, VIÑA ERRÁZURIZ **ACONCAGUA REGION** – *Deep violet. Hints of wild herbs, coffee, and smoke. The palate has plenty of blackberries and dark chocolate.*	**£15.50** EDC
NINQUEN 2002, VIÑA MONTGRAS RAPEL VALLEY – *Ripe plum aromas with rich blackberry, currant, and chocolate. Ripe tannins and a silky texture.*	**£17.00** ENO
UNUSUAL TERRAMATER 2002, TERRAMATER **MAIPO VALLEY** – *Pretty, sophisticated oak. The palate is intense and structured, with fresh blueberry fruit and delicate floral notes.*	**£17.00** YOB
WINE MAKERS RED 2000, VIÑA CARMEN MAIPO VALLEY – *Deep vermilion, with a fine hoisin sauce, smoke, and coal nose. Exceedingly full-bodied, sinewy, and long.*	**£18.00** FLY
CABO DE HORNOS 2001, SAN PEDRO CURICÓ VALLEY – *Deep, chocolately, and leathery. Concentrated bramble fruit, coffee, caramel, and pepper flavours buttressed by grippy tannins.*	**£25.00** RWM

BRONZE
CHILEAN RED

☆ **ANTU MAPU CABERNET SAUVIGNON 2003, WILLIAM COLE VINEYARDS CENTRAL VALLEY** – *Blackcurrants, barnyard nuances, cocoa, caramel, and earth. Warm cumin notes.*	**£4.00** MRN
☆ **CO-OP CHILEAN MERLOT 2004, VIÑEDOS SUTIL** **CENTRAL VALLEY** – *Deep cinnabar colour. Robust, with aromas of coal, cherries, and bay leaves.*	**£4.00** CWS
☆ **TERRAMATER MERLOT 2004, TERRAMATER** **CENTRAL VALLEY** – *Showy and open, with exotic sandalwood and clove notes on the nose and blackberry fruit flavours.*	**£4.10** YOB

☆ WINEMAKER'S SELECTION SYRAH 2004, VIÑA CANEPA **Rapel Valley** – *Leafy green pepper nose graduates to chewy, approachable blackberry palate. Some spice lingers and the finish is fruity.*	£4.50 THI
☆ DOÑA DOMINGA OLD VINES CABERNET CARMENÈRE 2004, VIÑA CASA SILVA **Rapel Valley** – *Spicy, heady, and layered, with cola, nutmeg, cherries, and dill. Eucalyptus notes.*	£5.00 JSM
☆ DOÑA DOMINGA OLD VINES CABERNET MERLOT 2004, VIÑA CASA SILVA **Rapel Valley** – *Mature garnet-brick red colour. Marjoram, pepper, and cherries on the nose. Smoky fruit flavours.*	£5.00 L&T
☆ PKNT MERLOT 2004, TERRAUSTRAL **Central Valley** – *Intense, with an exuberant, fresh raspberry and damson nose and palate. Forward. Herbal hints.*	£5.00 NTD
☆ RAVANAL CARMENÈRE 2003, VIÑA RAVANAL **Rapel Valley** – *A backbone of acidity supports the fleshy red cherry fruit palate. Soft hints of vanilla bean, toast, and violets.*	£5.00 BNK
☆ TESCO FINEST CHILEAN MERLOT RESERVE 2004, VIÑA VALDIVIESO **Central Valley** – *Grassy green pepper aromas. Bursting with youthful vigour. Ripe, intense, and edgy.*	£5.00 TOS
CASILLERO DEL DIABLO CARMENÈRE 2004, CONCHO Y TORO **Rapel Valley** – *Dark ruby red. Earth, crushed leaves, lavender, bonfire smoke, and red cherries flavour this structured, robust offering.*	£5.10 TOS/MWW FLA/JSM
CASA RIVAS MERLOT 2003, VIÑA CASA RIVAS **Maipo Valley** – *Blackcurrant leaf aromas. Flavours of cassis are seared by fresh acidity. Soft tannins.*	£5.30 ADN/JNW
CASILLERO DEL DIABLO CABERNET SAUVIGNON 2004, VIÑA CONCHA Y TORO **Central Valley** – *Smoked black fruit of good depth and complexity. Vibrant, full, and upfront. Some spice.*	£5.50 BGN/TOS RAV/JSM
CHILEAN CABERNET SAUVIGNON RESERVE 2003, LUIS FELIPE EDWARDS **Rapel Valley** – *Ruby cassis fruit laced with smoky oak. Fresh, bright acidity, fine oak, and long finish.*	£5.50 D&D

TOUCHSTONE CABERNET SAUVIGNON 2003, VIÑEDOS ORGANICOS EMILIANA Rapel Valley – *Savoury, peppery bramble fruit flavours are complemented by a bright streak of acidity. Long.*	£5.50 VRT
SAN MEDIN CABERNET SAUVIGNON 2003, VIÑA MIGUEL TORRES Central Valley – *Restrained nose. Mouthfilling and round, the palate has an approachable, smoky quality and lots of cassis fruit.*	£5.70 JEF
VALLE ANDINO RESERVE ESPECIAL MERLOT 2003, TERRANOBLE Maule Valley – *Notes of smoke, game, and spice on the nose. The palate has savoury red pepper flavours.*	£5.80 MCT
EXPLORER PINOT NOIR 2004, VIÑA CONCHA Y TORO Aconcagua Region – *Barnyard, tomato, vanilla, and strawberry flavours. Ripe, open, and round.*	£5.90 ESL/RAV FLA
AVENTURA ANDINA RESERVE SHIRAZ 2003, VINA LOS ACANTOS Colchagua Valley – *Seaweed, beet, creosote, and coffee bean nose. Earthy blackberry palate.*	£6.00 FEE
CASTILLO DE MOLINA CABERNET SAUVIGNON, LONTUE VALLEY 2003, SAN PEDRO Curicó Valley – *Cinnamon, blackberries, smoke, and almonds. Full and structured. Aromatic.*	£6.00 BUC
DOÑA DOMINGA RESERVE CABERNET SAUVIGNON 2004, VIÑA CASA SILVA Rapel Valley – *Tobacco, cedar, pepper, and chocolate aromas. Flavours of dark cassis. Ripe.*	£6.00 L&T
DOÑA DOMINGA SINGLE VINEYARD CARMENÈRE 2004, VIÑA CASA SILVA Rapel Valley – *Bright, fresh, and youthful. This medium-bodied beauty has mouthwatering currants, raspberries, and hints of loam.*	£6.00 L&T
LUIS FELIPE EDWARDS CABERNET SAUVIGNON 2004, LUIS FELIPE EDWARDS Rapel Valley – *Cassis liqueur essence on the nose and palate. The fruit is supported by youthful, powerful, oaky tannins.*	£6.00 D&D
LUIS FELIPE EDWARDS CARMENÈRE 2004, LUIS FELIPE EDWARDS Rapel Valley – *Floral and fruit driven, with elegant mocha and vanilla flavours lasting right through to the finish.*	£6.00 D&D

MONOS LOCOS MERLOT 2004, VIÑA CONCHA Y TORO **CENTRAL VALLEY** – *In its first flush of youth still, with a lush, spicy, medium-bodied plum palate. Will evolve.*	£6.00 VGN
PRIVATE RESERVE SYRAH 2002, VIÑA CANEPA **RAPEL VALLEY** – *Big, deep, scented fruit cordial and summer pudding nose. Approachable loganberry and liquorice palate.*	£6.00 THI
PUERTO VIEJO WOOD LABEL MERLOT 2003, VIÑA REQUINGUA **CURICÓ VALLEY** – *Ruby red. Bright, crisp, very attractive damson flavours, and charry oak aromas. Long.*	£6.00 CTL
RESERVE CABERNET SAUVIGNON 2003, VIÑA VENTISQUERO **MAIPO VALLEY** – *Full yet balanced and delicate, with spicewood, herb, and black cherry elements. Soft and warm.*	£6.00 PLB
VINA MAIPO RESERVE CABERNET SAUVIGNON 2004, VINA MAIPO **MAIPO VALLEY** – *Leather, cedar, cigar box, and plum scents and flavours. Young yet fully formed.*	£6.00 CYT
COLECCIÓN CARMENÈRE 2004, VIÑA CASA SILVA **RAPEL VALLEY** – *Vivid, mouthwatering, and juicy, this medium-full Carmenère is buoyed by a backbone of acidity. Sweetly ripe cherry flavours.*	£6.50 BBO
TRIO MERLOT 2004, VIÑA CONCHA Y TORO **RAPEL VALLEY** – *Clear, medium-bodied cherry and damson flavoured beauty with toffee aromas and chewy tannins.*	£6.50 POR/FLA
20 BARRELS PINOT NOIR 2003, CONO SUR **RAPEL VALLEY** – *Red plums, fresh herbs, and currants scent the fresh, medicinal nose. Youthful, pretty, and restrained.*	£7.00 TOS
ALTO DE TERRA ANDINA RESERVE SHIRAZ CABERNET SAUVIGNON 2002, TERRA ANDINA **MAIPO VALLEY** – *Blackcurrants, strawberries, fresh figs, and coconut whirl together in this robust, flavourful wine. Long and fresh.*	£7.00 PLE
CABERNET SAUVIGNON EL DELIRIO RESERVE 2003, VIÑA BOTALCURA **MAULE VALLEY** – *Ginger biscuit aromas on the nose. Firm, with ripe cherry flavours, vanilla undertones, and supple tannins.*	£7.00 TNG

CABERNET SYRAH RESERVE 2004, VIÑA MONTGRAS	£7.00
RAPEL VALLEY – *Unrestrained berry, liquorice and warm spice. Long finish with toasty oak and velvety tannins.*	ENO
CALITERRA CABERNET SAUVIGNON RESERVA 2003, CALITERRA **RAPEL VALLEY** – *Hints of red pepper and eucalyptus. Fruit, oak and alcohol are all in balance on the long, spiced finish.*	£7.00
	WIM
CALITERRA MERLOT RESERVA 2002, CALITERRA **RAPEL VALLEY** – *Ripe and juicy, with an evolved, integrated palate of sun-warmed currants and mulberries.*	£7.00
	HMA
COLECCIÓN PRIVADA MERLOT 2003, VIÑA CASABLANCA **MAIPO VALLEY** – *Notes of capsicum and charred wood decorate the nose. Vivid raspberry jam flavours. Long and structured.*	£7.00
	MOR
CONO SUR RESERVE MERLOT 2004, VIÑA CONO SUR **COLCHAGUA VALLEY** – *A whopping mouthful of textured chocolate-covered mulberry fruit tinged with liquorice.*	£7.00
	WST
CREMASCHI FURLOTTI SYRAH RESERVE 2003, CREMASCHI FURLOTTI **MAULE VALLEY** – *Blackberry, mineral and savoury Victoria plum nose. Spicy, firm, and young, this wine needs time to mature.*	£7.00
	CHN
DOÑA DOMINGA RESERVA CARMENÈRE 2004, VIÑA CASA SILVA **RAPEL VALLEY** – *Complex tobacco, stone, peony, chocolate, and currant flavours. Silky coconut texture. Robust and fresh.*	£7.00
	JSM
MERLOT ANGOSTURA GRAN RESERVA 2003, VIÑA CASA SILVA **RAPEL VALLEY** – *Deep, spicy, and intense, with notes of freshly crushed peppercorns and blackcurrants.*	£7.00
	BBO/FLY
MERLOT RESERVE 2003, CHATEAU LOS BOLDOS **RAPEL VALLEY** – *Spicy, mouthwatering, and reddish-black, with a round palate of blackberries and cherries.*	£7.00
	HBJ
MISIONES CABERNET SAUVIGNON 2003, TARAPACA **RAPEL VALLEY** – *Cinders, toffee, and cinnamon on the nose. The palate has plenty of ripe blackberry flavours.*	£7.00
	EHL

MONOS LOCOS CABERNET SAUVIGNON 2001, VIÑA LEYDA CENTRAL VALLEY – *Mincemeat, strawberries, black cherries, and earth. Approaching maturity. Drink now.*	**£7.00** VGN
RESERVA CABERNET SAUVIGNON 2003, SANTA RITA MAIPO VALLEY – *Pretty violet purple colour. Chewy, savoury, tightly coiled ripe black cherry palate. Will evolve further.*	**£7.00** MWW/JSM
SANTA RITA RESERVA MERLOT 2003, MAIPO VALLEY 2003, SANTA RITA MAIPO VALLEY – *Plums, mint, earth, and chocolate. Velvety mouthfeel. Persistent finish.*	**£7.00** MWW
TERRAMATER RESERVA 2003, TERRAMATER CURICÓ VALLEY – *Opaque. Forest floor and bramble fruit aromas. Soft currant fruit palate with an edge of acidity.*	**£7.10** YOB
TERRAMATER RESERVA 2003, TERRAMATER MAIPO VALLEY – *Displaying signs of maturity. Savoury cherry flavours. Liquorice, bark, and floral notes. Will keep another year or two.*	**£7.10** YOB
LOS ROSALES CHAPEL VINEYARD MERLOT 2004, VIÑA LA ROSA RAPEL VALLEY – *Full-bodied, with fresh cherry vanilla flavours and tobacco leaf notes. Sweet oak.*	**£7.20** LAI
TORREON DE PAREDES RESERVE MERLOT 2003, VINEDOS DE PAREDES RAPEL VALLEY – *Pine, orange peel, blackberries, star anise, and red apple characteristics. Concentrated.*	**£7.30** FTH
VALDIVIESO CABERNET SAUVIGNON RESERVE 2003, VIÑA VALDIVIESO CENTRAL VALLEY – *Intense and ripe, its forest fruits and chocolate oak possessing roundness, depth, and weight.*	**£7.40** FLY/JSM
TORO DE PIEDRA 2003, VIÑA REQUINGUA CURICÓ VALLEY – *Straightforward damson aromas on the nose. The palate has chewy black fruit flavours.*	**£7.50** CTL
DE MARTINO LEGADO RESERVA CABERNET SAUVIGNON 2003, DE MARTINO VINEYARDS MAIPO VALLEY – *Masses of ripe Ribena cassis aromas and flavours. Modern and structured.*	**£7.70** FHM/CEB EDC/DMV HAC

DE MARTINO LEGADO RESERVA CARMENÈRE 2003, DE MARTINO VINEYARDS Maipo Valley – *Summer fruit pudding flavours meld with crushed almond skin tannins on the slightly evolved nose and palate.*	**£7.70** EDC/DMV WDI/HAC
CARMENÈRE RESERVA ESPECIAL 2004, J BOUCHON Maule Valley – *Intense, complex, lifted tobacco, coffee, chocolate, blackberry, blackcurrant, and cedar aromas and flavours.*	**£7.80** H&H
DE MARTINO LEGADO RESERVA SYRAH 2003, DE MARTINO VINEYARDS Rapel Valley – *Intensely dark and bursting with black fruit flavour. Leather and earth hints and sweet floral notes.*	**£7.90** EDC/HAC
VALDIVIESO RESERVE SYRAH 2003, VIÑA VALDIVIESO Curicó Valley – *Steeped with berries, oak, and pepper. Firm tannins and balanced acid with a herbal edge.*	**£7.90** FLY
VIÑA CHOCALAN SYRAH RESERVE 2003, VIÑA CHOCALAN Maipo Valley – *Earthy, rich black wine gum nose and palate. Weighty and concentrated, with a long spicy finish.*	**£7.90** CCS/FLY
ALTO VUELO PINOT NOIR 2003, WILLIAM COLE VINEYARDS Aconcagua Region – *Ruby red. Stone, herb, animal, and flower nose and palate. Textured and long.*	**£8.00** HPW
CREMASCHI FURLOTTI CARMENÈRE RESERVA 2003, CREMASCHI FURLOTTI Maule Valley – *Complex notes of roast hazelnut, espresso, autumn leaves, and moist earth after a summer rain.*	**£8.00** CHN
ECHEVERRIA RESERVA MERLOT 2002, VINA ECHEVERRIA Curicó Valley – *Fresh plum and blueberry flavours. Hints of mocha and bonfire smoke. Medium-bodied.*	**£8.00** FHM
ELQUI VALLEY CARMENÈRE 2004, VIÑA FALERNIA Pisco – *Cedary, packed with red plums and scented with wild herbs. Smoothly textured, medium-bodied, and fresh.*	**£8.00** LAI
GRAND RESERVE CABERNET SAUVIGNON 2002, VIÑA VENTISQUERO Maipo Valley – *Cherry juice, cola, roast herb, and kirsch; chocolate, green pepper, mace, and clove.*	**£8.00** PLB

IN SITU RESERVA SYRAH 2003, VINA SAN ESTEBAN **ACONCAGUA REGION** – *Leather, coffee bean, smoked bacon, and dark raspberry flavours and scents.*	**£8.00** AWS
MARQUÉS DE CASA CONCHA MERLOT 2003, VIÑA CONCHA Y TORO RAPEL VALLEY – *Soft, with admirably complex creamy blackberry fruit, vanilla beans, and cinnamon spice.*	**£8.00** JSM
MARQUÉS DE CASA CONCHA SYRAH 2003, VIÑA CONCHA Y TORO RAPEL VALLEY – *A nose of mint, spices, and blackcurrants. Spicy and structured, with very good balance.*	**£8.00** MWW
MERLOT RESERVA DE GRAS 2004, VIÑA MONTGRAS RAPEL VALLEY – *Deep red cherry flavours. Hints of peppermint and baked earth on the nose. Powerful tannins.*	**£8.00** CTC
POTRO DE PIEDRA 2002, VIÑA REQUINGUA CURICÓ VALLEY – *Ruby garnet colour. Forest fruits, blackberries, and mint shine on the round palate. Smoky finish.*	**£8.00** CTL
RAVANAL RESERVA CARMENÈRE 2003, RAVANAL RAPEL VALLEY – *Rich scents of forest floor, raspberry coulis, stewed prunes, red apple, and tar. Medium-bodied, bright, and peppery.*	**£8.00** TCW
RESERVA ESPECIAL CARMENÈRE 2004, VISTAMAR WINES MAIPO VALLEY – *Good depth and balanced freshness. Excellent integration of fruit and wood. Full cassis and cedar flavours.*	**£8.00** VNO
TABALI RESERVA CABERNET SAUVIGNON 2003, VIÑA TABALI PISCO – *Minerals and mint lace the nose. The palate has charcoal and capsicum notes. Ripe, firm, and ready.*	**£8.00** JSM
TERRACED GRAN RESERVA CARMENÈRE 2003, LUIS FELIPE EDWARDS RAPEL VALLEY – *Hints of pepper lace the round cherry flavours with a smattering of vanilla. Velvety tannins.*	**£8.00** D&D
TERRACED GRAN RESERVA MERLOT 2003, LUIS FELIPE EDWARDS RAPEL VALLEY – *Tobacco leaf notes and cherries feature prominently on the bouquet. Dense, tarry, and heady.*	**£8.00** D&D

MARQUÉS DE CASA CONCHA CABERNET SAUVIGNON 2003, VIÑA CONCHA Y TORO Maipo Valley – *Mint and coffee tones dance above a palate of very dry blackcurrant fruit. Leathery notes.*	£8.40 TAN/FLA
CASA SILVA DOÑA DOMINGA MERLOT GRAN RESEVA 2003, VIÑA CASA SILVA S.A. Rapel Valley – *Cocoa, smoke, and Maraschino cherry flavour and scents. Firm and rich.*	£8.50 L&T
DOÑA DOMINGA GRAN RESERVE CABERNET 2003, VIÑA CASA SILVA Rapel Valley – *Dark purple-black hue. The nose is restrained and the palate has spicy, chewy redcurrant flavours.*	£8.50 L&T
NATIVA CABERNET SAUVIGNON 2002, VIÑA CARMEN Maipo Valley – *A soft attack leads to a palate of smoky, minty black and red fruit with eucalyptus notes.*	£8.50 FLY/WRW
MAX RESERVA SHIRAZ 2003, VIÑA ERRÁZURIZ Aconcagua Region – *Intense nose of tobacco smoke. Ripe palate of brambles, cherries, and grainy vanilla beans.*	£8.60 EDC/TOS MWW
SHIRAZ LOLOL GRAN RESERVA 2003, VIÑA CASA SILVA Rapel Valley – *Savoury game and grilled meat hints on the bouquet. Elegant yet structured and tannic, with deep purple damson flavours.*	£8.80 BBO
ARBOLEDA CARMENÈRE 2003, VIÑA ERRÁZURIZ Rapel Valley – *Pure, ripe, lush, concentrated blackcurrant and cranberry flavours. Aromas of milk chocolate and dried basil.*	£9.00 WIM
ARBOLEDA SYRAH 2002, VIÑA ERRÁZURIZ Rapel Valley – *Herbs and perfumed cherry fruit nose. Ripe, mouthwatering red plum and blueberry palate. Tarry notes.*	£9.00 HMA
CANATA PINOT NOIR PASO HONDO ALTA SELECCIÓN 2003, VIÑEDOS DE CANATA Bío-Bío – *Restrained, with a plateful of summer fruits and a nose of soft strawberries and currant leaves.*	£9.00 FUL
CONDE DE SUPERUNDA 2000, MIGUEL TORRES Curicó Valley – *Ripe strawberries, cranberries, and blackberries flavour this full, round wine. Notes of loam and spice.*	£9.00 JEF

DON RECA MERLOT 2004, VIÑA LA ROSA Rapel Valley *– Really rich! Many layers of liquorice, creamy vanilla, and little black berries.*	**£9.00** JSM
VISION CARMENÈRE 2003, CONO SUR Rapel Valley *– Spicy, with chocolate chunks, meaty red damsons, and fennel on the nose. Seductive blackcurrant flavours.*	**£9.00** WST
VISION SYRAH 2003, CONO SUR Rapel Valley *– Harmonious, clear, and soft, with crisp black fruit flavours and balancing acidity.*	**£9.00** WST
ERRÁZURIZ MAX RESERVA CABERNET SAUVIGNON 2003, VIÑA ERRÁZURIZ Aconcagua Region *– Garnet red. Briar, earth, chocolate, cigar, and cherry compôte flavours and aromas.*	**£9.10** BGN/EDC
GOLD ASSEMBLAGE 2003, VIÑA ESTAMPA Rapel Valley *– Oregano, basil, mint, and star anise scents. Flavours of blackberries, cream, dark plums, and coffee.*	**£9.10** NEC/TNG
ESTAMPA GOLD ASSEMBLAGE 2003, VIÑA ESTAMPA Rapel Valley *– Fine cassis mingles with wild juniper on the nose. The palate is linear, satiny, balanced, and long.*	**£9.30** TNG
ANAKENA ONA CABERNET/MERLOT/CARMENERE 2002, ANAKENA Rapel Valley *– Plums, strawberries, and kirsch emanate from the rich, robust palate. Woody notes.*	**£10.00** SWS
ANAKENA ONA SYRAH 2004, ANAKENA Rapel Valley *– Huge, deep purple colour, nose of amarettini biscuits, and rich flavours of blackberries, damsons, and charred wood.*	**£10.00** SWS
CABERNET SAUVIGNON ANTU NINQUEN 2002, VIÑA MONTGRAS Rapel Valley *– Smoke, meat, and earth rise from the glass. This wine is powerful yet elegant, and very long.*	**£10.00** ENO
GREY CABERNET SAUVIGNON 2002, VIÑA VENTISQUERO Maipo Valley *– Bright mulberry and blackberry fruits, mint, black pepper, and freshly ground spice elements.*	**£10.00** PLB

SANTA CAROLINA BARRICA SELECTION CARMENÈRE 2003, SANTA CAROLINA Rapel Valley – *Beautiful ripe dark fruit. Essence of chocolate covered cherries and pepper caress the palate with fine, smooth tannins.*	£10.00 PFC
DE MARTINO SINGLE VINEYARD CARMENÈRE 2003, DE MARTINO VINEYARDS Maipo Valley – *Vivid fresh red plum flesh, wild juniper scents, and delicate hints of vanilla define this smoothly textured wine.*	£10.60 FHM/EDC
DE MARTINO SINGLE VINEYARD SYRAH 2003, DE MARTINO VINEYARDS Rapel Valley – *Sensual fruitcake aromas rise from the nose. The palate has plenty of black cherry fruit on its long finish.*	£10.80 EDC
1865 CARMENÈRE 2002, SAN PEDRO Maule Valley – *Fresh, tight little redcurrants, cocoa powder, raspberry leaves, pipe tobacco, and cassis on nose and palate.*	£13.00 RWM
1865 MALBEC 2002, SAN PEDRO Curicó Valley – *There's an interplay of tart blackberries, rhubarb, freshly sliced fennel, and bonfire notes on nose and palate.*	£13.00 BUC
TERRAMATER ALTUM 2003, TERRAMATER Maipo Valley – *Vibrant palate with dense rich fruit and well integrated coconut oak. Soft buttery finish with hints of cocoa.*	£13.00 YOB
QUINTA GENERACIÓN 2002, VIÑA CASA SILVA Rapel Valley – *Rubber scents the nose. The palate is loaded with ripe cherries and hints of tomato and pepper.*	£13.50 BBO
COLECCIÓN PRIVADA DOÑA BERNARDA 2002, LUIS FELIPE EDWARDS Rapel Valley – *Earth, oak, black pepper, and cedar. Drink this maturing wine as soon as you wish.*	£15.00 D&D
CREMASCHI FURLOTTI VERNERE 2001, CREMASCHI FURLOTTI Maule Valley – *This masterful blend has juicy blue-black plum and cassis flavours. Pure lilac and toast aromas on the nose.*	£15.00 CHN
DE MARTINO GRAN FAMILIA CABERNET SAUVIGNON 2002, DE MARTINO VINEYARDS Maipo Valley – *Ripe, juicy and very warming, with dense, youthful, fiery blackcurrant flavours. Richly layered.*	£17.70 EDC

AMAYNA PINOT NOIR 2003, VIÑA GARCES SILVA **LEYDA VALLEY** – *Juicy and aromatic, its bright kirsch flavours spiked with tall summer grasses and notes of earth.*	**£18.50** HVN
DON AMADO 1998, VINEDOS TORREON DE PAREDES **RAPEL VALLEY** – *Ripe, smooth, plummy, and rich. Saddle leather and spice anoint the nose.*	**£19.00** FTH
DON MAXIMIANO FOUNDERS RESERVE 2001, VIÑA ERRÁZURIZ **ACONCAGUA REGION** – *Prunes, blueberries, wood, cocoa powder, cassis, and green pepper characteristics.*	**£20.80** EDC
VIÑEDO CHADWICK 2001, VIÑA ERRÁZURIZ **MAIPO VALLEY** – *Blackcurrants, leaves, and earth on the nose. Smooth berries and espresso on the palate.*	**£38.20** EDC/FLA

SEAL OF APPROVAL
CHILEAN RED

☆ TESCO CHILEAN MERLOT NV, VALDIVIESO **CENTRAL VALLEY** – *Bright, ripe, medium-bodied cherry flavours.*	**£3.00** TOS
☆ VINTNERS COLLECTION CABERNET SAUVIGNON 2004, CONSTELLATION **CENTRAL VALLEY** – *Cassis, kirsch, and chocolate. Medium-bodied.*	**£3.50** LCC
☆ SAN ANDRES CHILEAN VINO TINTO 2003, SAN PEDRO **CENTRAL VALLEY** – *Deep cassis and melting bitter chocolate.*	**£3.90** MHV
☆ VALLE ANDINO MERLOT 2003, TERRANOBLE **MAULE VALLEY** – *Bright plum juice with undergrowth notes.*	**£3.90** MCT
☆ 35 SOUTH CABERNET SAUVIGNON MERLOT 2004, SAN PEDRO **CENTRAL VALLEY** – *Ripe, soft, and full of sun-warmed raspberries.*	**£4.00** ASD

☆ 35 SOUTH CABERNET SAUVIGNON SHIRAZ 2004, SAN PEDRO CENTRAL VALLEY – *Aromas of toast. Ripe blackcurrant fruit.*	£4.00 TOS
☆ CHILEAN CABERNET SAUVIGNON 2004, VIÑA ERRÁZURIZ CENTRAL VALLEY – *Smoothly textured. Coconut and cherry flavours.*	£4.00 CWS
☆ FOOTSTEPS CABERNET SAUVIGNON NV, FOOTSTEPS CENTRAL VALLEY – *Brisk tannins buttress rich cassis.*	£4.00 MCT
☆ GATO NEGRO CABERNET SAUVIGNON 2004, SAN PEDRO CENTRAL VALLEY – *Fresh, vivid blackberry flavours and scents.*	£4.00 BUC
☆ LAS MONTAÑAS 2003, LAS MONTAÑAS CENTRAL VALLEY – *Deep cherry and plum flavours. Herbal hints.*	£4.00 BRZ
☆ LOS CAMACHOS CABERNET SAUVIGNON 2004, VIÑA SAN PEDRO CENTRAL VALLEY – *Bright, full, and packed with cassis.*	£4.00 WRT

GOLD
CHILEAN SWEET

☆ LATE HARVEST SAUVIGNON BLANC 2002, VIÑA CONCHA Y TORO MAULE VALLEY – *Orange blossom and apple nose. Weighty and sprinkled with spice, honey, elderflowers, lychees, white peach, and hints of caramel.*	£5.80 MWW/RAV FLA/WRW

EASTERN EUROPE

Not so long ago, before the arrival of wines from the New World, the countries on the other side of the old Iron Curtain were a reliable source of good value wines. Time has, sadly, not been kind to Bulgaria, Hungary, Romania, and former Yugoslavia. Stated bluntly, privatisation has not led to a leap in quality. There are still bargains to be found from these countries, but they tend to be inexpensive Seals of Approval rather than medals.

SILVER
EASTERN EUROPEAN WHITE

☆ ALBASTRELE PINOT GRIGIO 2004, ACOREX Moldova – *Composed, fresh, and attractive, with delicate tobacco leaf notes and a palate of fresh whitecurrants and greengages.*	£5.90 LAI

SEAL OF APPROVAL
EASTERN EUROPEAN WHITE

☆ CO-OP BULGARIAN CHARDONNAY 2004, DOMAINE BOYAR SHUMEN Bulgaria – *Bananas, grapefruit, lemons, and apples. Medium-bodied.*	£3.50 CWS
☆ PINOT GRIGIO RECAS 2004, CRAMELE RECAS Romania – *Delicate mineral notes. Fresh apple flavours.*	£3.50 WOW
☆ RIVERVIEW CHARDONNAY PINOT GRIGIO 2004, HILLTOP NESZMÉLY Hungary – *Fresh golden apple and whitecurrant flavours.*	£3.80 ASD/BGN JSM/MRN NTD
☆ CHAPEL HILL CHARDONNAY 2004, BALATONBOGLAR Hungary – *Fresh apples. Hints of white powder.*	£4.00 MYL

☆ CHAPEL HILL PINOT GRIGIO 2004, BALATONBOGLAR HUNGARY – *Elderflower cordial, whitecurrants, and limes.*	**£4.00** MYL
☆ JONJOSH CHARDONNAY 2003, BINDERER ST URSULA HUNGARY – *Fresh citrus, delicate spices, and flowers.*	**£4.00** THI
☆ SPICE TRAIL WHITE 2004, NAGYREDE ESTATE HUNGARY – *Ripe, youthful, peppery white fruit flavours.*	**£4.00** MYL
☆ TUK TAM SAUVIGNON BLANC 2003, LVK VINPROM BULGARIA – *Grassy, with plenty of peapod flavours.*	**£4.00** SPR

SILVER
EASTERN EUROPEAN RED

SOLITAIRE ELENOVO MERLOT 2003, BOYAR ESTATES BULGARIA – *Peppermint aromas waft from the nose. Silky vanilla softens the ripe palate of cherry and plum fruit.*	**£10.00** DBO

SEAL OF APPROVAL
EASTERN EUROPEAN RED

☆ HAWKS VIEW MERLOT NV, VINPROM SVISHTOV BULGARIA – *Fresh cranberry and roast herb characteristics.*	**£3.70** MHV
☆ BLUERIDGE XR MERLOT 2003, BOYAR ESTATES BULGARIA – *Blueberries, mint, and tobacco characteristics.*	**£4.00** TOS
☆ ORIACHOVITZA 2002, DOMAIN MENADA BULGARIA – *Deeply flavoured and firmly structured. Floral.*	**£4.00** WZD

☆ PERSONA MERLOT 2004, VINPROM YAMBOL **BULGARIA** – *Ripe plum and fresh thyme elements.*	£4.00 WZD
☆ PINOT NOIR RECAS RESERVA DOC 2003, CRAMELE RECAS **ROMANIA** – *Vibrant strawberry flavours. Ripe and medium-weight.*	£4.00 WOW
☆ SZEKSZARDI BULLS BLOOD 2003, HUNGAROVIN **HUNGARY** – *Powerful and packed with glowing red berries.*	£4.00 MYL
☆ VALLEY OF THE ROSES MERLOT 2004, STORK NEST ESTATES **BULGARIA** – *Brisk acidity lifts dark cherry flavours.*	£4.00 WZD

SEAL OF APPROVAL
EASTERN EUROPEAN ROSÉ

☆ VALLEY OF THE ROSES CABERNET SAUVIGNON ROSÉ 2004, STORK NEST ESTATES **BULGARIA** – *Bright pink. Deep cassis and herb elements.*	£4.00 WZD

BRONZE
EASTERN EUROPEAN SPARKLING

☆ CHAPEL HILL SPARKLING CHARDONNAY PINOT NOIR NV, BALATONBOGLAR **HUNGARY** – *Fresh white fruits, summer pudding berries, and crushed almonds mingle with notes of mint on this wine.*	£5.50 MYL/CTC

BRONZE
EASTERN EUROPEAN SWEET

DISZNÓKÖ TOKAJI ASZÙ 5 PUTTONYOS 2000, DISZNÓKÖ ESTATE **HUNGARY** – *Slightly oxidised with bright and bitter Seville orange flavours. This has plenty of depth on its full palate.*	£15.90 CCH

DOBOGO TOKAJI ASZÚ 6 PUTTONYOS 2000, DOBOGO	**£38.00**
HUNGARY – *Bright gold, with a sweet, spicy white mushroom nose. A well-balanced, lush, attractive Tokaj.*	LIB

GOLD MEDALS HAVE SCORED the equivalent of at least 18.5/20 (or 95/100) and are exceptional. Silver has scored over 17/20 (or 90/100), bronze over 15.5/20 (or 85/100), and seals of approval over 14/20 (or 80/100).
☆ particularly good value
★ truly great value

FOR STOCKIST CODES turn to page 317. For regularly updated information about stockists and the International Wine Challenge, visit wineint.com. For a full glossary of wine terms and a complete free wine course, visit robertjoseph-onwine.com

F R A N C E

French wine continues to slide down the UK popularity charts. At the current rate, it will soon be pushed into third place by California. But this is still the place to go hunting for non-branded bargains. The figures speak for themselves; this year France offered around one and a half times as many value-for-money award winners as Australia or Chile. Add to that the extraordinary range of traditional styles that are not to be found elsewhere, and the way so many of these wines accompany food, and France unquestionably deserves to be doing better than it is. Now's the time to go out to explore some of these wines before the New World sweeps them off the shelves.

T R O P H Y
ALSACE WHITE

GEWURZTRAMINER ROSENBERG 2003, BARMÈS-BUECHER **ALSACE** – *Petal and powdered mineral scents, and a textured palate of soft peach and apple fruit. Rich yet balanced.*	**£19.50** GON

G O L D
ALSACE WHITE

☆ GEWURZTRAMINER GRAND CRU BRAND 2001, CAVE VINICOLE DE TURCKHEIM **ALSACE** – *Rosewater, lychee, and saffron perfume. The palate is round and unctuous yet the lush fruit is held in check by fine acidity.*	**£12.10** FHM/OCM FLA/ICL WRK
GEWURZTRAMINER HENGST 2003, ZIND HUMBRECHT **ALSACE** – *Rosewater, lychee, and honeysuckle on the nose. Opulent and glycerol rich but balanced by fine mineral acidity.*	**£34.50** GON

SILVER
ALSACE WHITE

GEWURZTRAMINER VIEILLES VIGNES 2004, DOMAINE GRUSS & FILS **Alsace** – *Peaches, Turkish Delight, white pepper, and powdered minerals. Ripe stone fruits and lychees. Rich and voluptuous.*	**£11.20** 3DW
RIESLING GRAND CRU BRAND 2000, CAVE VINICOLE DE TURCKHEIM **Alsace** – *Cinnamon, Sicilian lemons, orange blossom, and mineral nose. Greengage and citrus flavours. Long and complex.*	**£12.30** FHM/PBA FLA/JSM WSO/THS
TOKAY PINOT GRIS SCHWARZBERG 2002, DOMAINE DIRLER-CADÉ **Alsace** – *Enormous, with a bountiful array of green apples, pineapples, acacia blossoms, and sweet pear fruit.*	**£15.00** CCS
RIESLING HEIMBOURG 2001, ZIND HUMBRECHT **Alsace** – *Rich, unctuous, honeyed, and buttery, with fine intensity, balanced weight, and a long finish.*	**£16.50** GON
RIESLING SAERING GRAND CRU 2002, DOMAINE DIRLER-CADÉ **Alsace** – *Little white hedgerow flowers, minerals, and ground nutmeg nose. Limes, papaya, and mangosteen. Excellent balance.*	**£18.00** BBR/CCS

BRONZE
ALSACE WHITE

KUEHN RIESLING 2004, VINS D'ALSACE KUEHN **Alsace** – *Fresh, youthful apple and lemon flavours. Textured, with aromatic white peach scents.*	**£6.00** PLB
KUEHN RIESLING COLLECTION PRIVÉE 2004, VINS D'ALSACE KUEHN **Alsace** – *Vivid ripe lemon flavours coalesce with green apples and talc on nose and palate. Young yet refined.*	**£6.50** PLB
PINOT BLANC ROSENBERG 2003, BARMÈS-BUECHER **Alsace** – *A sweet nose with fragrant elderflower nuances. Waxy ripe fruit and a lean finish.*	**£12.00** GON

RIESLING GRAND CRU OLLWILLER 2002, CAVE VINICOLE DE TURCKHEIM ALSACE – *A pronounced citrus nose with a touch of peach. The palate is mid-weight, straightforward, and well made.*	£13.00 PBA
RIESLING GRAND CRU SOMMERBERG 2002, CAVE VINICOLE DE TURCKHEIM ALSACE – *A ripe and spicy nose leads to a rich ripe stonefruit palate. Very good freshness and length.*	£13.00 PBA
WEINBACH RIESLING GRAND CRU SCHLOSSBERG 2002, WEINBACH ALSACE – *Iodine and the smell of the sea. Rich and ripe with a juicy mid-palate, and a long mineral finish.*	£17.70 TNG
TOKAY PINOT GRIS CUVÉE LAURENCE 2001, DOMAINE WEINBACH ALSACE – *Bright, lively flavours of red apple skin and minerals. Full aromatic bouquet. Textured roundness.*	£24.70 TNG

SILVER
ALSACE SPARKLING

☆ MAYERLING BRUT CREMANT D'ALSACE BLANC DE BLANCS NV, CAVE VINICOLE DE TURCKHEIM ALSACE – *Fresh green and white berries on nose and palate. Scents of spring blossom perfume the bouquet.*	£9.10 V&C/FLA WRK

GOLD
ALSACE SWEET

☆ GEWURZTRAMINER VENDANGES TARDIVES 2002, CAVE VINICOLE DE TURCKHEIM ALSACE – *Rich apricot, pinepple, cigar, beeswax, lemon curd, white flower, pear, and caramelised lemon rind flavours. This is the business!*	£13.00 PBA
PINOT GRIS CLOS JEBSAL 2003, ZIND HUMBRECHT ALSACE – *Roast aubergine, oil, poached pear, honeysuckle, and cooking apple aromas and flavours. Finely textured.*	£27.50 GON

BRONZE
ALSACE SWEET

GEWURZTRAMINER GRAND CRU EICHBERG 2003, PHILIPPE ZINCK ALSACE – *Minerals, ripe pears, fresh flowers, and grapefruit. Concentrated, long, and very well balanced.*	£10.00
	MWW

BRONZE
BEAUJOLAIS RED

BEAUJOLAIS VILLAGES COMBE AUX JACQUES 2003, LOUIS JADOT BEAUJOLAIS – *This winner reflects the excellent 2003 vintage in Beaujolais: ripe, tight blackberry fruit, floral scents, and quartzite minerals.*	£7.50
	FHM

SILVER
BORDEAUX WHITE

★ CALVET LIMITED RELEASE 2004, CALVET BORDEAUX – *Loaded with complex fruit. A salmagundi of different aromas and flavours which really slakes the thirst.*	£5.00
	GYW/JSM

BRONZE
BORDEAUX WHITE

☆ CHÂTEAU BEAU MAYNE SAUVIGNON BLANC 2004, CVBG DOURTHE KRESSMANN BORDEAUX – *Pea pod and mineral nose and palate. A fresh, grassy wine, crisp, and well-balanced.*	£5.00
	DOU
MERCHANTS BAY 2004, GINESTET BORDEAUX – *Crisp, dry, and aromatic. Grassy apple flavours.*	£5.00
	WAV
☆ YVECOURT BLANC 2004, YVON MAU BORDEAUX – *A powerful fruit salad nose with white pepper notes. The palate has green plums, good concentration, and length.*	£5.00
	TOS

PREMIUS BLANC 2004, YVON MAU Bᴏʀᴅᴇᴀᴜx – *Fresh green fruit on the nose leads to a lovely lemon tart palate. A delightful summer-drinking wine.*	£6.00 TOS

TROPHY
BORDEAUX RED

CHÂTEAU MAGREZ-TIVOLI 2002, CHÂTEAU LES GRANDS CHÊNES Bᴏʀᴅᴇᴀᴜx – *Rich, round, silky, mouth-coating prune, and plum flavoured, with scents of crumbled earth and spice.*	£.00 NOT AVAILABLE IN THE UK

GOLD
BORDEAUX RED

CHÂTEAU CLÉMENT PICHON 2001, CHÂTEAU CLÉMENT PICHON Bᴏʀᴅᴇᴀᴜx – *Truffles, gravel, leather, cedar, and flowers scent its heady bouquet. Chocolate, redcurrants, and coffee flavour its expressive palate.*	£14.00 ADN/JSM
CHÂTEAU LA GRAVE FIGEAC 2000, CHÂTEAU LA GRAVE FIGEAC Bᴏʀᴅᴇᴀᴜx – *Pepper, graphite, and cinnamon complement the chewy red berry flavours. Complex, satisfying, stylish and extremely well made.*	£17.00 MWW
CHÂTEAU GRAND-PUY-LACOSTE 2001, CHÂTEAU GRAND-PUY-LACOSTE Bᴏʀᴅᴇᴀᴜx – *Chocolate-covered cassis, spice, powdered earth, and graphite flavours reined in by firm tannins. Leafy, restrained, and powerfully built.*	£25.10 ESL/LAI
CHÂTEAU ROL VALENTIN 2001, CHÂTEAU ROL VELENTIN Bᴏʀᴅᴇᴀᴜx – *Opulent blackcurrant, damson, and truffle notes. Ripe tannins. The finish is elegant and refined with good depth and length.*	£49.50 JNW

SILVER
BORDEAUX RED

CHÂTEAU LE PEY 2002, COMPAGNET VINS Bᴏʀᴅᴇᴀᴜx – *Deep cassis and plum flavours mingle with scents of undergrowth and flowers on the nose.*	£5.80 TOS

CHÂTEAU CLOS DE LA TOUR RÉSERVE DU CHÂTEAU 2002, CVBG DOURTHE KRESSMANN Bordeaux – *Scents of earth and cigars. Round, vivid flavours of black plums and redcurrants. Balanced, clear, firm, and dry.*	£9.00 DOU
CHÂTEAU DE LA GARDE 2001, CHÂTEAU DE LA GARDE Bordeaux – *Mulberry and blackcurrant jam. The palate is exceptionally firm, with sweet spice and black cherry fruit. Long, toasty finish.*	£9.00 JSM
CHÂTEAU PATACHE D'AUX 2002, DOMAINES LAPALU Bordeaux – *Gravel, moist tobacco, prunes, and plums. An attack of blackberries and cherries laced with toast and inkwell.*	£9.50 TAN
CHÂTEAU REYNIER CUVÉE HERITAGE 2002, VIGNOBLES MARC LURTON Bordeaux – *Deep raspberry red. Hints of almond blossom and marzipan. Ripe, perfumed plum palate with high tannins and a long finish.*	£10.00 FWM
CHÂTEAU LA GARDE 2002, VINS ET VIGNOBLES DOURTHE Bordeaux – *Delicately perfumed small dark berries. Cigars, pencil shavings, and earth. Big, full-bodied, and long.*	£15.00 LAI
LE PRESBYTÈRE 2002, LAITHWAITES Bordeaux – *Big and deeply coloured, with a classic nose of pencil shavings. Spiced wood and liquorice notes. Plenty of cassis.*	£20.00 LAI
LA RÉSERVE DE LEOVILLE-BARTON 2000, CHÂTEAU LEOVILLE-BARTON Bordeaux – *Ceps scent the compelling nose. Red berry jam and game flavours. Glorious with harvest foods.*	£20.30 MWW/TAN

BRONZE
BORDEAUX RED

☆ MONTENEY 2004, BENOIT ET VALÉRIE CALVET Bordeaux – *Deep currant and fresh herb elements.*	£3.00 ALD
☆ YVON MAU YVECOURT 2003, YVON MAU Bordeaux – *Medium-bodied and accessible, with a pretty, balanced palate of strawberry leaves and fruit.*	£5.00 TOS

LES TOURELLES DE SIPIAN 2001, CHÂTEAU ROUSSEAU DE SIPIAN Bordeaux – *Vanilla, spices, and smoke scent the nose. The palate has plenty of leathery blackberry fruit.*	**£5.80** STH
AVERY'S FINE CLARET 2003, AVERY'S Bordeaux – *The plush palate of plums and blackberries has the softest tannic structure. Fresh and youthful.*	**£6.00** AVB
CORDIER COLLECTION PRIVÉE BORDEAUX ROUGE 2003, CORDIER MESTREZAT & DOMAINES Bordeaux – *The lifted nose of sugar plums boasts lavender nuances and racy acidity. Chewy and ripe.*	**£6.00** MTC
CALVET RESERVE 2002, CALVET Bordeaux – *Full and vibrant, its taut damson flavours laced with rich fruitcake spices. Balanced and long.*	**£7.00** GYW/JSM
CHÂTEAU JOUANIN 2003, CHÂTEAU JOUANIN Bordeaux – *Peppery nose. The palate is full of mouthwatering redcurrant flavour and firm, uncompromising tannins.*	**£7.00** JSM
CHÂTEAU PUY BARDENS 2002, VIGNOBLES LAMIABLE Bordeaux – *Spicy, youthful, and full-bodied, with plenty of red cherries and cigars. Mineral hints.*	**£7.00** FCA
CHÂTEAU REYNIER 2003, VIGNOBLES MARC LURTON Bordeaux – *Ripest blackcurrant and fresh damson flavours. Herbal overtones. Clear and persistent.*	**£7.00** FWM
LAITHWAITES MERLOT 2003, LAITHWAITES Bordeaux – *Damsons, roast herbs, flowers, chocolate, cedar, and smoke. A fresh, ripe wine.*	**£7.00** LAI
CUVÉE PRESTIGE 2002, CHÂTEAU DE LISENNES Bordeaux – *Spicebox aromatics on the nose. Brisk acidity etches the ripe blackcurrant fruit palate.*	**£7.20** BBS
MASCARON PAR GINESTET 2003, GINESTET Bordeaux – *Concentrated and long, with an extremely spicy palate of warm smoky redcurrants.*	**£8.00** WAV

CHÂTEAU DE LA GARDE 2002, CHÂTEAU DE LA GARDE Bordeaux – *Toasty oak, violet, and cigar box notes on the nose complement the damson-infused palate.*	**£9.00** JSM
CHÂTEAU GRAND BERTIN DE ST CLAIR 2002, COMPAGNET VINS Bordeaux – *Balanced, firm, and generously fruited, with rich cassis, cedar, and chocolate flavours.*	**£9.00** H&H
DOURTHE BARREL SELECT MÉDOC 2003, CVBG DOURTHE KRESSMANN Bordeaux – *Ripest kirsch and cassis flavours. Aromas of bonfire smoke. Ready to drink now.*	**£9.00** THS
DOURTHE BARREL SELECT ST-EMILION 2003, CVBG DOURTHE KRESSMANN Bordeaux – *Soft and delicate, with tarry notes. Appealing brick red colour. Mature and integrated.*	**£9.00** DOU
TOUR DES VINS ST-EMILION 2003, BARTON & GUESTIER Bordeaux – *Hints of pencil lead and undergrowth on the nose. Flavours of cherries and currants.*	**£9.00** DGO
CHÂTEAU LEBOSCQ 2003, DOMAINES LAPALU Bordeaux – *Firm yet ripe, with powerful kirsch flavours and a mouthcoating texture. Herb and smoke overtones.*	**£10.00** LAI
CORDIER COLLECTION PRIVÉE BORDEAUX SUPERIEUR 2002, CORDIER MESTREZAT & DOMAINES Bordeaux – *Notes of undergrowth, minerals, and herbs lift the palate of structured redcurrant fruit.*	**£10.00** JSM
CHÂTEAU LABAT 2002, CHÂTEAU LABAT Bordeaux – *Red cherry and pepper nose. Balanced, its red fruits interwoven with firm tannins. A food wine.*	**£11.00** LAI
CHÂTEAU MONCONSEIL-GAZIN 2003, CHÂTEAU MONCONSEIL-GAZIN Bordeaux – *Dark cherry pie nose. The open-knit palate is crammed with deep bramble fruit flavour.*	**£11.50** 3DW
CHÂTEAU ROUSSEAU DE SIPIAN 2001, CHÂTEAU ROUSSEAU DE SIPIAN Bordeaux – *Cassis, chocolate, and clove scent this wine. Complex notes of game and leather. Mature.*	**£11.60** STH

CHÂTEAU ROUSSEAU DE SIPIAN 2002, CHÂTEAU ROUSSEAU DE SIPIAN Bordeaux – *Very forward nose of fruitcake and clove buds. The warm, grippy cherry palate is tinged with vanilla.*	£11.60 STH
CHÂTEAU LABAT 2003, CHÂTEAU LABAT Bordeaux – *Weighty and concentrated, with round tannins and aromas of pencil lead. Mature and medium-bodied.*	£12.00 LAI
CHÂTEAU LA CLARIÈRE LAITHWAITE 2003, CHÂTEAU LA CLARIÈRE Bordeaux – *Intense plum flavours. Firmly oaked, harmonious, and concentrated, its rich fruit etched with pencil shavings.*	£15.00 LAI
CHÂTEAU TOURNEFEUILLE 2002, CHÂTEAU TOURNEFEUILLE Bordeaux – *Classic Bordeaux nose and palate, with big yet restrained sweetly ripe cassis and pine tree elements.*	£19.00 MKV
LE PRESBYTÈRE 2003, LAITHWAITES Bordeaux – *Deep ruby red. Perfume of damsons and cherries, smooth texture and medium body.*	£20.00 LAI
CHÂTEAU PIBRAN 1997, CHÂTEAU PIBRAN Bordeaux – *Mature, with plenty of cassis and a fine tannic backbone. Perfectly ready to drink this Christmas.*	£23.50 BNK

GOLD
BORDEAUX SWEET

☆ TESCO FINEST SAUTERNES 2002, TESCO Bordeaux – *Honeyed sweetness showing exotic apricot, saffron, and quince aromas on the nose. The palate has tremendous fruit richness allied to fine refreshing acidity.*	£12.00 TOS

SILVER
BORDEAUX SWEET

☆ MASCARON PAR GINESTET 2003, GINESTET Bordeaux – *Bright honey and perfumed flower nose. Soft marmalade and candied citrus flavours lifted by invigorating acidity.*	£6.00 WAV

☆ CHÂTEAU LIOT 2003, CHÂTEAU LIOT Bordeaux – *Herbs de Provence, whitecurrants, orange flowers, and lemons. Characterful and very ripe, an expressive, textured wine.*	£9.80
	WTS

BRONZE
BORDEAUX SWEET

☆ LA CHAPELLE DE LAFAURIE-PEYRAGUEY 2002, CHÂTEAU LAFAURIE-PEYRAGUEY Bordeaux – *A restrained wine with easy drinking honeyed flavours. Pleasant, approachable, and soft.*	£7.00
	JSM
CHÂTEAU DOISY-DAËNE SAUTERNES 2003, CHÂTEAU DOISY-DAËNE Bordeaux – *This has some style, an appealing viscous mouth feel, a good depth of flavour, and satisfying length.*	£12.00
	WTS
SUBLIME STE-CROIX-DU-MONT 2001, CHÂTEAU LA RAME Bordeaux – *Lemon rind, honeycomb, flower, and gooseberry flavours and scents. Powerfully sweet.*	£13.00
	WTS

TROPHY
BURGUNDY WHITE

☆ CHABLIS VIEILLES VIGNES 2003, JEAN-MARC BROCARD Burgundy – *Complex, pure, and perfumed, with citrus zest and lime blossom and delicate hints of flint. Impressive concentration.*	£10.50
	POR/CEB
LOUIS JADOT MEURSAULT 2002, LOUIS JADOT Burgundy – *Roast almond and mineral aromas. Tangy lemon fruit, supple, silky texture, and rich, opulent flesh. Drinking very well now.*	£27.00
	EDC/JSM

GOLD
BURGUNDY WHITE

☆ CUVÉE AL'ANCIENNE POUILLY-FUISSÉ 2003, PAUL BOUTINOT Burgundy – *Measured and elegant, with crushed cobnuts and almond kernels on the nose. Rich candlewax texture. Spikes of tarragon.*	£9.50
	PBA

☆ CHABLIS RESERVE CROIX ST JOSEPH 2000, J MOREAU BURGUNDY – *Minerals and citrus blossom scents. Apricot and peach palate. Elegant and honeyed, its finish sprinkled with grated lemon zest.*	**£10.70** MCT
BOURGOGNE BLANC LE CLOS 2002, CHÂTEAU DE PULIGNY BURGUNDY – *Apple, sugared almond, and pear tart aromas. Surpassingly beautiful white stone fruits, powdered minerals and runny honey.*	**£14.00** BBR
ROPITEAU MEURSAULT 2003, ROPITEAU BURGUNDY – *Bright, palest gold. Soft, with gently ripe pear fruit and cinnamon spice. Savoury peaches and candied grapefruit.*	**£20.00** WAV
PULIGNY-MONTRACHET LES MEIX LEFLAIVE 2002, OLIVIER LEFLAIVE FRÈRES BURGUNDY – *Astounding focus, power, and restraint. Fabulous grapefruit, pineapple, lemon, and ginger elements. Tremendous finesse and longevity. Santé!*	**£21.50** C&B
CHABLIS GRAND CRU LES CLOS 2003, JEAN-MARC BROCARD BURGUNDY – *Pungent, sweetly ripe quince, with a seam of minerals, nutty elements, and bright lime flavours.*	**£23.00** GSL
MEURSAULT MOREY-BLANC 2000, MOREY-BLANC BURGUNDY – *Round, with a dry, developed palate of lemon peel and jasmine blossom. Sultry cream and explosive citrus.*	**£29.00** TAN

SILVER
BURGUNDY WHITE

BOURGOGNE DE VIGNE EN VERRE 2004, DOMAINE TOUZOT BURGUNDY – *Light touches of toast complement the lychee, satsuma, and jackfruit flavours. Lemon zest nose. A wine of power.*	**£8.50** LAI
POUILLY-VINZELLES LES LONGEAYS 2002, ANTHONY BYRNE FINE WINES BURGUNDY – *Delicate, elegant, and integrated. The palate is crisp and dry, with a delicious seam of minerals.*	**£9.00** WTS
CHABLIS CUVÉE LC 2003, LA CHABLISIENNE BURGUNDY – *Pale and pungent, with aromas of greengages, chalk, and freshly picked lemons. Fine texture and hints of vanilla.*	**£9.50** WWT

MONTAGNY 1ER CRU MONTCUCHOT 2003, LA BUXYNOISE **Burgundy** – *A clear, elegant nose of stone fruits. Flavours of creamy oak and crisp red apples line the palate.*	**£11.00** HWL
EMOTION DE TERROIRS BLANC 2002, VINCENT GIRARDIN **Burgundy** – *Creamy and expressive, with good complexity and integration. Built to last. Orange zest, fresh hay, and grapefruit.*	**£12.50** ODD
CHABLIS 1ER CRU VAILLONS 2002, DOMAINE LOUIS MOREAU **Burgundy** – *The nose has baked apple pie aromas. The edgy palate is firm and dry, with refreshing acidity and a whisper of chalkdust.*	**£14.00** PBA/TAN ICL
CHABLIS PREMIER CRU SENSUEL 2003, JEAN-MARC BROCARD **Burgundy** – *Delicate tones of ginger and cardamom. The mid-weight palate has a spark of minerality and soft peach flesh.*	**£14.00** JBF
VALLET FRÈRES PERNAND-VERGELESSES BLANC 2003, VALLET FRERES **Burgundy** – *Full of candied lemons and may flowers, with a soft, sensual mouthfeel. Citrus fruit and oak flavours.*	**£16.00** PBA
MONTHELIE BLANC 2003, JEAN-CLAUDE BOISSET **Burgundy** – *Luscious yet tangy, with smouldering oak and pineapple fruit flavours. Restrained, toasty, and classic.*	**£16.90** CCS/BEN FLY
CHÂTEAU DE MEURSAULT CLOS DU CHÂTEAU BOURGOGNE BLANC 2003, DOMAINE DU CHÂTEAU DE MEURSAULT **Burgundy** – *Touches of spice on a fresh, fruity nose. Firm lemon and pear flavours and dried lavender.*	**£18.50** PAT/FLA
CHASSAGNE-MONTRACHET HENRI DE VILLAMONT 2001, HENRI DE VILLAMONT **Burgundy** – *A wine of pedigree. Deep musky lemon flavours and hazelnut and spring blossom aromas. Voluptuous.*	**£21.60** BBO
VALLET FRERES MEURSAULT 2002, VALLET FRERES **Burgundy** – *Scents of toast and caramel. A powerfully complex and elegant array of roast nuts and silky lemon fruit.*	**£22.50** PBA
CHABLIS GRAND CRU LES CLOS 2002, DOMAINE LOUIS MOREAU **Burgundy** – *Deep hazelnut, pear, starfruit, and Fuji apple flavours. Lifted and fine, with a streak of flint.*	**£27.00** PBA

BRONZE
BURGUNDY WHITE

BOURGOGNE CHARDONNAY 2002, MARIE-LOUISE PARISOT **Burgundy** – *Big and buttery, with vanilla bean richness. Toasty, rich, and tropical, with jackfruit and melon flavours.*	£5.80 MCT
BLASON DE BOURGOGNE CÔTE CHALONNAISE 2004, BLASON DE BOURGOGNE **Burgundy** – *Clear, appealing lemon bonbon flavours and a nose scented with citrus flowers. Delicate prickle of lemon zest notes.*	£6.70 BGN/JSM THS
UNITE WHITE BURGUNDY 2003, CAVE DE LUGNY **Burgundy** – *Fresh citrus fruit flavours and scents. Lime juice acidity provides a steely backbone.*	£7.00 JSM
PETIT CHABLIS J MOREAU 2004, J MOREAU **Burgundy** – *Delicate hints of chalk. The palate is steely yet warming, with Macintosh apple flavours.*	£7.60 MCT
ST-VÉRAN MORIN PÈRE & FILS 2004, MORIN PÈRE & FILS **Burgundy** – *Pineapples and peaches flavour this delicious offering. Lemon flowers and butterscotch scent the nose.*	£7.70 MHV
BLASON DE BOURGOGNE ST-VÉRAN 2004, BLASON DE BOURGOGNE **Burgundy** – *Lemons, grapefruit, and bananas flavour this wine. Light floral notes on the nose.*	£8.00 TOS
CHABLIS LES MANANTS 2004, JEAN-MARC BROCARD **Burgundy** – *Tropical and inviting, its candied citrus palate lifted by the spicy scent of gardenia blossoms.*	£8.00 POR
RESERVE PERSONNEL VIRÉ-CLESSÉ 2003, PAUL BOUTINOT **Burgundy** – *Pleasing banana and biscuit flavours and scents make this a delicious drop indeed. Creamy and ripe.*	£8.00 PBA
SAINSBURY'S CLASSIC SELECTION CHABLIS CUVÉE STE CÉLINE 2004, BROCARD **Burgundy** – *Youthful yet elegant and balanced, with a flowery nose and a fresh palate of pears and limes.*	£8.00 JSM

MACON UCHIZY RAPHAEL SALLET 2004, RAPHAEL SALLET BURGUNDY – *Sweet pineapple fruit and lime oil nose. The palate has balanced acidity and persistent lemon flavours.*	**£8.10** ROG
BLASON DE BOURGOGNE POUILLY-FUISSÉ 2004, BLASON DE BOURGOGNE BURGUNDY – *Intense and well-defined, with a balanced, layered palate of pear fruit and a backbone of minerality.*	**£9.00** TOS
CHABLIS FLEUR D'ACACIA 2003, LAMBLIN FILS BURGUNDY – *The expansive nose has a mineral thrust and tropical warmth. The palate is appley and crisp.*	**£9.00** BAB
SOMERFIELD CHABLIS 2003, LA CHABLISIENNE BURGUNDY – *Some development is displayed on the peachy nose. The tropical palate is long, lemony, and exotic.*	**£9.00** SMF
TESCO FINEST CHABLIS 1ER CRU 2001, LA CHABLISIENNE BURGUNDY – *Developed. Delicate aromas of flowers and lime fruit. The palate is elegant, complex, and long.*	**£9.00** TOS
CHÂTEAU DE MARSANNAY 2001, CHÂTEAU DE MARSANNAY BURGUNDY – *Nearly five years on and still this wine is holding up well, buoyed by elegant lemon oil acidity.*	**£9.50** PAT/MWW
DOMAINE DE VAUROUX CHABLIS 2003, DOMAINE DE VAUROUX BURGUNDY – *Fresh talc and white flowers on the nose. Crisp acidity supports soft peachy flesh. Mineral. Expressive.*	**£9.50** CNL/ENO ICL
LABOURÉ ROI CHABLIS 2004, LABOURÉ ROI BURGUNDY – *Fresh flowers on the nose. Dry, minerally, and silky, with lively acidity and well-defined greengage fruit.*	**£9.50** TOS/THI
CHABLIS LAROCHE 2004, LAROCHE BURGUNDY – *Papaya and pineapple nose. The palate is crisp and clear, with green and red apples. Warming.*	**£9.60** TOS/BWL FLY/JSM
BARTON & GUESTIER CHABLIS 2004, BARTON & GUESTIER BURGUNDY – *Pear drops and butterscotch aromas and flavours. Minerals and zesty lemons infuse the palate.*	**£10.00** DGO

CHABLIS SIMONNET-FEBVRE 2004, SIMONNET-FEBVRE **Burgundy** – *The nose is steely and sophisticated. The still-young palate is flinty, fresh, and packed with apples.*	£10.00 LOL
PASCAL BOUCHARD CHABLIS 2004, VINS PASCAL BOUCHARD **Burgundy** – *Steely yet full, this wine has enormous quantities of citrus flesh on its zesty acidic backbone.*	£10.00 TPE
CÔTE DE NUITS-VILLAGES 2003, DOMAINE DESERTAUX-FERRAND **Burgundy** – *A whiff of minerality, delicate nutty oak, bright lemon flavours, and a long finish.*	£10.60 3DW
SÉGUINOT-BORDET CHABLIS 2003, DOMAINE SÉGUINOT-BORDET **Burgundy** – *A seam of acidity supports the ripe pear flesh. Aromas of minerals, flowers, and ripe citrus fruit.*	£10.90 3DW
CHABLIS 1ER CRU FOURCHAUMES 2003, LAMBLIN FILS **Burgundy** – *Flint, lemons, and powdery white flowers decorate the nose. Ripe lemon flavours and a tingle of lime juice acidity.*	£11.00 BAB
POUILLY FUISSÉ LES VIEUX MURS 2003, LORON & FILS **Burgundy** – *The weight is perfectly balanced, the flesh rich and drenched in poached pear flavour. Delicate and refreshing.*	£11.20 ESL
CHABLIS 1ER CRU VAILLONS 2003, J MOREAU **Burgundy** – *Pale straw yellow, with mineral hints, green apples, and citrus fruit. Long and soft. Balanced.*	£12.40 MCT
HAUTES-CÔTES DE NUITS BLANC 2003, JEAN-CLAUDE BOISSET **Burgundy** – *Mineral and toasty oak nose. Opulent mouthful of vibrant, textured, buttery lemon fruit.*	£12.40 RSV/CCS BEN/FLY
POUILLY-FUISSÉ LES VIEILLES PIERRES 2003, PIERRE ANDRE **Burgundy** – *Redolent of crushed hazelnut, banana, and guava. Soft, concentrated, and dense, with a long finish.*	£12.50 RBC
CHABLIS 1ER CRU FOURCHAUME 2003, DOMAINE SÉGUINOT-BORDET **Burgundy** – *Bright, sun-warmed peach fruit flavours. Creamy and lively, with a mouthcoating texture.*	£12.70 3DW

BROCARD CHABLIS PREMIER CRU 2003, BROCARD **Burgundy** – *Bright gold colour. Round and soft, with ripe mouthwatering citrus fruit and rich vanilla overtones.*	£13.00 POR/V&C JSM
CHABLIS DOMAINE DE LA BOISSONNEUSE 2003, JEAN-MARC BROCARD **Burgundy** – *Smoky wood and minerals on the nose. The toasty, medium-bodied palate is infused with lemon fruit.*	£13.00 ADN
CHABLIS 1ER CRU VAILLONS 2003, BOISSET **Burgundy** – *Ripe and full, with lifted mineral notes. This mature wine has citrus fruit flavours and aromas.*	£13.10 MHV
CHABLIS PREMIER CRU FOURCHAUME 2003, JEAN-MARC BROCARD **Burgundy** – *Minerally and restrained, its ripe yet youthful greengage fruit buttressed by lively acidity.*	£13.50 CEB
CHABLIS PREMIER CRU EXTREME 2003, JEAN-MARC BROCARD **Burgundy** – *Pale lemony green, with leesy notes of green apple and yeast. Grippy, creamy palate of lime fruit and flowers.*	£14.00 JBF
CHABLIS PREMIER CRU VAILLONS 2003, JEAN-MARC BROCARD **Burgundy** – *Beautiful candied lemon fruit mingles with grassy elements on the nose and palate. Soft and pale.*	£14.00 COE
AUVIGUE POUILLY-FUISSÉ VIEILLES VIGNES 2003, AUVIGUE **Burgundy** – *Toasted almond aromas. Its lemon and mandarin orange flavours are evolved and persistent.*	£18.00 CCS
LOUIS JADOT ST AUBIN 2000, LOUIS JADOT **Burgundy** – *Light, bright gold. Evolved, with warm, very appealing pear drop and tangerine fruit flavours and scents.*	£18.00 THS
CHABLIS GRAND CRU VALMUR 1998, J MOREAU **Burgundy** – *Wet stone terroir on the nose. Long and weighty yet crisp, with rich honeyed notes.*	£22.00 MCT
CHABLIS GRAND CRU BOUGROS 2003, JEAN-MARC BROCARD **Burgundy** – *Minerals, yeast, and Granny Smith apples on the nose. Softly textured, with fine acidity. Rich and long.*	£23.50 POR/JSM

MEURSAULT BLAGNY LA GENELOTTE 1ER CRU 2002, MARTELET DE CHERISEY Burgundy – *Complex flint, matchstick, and fruit compôte nose. Big, firm, crunchy, and fresh, with apple blossom and pear notes.*	£35.00 J&B

T R O P H Y
BURGUNDY RED

BEAUNE 1ER CRU LES GRÈVES 2003, JEAN-CLAUDE BOISSET Burgundy – *Shredded coconut, cool pine forest, black cherry, tobacco, and inkwell scents and flavours. Very long.*	£30.00 LIB

G O L D
BURGUNDY RED

GEVREY-CHAMBERTIN VIEILLES VIGNES DOMAINE HERESZTYN 2003, LA COMPAGNIE DES VINS D'AUTREFOIS Burgundy – *A perfectly weighted body of richly rendered, modern, stylish summer fruits.*	£20.00 WTS
CHAMBOLLE-MUSIGNY MICHEL GROS 2003, DOMAINE MICHEL GROS Burgundy – *This enormous, dark, structured burgundy has plenty of full, ripe fruit, tobacco smoke, fresh hay, and wildflower nuances. Towering.*	£25.00 HBJ
NUITS-SAINT-GEORGES LES CHALIOTS 2003, DOMAINE MICHEL GROS Burgundy – *Ripe strawberries, violets, and espresso on the nose. Flavours of cherry liqueur, pine nuts, and tree bark.*	£25.00 HBJ
VOSNE-ROMANÉE 1ER CRU AUX BRÛLÉES 2003, DOMAINE MICHEL GROS Burgundy – *This wine is packed with vibrant, chewy blackberries and mulberries. Perfectly concentrated and ripe.*	£35.00 HBJ
CLOS VOUGEOT 2003, DOMAINE MICHEL GROS Burgundy – *Deep layers of eucaulyptus, leather, charcoal, and raspberries. Fine-grained tannins, bright strawberry fruit, forest floor notes, and cinnamon spice.*	£45.00 HBJ

SILVER
BURGUNDY RED

CÔTE DE NUITS-VILLAGES LES PERRIÉRES 2003, DOMAINE DÉSERTAUX-FERRAND Burgundy – *Lively pepper, coffee, hay, and earth scents rise from the nose. Raspberry compote and freshly made toast flavours.*	£12.20 3DW
GEVREY-CHAMBERTIN EN SONGE 2003, DOMAINE LUCIEN JACOB Burgundy – *Top class cherry stone, autumn berry, and bonfire scents. The palate is medium-bodied, crisp, and long.*	£14.60 3DW
BEAUNE 1ER CRU LES AVAUX 2003, DOMAINE LUCIEN JACOB Burgundy – *Ripe and expressive, its strawberry fruit laced with moist earth scent. Firm, and replete with savoury nuances.*	£17.00 3DW
BEAUNE 1ER CRU LES BRESSANDES 2002, DOMAINE ALBERT MOROT Burgundy – *Earth and beetroot scents. Strawberry fruit flavours dusted with flecks of vanilla bean. Grippy and gravelly.*	£28.00 CAB
GEVREY-CHAMBERTIN LES EVOCELLES DOMAINE DE LA VOUGERAIE 2000, DOMAINE DE LA VOUGERAIE Burgundy – *Herbaceous and savoury, this wine is ripe and mature, with steak juice and tar flavours and a floral perfume.*	£28.50 CCS
CHAMBOLLE MUSIGNY 1ER CRU DU DOMAINE 2003, HENRI DE VILLAMONT Burgundy – *Seductive freshly picked blueberries, crushed leaves, and coffee. Juicy fruit buttressed by firm tannins. Long finish.*	£29.00 BBO
BEAUNE CLOS DES MOUCHES JOSEPH DROUHIN 2002, DREYFUS ASHBY & CO Burgundy – *Spiced cherries, leaves of mint, and bitter almond notes. Complex, elegant, and classic, with delectable hints of mushroom.*	£30.00 WTS
GEVREY-CHAMBERTIN 2003, JEAN-CLAUDE BOISSET Burgundy – *Ripe black cherry and charcoal aromas. The palate has integrated tannins married to ripe, silky red stone fruits.*	£32.20 CCS/LIB FLY

BRONZE
BURGUNDY RED

BOURGOGNE HAUTES CÔTES DE BEAUNE 2003, DOMAINE CHEVROT Burgundy – *Warm, rich oak bouquet. The Black Forest palate has very good extract. Deep and long.*	**£8.60** 3DW
LOUIS JADOT BOURGOGNE PINOT NOIR 2001, LOUIS JADOT Burgundy – *This gem has a soft red fruit nose and a crisp palate of delicate raspberry pips and smoke.*	**£9.60** FHM/EDC FLA/THS
CÔTE DE BEAUNE VILLAGES 1999, BOISSET Burgundy – *Pretty garnet gemstone colour. Baked plum tart flavours are underscored by fine grainy tannins. Delicate.*	**£9.90** MHV
MARANGES SUR LE CHÊNE 2003, DOMAINE CHEVROT Burgundy – *Fresh alpine strawberry flavours melt into silky oak. Hints of tobacco, coffee, and loam. Ripe.*	**£10.80** 3DW
SAVIGNY-LES-BEAUNE 2003, DOMAINE LUCIEN JACOB Burgundy – *Sound and beautifully structured, with aromas of wet stone and blackcurrants and flavours of sun-warmed blackberries.*	**£11.70** TNG/3DW
MERCUREY 1ER CRU CLOS DES MONTAIGUS 2002, DOMAINE J-M ET L PILLOT Burgundy – *Fine red berry fruit flavours are supported by a taut web of tree bark tannins. Farmyard scents.*	**£15.40** 3DW
SAVIGNY-LÈS-BEAUNE 1ER CRU CLOS DES GUETTES 2003, HENRI DE VILLAMONT Burgundy – *Strawberry fields forever. Wood and earth scents. Vibrant, ripe, and smoky.*	**£15.40** BBO
GEVREY CHAMBERTIN 2003, PATRIARCHE PÈRE ET FILS Burgundy – *Intense, youthful, and deeply coloured, with warm, vibrant strawberry fruit and fine, firm tannins.*	**£16.00** PAT
SAVIGNY-LÈS-BEAUNE CLOS DES GUETTOTES MONOPOLE 2003, CHÂTEAU DE CORTON ANDRÉ Burgundy – *Ripe, its sultry redcurrant flavours laced with scents of smoke and leather. Enjoy now.*	**£16.50** RBC

LOUIS JADOT BEAUNE 2000, LOUIS JADOT **Burgundy** – *This medium-bodied Burgundy has perfumed strawberry fruit and notes of charcoal.*	**£17.00** HMA/THS
BEAUNE DU CHÂTEAU 2003, BOUCHARD **Burgundy** – *Juicy and fresh, with floral notes, vanilla oak, and tangy acidity enfolding the textured cherry fruit.*	**£20.00** JEF
SANTENAY 1ER CRU LA COMME 2003, JEAN-CLAUDE BOISSET **Burgundy** – *Nose and palate of bright black cherries and raspberries. Spicy, fresh, and delicate, this is a toasty, pretty wine.*	**£20.00** LIB
CHAMBOLLE MUSIGNY 1ER CRU LES CHARMES 2003, JEAN-CLAUDE BOISSET **Burgundy** – *A soft pillow of raspberry fruit with firm, integrated tannins. Feminine and silky, with woody overtones.*	**£35.00** CCS/LIB FLY

TROPHY
CHAMPAGNE

CHARLES HEIDSIECK BLANC DES MILLÉNAIRES 1983, CHAMPAGNES P & C HEIDSIECK **Champagne** – *Very complex yeast and brioche aromas. Rich buttery fruit and mouth-watering acidity. The finish is deep and hedonistic.*	**£.00** NOT AVAILABLE IN THE UK
★ TESCO PREMIER CRU CHAMPAGNE NV, TESCO **Champagne** – *Elegant and harmonious with a lovely fresh nose showing light citrus, yeast, and hay aromas. The palate is weighted with fruit intensity and fine acidity.*	**£14.80** TOS
GAUTHIEN BRUT MILLÉSIMÉ 1998, MARNE ET CHAMPAGNE **Champagne** – *Finely balanced wine with an aromatic nose showing hay, butter, and citrus notes. The palate is clean and fresh with some yeasty depth and complexity.*	**£23.00** MCD
DOM RUINART BLANC DE BLANCS 1996, CHAMPAGNE RUINART **Champagne** – *Intense butterscotch, biscuit, and yeast aromas. The palate is hugely concentrated yet delicate and elegant.*	**£70.50** TNG/ICL WDI
GRAND SIÈCLE ALEXANDRA ROSÉ 1997, LAURENT-PERRIER **Champagne** – *Lovely freshness on the nose. The refined, elegant palate shows creamy fruit accentuated by fine effervescence.*	**£145.00** EDC

GOLD
CHAMPAGNE

☆ ANDRÉ SIMON CHAMPAGNE DEMI-SEC 1983, MARNE ET CHAMPAGNE DIFFUSION CHAMPAGNE – *Buttery tones and evolved biscuity depth. Concentrated fruit married to refreshing acidity. Long and deliciously honeyed.*	**£14.00** WRT
★ PAUL LANGIER CHAMPAGNE ROSÉ NV, CHAMPAGNES P&C HEIDSIECK CHAMPAGNE – *Elegant salmon colour. Crisp, toasty, delicate, and long, with a lively palate of currants, strawberries, and roast nuts.*	**£16.60** MHV
GIMONNET BRUT GASTRONOME 2000, GIMONNET CHAMPAGNE – *Racy, cristalline, and superbly elegant, with frothy mousse, lime, pear, and blossom flavours and a fine mineral backbone.*	**£20.50** ODD
LE BRUN DE NEUVILLE CUVÉE MILLÉSIME 1997, LE BRUN DE NEUVILLE CHAMPAGNE – *Honeyed wine with complex bready aromas. Elegant and poised with fruit richness, a fine mousse, and fresh acidity.*	**£23.00** WAW
CHARLES LAFITTE 1834 ROSÉ NV, VRANKEN POMMERY MONOPOLE CHAMPAGNE – *The bready nose leads to a complex palate of honeyed citrus fruit, rich yeast, and refreshing acidity. The finish is long and creamy.*	**£26.00** PFC
POMMERY BRUT VINTAGE 1996, POMMERY CHAMPAGNE – *Complex hay, honey, and brioche aromas. Rich and creamy with excellent fruit intensity, lively acidity, and persistent mousse.*	**£29.00** PFC/TNG
RUINART BLANC DE BLANCS NV, CHAMPAGNE RUINART CHAMPAGNE – *Intense butter, noisette, and fresh citrus aromas. Creamy yet balanced thanks to fine bubbles and refreshing acidity.*	**£33.60** WIDELY AVAILABLE
VEUVE CLICQUOT VINTAGE RESERVE ROSÉ 1999, VEUVE CLICQUOT PONSARDIN CHAMPAGNE – *Aromas of raspberry, strawberry, and hay. The palate has excellent balance and complexity with intense fruit supported by fine linear acidity.*	**£43.90** FHM/ESL EDC/MWW CNL
CHAMPAGNE JOSEPH PERRIER CUVÉE JOSEPHINE 1995, JOSEPH PERRIER CHAMPAGNE – *A rich nose showing notes of brioche and yeast. Fruit intensity, a fine beaded mousse, and mouth-watering acidity.*	**£58.20** ESL/CHN FLY

CUVÉE DES ENCHANTELEURS 1990, CHAMPAGNE HENRIOT CHAMPAGNE – *Bready nose with heady yeast and brioche aromas. Balanced and concentrated with great fruit depth and intensity.*	£67.30 JEF/FLY
DOM RUINART ROSÉ VINTAGE 1990, CHAMPAGNE RUINART CHAMPAGNE – *Lush grapefruit and red apple flavours accentuated by aromas of plum tart and smoke. Mature, ripe, and full-bodied.*	£83.20 TNG/MW W RAV/LEA WDI/HAC

SILVER
CHAMPAGNE

★ PRINCE WILLIAM PREMIER CRU CHAMPAGNE NV, SOMERFIELD CHAMPAGNE – *White orchard blossom, hawthorn, strawberry, digestives, and almonds. Mouthwatering acidity and crisp finish.*	£15.00 SMF
CHANOINE FRÈRES VINTAGE 1998, CHAMPAGNE CHANOINE FRÈRES CHAMPAGNE – *Creamy aromas of brioche, toffee apple, and butter. Long, lively lemon and lime flavours with hints of yeast.*	£20.00 TOS
ROSÉ DE SAIGNÉE BRUT NV, CHAMPAGNE DUVAL LEROY CHAMPAGNE – *Fresh strawberry and redcurrant fruit flavours. Deep salmon pink colour. Lively mousse.*	£20.00 SMF
LANSON IVORY LABEL DEMI-SEC NV, MARNE ET CHAMPAGNE DIFFUSION CHAMPAGNE – *Ripe, elegant pear and apple flavours, scents of flowers and mulling spices, and fine, persistent mousse.*	£21.00 MCD
NOSTALGIE VINTAGE 1997, CHAMPAGNE BEAUMONT DES CRAYÈRES CHAMPAGNE – *Fine, slow-rising bread and delicate acacia blossom aromas. Red apple pie, honey, biscuit, and currant flavours.*	£21.30 TAN
GRANDE SENDRÉE 1999, CHAMPAGNE DRAPPIER CHAMPAGNE – *Complex toasty nose and delicate tawny hue. Fresh, autolytic, and nutty. Textured whitecurrant and lime fruit.*	£25.20 JNW
GRANDE CUVÉE CHARLES VII NV, CANARD-DUCHÊNE CHAMPAGNE – *Bananas, lemons, starfruit, limes, sweet hedgerow flowers, and mineral aromas and flavours. Crisp, refreshing, and long.*	£25.30 BNK/EDC PRG

CHARLES LAFITTE 1834 MILLÉSIMÉ 1999, VRANKEN POMMERY MONOPOLE CHAMPAGNE – *Lavender and sage scents. Rich candied lemon and whitecurrant fruit. Balanced, creamy, and robust.*	**£28.00** PFC
CUVÉE ROYALE BRUT VINTAGE 1996, CHAMPAGNE JOSEPH PERRIER CHAMPAGNE – *Bright golden yellow, with elegant, rich mousse. The apple-flavoured palate has delicious notes of toast. Yeasty and long.*	**£28.50** ESL/CHN FLY
CHARLES LAFITTE 1834 BLANC DE BLANCS NV, VRANKEN POMMERY MONOPOLE CHAMPAGNE – *Youthful and lemony, with refreshing zesty citrus scents and flavours and fine, persistent mousse.*	**£30.00** PFC
JACQUART BRUT ROSÉ MILLÉSIMÉ 1999, CHAMPAGNE JACQUART CHAMPAGNE – *Yeasty strawberry flavours, hints of white chocolate, and touches of roast hazelnut. Fresh, medium-bodied, concentrated, and long.*	**£30.00** FLA
LAURENT-PERRIER BRUT MILLÉSIMÉ 1996, CHAMPAGNE LAURENT-PERRIER CHAMPAGNE – *Autolytic nose of gunflint and ripe limes. Citrus fruit, grapefruit, and strawberry flavours. Firm backbone of acidity.*	**£31.20** WRI/EDC MWW
PERRIER-JOUËT BLASON ROSÉ NV, CHAMPAGNE PERRIER-JOUËT CHAMPAGNE – *Fresh strawberry flavours are propelled by a persistent mousse. Elegant currant flavours. Hints of cinnamon and fresh pastry.*	**£32.10** POR/EDC MWW/RAV
D DE DEVAUX LE ROSÉ NV, CHAMPAGNE DEVAUX CHAMPAGNE – *A rich onion skin colour and a steady stream of bubbles. Restrained floral nose. Flavours of summer fruits.*	**£32.50** HWL
CHAMPAGNE POMMERY VINTAGE 1995, VRANKEN POMMERY MONOPOLE CHAMPAGNE – *Dough and strawberry scents. Persistent, its citrus flavours possessing a touch of earth and a creamy texture.*	**£33.00** PFC
MOËT ET CHANDON VINTAGE 1999, MOËT ET CHANDON CHAMPAGNE – *Candied lemons, biscuits, hazelnuts, and mandarin oranges. Flavours of citrus. An explosion of bubbles.*	**£33.40** WIDELY AVAILABLE
VEUVE CLICQUOT RICH RESERVE VINTAGE 1998, VEUVE CLICQUOT PONSARDIN CHAMPAGNE – *Intensely rich strawberries and cream, roast nuts, brioche, pear blossom, and lemon zest. Opulent.*	**£40.00** MWW/JSM LEA

CLOS DES GOISSES 1991, CHAMPAGNE PHILIPPONNAT CHAMPAGNE – *Greengage and golden apple perfume. Plenty of yellow and ruby grapefruit flavours with an edge of toast.*	**£50.00** CEL
CUVÉE WILLIAM DEUTZ VINTAGE 1996, CHAMPAGNE DEUTZ CHAMPAGNE – *Vivid, long, rich, and dry, this stunning cuvée possesses dense apple flavours, bright acidity and good definition.*	**£55.00** BWC
DOM PÉRIGNON 1996, MOËT ET CHANDON CHAMPAGNE – *Burnished gold. Toasty and savoury, with chalky tannins, delicate citrus fruit, and notes of mushroom. Complex, yet young.*	**£77.90** WIDELY AVAILABLE
TAITTINGER COMTES DE CHAMPAGNE ROSÉ 1999, CHAMPAGNE TAITTINGER CHAMPAGNE – *Pretty redcurrant jam, pineapple, and cream nose. The delicate palate of red and white fruit is ethereal and elegant.*	**£91.30** POR/EDC MWW
LA GRANDE DAME ROSÉ 1995, VEUVE CLICQUOT PONSARDIN CHAMPAGNE – *Dense, ripe, and tightly-wound, with aromas of bonfire, flowers, and marzipan, and flavours of redcurrants and mandarin oranges.*	**£165.00** EDC

BRONZE
CHAMPAGNE

JOHN ARMIT CHAMPAGNE NV, CHAMPAGNE BOIZEL CHAMPAGNE – *This excellent little Champagne is fresh, lively, and round, with elegant candied lemon flavours and bright acidity.*	**£13.10** JAR
SAINSBURY'S EXTRA DRY NV, CHAMPAGNE DUVAL LEROY CHAMPAGNE – *Fine, biscuity and packed with fruit, this classic Champagne has fresh citrus, delicate meringue, and pretty floral elements.*	**£13.50** JSM
ALBERT ETIENNE BRUT NV, MARNE ET CHAMPAGNE DIFFUSION CHAMPAGNE – *Balanced, fresh, golden yellow fizz with restrained pear drop flavours and scents. Lively mousse. Floral notes.*	**£14.00** MCD
CARTE D'OR BRUT NV, CHAMPAGNE JEAN MOUTARDIER CHAMPAGNE – *A bright basketful of citrus and raspberry flavour with a fresh backbone of cleansing acidity. Hints of spice.*	**£15.00** GRT

CARTE NOIR BRUT NV, CHAMPAGNE RAOUL COLLET **CHAMPAGNE** – *Delicate hints of baking bread and nutmeg. Mouthwatering red berry and grapefruit flavours.*	**£15.00** FUL
JEAUNAUX-ROBIN NV, CHAMPAGNE CYRIL JEAUNAUX **CHAMPAGNE** – *Scents and flavours of red summer fruits are laced with hints of spice. Persistent mousse.*	**£16.00** BLC
LOUIS BELMANCE BLANC DE BLANCS NV, CHAMPAGNES P&C HEIDSIECK **CHAMPAGNE** – *Austere, elegant, and packed with citrus and pear flavours. Clear lemon yellow. Ebullient mousse.*	**£16.50** MHV
BEAUMONT DES CRAYÈRES GRANDE RÉSERVE NV, CHAMPAGNE BEAUMONT DES CRAYÈRES **CHAMPAGNE** – *Biscuits, hazelnuts, limes, lemon zest, and wildflowers spill from this wine. Bright, balanced and medium-bodied.*	**£16.90** CCS/JAR
FINEST VINTAGE CHAMPAGNE 2000, TESCO **CHAMPAGNE** – *Fresh, textured, aromatic bubbly. Floral notes and roast almonds scent the nose. The palate is round and ripe.*	**£16.90** TOS
GAUTHIEN BRUT GRANDE RESERVE NV, MARNE ET CHAMPAGNE DIFFUSION **CHAMPAGNE** – *Roast nuts, grilled lemons, ruby grapefruit, and golden apples whirl together on the palate. Balanced and attractive.*	**£17.00** MCD
WAITROSE BLANC DE BLANCS NV, CHAMPAGNES P&C HEIDSIECK **CHAMPAGNE** – *Linear lemon, brioche, apricot kernel, honey, and lime zest elements. Creamy mousse lifts this steely, elegant fizz.*	**£17.00** WTS
FLEUR DE PRESTIGE VINTAGE 1998, CHAMPAGNE BEAUMONT DES CRAYÈRES **CHAMPAGNE** – *Sweet honeysuckle, may blossom, green apple, lime, lemon, grapefruit, and pear flavours grace this refreshing wine.*	**£17.70** TAN
ALBERT ETIENNE MILLÉSIMÉ 1999, CHAMPAGNE ALBERT ETIENNE **CHAMPAGNE** – *Fresh and youthful, with hints of nuts and fresh citrus flavours galore. Persistent, lively mousse. Lemon yellow hue.*	**£18.00** MCD
B DE BESSENAT DE BELLEFON BRUT NV, MARNE ET CHAMPAGNE DIFFUSION **CHAMPAGNE** – *Fine mousse of lemons and raspberries rises from the glass. Hints of nougat enrich the flavours.*	**£18.00** MCD

BRUT TRADITION VINTAGE 1983, CHAMPAGNE HENRI BLIN Champagne – *This quality grower's cooperative consistently produces delicious wines at reasonable prices. Spicy, dense, and lemony.*	**£18.00** ODD
MICHEL LENIQUE MILLÉSIMÉ 1999, CHAMPAGNE MICHEL LENIQUE Champagne – *Delicate roast nut and acacia aromas and a palate of citrus fruit and baked bread. Light and refreshing.*	**£18.00** 3DW
SELECTION BRUT PREMIER CRU NV, CHAMPAGNE BAUCHET PÈRE ET FILS Champagne – *White peach, tangerine, candied lemon, and acacia flowers flavour and perfume this attractive, balanced wine.*	**£18.00** AVB
PANNIER BRUT SELECTION NV, CHAMPAGNE PANNIER Champagne – *Fresh lemons, peaches, pistachios, and brioche scent and flavour this balanced, refreshing, attractive wine.*	**£18.70** HBJ/LAI
BROSSAULT NV, CHAMPAGNES P&C HEIDSIECK Champagne – *Fresh, textured, and light-bodied, with attractive strawberry and pear flavours and sweet elderflower scents on the nose.*	**£18.80** MWW
CANARD-DUCHÊNE BRUT NV, CHAMPAGNE CANARD-DUCHÊNE Champagne – *Delicate acacia blossom, biscuit, freshly squeezed lemon, and hazelnut scents and flavours. Light straw yellow.*	**£18.90** WIDELY AVAILABLE
GREEN TOP DEMI-SEC NV, HEIDSIECK MONOPOLE Champagne – *Lovely melon fruit, with ripe sweet pear and citrus overtones. Rich creamy palate. Lively acidity.*	**£19.00** PFC
BRUT CUVÉE DES DAMES NV, CHAMPAGNE GREMILLET Champagne – *Ripe citrus and wild strawberry flavours. Persistent mousse rises through the golden liquid.*	**£19.50** PBA/RSV
DEVAUX GRANDE RÉSERVE NV, CHAMPAGNE DEVAUX Champagne – *Zingy acidity rends the juicy apple, lemon, nectarine, and pear flesh. Aromas of flowers and nuts.*	**£19.50** HWL
ANDRE SIMON CHAMPAGNE BRUT VINTAGE 1998, MARNE ET CHAMPAGNE DIFFUSION Champagne – *Balanced, textured, and harmonious, with light roast hazelnut and acacia blossom, summer fruits, and spice.*	**£20.00** WRT

JEAN MOUTARDIER MILLÉSIME 1997, CHAMPAGNE JEAN MOUTARDIER CHAMPAGNE – *Deep pockets of whitecurrant and cranberry flavour are rounded out by hints of baked bread. Floral notes.*	**£20.00** GRT
RAYMOND BOULARD VINTAGE 1999, CHAMPAGNE RAYMOND BOULARD CHAMPAGNE – *Many 1999s are drinking well now. This youthful wine has plenty of citrus zest flavours and floral scents.*	**£20.00** OCM
WAITROSE VINTAGE 1999, CHAMPAGNES P&C HEIDSIECK CHAMPAGNE – *Toast, cherries, piecrust, and caramel ooze from this wine. Textured, smooth, and long, with bright, balancing acidity.*	**£20.00** WTS
MASSE MILLÉSIMÉ 1999, CHAMPAGNE MASSE CHAMPAGNE – *Bright, textured red berry flavours wind their way round a seam of citric acidity. Nutty and biscuity.*	**£21.00** MCD
CHAMPAGNE MERCIER BRUT ROSE NV, MOËT ET CHANDON CHAMPAGNE – *Some yeast autolysis, with baskets of fresh strawberries. A hint of nuttiness and generous dosage round out the palate.*	**£21.20** ICL/THS
PANNIER VINTAGE 1998, CHAMPAGNE PANNIER CHAMPAGNE – *Freshly baked bread, hints of clove and cinnamon, and delicate raspberry and lime flavours.*	**£21.30** HBJ
JOSEPH PERRIER CUVÉE ROYALE BRUT NV, JOSEPH PERRIER CHAMPAGNE – *Rich roast nut, baguette, and smoke notes scent the nose of this bright gold, lemon and lime flavoured beauty.*	**£21.40** ESL/CHN FLY
DEVAUX BLANC DE NOIRS NV, CHAMPAGNE DEVAUX CHAMPAGNE – *The texture of silk, scents of raspberry leaves and honeysuckle, and flavours of juicy red cherries.*	**£21.50** HWL
BRUT MOSAÏQUE NV, CHAMPAGNE JACQUART CHAMPAGNE – *Marzipan, candied lemon, yeast, and fresh croissants rise from the nose. Fresh and balanced, with lively mousse.*	**£21.70** MWW/FLA
PRIVILÈGE DES MOINES NV, JM GOBILLARD & FILS CHAMPAGNE – *Vibrant lemon fruit, roast nuts, and brioche on nose and palate. Rich, mouthcoating, and toasty.*	**£22.00** FEE

DE CASTELLANE VINTAGE 1999, CHAMPAGNE DE CASTELLANE **Champagne** – *Vibrant redcurrants, juicy pears, pineapples, limes, and meringue. Beginning to evolve. Bright.*	**£22.60** EDC
CHARLES LAFITTE 1834 DEMI-SEC NV, VRANKEN POMMERY MONOPOLE **Champagne** – *Sensuous fizz. Flowers, biscuit, and marzipan scents. Silky palate of lemons and strawberries sprinkled with caster sugar.*	**£23.00** PFC
CUVÉE DES MOINES BLANC DE BLANCS NV, BESSENAT DE BELLEFON **Champagne** – *Pears, golden apples, pineapples, and lime on nose and palate. Delicate floral notes. Steely acidity.*	**£23.00** MCD
HENRI BLIN VINTAGE 1999, CHAMPAGNE HENRI BLIN **Champagne** – *Henri Blin knows a thing or two about red wine. Dense strawberry and grapefruit flavours and bold spices.*	**£23.00** ODD
PERRIER-JOUËT GRAND BRUT NV, CHAMPAGNE PERRIER-JOUËT **Champagne** – *Fresh lemons, limes, and hints of mandarin orange flavour this refreshing bubbly. Persistent mousse. Floral notes.*	**£23.00** EDC/MWW RAV
LAURENT-PERRIER BRUT NV, CHAMPAGNE LAURENT-PERRIER **Champagne** – *A classic. Red and white berries crowd the balanced, refreshing palate. Persistent mousse. Lemony gold.*	**£23.20** WIDELY AVAILABLE
BRUT VINTAGE 1999, CHAMPAGNE CANARD-DUCHÊNE **Champagne** – *Youthful lemon fruit, grilled walnut, marzipan, and smoke notes. Hints of evolution are displayed in this fresh bubbly.*	**£23.80** BNK/EDC HAC
CHARLES HEIDSIECK BRUT RESERVÉE MIS EN CAVE EN 2000 NV, CHAMPAGNES P&C HEIDSIECK **Champagne** – *Masterful. Currants, lemons, hazelnuts, nougat, meringue, may flowers, and lime cordial. Fine bubbles rise lazily in the glass.*	**£26.00** TOS
DRAPPIER BLANC DE BLANCS NV, CHAMPAGNE DRAPPIER **Champagne** – *Sliced green apples, golden grapefruit, and aromatic pear flavours. Balanced, clear, and very fresh.*	**£26.70** TNI
LANSON ROSÉ VINTAGE 1997, MARNE ET CHAMPAGNE **Champagne** – *This salmon-coloured beauty has crisp strawberry aromas and flavours, fine, persistent mousse, and a soft, elegant roundness.*	**£26.80** TOS/MWW

TAITTINGER DEMI-SEC NV, CHAMPAGNE TAITTINGER CHAMPAGNE – *Delicately sweet, with enchanting aromas of meringue, honeysuckle, and orange peel. Fresh, lush, and attractive.*	£27.00 ODD
DIAMANT BLANC 2000, HEIDSIECK MONOPOLE CHAMPAGNE – *Elegant nose with fresh baked bread and citrus aromas. Full foaming mousse and remarkably fresh finish.*	£28.00 PFC
DE VENOGE BLANC DE BLANCS VINTAGE 1998, CHAMPAGNE DE VENOGE CHAMPAGNE – *Peach, yellow plum, acacia, hazelnut, chalky minerals, and fresh golden grapefruit scents and flavours.*	£29.00 PBA/RSV
DE VENOGE VINTAGE 1995, CHAMPAGNE DE VENOGE CHAMPAGNE – *Rich, satiny strawberries and cream flavours fill the mouth. The nose has delicate nuttiness and lifted floral notes.*	£29.00 PBA/RSV
POMMERY SUMMERTIME NV, CHAMPAGNE POMMERY CHAMPAGNE – *Fresh, youthful lemon flesh is seared by lime juice acidity and chalky minerals. Steely and vivid.*	£29.70 PFC/TNG RSV
BRUT MOSAÏQUE VINTAGE 1998, CHAMPAGNE JACQUART CHAMPAGNE – *Yeast autolysis marries meaty lemon aromas. Creamy mousse, firm acidity, and ripe white fruit flavours.*	£30.00 MWW/FLA
TAITTINGER NOCTURNE SEC NV, CHAMPAGNE TAITTINGER CHAMPAGNE – *Dough, cashews, red vine fruits, and subtle spice notes. Tawny gold. Balanced, sweet, and refreshing.*	£30.70 FHM/EDC
PERRIER-JOUËT GRAND BRUT VINTAGE 1997, CHAMPAGNE PERRIER-JOUËT CHAMPAGNE – *Nuts, marzipan, and flower aromas. The palate is a balanced mouthful of ruby grapefruit and strawberries.*	£30.80 EDC/RAV HAC
BLANC DE BLANCS BRUT VINTAGE 1996, CHAMPAGNE PANNIER CHAMPAGNE – *White peach, lemon, grapefruit, and minerals mingle with toasted almonds and meringue. Balanced, steely, and elegant.*	£31.00 HBJ
TAITTINGER BRUT VINTAGE 1999, CHAMPAGNE TAITTINGER CHAMPAGNE – *Freshly baked biscuits, lemon meringue pie, honeysuckle, and tangerines commingle on the nose and palate.*	£31.30 WIDELY AVAILABLE

PRELUDE GRANDS CRUS NV, CHAMPAGNE TAITTINGER Champagne – *A classic blend, with delicate strawberry flavours, freshly picked lemons, roast nuts, and minerals all whirled together.*	**£35.10** EDC/MWW
D DE DEVAUX LE MILLÉSIMÉ 1996, CHAMPAGNE DEVAUX Champagne – *All the merits of 1996. Dense white fruit flavours seared by a backbone of acidity. Youthful and refined.*	**£36.50** HWL
VEUVE CLICQUOT VINTAGE RESERVE 1998, VEUVE CLICQUOT PONSARDIN Champagne – *Dried fruit, hazelnut, and fig characteristics. Hints of exotic flora. Pronounced, toasty, long, and elegant.*	**£39.30** WIDELY AVAILABLE
GRAND SIÈCLE CUVÉE NV, CHAMPAGNE LAURENT-PERRIER Champagne – *Rich hazelnut, lemon, grapefruit, strawberry, and whitecurrant flavours. Aromas of acacia blossom, lime zest and minerals.*	**£51.70** WRI/EDC MWW/JSM
LANSON NOBLE CUVÉE BLANC DE BLANCS VINTAGE 1996, MARNE ET CHAMPAGNE DIFFUSION Champagne – *Flowers, lemons, toasted almonds, nougat, minerals, and racy acidity. Fine blanc de blancs from an excellent vintage.*	**£62.00** MCD
COMTES DE CHAMPAGNE BLANC DES BLANCS 1995, CHAMPAGNE TAITTINGER Champagne – *Delicious coffee and almond nose. Very rich ripe apple and honey flavours. Biscuity elegance and graceful development.*	**£73.50** POR/TPE CEB/EDC LEA
L'AMOUR DE DEUTZ BLANC DE BLANCS MILLÉSIMÉ 1998, CHAMPAGNE DEUTZ Champagne – *It's good to see medium-sweet Champagne performing so well. Bursting with passion-fruit and piecrust flavours.*	**£75.00** BWC
CUVÉE LOUISE VINTAGE 1995, CHAMPAGNE POMMERY Champagne – *Ripe, refined, and tightly wound, with flavours of nougat, lemons, and Cox's Orange Pippin apples. Lengthy.*	**£78.00** PFC/TNG RSV
LA GRANDE DAME 1996, VEUVE CLICQUOT PONSARDIN Champagne – *Pear, yeast, and nuts. Fine, delicate mousse. Almonds, figs, peaches, and warm biscuits. Complex.*	**£80.40** ESL/EDC MWW/CNL JSM/LEA

B R O N Z E
LANGUEDOC-ROUSSILLON WHITE

☆ CHARDONNAY HERRICK 2004, JAMES HERRICK **LANGUEDOC-ROUSSILLON** – *Sweet pear and yellow plum fruit flavours. The texture is soft. Hints of cinnamon spice add lift.*	**£5.00** BGN/TOS
☆ DOMAINE DE LUC SAUVIGNON BLANC 2004, LOUIS FABRE **LANGUEDOC-ROUSSILLON** – *A very herbaceous nose and palate with an excellent grassy character offset by zingy acidity.*	**£5.00** FXT
☆ DOMAINE DU BOIS VIOGNIER 2003, MAUREL VEDEAU **LANGUEDOC-ROUSSILLON** – *Fresh fuzzy peaches, honeysuckle, and cream. Subtle vanilla nuances. Round and fleshy.*	**£5.00** THI
☆ L'IF GRENACHE BLANC 2004, MONT TAUCH **LANGUEDOC-ROUSSILLON** – *Orange blossom richness to the nose and palate, off-set by a seam of mineral flavours.*	**£5.00** THI
PAUL MAS CHARDONNAY 2004, LES DOMAINES PAUL MAS **LANGUEDOC-ROUSSILLON** – *Fresh, ripe, and youthful, with lots of lemons and pineapples on nose and palate. Clear and balanced.*	**£5.00** TNG
SAUVIGNON BLANC LES JAMELLES 2004, BADET CLÉMENT **LANGUEDOC-ROUSSILLON** – *A low-key nose and sweetly ripe palate with exotic fruit. Pretty, fresh, and lively Sauvignon Blanc.*	**£5.20** CCS/JSM
CHARDONNAY L LAROCHE 2004, LAROCHE **LANGUEDOC-ROUSSILLON** – *Restrained fresh lemonade nose. The medium-bodied palate has candied lemon flavours and floral notes.*	**£6.00** FLY
CHARDONNAY LAROCHE 2004, LAROCHE **LANGUEDOC-ROUSSILLON** – *Sweetly ripe, this wine offers lime juice and peach flavours accented by coconut oak.*	**£6.50** FLY/JSM
ETOILE FILANTE VIOGNIER 2003, DOMINE VIRGINIE **LANGUEDOC-ROUSSILLON** – *Peach, apricot, and pear aromas. Smooth palate of ripe fruit that lingers in the mouth.*	**£7.00** ODD

LES FLACONS LA BRIFFAUDE WHITE 2002, MAUREL VEDEAU **Languedoc-Roussillon** – *Hazelnut and oak aromas show some development, the palate is equally nutty with ginger and spice notes.*	£10.00 THI
MAS LA CHEVALIÈRE CHARDONNAY 2003, LAROCHE **Languedoc-Roussillon** – *Subtle mineral and honeycomb nose. Flavours of crisp, tangy citrus and pear drops. Light-bodied and refreshing.*	£10.80 FLY
LAURENT MIQUEL VIOGNIER VERITÉ 2004, LARENT MIQUEL **Languedoc-Roussillon** – *Apricot and orange blossom aromas. Light tropical palate with subtle nuttiness and a lengthy finish.*	£12.00 HWL

SEAL OF APPROVAL
LANGUEDOC-ROUSSILLON WHITE

☆ LA CAMPAGNE VIN DE PAYS D'OC VIOGNIER 2004, LGI **Languedoc-Roussillon** – *Lush stone fruit flavours and scents.*	£4.00 MCT
☆ MHV VIN DE PAYS DU JARDIN DE LA FRANCE SAUVIGNON BLANC NV, PRODIS **Languedoc-Roussillon** – *Bright, tropical pineapple, and peapod flavours.*	£4.00 MHV

TROPHY
LANGUEDOC-ROUSSILLON RED

☆ DOMUS MAXIMUS 2000, DOMAINE MASSAMIER LA MIGNARDE **Languedoc-Roussillon** – *A mind-blowing spectrum of meat juice, hot stone, grilled spice, mulberries, and forest floor elements.*	£11.10 BBR/CCS FLY

GOLD
LANGUEDOC-ROUSSILLON RED

CORBIÈRES LA FORGE 2001, GERARD BERTRAND **Languedoc-Roussillon** – *Evolved leather, toast, and blackcurrants. Black fruits and a fine mouthcoating texture. Chewy, deep, and spicy.*	£20.00 THI

CORBIÈRES LA FORGE 2001, GERARD BERTRAND **Languedoc-Roussillon** – *Evolved aromas of leather, toast, and blackcurrants. Sweetly ripe black fruits and a fine mouthcoating texture.*	£22.00 WTS

SILVER
LANGUEDOC-ROUSSILLON RED

☆ **MALBEC MAISON MAUREL VEDEAU 2003, MAUREL VEDEAU Languedoc-Roussillon** – *Baked plums, bitter almonds, and bonfire scents appear on nose and palate. Concentrated, long, and firm.*	£5.00 THI
☆ **RESERVE ANGLAIS 2003, RICHARD SPEIRS & PIERRE ROQUE Languedoc-Roussillon** – *Scents of wild Mediterranean herbs. Long, appealing, and complex with capsicum flavours and hints of liquorice.*	£7.00 RSN
☆ **DOMAINE DE ROUDENE FÛTS DE CHÊNE 2003, DOMAINE DE ROUDENE Languedoc-Roussillon** – *Green peppercorns, smoke, coffee, strawberries, and coconut. Leaves lasting streaks of colour in the glass.*	£7.50 GRT
FITOU LES QUATRE MONT TAUCH 2003, THIERRYS Languedoc-Roussillon – *Dense, layered, and smoky, with brooding black fruit flavours and scents of flowers, pepper, and herbs.*	£9.00 WTS
MINERVOIS LA LIVININIERE CHÂTEAU MARIS VIEILLES VIGNES 2002, FOLLY WINES Languedoc-Roussillon – *Scents of maquis and lush red and black vine fruit flavours. Mineral notes, bark, and sweet flowers. Layered.*	£9.00 WTS
DOMAINE SILÈNE 2003, SILÈNE DES PEYRALS Languedoc-Roussillon – *Lavish oak on the nose and palate. Finishes with a big fruity wallop of cherries.*	£15.00 MCT

BRONZE
LANGUEDOC-ROUSSILLON RED

☆ **CARIGNAN SYRAH VIN DE PAYS CÔTEAUX DE FONCAUDE 2004, CRUSAN Languedoc-Roussillon** – *Balanced, soft, and very approachable, this comely blend has raspberries, blueberries, and hints of vanilla.*	£3.60 MCT

☆ CORBIÈRES MONT TAUCH 2004, MONT TAUCH **LANGUEDOC-ROUSSILLON** – *Redcurrants, loganberries, and sloes collide on the dense, youthful, medium-bodied palate. Deep ruby red.*	£5.00 THI
☆ LE TRÉSOR GRENACHE NOIR 2004, ANDRE QUANCARD ANDRE **LANGUEDOC-ROUSSILLON** – *Sweet tropical coconut and violet nose. Cherry and bubble gum palate. A juicy wine with a pleasing finish.*	£5.00 THI
☆ MOULIN DE DAUDET SYRAH 2003, BOUTINOT **LANGUEDOC-ROUSSILLON** – *Balanced palate of red fruits, licquorice, and tobacco. Firm tannins and a long finish.*	£5.00 VGN
☆ OC CUVÈE 178 MERLOT 2004, LES CHAIS BEAUCAIROIS **LANGUEDOC-ROUSSILLON** – *Ripe, with an impressively deep colour and a medium-weight palate of mouthwatering plum jam.*	£5.00 THI
PAUL MAS MERLOT 2004, LES DOMAINES PAUL MAS **LANGUEDOC-ROUSSILLON** – *Plums, chocolate, and cherries flavour this medium-bodied, clear, youthful wine.*	£5.00 SWS
DOMAINE DE SÉRAME MERLOT RÉSERVE 2004, CHÂTEAU DE SÉRAME **LANGUEDOC-ROUSSILLON** – *Maquis, capsicum, deep plum, and chocolate mingle in this vivid, youthful wine.*	£5.50 DOU
ORIGIN MERLOT 2004, BADET CLÉMENT **LANGUEDOC-ROUSSILLON** – *Young and elegant. Deep purple-black colour, a nose of some delicacy and a palate of vibrant blackberries.*	£5.50 THS
CHÂTEAU DE SÉRAME CORBIÈRES 2003, CVBG DOURTHE KRESSMANN **LANGUEDOC-ROUSSILLON** – *Deeply coloured. Peppercorn and raspberry nose. Intense, sweetly ripe, and fresh, with poise and balance.*	£6.00 DOU
FITOU MAS CAPITEL 2003, MAUREL VEDEAU **LANGUEDOC-ROUSSILLON** – *Pulverised white pepper, black olive, and rosemary scents. The palate is a ripe mix of strawberries and vanilla pods.*	£6.00 THI
LA COMBE DES OLIVIERS 2003, VIGNOBLES LORGERIL **LANGUEDOC-ROUSSILLON** – *Moist soft prunes, plums, saddle leather, dark earth, and sweet fresh leather mingle in this flavourful wine.*	£6.00 L&T

MERLOT LAROCHE 2004, LAROCHE LANGUEDOC-ROUSSILLON – *Baked fruit and minerals scent the nose, whilst the palate is an approachable ripe plum and cherry delight.*	£6.00 FLY
ST-CHINIAN DOMAINE DE COMBEBELLE 2004, FONCALIEU LANGUEDOC-ROUSSILLON – *Try this red berry fruited, delicately spiced wine with grilled lamb and a sprig of rosemary. Clear, focused, and earthy.*	£6.00 PLB
LA FORGE ESTATE CABERNET SAUVIGNON 2004, LES DOMAINES PAUL MAS LANGUEDOC-ROUSSILLON – *Hints of liquorice and a palate of ripe blackcurrants. A wine that will repay those who wait.*	£6.70 WPR/TNG
GERARD BERTRAND TERROIR LES TERRASSES QUATERNAIRES 2002, GERARD BERTRAND LANGUEDOC-ROUSSILLON – *A rich onslaught of garrigue, pepper, and vine fruits. The palate is meaty, herbal and utterly charming.*	£7.00 THI
CHÂTEAU DE SÉRAME MINERVOIS 2003, CVBG DOURTHE KRESSMANN LANGUEDOC-ROUSSILLON – *Toast, vanilla, maquis, bright raspberries, cracked pepper, and sensual prune flavours. Ripe.*	£8.00 DOU
LES FAISSES 2004, LES DOMAINES PAUL MAS LANGUEDOC-ROUSSILLON – *Fresh perfumed fruit is well integrated with oak. The wine displays good balance and finishes clean.*	£8.00 SWS
LA CUVÉE DU BARON ILL SAINT-AURIOL 2002, SAINT-AURIOL LANGUEDOC-ROUSSILLON – *Crushed herbs, capsicum, tree bark, and wildflower scents. Rich blackberry flavours.*	£8.30 ABY
LES HAUTS DE L'ENCLOS DES BORIES 2002, VIGNOBLES LORGERIL LANGUEDOC-ROUSSILLON – *Cherry red with pink glints. Dry, fresh, grippy, and young, its currant flavours peppered with spice.*	£9.00 L&T
LES FLACONS CLOS DE FONTEDIT 2002, MAUREL VEDEAU LANGUEDOC-ROUSSILLON – *Peppermint, loganberries, and scents of wet earth. Flavours of youthful blackberry fruit. Will age well.*	£10.00 THI
MAS LA CHEVALIÈRE LAROCHE 2003, LAROCHE LANGUEDOC-ROUSSILLON – *Young and densely packed with mulberries, mocha, and spice. Full and lusciously ripe, with a fresh, lifted finish.*	£10.40 FLY/JSM

CIGALUS ROUGE 2001, GERARD BERTRAND **Languedoc-Roussillon** – *A modern, sophisticated blend with many layers of blackberries, cedar, gravel, herbs, and spice.*	£15.00 MWW
LA VIALA 2001, GERARD BERTRAND **Languedoc-Roussillon** – *Deep pockets of raspberries, mulberries, and redcurrants. Scents of spice. Peppery, floral notes.*	£20.00 THI

SEAL OF APPROVAL
LANGUEDOC-ROUSSILLON RED

☆ MAISON ROUGE MEDIUM DRY RED TABLE WINE NV, VINIVAL **Languedoc-Roussillon** – *Juicy plums and currants and a grinding of pepper.*	£3.30 MHV
☆ LE CAPRICE CABERNET SAUVIGNON 2004, FONCALIEU **Languedoc-Roussillon** – *Fresh redcurrants, lifted herbs, and leather.*	£3.50 MCT
☆ CO-OP VIN DE PAYS D'OC SHIRAZ 2004, FONCALIEU **Languedoc-Roussillon** – *Vibrant barnyard aromas. Blackberry flavours.*	£3.90 CWS

GOLD
LANGUEDOC-ROUSSILLON SWEET

☆ RIVESALTES AMBRÉ HORS D'AGE 1982, ARNAUD DE VILLENEUVE **Languedoc-Roussillon** – *Complex rancio nose shows notes of raisin, tar, and molasses. Nutty depths married to sweetness and acidity.*	£11.00 WTS

BRONZE
LANGUEDOC-ROUSSILLON SWEET

☆ SAINSBURY'S MUSCAT DE ST JEAN DE MINERVOIS NV, LES VIGNERONS DE LA MÉDITERRANÉE **Languedoc-Roussillon** – *Honeycomb, jasmine flowers, Seville oranges, and ripe juicy scented melons flavour this sweet wine.*	£4.00 JSM

GOLD
LOIRE WHITE

☆ **DOMAINE MICHEL THOMAS 2004, DOMAINE MICHEL THOMAS & FILS** Loire – *Gooseberry and citrus aromas on the nose. The palate has lively citrus fruit, deep mineral complexity, and fine acidity. Good persistence and depth.*	**£11.00** LAI

SILVER
LOIRE WHITE

☆ **MARKS & SPENCER SAUVIGNON BLANC VIN DE PAYS DU JARDIN DE LA FRANCE 2004, VINIVAL** Loire – *Good varietal character with green fruit and zippy acidity. Straightforward but satisfying wine.*	**£4.50** M&S
★ **MUSCADET DE SÈVRE-ET-MAINE SUR LIE 2004, DOMAINE DES HAUTES NOELLES** Loire – *Nutty, yeasty aromas and some structure to the palate of fresh tropical fruit. Perfect with shellfish.*	**£4.80** MWW
☆ **DOMAINE DOUILLARD MELON 2004, DOMAINE JEAN DOUILLARD** Loire – *Ripe and mineral, with wet stone and sea air perfume. Lean and crisp with apple and pear fruit.*	**£5.80** LAI
SANCERRE BLANC LA FUZELLE 2004, JOSEPH MELLOT Loire – *Nettles and nuts on the nose. The robust balance of acidity and fruit mean this has good ageing potential.*	**£8.70** MCT
POUILLY-FUMÉ JEAN PABIOT 2004, DOMAINE JEAN PABIOT Loire – *This is a grassy, herbaceous wine with an undercurrent of minerals and a hint of barrel age.*	**£9.20** POR/MWW
DOMAINE DES COTTEREAUX 2004, REVERDY-FERRY Loire – *Aromatic elderflower, lemon zest and wet stone scents. The palate is austere and thirst quenching. Benchmark Sancerre.*	**£10.50** LAI
DOMAINE MERLIN-CHERRIER 2004, DOMAINE MERLIN-CHERRIER Loire – *Medium-weight, with citrus, mineral, fresh asparagus flavours, and a hint of gun smoke. Long, refreshing finish.*	**£11.00** LAI/RWD

DOMAINE RAIMBAULT-PINEAU LES CHASSEIGNES 2004, DOMAINE RAIMBAULT-PINEAU Loire – *An aromatic and minty nose. Good citrus acidity, apples and pears, plus fresh herbaceous notes.*	**£11.00** LAI
VACHERON SANCERRE BLANC 2004, DOMAINE VACHERON Loire – *Pea pod, flint and gooseberry scents. Youthful fresh limes and green plums fills the mouth with bright, sensuous flesh.*	**£13.60** MWW/FLY WSO

BRONZE
LOIRE WHITE

☆ WAITROSE TOURAINE SAUVIGNON 2004, VINIVAL Loire – *A light aroma of melons and kiwi fruit. Some warm yeasty notes with a fresh crunch of gooseberries.*	**£4.70** WTS
☆ MOULIN DES COSSARDIÈRES MUSCADET DE SÈVRE-ET-MAINE SUR LIE 2004, VINIVAL Loire – *Straightforward fruit with good floral flavours. A crisp thirst-quencher which is crying out for seafood.*	**£5.00** M&S
☆ MUSCADET COTES DE GRANDLIEU SUR LIE FIEF GUERIN 2004, FIEF GUERIN Loire – *An inviting mineral and herbaceous nose with a dry and austere palate, with tight fruit and acidity.*	**£5.00** WTS
☆ TOURAINE SAUVIGNON BLANC 2004, ACKERMAN RÉMY PANNIER Loire – *Tropical notes on the nose and palate with a fruity, mouthfilling flavour and a minerally aftertaste.*	**£5.00** WAV
COLLECTION LOIRE 756 TOURAINE SAUVIGNON 2004, DONATIEN BAHUAUD Loire – *Clean elderflower nose with elegant elderflower and citrus notes on the palate. Dry with good length.*	**£5.50** MCT
CHEVERNY LE VIEUX 2004, CLOS DELAILLE Loire – *A mineral and flint nose with a sweet hint of sherbet. Poised. This wine is very youthful still.*	**£6.00** WTS
POUILLY FUMÉ LES GRIOTTINES 2004, DOMAINE BAILLY & FILS Loire – *Smoky grassy notes on the nose and palate. A fresh finish rounds off this appetising wine.*	**£8.00** THI

HENRI VALLON SANCERRE LES FRESNAIES 2004, JEAN BEAUQUIN Loire – *A savoury nose with clear lemon fruit on the palate and nutty edge. Good balance and great length.*	**£8.50** WRT
DOMAINE DU CARROIR PERRIN SANCERRE 2004, DOMAINE DU CARROIR PERRIN Loire – *Touch of gooseberry and grass on the nose and palate. Attractive ripe fruit roundness, balanced acidity, elegant finish.*	**£8.90** 3DW
PASCAL JOLIVET ATTITUDE SAUVIGNON BLANC 2003, PASCAL JOLIVET Loire – *Buttery hazelnuts on the nose. Grilled buttery pineapple on the palate with some ripe fruit.*	**£10.00** BTH
SANCERRE LES BLANCS GÂTEAUX 2004, DOMAINE LA CROIX CANAT Loire – *Fragrant. This Sancerre is piled high with nettles and limes and flinty mineral scents.*	**£10.00** JSM
DOMAINE REVERDY-DUCROUX 2004, DOMAINE REVERDY-DUCROUX Loire – *Modern, crisp Sauvignon Blanc character. Good acidity lifts the lemon, lime, and melon fruit.*	**£10.50** LAI
SANCERRE BLANC LES COLLINETTES 2003, JOSEPH MELLOT Loire – *Freshly picked peas, citrus, greengages, and nettles scent and flavour this flinty Sancerre. Ripe for enjoyment.*	**£10.70** WPR/CTC
POUILLY-FUMÉ LA RENARDIÈRE 2004, BOUCHIE CHATELLIER Loire – *A distinctive note of citrus, herbal tea, and celery. These elements reappear on the palate. An unusual, stylish wine.*	**£11.00** NEC/PBA
POUILLY-FUMÉ LA MOYNERIE 2003, MICHEL REDDE ET FILS Loire – *Herb and spice nose. Intensely aromatic. Its white peach and lime flavours have a hint of flint.*	**£12.00** LOL
DOMAINE MICHEL THOMAS SILEX 2003, DOMAINE MICHEL THOMAS Loire – *A fat, warm, lemon, and honey palate. The palate adds pineapple to the mix. A good juicy, warm style Sauvignon Blanc.*	**£13.00** LAI
RADCLIFFE'S POUILLY-FUMÉ 2002, FOURNIER PÈRE ET FILS Loire – *Smoking gun and flint nose. The palate is subtle with complex herbaceous and mineral tones.*	**£13.00** THS

SEAL OF APPROVAL
LOIRE WHITE

☆ ANJOU BLANC 2004, VINIVAL LOIRE – *Fresh apricots and lemon flavours with a pleasing rich texture.*	**£3.10**
	JSM
☆ SAUVIGNON VDPJF BLANC 2004, VINIVAL LOIRE – *Fresh gooseberry flavours with a burst of balancing acidity.*	**£3.10**
	CWS

BRONZE
LOIRE RED

☆ VALLÉE LOIRE RED SAUMUR 2003, CAVE DE SAUMUR LOIRE – *Fresh strawberry flavours mingle with leather, pencil lead, and a tangle of herbs on nose and palate.*	**£5.00**
	TOS
DOMAINE DE LA CUNE SAUMUR-CHAMPIGNY 2003, DOMAINE DE LA CUNE LOIRE – *Vivid cherry fruit and hints of stony minerals scent the bouquet. The palate is structured, fresh and ripe.*	**£7.80**
	3DW
BOURGUEIL VIEILLES VIGNES 2004, DOMAINE DE LA CHEVALERIE LOIRE – *Pretty summer fruit flavours. Clove and lavender scents. Firm, youthful tannins.*	**£8.50**
	3DW
CUVÉE CARINE 2002, JEAN-CLAUDE MABILEAU ET DIDIER REZÉ LOIRE – *Rich and structured, this delicious Cabernet Franc has classic pencil shaving, currant leaf, cassis, and moist earth elements.*	**£8.60**
	3DW

BRONZE
LOIRE ROSÉ

☆ ROSÉ DE LA LOIRE DE VINIVAL 2004, VINIVAL LOIRE – *Fresh, youthful and bursting with plums and strawberries. Firm, integrated tannins provide support. Herbal hints.*	**£5.00**
	MHV

B R O N Z E
LOIRE SPARKLING

☆ SAUMUR MOUSSEUX 1811 ACKERMAN NV, ACKERMAN RÉMY PANNIER Loire – *Characterful, fresh and packed with flavour, this medium-sweet beauty has plenty of waxy lemons, honeysuckle, and hints of cassis.*	£6.00 WAV

S E A L O F A P P R O V A L
LOIRE SPARKLING

☆ CO-OP SPARKLING CHARDONNAY NV, VARICHON ET CLERC Loire – *Lushly fruited, with zesty acidity.*	£5.30 CWS
☆ SAUMUR BRUT SPARKLING NV, CAVE DE SAUMUR Loire – *Floral notes. White apple and cassis flavours.*	£6.90 CWS

S I L V E R
LOIRE SWEET

☆ CHAUME 1ER CRU DES CÔTEAUX DU LAYON 2003, DOMAINE DES FORGES Loire – *Classic waxy notes and fragrant lemon fruit. Fine balance and weight. Nutty and viscous. Long.*	£6.80 FLY

B R O N Z E
LOIRE SWEET

☆ VOUVRAY DEMI-SEC LA BOURDONNERIE 2004, DOMAINE BOURILLON D'ORLEANS Loire – *Sweet candied lemons and delicate white flowers flavour this sweet, textured, mouthcoating Vouvray.*	£7.00 MWW/THI

BRONZE
RHÔNE WHITE

CAVE DE TAIN L'HERMITAGE HERMITAGE BLANC 2001, CAVE DE TAIN L'HERMITAGE Rhône – *White apple, fuzzy peach, white chocolate, and clove bud elements. Aristocratic, with fresh zesty acidity and lavish flesh.*	£21.00 PBA
HERMITAGE MARQUISE DE LA TOURETTE 2001, DELAS FRÈRES Rhône – *Profound, robust, and beginning to mature. Deep pockets of apricot and white peach. Seriously long and... serious.*	£26.00 BWC

TROPHY
RHÔNE RED

HERMITAGE MARQUISE DE LA TOURETTE 2000, DELAS FRÈRES Rhône – *Spiciness radiates from the nose of blackberry and strawberry fruit. Classic savoury game notes and perfumed berry flavours.*	£28.50 BWC

GOLD
RHÔNE RED

CROZES-HERMITAGE TOUR D'ALBON 2003, DELAS FRÈRES Rhône – *Ripe blackberry and blue plum fruit compete with cloves, malt, and grass. Christmas cake spices and dusky damson flavours.*	£13.00 BWC
CHÂTEAUNEUF-DU-PAPE ROUGE 2003, FONT DE MICHELLE Rhône – *Youthful, intense, and opulent. Elegant and softly textured, with red pepper notes, mineral elements, and a persistent finish.*	£16.00 POR
LAURUS HERMITAGE 2003, GABRIEL MEFFRE Rhône – *Leather, spice, blackberry, and truffle aromas. Intense, tarry fruit married to well-integrated tannins and subtle oak.*	£22.00 GYW
CÔTE RÔTIE SEIGNEUR DE MAUGIRON 2001, DELAS FRÈRES Rhône – *Smooth plums, pink roses, granite, and spiced almond oak. Savoury red and black fruits, star anise and baked earth.*	£31.00 BWC

SILVER
RHÔNE RED

★ PRÉFÉRENCE CÔTES DU RHÔNE ROUGE 2004, CAVES ST PIERRE Rhône – *Plenty of wild red berry flavours tempered with aromatic scents of garrigue. Balanced by a welcome backbone of acidity.*	£5.00 THI
☆ DARRIAUD CAIRANNE 2001, PAUL BOUTINOT Rhône – *Lavish cherry flavours are underpinned by firm, ripe tannins. This wine has delicious hints of chocolate and coffee.*	£6.50 PBA/FLA
☆ CÔTES DU RHÔNE VILLAGES SEGURET 2004, LES VIGNERONS DE BEAUMES DE VENISE Rhône – *Scattered with fresh pink peppercorns and emblazoned by crisp acidity, with delicate hints of chocolate for good measure.*	£7.00 THI
☆ PRÉFÉRENCE CÔTES DU RHÔNE VILLAGES RASTEAU 2004, CAVES ST PIERRE Rhône – *Big, its flavours of rich blackcurrants and raspberries underscored by chocolate, tobacco, and fruitcake. Youthful and robust.*	£7.00 THI
☆ CÔTES DU RHÔNE VILLAGES RASTEAU 2004, LES VIGNERONS DE BEAUMES DE VENISE Rhône – *Peppery, youthful and structured, with plenty of ripe red fruits, mineral hints, and touches of prune. Medium-bodied.*	£7.50 THI/JSM
CROZES-HERMITAGE ROUGE 2003, CAVE DE TAIN L'HERMITAGE Rhône – *Notes of undergrowth and pepper etch the bright raspberry fruit. Pine needles rise from the nose. Excellent grip.*	£7.90 HBJ/ICL JSM
CROZES-HERMITAGE SELECTION PREMIÈRE 2003, CAVE DE TAIN L'HERMITAGE Rhône – *Youthful, ripe, and intense, its nose etched with warm vanilla. Laden with weighty bramble fruit. Brisk tannic backbone.*	£8.00 RSV
CHATEAUNEUF DU PAPE LA VOLONTÉ DES PAPES 2004, LES VIGNERONS DE BEAUMES DE VENISE Rhône – *A well balanced bouquet entices your palate to enjoy rounded fruity and spicy tastes with a velvet texture.*	£10.00 THI
CROZES-HERMITAGE 2002, DOMAINE MICHELAS ST JEMMS Rhône – *Robust mouthful of vibrant black fruit and hints of spice. Good grip and structure distinguishes this wine.*	£10.00 CAB

LAURUS GIGONDAS 2003, GABRIEL MEFFRE Rhône – *Traditional Demi-Queue de Vaucluse age this wine. Seductively ripe, smoothly textured, and packed with red berries.*	**£13.00** GYW
CUVÉE DU VATICAN 2003, VIGNOBLES DIFFONTY Rhône – *White pepper powder, cloves, and chocolate nose. Soft, supple cherry fruit palate with notes of prunes.*	**£14.00** LAI
SERINAE 2003, DOMAINE DE SEYSSUEL Rhône – *Sweet fruit, shades of chocolate, and jam. Long, with a touch of spice. An experience to remember.*	**£28.00** WSG

B R O N Z E
RHÔNE RED

☆ VINTNERS COLLECTION CÔTES DU RHÔNE 2003, CAVES ST PIERRE Rhône – *Juicy plum, cloves, and pepper flavours stride across the palate and integrate into the oak. Long sweet finish.*	**£3.80** LCC
☆ OLD GIT CÔTES DU VENTOUX 2003, PAUL BOUTINOT Rhône – *Soft and elegant. Sweetly ripe, with balanced tannins and a long, thirst-quenching finish.*	**£4.20** PBA/BGN
ECLAT DU RHÔNE 2004, LES CHAIS BEAUCAIROIS Rhône – *Plums, cranberry jelly, redcurrants, and wild herbs scent the nose. Clear, bright, and balanced.*	**£5.00** THI
LA SIRÈNE CÔTES DE VENTOUX 2003, BOUTINOT Rhône – *Violets and perfume on the nose and palate, which displays ripe fruit and a firm tannic structure.*	**£5.50** VGN
PURE SYRAH VIN DE PAYS DES COLLINES RHODANIENNES 2003, CAVE DE TAIN L'HERMITAGE Rhône – *A taste of pepper and clove and a powerful kick of black fruit. A wine with ample tannins.*	**£5.50** PBA
DOMAINE LA COURANÇONNE 2003, CAVES ST PIERRE Rhône – *Ruby colour. Soft nose and strong attack of prominent fruit. Herbal touches. Displays good length and elegance.*	**£5.70** LAI

CHÂTEAU GRAND ESCALION 2003, GABRIEL MEFFRE RHÔNE – *Warm, sweet, and juicy. A touch of spice and tobacco. Rich with firm structure and medium length.*	£6.00 GYW
LA CHASSE DU PAPE GRANDE RESERVE 2004, GABRIEL MEFFRE RHÔNE – *Medium-bodied cherry and plum flesh is seared by cleansing acidity. Warm prune undertones.*	£7.00 GYW
PREFERENCE CÔTES DU RHÔNE VILLAGES 2004, CAVES SAINT-PIERRE RHÔNE – *Peppery redcurrants and youthful mulberries flow from the balanced, flavourful palate. Medium-bodied.*	£7.00 TOS
VIGNERONS DE BEAUMES DE VENISE CÔTES DU RHÔNE VILLAGES 2004, LES VIGNERONS DE BEAUMES DE VENISE RHÔNE – *Lively and vibrant, with a ripe fruit palate and bursts of licquorice. The finish lingers.*	£7.00 THI
BARQUE VIEILLE 2004, CAVE DES VIGNERONS DE CHUSCLAN RHÔNE – *Winemaker Andre Roux comes up trumps again. A rustic yet well-crafted effort with deep, smoky black fruit flavours.*	£7.20 LAI
ALAIN PARET VALVIGNEYRE 2003, ALAIN PARET RHÔNE – *Leather, liquorice, and sweet vanilla notes on the nose. The black fruit palate is full and powerful.*	£7.80 BNK
CHAPOUTIER RASTEAU COTES-DU-RHONE VILLAGES 2003, CHAPOUTIER RHÔNE – *A soft, delicate nose of cranberries and redcurrants. Coffee and elderberries mingle with meat. Excellent length.*	£10.00 EDC/WDI
VACQUEYRAS MONTIRIUS 2003, CHRISTINE ET ERIC SAUREL RHÔNE – *An understated, medium bodied, dry, spicy wine with summer fruit flavours and a long clean finish.*	£10.30 VER/3DW
CROZES-HERMITAGE CUVÉE LOUIS BELLE 2001, DOMAINE BELLE RHÔNE – *Deep, layered, and intense, with damsons, lilacs, vanilla pod, bonfire, and herb flavours and scents.*	£12.00 ALL
PRÉFÉRENCE ST JOSEPH 2004, CAVES ST PIERRE RHÔNE – *Near opaque, with plentiful red fruit and pleasing tannins, this wine has herbal characteristics and a peppery finish.*	£12.00 THI

VERSINO CHÂTEAUNEUF-DU-PAPE 1999, VERSINO Rhône – *Traditional earth, chocolate, and sweet fruit flavours. Firm tannins and a long finish.*	£12.00 J&B
CÔTES DU VENTOUX QUINTESSENCE 2001, CHÂTEAU PESQUIE Rhône – *A blackberry flavoured, elegant, refined wine. Hints of red pepper, maquis, and juniper.*	£12.90 OWL
ST-JOSEPH LES LARMES DU PÈRE 2003, ALAIN PARET Rhône – *Mulling spices and dense strawberry and cassis fruit nose. Minerals and toasty oak enhance the textured palate.*	£13.00 CCS
CHÂTEAUNEUF-DU-PAPE GRANDE RESERVE 2003, CHÂTEAU BEAUCHENE Rhône – *Elegant pale ruby red. Brisk acid supports the plush red cherry and prune fruit. Ripe tannins.*	£15.00 GAL
DOMAINE GRAND TINEL CHÂTEAUNEUF-DU-PAPE 2003, DOMAINE GRAND TINEL Rhône – *Flavours of cocoa and ripe strawberries. Aromas of grass, black cherries, and freshly ground pepper.*	£15.00 WRK
PRÉFÉRENCE CHÂTEAUNEUF-DU-PAPE 2003, CAVES ST PIERRE Rhône – *Ripe redcurrant and loganberry scents and flavours. Delicate raisined notes. Appetising, full, soft, focused, and long.*	£15.00 THI

B R O N Z E
RHÔNE ROSÉ

CHÂTEAU D'AQUERIA TAVEL ROSÉ 2004, CHÂTEAU D'AQUERIA Rhône – *Ripe strawberries, cassis, and rosemary scent and flavour this delicious, impeccably made, robust Tavel rosé.*	£9.00 MWW

B R O N Z E
RHÔNE FORTIFIED

LAURUS MUSCAT 2003, GABRIEL MEFFRE Rhône – *Fiery, honeyed flavours of tangerine, rose petal, lemon peel, and candied grapefruit. Sweet and unctuous.*	£10.00 GYW

TROPHY
SOUTHWEST WHITE

☆ CHANT DES VIGNES 2003, DOMAINE CAUHAPÉ **Southwest** – *Crammed with greengages, grapefruit, and lemons. Exotic satsuma and marjoram notes. Long, clear and characterful.*	**£12.00** CCS/FLY

GOLD
SOUTHWEST WHITE

☆ BLANC SEC PRESTIGE 2003, CHÂTEAU DES EYSSARDS **Southwest** – *Marmalade, lavender, and peaches scent the nose. Waxed lemon flavours. Intense yet restrained. Mellow spices.*	**£8.00** FLA

BRONZE
SOUTHWEST WHITE

☆ DOMAINE VIGNÉ-LOURAC SAUVIGNON PRESTIGE 2004, DOMAINE VIGNÉ-LOURAC **Southwest** – *Crisp, fresh Sauvignon Blanc perfume. Grass and limes flavour the palate. Bright and clear.*	**£5.00** GRT
LES VIGNES RETROUVÉES BLANC 2004, PLAIMONT **Southwest** – *A mineral and steely nose is matched by a crisp palate with sharp Granny Smith apple notes.*	**£5.70** ESL/POR
VIN DE PAYS DES CÔTES DE THONGUE 2004, DOMAINE DE MONT D'HORTES **Southwest** – *Grassy and herbaceous. Mouthfilling, with good balance between green berry fruit and acidity.*	**£5.80** WDS
FRENCH CONNECTION SAUVIGNON BLANC 2004, VIGNOBLES DU PELOUX **Southwest** – *A good floral, fresh nose is lifted by zesty grapefruit and lime flavours on the palate.*	**£6.00** TOS
TARIQUET SAUVIGNON BLANC 2004, DOMAINE GRASSA **Southwest** – *Apples, lemons, and hints of tropical fruit. The palate has a piercing seam of acidity.*	**£6.20** POR/THI

BERGERAC BLANC SEC 2004, CHÂTEAU DES EYSSARDS Southwest – *Smooth and balanced with pleasant aromas of honey, flowers, and peaches. Well-rounded wine.*	£6.40 ADN/FLA

SEAL OF APPROVAL
SOUTHWEST WHITE

☆ BARON SAINT JEAN 2004, LES GRANDS CHAIS DE FRANCE Southwest – *Floral perfume. Youthful citrus and almond palate.*	£2.40 ALD
☆ CUVÉE JEAN-PAUL SEC 2004, PAUL BOUTINOT Southwest – *Wildflowers scent the nose. Pear flavours.*	£4.00 PBA/WRK
☆ GASTON DE VEAU 2004, PRODUCTEURS PLAIMONT Southwest – *Cut grass, nettles, and pea pod flavours.*	£4.00 M&S
☆ PIAT D'OR MEDIUM DRY WHITE NV, PIAT D'OR Southwest – *Luscious ripe pears and golden apples.*	£4.00 BGN/PFC TOS/JSM

GOLD
SOUTHWEST RED

☆ CHÂTEAU HAUT-MONPLAISIR PRESTIGE 2001, LE CÈDRE DIFFUSION Southwest – *Spice, tea, flowers, wild scrub, and black cherries. Lavender, toast, and coconut. A force to be reckoned with.*	£9.50 L&T
☆ CHÂTEAU LES HAUTS D'AGLAN CUVÉE A 2002, CHÂTEAU LES HAUTS D'AGLAN Southwest – *Classic Cahors. Mint, stone, and dark damsons. Bright acidity, integrated tannins, and vanilla pods. Lingering, smoky finish.*	£12.00 L&T

SILVER
SOUTHWEST RED

GRANDE MAISON CUVÉE ANTOINETTE 2003, **DESPRES** SOUTHWEST – *Christmas cake spices, earth, and cedar. The palate is a stunning marriage of raspberry fruit and oak.*	**£8.00** VER
GRAND VIN DU CHÂTEAU GRINOU 2003, GUY CUISSET SOUTHWEST – *Plums, chocolate, coffee, and herbs grace the nose, whilst raspberry compôte and cinnamon oak line the palate*	**£9.50** ALZ
PARADIS 2000, SUD OUEST MILLÉSIMÉS SOUTHWEST – *Dark cherries and violets. The palate is restrained, smoky, and long, with baked pie flavours and firm tannins.*	**£16.00** THI

BRONZE
SOUTHWEST RED

☆ **CUVÉE DES ARCADES 2004, SUD OUEST** **MILLÉSIMÉS** SOUTHWEST – *Strawberries, pencil lead, bales of straw, leather, and aniseed aromas and flavours. Deep and structured.*	**£4.50** THI/JSM
☆ **BUZET CUVÉE 44 2003, LES VIGNERONS DE BUZET** SOUTHWEST – *Full and ripe and brimming with approachable, unadulterated, clear aromas and flavours of cherry fruit.*	**£5.00** THI
CHÂTEAU BEAUPORTAIL 2002, FABRICE FEYTOUT SOUTHWEST – *Dark berry fruit aromas and flavours. Long, earthy, and ripe, with fresh notes of Herbs de Provence.*	**£8.00** ALZ
MONASTERE DE SAINT MONT 2002, PLAIMONT SOUTHWEST – *Soft prunes, dark plums, and sloes perfume and flavour this deeply coloured, velvety wine. Nuances of grilled meat.*	**£10.50** HWL

BRONZE
SOUTHWEST ROSÉ

☆ FONCAUSSADE 2004, LES VIGNERONS DE SIGOULÈS Southwest – *Fine black plum, cherry, and kirsch flavours. Fresh, cleansing acidity. Firm tannins. A delicious drop.*	£5.00 WTS

GOLD
SOUTHWEST SWEET

QUINTESSENCE 1999, DOMAINE CAUHAPÉ Southwest – *The masculine palate of candied lemon and treacle tingles with enervating acidity. Superb waxy texture and notes of herbs.*	£24.00 SGL

SILVER
SOUTHWEST SWEET

CLOS D'YVIGNE SAUSSIGNAC 1999, CLOS D'YVIGNE Southwest – *Rich grapefruit and lemon flavours seared by fresh acidity. Delicate herbal notes and hints of spice.*	£20.00 J&B
NOBLESSE DU TEMPS 2001, DOMAINE CAUHAPÉ Southwest – *Vibrant green-gold. Nose of barley sugar and flowers. Sweet grapey flavours mingle with peaches and herbs on the palate.*	£20.90 RSV/FLY
GRANDE MAISON CUVÉE DES MONSTRES 2002, DESPRÉS Southwest – *The pineapple flesh is lush and lifted by delicate orange blossom nuances. Long, poised, and balanced.*	£32.00 VER

BRONZE
SOUTHWEST SWEET

SAUSSIGNAC CUVÉE FLAVIE 2003, CHÂTEAU DES EYSSARDS Southwest – *Complex flavours of vanilla and cinnamon. Fresh pear fruit and a light touch of toast.*	£9.50 ADN/FLA JSM

CHATEAU GRINOU SAUSSIGNAC 2001, GUY CUISSET **SOUTHWEST** – *Complex spice matched with citrus fruit, baked apples, and a lovely ripe peach finish.*	**£13.00** ALZ
SAUSSIGNAC CHÂTEAU GRINOU 2002, CHÂTEAU GRINOU **SOUTHWEST** – *Deep, opulent honey, and mushroom aromas. Flavours of lanolin and navel oranges.*	**£13.00** ALZ

SEAL OF APPROVAL
SOUTHWEST SWEET

☆ DOMAINE HAUT RAULY MONBAZILLAC 2003, PIERRE ALARD **SOUTHWEST** – *Ripe, unctuous, and packed with lemon marmalade.*	**£4.80** CWS

SILVER
OTHER FRENCH WHITE

☆ CUVÉE PECHEUR VIN DE PAYS DE COMTE TOLOSAN 2004, LGI **GERS** – *Attractive peach and cantaloupe nose and palate. A thirst-quenching seam of acidity refreshes the viscous mouthfeel. Fresh finish.*	**£3.50** WTS

BRONZE
OTHER FRENCH WHITE

☆ FRENCH CONNECTION SAUVIGNON BLANC GRENACHE 2004, VIGNOBLES DU PELOUX **SOUTHWEST FRANCE** – *Pepper powder and capsicum aromas. Bright and grassy, with flavours of lime cordial. Thirst-quenching.*	**£4.30** TOS
☆ AVERY'S FRENCH COUNTRY WHITE 2004, AVERY'S **LANGUEDOC-ROUSSILLON** – *Some fresh fruit flavours on the nose and palate. Gooseberry character stands out with particular focus.*	**£4.50** AVB

SEAL OF APPROVAL
OTHER FRENCH WHITE

☆ VINTNERS COLLECTION CHARDONNAY VIN DE PAYS DU JARDIN DE LA FRANCE 2003, DONATIEN BAHUAUD **Loire** – *Delicate vanilla notes complement lemon flavours.*	£3.70 LCC

SILVER
OTHER FRENCH RED

CHÂTEAU LA BRANNE CUVÉE FERNAND GINESTET 2003, GINESTET **Bordeaux** – *Bright, pretty violet colour. Perfumed with caramel and toast and swathed in firmest tannins.*	£8.00 WAV

BRONZE
OTHER FRENCH RED

CHÂTEAU VIGNELAURE 2001, CHÂTEAU VIGNELAURE **Provence** – *Complex mint, violets, and cherry fruit. Perfect for ageing, with a sweet nose and great length and structure.*	£11.70 JNW

SEAL OF APPROVAL
OTHER FRENCH SPARKLING

☆ CHRISTIAN SACCARD BLANC DE BLANCS BRUT NV, CFGV **Regional Blend** – *Almond skin scents. Citrus flavours.*	£4.50 MHV
☆ PHILIPPE MICHEL CRÉMANT DU JURA 2002, COMPAGNIE DES VINS DU JURA **Jura** – *Flavours of white apples. Firm acidity.*	£6.00 ALD
☆ VEUVE DU VERNAY BRUT 2003, SORVEI **Loire** – *Fresh citrus flavours laced with floral notes.*	£6.00 CWS

GERMANY

If Eastern Europe has neen treading water since the mid 1980s, Germany has undergone a quiet vinous revolution. The quality of the most basic wines – even the Liebfraumilchs – has improved, but far more importantly, has been the move to offer approachable dry wines like the Domdechant Werner Hochheimer Holle Reslings, and the Deinhard classic Pinot Blanc listed below. Labels, thank goodness, are becoming much more readable, too.

TROPHY
GERMAN WHITE

☆ DOMDECHANT WERNER RIESLING CLASSIC 2003, DOMDECHANT WERNER **R**HEINGAU – *Dried lavender, delicate orange blossom, and pear aromas. Weighty, textured lychee fruit assaults the senses. Vivid minerality.*	**£8.00** WDI

GOLD
GERMAN WHITE

BRAUNEBERG JUFFER-SONNENUHR RIESLING SPÄTLESE 2002, FRITZ HAAG **M**OSEL-**S**AAR-**R**UWER – *A sweet/sour tang. Lemons and limes, crystalline minerals, orange blossoms, and green apples.*	**£15.00** J&B
IPHÖFER JULIUS-ECHTER-BERG GRAUBURGUNDER AUSLESE TROCKEN 2003, WEINGUT HANS WIRSCHING **F**RANKEN – *Notes of lavender and new-mown hay. Tea leaves, powdered minerals, and rich chocolate nuances.*	**£25.40** WBN

SILVER
GERMAN WHITE

RIESLING KABINETT 2002, SA PRUM **M**OSEL-**S**AAR-**R**UWER – *Warm, feminine aromas of peaches, clove, rose petals, and lychees. Smoke and rich petrol notes.*	**£14.50** CEB

ESCHERNDORFER LUMP RIESLING SPÄTLESE TROCKEN 2004, HORST SAUER FRANKEN – *Vivid spices, crisp candied lemons, and minerals. The palate is solidly built, with mature, lavish pear and lime flavours.*	£15.00 NYW
HOCHHEIMER KIRCHENSTUCK RIESLING SPÄTLESE 2003, KÜNSTLER ESTATE RHEINGAU – *Intensely aromatic, with minerals, flowers, limes, and apricots. The palate has zingy acidity, impressive in such a warm vintage.*	£16.00 WTS
JULIUS-ECHTER-BERG RIESLING TROCKEN GROSSES GEWÄCHS 2003, WEINGUT HANS WIRSCHING FRANKEN – *Lime and apple palate with a firm mineral backbone. Perfumed ripe peach, flower, and grapefruit scents.*	£24.10 WBN

BRONZE
GERMAN WHITE

☆ RIESLING KABINETT 2003, MOSELLAND MOSEL-SAAR-RUWER – *A nicely developed nose and palate with fresh fruit and kerosene notes. Off-dry and long.*	£4.40 POR/TAN
☆ PINOT BLANC CLASSIC 2004, DEINHARD RHEINHESSEN – *Pretty whitecurrant, apricot, honey, and marzipan flavours. A mouthcoating texture extends the finish.*	£4.50 HOH
VILLA WOLF PINOT GRIS 2004, JL WOLF PFALZ – *Smooth lime and elderflower flavours. Hints of pepper powder and minerals. Youthful yet rich.*	£6.10 CCS/JNW
KENDERMANN DRY RIESLING ROTER HANG 2003, REH KENDERMANN RHEINHESSEN – *Pretty apricot and orange blossom nose. Lemon zest and savoury spice. Long finish.*	£7.00 WTS
ESCHERNDORFER LUMP SILVANER SPÄTLESE TROCKEN 2004, HORST SAUER FRANKEN – *Great freshness combined with good ripeness and minerality. Clean, spicy, fruity finish.*	£14.00 NYW
HATTENHEIM WISSELBRUNNEN RIESLING ERSTES GEWÄCHS 2003, WEINGUT HANS LANG RHEINGAU – *Big aromas and flavours of lime zest, white peach, apricot, and starfruit. Very ripe and aromatic. Zippy acidity.*	£16.00 TWK

KALKOFEN DEIDESHEIM 2003, WEINGUT DR VON BASSERMANN-JORDAN **Pfalz** – *A zingy, spritzy nose with lively green lime scents. Flowers and fruit flavour the fresh, off-dry palate.*	£19.90 WBN

SEAL OF APPROVAL
GERMAN WHITE

☆ VINTNERS COLLECTION LIEBFRAUMILCH 2003, SCHMITT SÖHNE **Rheinhessen** – *Orange blossom scents. Lush yet fresh.*	£3.00 LCC
☆ VINTNERS COLLECTION NIERSTEINER GUTES DOMTAL 2003, SCHMITT SÖHNE **Rheinhessen** – *Lime flowers, citrus flavours, and mineral hints.*	£3.30 LCC
☆ BLACK TOWER DRY RIESLING 2004, REH KENDERMANN **Rheinhessen** – *Fresh flowers, ripe apples, and mineral notes.*	£3.80 TOS
☆ FOOTSTEPS LIEBFRAUMILCH NV, CONSTELLATION **Rheinhessen** – *White roses, crisp pears, and talcum powder.*	£4.00 MCT
☆ KENDERMANN DRY RIESLING 2004, REH KENDERMANN **Pfalz** – *Apples, grapefruit, and lush pears galore.*	£4.00 BGN/TOS JSM

SEAL OF APPROVAL
GERMAN SPARKLING

☆ HENKELL TROCKEN ROSÉ NV, HENKELL & CO WEISBADEN **Regional Blend** – *Dry, frothy, and packed with raspberry flavours.*	£6.00 MYL
☆ DEINHARD LILA RIESLING TROCKEN NV, DEINHARD **Mittelrhein** – *Balanced, aromatic, and very fresh. Lemony.*	£7.00 CTC

TROPHY
GERMAN SWEET

ERDENER PRÄLAT RIESLING AUSLESE 2004, DR LOOSEN **MOSEL-SAAR-RUWER** – *Red slate soils and optimal exposure contribute to the vivid minerality and pear and spice flavours in this aristocratic entry.*	**£35.70** CNL/CCS FLY/NYW

GOLD
GERMAN SWEET

☆ DOMDECHANT WERNER HOCHHHEIMER HÖLLE RIESLING 1999, DOMDECHANT WERNER **RHEINGAU** – *Peaches, flint, and candied lemons. Citrus, apples, and bracing minerality. Would accompany highly spiced Asian cuisine.*	**£10.50** LAI
☆ RÜDESHEIMER MAGDALENENKREUZ RIESLING SPÄTLESE 2004, LEITZ **RHEINGAU** – *Talented Johannes Leitz. Orange peel, honey, and limes. Apricots and minerals. Firm, young, well-structured, and achingly fresh.*	**£11.70** CCS/WAW NYW
RÜDESHEIMER BERG SCHLOSSBERG RIESLING SPÄTLESE 2004, LEITZ **RHEINGAU** – *Sweet red cherries, candied lemons, slatey minerals, smoke, honeycomb, powder puff, and grapefruit. Unctuous yet fresh.*	**£16.60** CCS/FLY WAW/NY W
HOCHHEIMER DOMDECHANEY RIESLING AUSLESE 2003, DOMDECHANT WERNER **RHEINGAU** – *The heavy soils of Domdechaney produce wines of character. Perfume of limes and honey. Flavours of soft stone fruit.*	**£25.00** WDI
JOHANNISBERGER KLAUS AUSLESE 2003, WEINGUT PRINZ VON HESSEN **RHEINGAU** – *Honeyed pear notes scent the feminine nose. Lush apricot fruit is balanced by fine ruby grapefruit acidity.*	**£60.00** OWL
HOCHHEIMER KIRCHENSTUCK RIESLING TBA 2003, DOMDECHANT WERNER **RHEINGAU** – *Opulent apricot, marmalade, and honey characteristics define this rich, weighty, luscious wine.*	**£100.00** WDI

SILVER
GERMAN SWEET

☆ ILBESHEIMER HERRLICH BEERENAUSLESE 2001, LAITHWAITE PRIVATE CELLARS PFALZ – *Brass colour. Rich honey and barley sugar, elderflowers, caramel, limes, and toffee. An almost oily texture.*	£7.00 LAI
JOHANNISBERGER KLAUS BEERENAUSLESE 2003, WEINGUT PRINZ VON HESSEN RHEINGAU – *Grapefruit galore. Warm nose of pear, tangerine, and golden apple fruit. Long, concentrated, ripe, and fine.*	£12.00 OWL
RIESLING AUSLESE HATTENHEIMER WISSELBRUNNEN 2003, WEINGUT HANS LANG RHEINGAU – *Restrained aromas of lime, lemon sherbet, minerals, and pear fruit. Etched with filigree acidity. Perfectly balanced.*	£16.30 TWK
WINKELER HASENSPRUNG SPÄTLESE 2003, WEINGUT PRINZ VON HESSEN RHEINGAU – *Fully ripe. Pure, zesty, honeyed, and bursting with Conference pear flavours. Long and very luscious.*	£18.00 OWL
ÜRZIGER WÜRZGARTEN RIESLING SPÄTLESE 2004, DR LOOSEN MOSEL-SAAR-RUWER – *Delicate lime blossom, mineral, and green apple aromas. Peaches, pineapples, and papaya flavours seared by fresh acidity.*	£19.30 CNL/CCS FLY/NYW

BRONZE
GERMAN SWEET

HOCHHEIMER DOMDECHANEY RIESLING SPÄTLESE 2003, DOMDECHANT WERNER RHEINGAU – *Ripe and aristocratic. Crisp apples, lush peaches, and fresh lemons appear on nose and palate. Elegant.*	£14.00 TAN
RIESLING EISWEIN 2001, WINZERVEREIN RUPPERTSBERG PFALZ – *Perfumed key lime, petrol, sweet apple, hawthorn, and lemon marmalade aromas and flavours.*	£15.00 JSM
RUPPERTSBERG RIESLING EISWEIN 2001, WINZERVEREIN RUPPERTSBERG PFALZ – *Vivid acidity sears the mouthcoating honey, pear, lemon, marmalade, and mineral-rich flesh. Balanced.*	£15.00 JSM

WINKELER HASENSPRUNG TBA 2003, WEINGUT PRINZ VON HESSEN Rheingau – *Opulent. Sweet apricot, Seville orange, lemon zest, smoke, and golden syrup lavours and aromas.*	£24.00 OWL
PENGUIN EISWEIN SILVANER 2003, LOUIS GUNTRUM Rheinhessen – *Full-bodied, with earthy, mineral-infused flavours of whitecurrants, pears, and golden grapefruit. Poised, lush, and long.*	£26.00 SOH
HATTENHEIMER NUSSBRUNNEN RIESLING AUSLESE 2003, BALTHASAR RESS WEINGUT Rheingau – *Intense, its lavish yet focused flavours of apricot, lemon, marmalade, and apple a veritable wall of flavour.*	£28.00 TNG

SEAL OF APPROVAL
GERMAN SWEET

☆ PIESPORTER MICHELSBERG 2004, MOSELLAND Mosel-Saar-Ruwer – *Elderflowers, limes, and pears flavour this wine.*	£2.80 SMF
☆ GREEN LABEL RIESLING 2004, DEINHARD Mosel-Saar-Ruwer – *Fresh peaches, powdered minerals, and kerosene.*	£4.00 HOH

FOR STOCKIST CODES turn to page 317. For regularly updated information about stockists and the International Wine Challenge, visit **wineint.com**. For a full glossary of wine terms and a complete free wine course, visit robertjoseph-onwine.com

GREECE + CYPRUS

Sadly, despite the efforts to persuade us all to explore Greek wines, and the brief flurry of excitement that folllowed Greece's successful Olympics, the wines of this ancient vinous heartland are hard to find in Britain. Too many people seem to imagine that the wines on offer here are still restricted to Retsina and basic taverna reds unaffectionately known as "Domestos". But wines like the award-winning Mavrodaphne, made from a grape exclusive to Greece, are well worth seeking out.

BRONZE
GREEK + CYPRIOT WHITE

☆ CO-OP ISLAND VINES CYPRUS WHITE NV, SODAP **Paphos** – *Fruit salad aromas greet the nostrils. The palate has austere white fruit and crisp lime acidity.*	£4.00 CWS
DOMAINE EVHARIS WHITE 2004, DOMAINE EVHARIS **Attica** – *A simple nose with fresh lean apple aromas. A terse, crisp palate is off-set by sweet pear fruit.*	£7.60 CCS/FLY NYW

SILVER
GREEK + CYPRIOT RED

ALPHA XINOMAVRO 2003, ALPHA ESTATE **Macedonia** – *Rich animal notes complement the palate of red apple fruit and strawberry pip tannins. Very firm, with excellent concentration.*	£18.00 VKB

BRONZE
GREEK + CYPRIOT RED

MOUNT ATHOS VINEYARDS 2002, EVANGELOS TSANTALIS **Chalkidiki** – *Muscular and big, with loads of black cherry fruit and a firm framework of tannins. Still young.*	£7.50 LAI

KTIMA PAVLIDIS 2003, CHRISTOFOROS PAVLIDIS	£10.00
MACEDONIA – *Lots of little blackcurrants flavour the firm palate. Brooding, structured, and long.*	VKB

BRONZE
GREEK + CYPRIOT FORTIFIED

☆ KOURTAKIS MAVRODAPHNE OF PÁTRAS NV, D	£4.30
KOURTAKIS **PELOPONNESE** – *Sweet, rich, and complex. Flavours of currants, red apples, cinnamon, and nutmeg. Long, layered, and fresh. Well balanced.*	ADE/TOS JSM

GOLD MEDALS HAVE SCORED the equivalent of at least 18.5/20 (or 95/100) and are exceptional. Silver has scored over 17/20 (or 90/100), bronze over 15.5/20 (or 85/100), and seals of approval over 14/20 (or 80/100).
☆ particularly good value
★ truly great value

FOR STOCKIST CODES turn to page 317. For regularly updated information about stockists and the International Wine Challenge, visit wineint.com. For a full glossary of wine terms and a complete free wine course, visit robertjoseph-onwine.com

ITALY

Another under-appreciated source of great value wines, Italy came up with more bargains this year than Australia. Revealingly, many of these came from parts of the country that no one took seriously a few years ago. The South of Italy and Sicily are, in some ways, New World regions in Europe, where modern methods are bringing the best out of grapes like the Syrah and Chardonnay. But traditional local varieties are shining here too. Look out for examples of Nero d'Avola, Falanghina, and Primitivo among the winners listed here. In the more famous, more northerly, regions there are, of course, great classic wines - and novelties like Tuscan Syrah.

GOLD
PIEDMONT + NORTHWEST WHITE

☆ MINAIA GAVI DI GAVI 2004, NICOLA E GIANLUIGI BERGAGLIO Piedmont – *Fragrant ripe peach, nectarine, and almond characteristics. Beautifully weighted, long, and complex.*	£9.90 ICL/ENO
MONTALUPA BIANCO VIOGNIER 2003, CANTINE ASCHERI GIACOMO Piedmont – *Exotic notes of peach, apricot, and honeysuckle. Fine acidity and minerals. The finish is long and balanced.*	£22.50 V&C/BBL ENO

SILVER
PIEDMONT + NORTHWEST WHITE

GAVI DI GAVI MASSERIA DEI CARMELITANI 2004, TERRE DA VINO Piedmont – *Exotic, minerally, and long. The palate is taut and balanced, with zingy pineapple fruit and fresh lime cordial acidity.*	£9.00 V&C
GAVI DI GAVI TOLEDANA 2004, DOMINI VILLAE LANATA Piedmont – *Quartz, almonds, lemons, and green melons scent the nose and flavour the palate. Clean, balanced, long, and refreshing.*	£24.00 D&D

BRONZE
PIEDMONT + NORTHWEST WHITE

TESCO FINEST GAVI 2004, FRATELLI MARTINI SECONDO LUIGI PIEDMONT – *Juicy apple, elderflower, honeysuckle, and greengage flavours and scents. Vibrant acidity. Very intense.*	£6.00 TOS/D&D
GAVI DI GAVI CASCINA LA TOLEDANA 2003, VILLA LANATA PIEDMONT – *Finely textured white peach and lime cordial flavours. Scents of almonds and pea pods.*	£8.00 MWW

SEAL OF APPROVAL
PIEDMONT + NORTHWEST WHITE

☆ VINTNERS COLLECTION PINOT GRIGIO 2003, FRATELLI MARTINI LOMBARDY – *Fresh little green berries covered in floral scents.*	£4.00 LCC

TROPHY
PIEDMONT + NORTHWEST RED

BARBARESCO MORASSINO 2001, CASCINA MORASSINO PIEDMONT – *Tea, roses, leather, and iodone nose. Black bramble fruit flavours underscored by firm tannins. Coffee notes.*	£20.00 VIN

GOLD
PIEDMONT + NORTHWEST RED

☆ ARALDICA D'ADRIA BARBERA D'ASTI 2003, ARALDICA PIEDMONT – *Mulberries, damsons, cardamom, tamarind, tobacco, leather, and crumbled earth. Creamy oak and ruby bramble fruits.*	£10.00 MDN

SILVER
PIEDMONT + NORTHWEST RED

BARBERA D'ALBA SUCULE 2001, VILLA LANATA **Piedmont** – *Black damson flavours seared by lifted acidity. Delicately structured, with bruised plum, honey, and smoke perfume.*	£8.00 MWW
PODERI ALASIA RIVE BARBERA 2003, ARALDICA VINI PIEMONTESI **Piedmont** – *Undergrowth and tar. A handful of Chinese five spice powder and chocolate covered cherry flavours.*	£10.30 MDN/POR FLA
SAINSBURY'S CLASSIC SELECTION BAROLO 2000, ASCHERI **Piedmont** – *Warm plum tart, wildflower, spicebox, and tarmac. Mouthcoating cherry flavours. Gamey notes.*	£13.00 JSM
BARBARESCO PAJE 2000, PRODUTTORI DEL BARBARESCO **Piedmont** – *Chestnut red. Vanilla pods, tar, red cherries, wild herbs, and scorched earth. Layered and fine.*	£23.00 V&C
BAROLO LO ZOCCOLOLAIO 2000, DOMINI VILLAE LANATA **Piedmont** – *Raisined, spicy, and port-like, with rose, soot, and cinnamon aromas. Herbal tea undertones. Smooth, chalky tannins.*	£25.50 D&D

BRONZE
PIEDMONT + NORTHWEST RED

LE TERRE BARBERA D'ALBA 2001, TERRE DEL BAROLO **Piedmont** – *Lively, fresh, complex, and balanced, with plums, leather, and spice flavours and aromas. Delicate, crunchy texture.*	£6.00 WAV
VALLE BERTA BARBERA D'ASTI 2003, ARALDICA **Piedmont** – *Pretty summer fruit pudding aromas. Bright pigeon-blood ruby colour. Flavours of kirsch and rhubarb.*	£6.00 MDN
ALASIA BARBERA D'ASTI SUPERIORE 2003, ARALDICA VINI PIEMONTESI **Piedmont** – *Tight red cherry nose. The palate is austere yet attractive, with firm tannins and perfumed strawberry flavours.*	£7.00 MDN

BARBERA D'ALBA SUCULE 2002, DOMINI VILLAE LANATA PIEDMONT – *Flowers, tar, liquorice, and cloves. Medium-bodied and elegant, with warm peppery bramble fruit.*	**£8.00** MWW/D&D
BARBARESCO CONTE DI MARESCO RISERVA 2000, FRATELLI MARTINI PIEDMONT – *Garnet red. Cherries, earth, tea leaves, and tobacco. Fresh and long. This youthful wine shall develop further.*	**£8.60** MCT
BAROLO TERRE DEL BAROLO 2000, TERRE DEL BAROLO PIEDMONT – *Ink, leather, cherry, and smoke. Elegant and gently ageing, with a long, medium-bodied palate of hedgerow fruit.*	**£9.00** BNK/WAV
EREMO 2003, FONTANAFREDDA PIEDMONT – *Mouthwatering loganberry fruit supported on a fine tannic backbone. Fresh, approachable, and very pretty.*	**£10.40** FHM
ASDA EXTRA SPECIAL BAROLO 2000, CANTINA TERRE DEL BAROLO PIEDMONT – *Dark prune, flower and cherry nose. The palate is long, solidly constructed, and mature.*	**£11.00** ASD
BARBERA D'ALBA SOVRANA 2003, BENI DI BATASIOLO PIEDMONT – *Deep. The meaty nose has beef and dried herb notes. Soft, spicy, and lingering. A good food wine.*	**£11.00** MON
BAROLO PAESI TUOI 2000, TERRE DA VINO PIEDMONT – *Lots of nuts, dried cherries, leather, espresso, and melted chocolate. Sweet vanilla hints. Will evolve further.*	**£18.00** VIN
BENI DI BATASIOLO BAROLO 2000, BENI DI BATASIOLO PIEDMONT – *Earthy yet ethereal, with delicate rose petal, tar, and iodone aromas. Fresh acidity lifts the velvety texture.*	**£18.00** MON
BAROLO CEREQUIO SINGLE VINEYARD 2000, BENI DI BATASIOLO PIEMONT – *Spicy. Very firm tree bark tannins, notes of leather and sweet blackberry fruit flavours.*	**£28.00** MON
BAROLO LA CORDA DELLA BRICCOLINA SINGLE VINEYARD 2000, BENI DI BATASIOLO PIEMONT – *Densely perfumed with flowers, spice, and pencil lead. Evolved blueberry flesh with a firm tannic backbone. A classic.*	**£37.00** MON

B R O N Z E
PIEDMONT + NORTHWEST SPARKLING

☆ MOSCATO D'ASTI 2004, BENI DI BATASIOLO **PIEDMONT** – *Delicate rose petal scents mingle with honeycombed mandarin oranges. The luscious frizzante palate has a tingle of acidity.*	£6.80 MON

S E A L O F A P P R O V A L
PIEDMONT + NORTHWEST SPARKLING

☆ CAPETTA MOSCATO SPUMANTE , CAPETTA **PIEDMONT** – *Runny honey, orange zest, and fresh apples.*	£3.00 MRN
☆ CAPETTA ASTI 2003, CAPETTA **PIEDMONT** – *Sweet Turkish Delight and tangerines.*	£4.00 MRN
☆ SOMERFIELD ASTI SPUMANTE NV, CAPETTA **PIEDMONT** – *Lifted, aromatic, and sweet. Grapey flavours.*	£4.00 M&M
☆ VILLA JOLANDA MOSCATO D'ASTI NV, SANTERO **PIEDMONT** – *Honey, lemons, and starfruit flavours.*	£4.00 WAV
☆ SANTERO ASTI NV, SANTERO **PIEDMONT** – *Rose petal aromas. Flavours of honeyed apples.*	£5.00 TOS
☆ VILLA AUGUSTA ASTI SPUMANTE NV, CAPETTA **PIEDMONT** – *Heady satsuma and rose petal elements.*	£6.00 SMF

BRONZE
PIEDMONT + NORTHWEST SWEET

MOSCATO D'ASTI DI STREVI 2004, CONTERO PIEDMONT – *Lush yet delicate. Flavours of bruised apples, Turkish Delight and honeycomb.*	£7.60 AWO/FLY LIB
MOSCATO D'ASTI 2004, GD VAJRA PIEDMONT – *Delicate rose petal, honey, mandarin orange, and apple scents and flavours.*	£9.40 LIB/NYW

BRONZE
PIEDMONT + NORTHWEST FORTIFIED

☆ TOSTI VERMOUTH BIANCO NV, BOSCA TOSTI PIEDMONT – *Tart, aromatic, and packed with herbs. Sweet lavender, lemons, and green apples.*	£4.00 PLB

GOLD
VENETO + NORTHEAST WHITE

☆ CASATA MONFORT TRENTINO PINOT GRIGIO 2004, CANTINE MONFORT TRENTINO-ALTO ADIGE – *Creamy citrus blossom, slivered almond, roast hazelnut, quartz, and green plums. Restrained and harmonious.*	£9.00 JNV

SILVER
VENETO + NORTHEAST WHITE

★ CANTI CHARDONNAY PINOT GRIGIO VENETO 2004, FRATELLI MARTINI SECONDO LUIGI VENETO – *Elegant, aromatic floral flavours and attractive bitter almond notes. Balanced and lingering.*	£4.30 BGN/TOS D&D/NTD
☆ CANALETTO PINOT GRIGIO GARGANEGA DEL VENETO 2004, CASA GIRELLI VENETO – *Dry and peachy, with ripe cantaloupe melon aromas. The palate has plenty of soft stone fruit flavour.*	£5.00 BGN

☆ MONTECLETHA SOAVE CLASSICO SUPERIORE 2003, **CANTINA MONTECCHIA** VENETO – *Minerals, almonds, bananas, wildflowers, melons, and walnuts reel across the nose and palate of this wine.*	£7.50 ENO
LIBER 2001, FASOLI GINO VENETO – *Smoky golden grapefruit nose. Grip and admirable balance, with candied lemon fruit and almond hints.*	£8.00 VRT

B R O N Z E
VENETO + NORTHEAST WHITE

MHV FRIULI GRAVE CHARDONNAY 2004, BIDOLI FRIULI-VENEZIA GIULIA – *Cashews and lemons scent and flavour this pretty wine. Perfect with a roast chicken supper.*	£5.10 MHV
SAINSBURY'S SOAVE CLASSICO SELECTION 2002, INAMA VENETO – *Bitter almond, hawthorn blossom, sweet honeysuckle, and juicy pear elements flavour this aristocratic Soave Classico.*	£8.00 JSM
MASIANCO 2004, MASI AGRICOLA FRIULI-VENEZIA GIULIA – *Sophisticated and poised, this smoothly textured wine has plenty of mouthcoating pear and apple flavours with rosemary aromas.*	£8.50 BWC
VIRTUOSO CHARDONNAY TRENTINO 2003, CASA GIRELLI TRENTINO-ALTO ADIGE – *Luxuriant sweet oak aromas and flavours envelop the tropical palate of passion fruit and satsumas.*	£10.00 VLW

S E A L   O F   A P P R O V A L
VENETO + NORTHEAST WHITE

☆ VENIER SOAVE 2004, GRUPPO ITALIANO VINI VENETO – *Crushed almonds mingle with green apples.*	£2.50 KWI
☆ CO-OP SOAVE 2004, FRATELLI MARTINI VENETO – *Crisp pear fruit mingles with bitter almonds.*	£2.90 CWS

T R O P H Y
VENETO + NORTHEAST RED

VIGNETI DI JAGO AMARONE VALPOLICELLA DOMINI VENETI 2000, CANTINA VALPOLICELLA NEGRAR VENETO – *Blackberry, rosemary, and shredded coconut. Refined, concentrated cassis, chocolate flavours. Fresh, ripe, and intense.*	£32.00 BRA

G O L D
VENETO + NORTHEAST RED

☆ **VALPOLICELLA VALPANTENA RIPASSO FALASCO 2003, CANTINA SOCIALE DELLA VALPANTENA** VENETO – *Coffee, charred wood, and dried black cherry palate. Silky, with chocolate oak, mulling spices, and red stone fruit.*	£9.00 FLA/ICL DEF/ENO NYW
☆ **LA CASETTA VALPOLICELLA CLASSICO SUPERIORE RIPASSO 2002, CANTINA VALPOLICELLA NEGRAR** VENETO – *Concentrated blackberry, ginger, prune, and espresso aromas. Delicate sweet blackberry flavours flesh out the palate.*	£10.00 MWW
☆ **VALPOLICELLA RIPASSO QUINTUS 2003, CANTINA SOCIALE DELLA VALPANTENA** VENETO – *Victoria plums, cranberries, raspberries, mace, cumin, and wildflowers. Heady stuff, its ample flesh tempered by fresh acidity.*	£10.00 ENO
COSTASERA AMARONE 2001, MASI VENETO – *Concentrated, seductive molasses, mocha, raisins, and meadow flower scents. Ripe blackberry fruit.*	£21.40 V&C/CEB TNG/NYW
AMARONE DELLA VALPOLICELLA VALPANTENA 2002, CANTINA SOCIALE DELLA VALPANTENA VENETO – *Cinnamon bark and ginger powder and currant scents. Rich yet fresh fruitcake, crushed strawberries, and baked earth.*	£23.00 ENO
AMARONE CLASSICO CA' FLORIAN 2001, TOMMASI VITICOLTORI VENETO – *Tremendously grippy redcurrant and cherry fruit laden with brooding liquorice, rosemary, and spice scents.*	£24.00 EOR
ZENATO AMARONE 2000, ZENATO VENETO – *Densely layered and crammed with soft prunes and plums, wildflowers, Havana cigars, and cloves. Satin texture.*	£25.80 EUW/WAW

AMARONE DELLA VALPOLICELLA CLASSICO 2001, ALLEGRINI **Veneto** – *Sweet currants, sultanas, and prunes. Cloves, cinnamon, and scorched earth. Aromatic. Balanced and concentrated.*	**£34.10** WIDELY AVAILABLE

SILVER
VENETO + NORTHEAST RED

☆ LISON PRAMAGGIORE REFOSCO DAL PEDUNCOLO ROSSO VALENTINO PALADIN 2004, PALADIN & PALADIN **Veneto** – *Violet colour. Vivid black plum flavours. Young, playful, and zippy, with an approachable quality.*	**£5.00** CMB
☆ BOTTEGA VINAI TEROLDEGO ROTALIANO 2003, CAVIT **Trentino-Alto Adige** – *Redcurrant nose. Full, dry wine with dusty tannins, game, plums, and bonfire. Tart acidity and excellent grip.*	**£7.00** ICL
☆ BOTTEGA VINAI TRENTINO MERLOT 2002, CAVIT **Trentino-Alto Adige** – *Ripe currants, melted chocolate, herbs, and cherries. Firmly structured and layered. Admirable freshness and integration.*	**£7.00** ICL
VALPOLICELLA RIPASSO TERRE DI VERONA 2003, CANTINA SOCIALE DELLA VALPANTENA **Veneto** – *Black cherry and earth elements mingle on nose and palate. Medium-bodied, fresh, ripe, and long. Integrated tannins.*	**£10.00** ENO
VALPOLICELLA CLASSICO SUPERIORE DI RIPASSO 2001, CORTE RUGOLIN **Veneto** – *Black cherries, roast coffee beans, and bittersweet chocolate. Deep, rich, and balanced, with a mouthcoating texture.*	**£12.50** BBR
PALAZZO DELLA TORRE 2001, ALLEGRINI **Veneto** – *Silky raspberry flavours and scents of raisins, dark chocolate, prunes, and olives. Robust and warming.*	**£13.40** WIDELY AVAILABLE
LA GROLA 2001, ALLEGRINI **Veneto** – *Red plum and black cherry fruit. Mint, ink, and chocolate weave in and out of the firm tannins.*	**£14.00** WIDELY AVAILABLE
AMARONE CLASSICO LE VIGNE 2002, CANTINA SOCIALE DELLA VALPANTENA **Veneto** – *Deep and mature. Intense, pure raisin, sweet hay, and herb nose. Black cherry palate. Seductive mouthfeel. Well made.*	**£18.60** ICL/ENO NYW

A AMARONE DELLA VALPOLICELLA 2001, ALPHA ZETA **Veneto** – Raisin, fig, and Christmas cake nose. Ripe sultanas and red plums. Invigorating mint notes.	£19.70 CCS/FLY LIB/NYW VLW
AMARONE CLASSICO DELLA VALPOLICELLA DOMINI VENETI 2001, CANTINA VALPOLICELLA NEGRAR **Veneto** – Sharp, lifted redcurrant, roast coffee, and earth notes. Dense, smoky blueberry fruit and smooth, mouthcoating texture.	£20.00 WRK
AMARONE DELLA VALPOLICELLA CLASSICO 1999, FRATELLI BOLLA **Veneto** – Long and deep, with chocolate, caramel, and a port-like palate of Morello cherry fruit. Brisk tannins. Mature.	£20.40 RAV
AMARONE DELLA VALPOLICELLA FALASCO 2001, CANTINA SOCIALE DELLA VALPANTENA **Veneto** – Tinned cherries and raisins meld with ginger. Smoothly textured, with elegant coconut oak flavours.	£22.70 FLA/DEF ENO
AMARONE DELLA VALPOLICELLA CLASSICO 1998, CORTEFORTE **Veneto** – Black cherries and chocolate nose. Fresh and bright, with herbal notes, spices, and red plum flavours.	£26.30 SWG/P&S SMC
SEREGO ALIGHIERI VAIO ARMARON AMARONE 1999, MASI AGRICOLA **Veneto** – Rich prune and fig aromas and savoury overtones. Grippy, with coffee, herb, and chocolate flavours.	£28.00 BWC/NYW
LA POJA 2000, ALLEGRINI **Veneto** – Brick-black. Fabulous cocoa powder and black plum nose. Grainy tannins and chocolatey fruit.	£39.60 WIDELY AVAILABLE

B R O N Z E°
VENETO + NORTHEAST RED

SARTORI VIGNETI DI MONTEGRADELLA VALPOLLICELLA CLASSICO 2002, SARTORI **Veneto** – Milk chocolate aromas. Freshly baked pain au chocolate and black cherry jam flavours.	£6.00 TOS/WAV
AMARONE DELLA VALPOLICELLA NINFEO 2002, CANTINA SOCIALE DELLA VALPANTENA **Veneto** – Obvious wood ageing and cocoa butter notes on the nose are offset with ripe plum fruit on the palate.	£7.50 ENO

ASDA EXTRA SPECIAL VALPOLICELLA RIPASSO 2001, MARCO DELL'EVA VENETO – *Cheerful red fruit, warm cinnamon, and creamy chocolate flavours make this an easy wine to enjoy.*	**£8.00** ASD
BRICCOLO MERLOT 2003, BIDOLI FRIULI-VENEZIA GIULIA – *Brisk tannins buttress the palate of damson fruit. Mouthwatering, firm, and aromatic.*	**£8.00** WST
REGOLO, SARTORI 2001, SARTORI VENETO – *Soft and tart with a bitter almond note on the restrained, balanced palate. Refreshing.*	**£9.00** WAV/THS
MARA VALPOLICELLA CLASSICO VINO DA RIPASSO 2002, CESARI VENETO – *Grated nutmeg, white pepper powder, and delicate tobacco notes scent the nose. Luscious cherry palate.*	**£9.30** AFI
MERLOT ISONZO 2003, I FEUDI DI ROMANS FRIULI-VENEZIA GIULIA – *Bright, ripe black cherry flavours permeate the young, grippy, elegant palate. Long.*	**£9.50** V&C/LIB
CAMPOFIORIN 2002, MASI AGRICOLA VENETO – *Light crimson colour with crisp raspberry and strawberry flavours and a real crunch to the finish.*	**£10.70** TRO
AMARONE DELLA VALPOLICELLA VIA NOVA 2002, CANTINA SOCIALE DELLA VALPANTENA VENETO – *Caramel and nuts on the nose. Packed with red fruit and dark chocolate flavours. Very rich and robust.*	**£11.00** ENO
BROLO DI CAMPOFIORIN 2000, MASI AGRICOLA SPA VENETO – *Crisp cranberry fruit on the nose is matched with a refreshing swish of acidity on the palate.*	**£12.00** BWC
AMARONE DELLA VALPOLICELLA TERRE DI VERONA 2002, CANTINA SOCIALE DELLA VALPANTENA VENETO – *High alcohol and chestnut flavours mark this wine out as classic Amarone. One for the connoisseur.*	**£15.00** ENO
AMARONE CLASSICO 2001, TEDESCHI VENETO – *A distinctive aroma of roast chestnuts on the nose. Warm chocolate-covered red fruit palate.*	**£18.50** BNK/MW W

AMARONE DELLA VALPOLICELLA CLASSICO 2001, CESARI Veneto – *Plum, spice, chocolate, and coffee nose and palate. Smoothly textured and very long, with farmyard notes.*	£19.50 AFI
AMARONE DELLA VALPOLICELLA CLASSICO LE ORIGINI 1999, FRATELLI BOLLA Veneto – *Delicate savoury tones, robust tannins, and firm blackberry flavours. Liquorice, fruitcake, coconut, and prune scents.*	£20.00 BRF
AMARONE DELLA VALPOLICELLA CLASSICO 1999, ALLEGRINI Veneto – *Rich yet fresh, with cranberry, graphite and cloves. The gamey prune flesh has a mouthcoating texture.*	£33.40 NEC/POR RSV/FLY WRW/VLW
BOSAN VALPOLICELLA SUPERIORE RIPASSO 2001, CESARI Veneto – *Cocoa powder, raisin, and violet scents. Intensely ripe red cherry flavours. Silky, and very well made.*	£40.00 V&C

SEAL OF APPROVAL
VENETO + NORTHEAST RED

☆ **CORTE VIGNA MERLOT DELLE VENEZIE 2004, ENOITALIA** Veneto – *Hints of spicewood hover over raspberry fruit.*	£3.40 MCT
☆ **GAVIOLI CABERNET SAUVIGNON NV, DONELLI VINI** Veneto – *Bright cherry, tobacco, and cinnamon nuances.*	£4.00 KWI
☆ **SOMERFIELD MERLOT DELLE VENEZIE 2002, DONELLI VINI** Veneto – *Bright red plum flavours laced with herbs.*	£4.00 SMF

BRONZE
VENETO + NORTHEAST SPARKLING

☆ **PROSECCO DE CONEGLIANO CUVÉE EXTRA DRY NV, CARPENE MALVOLTI** Veneto – *Delicate bitter almond notes mingle with wild herbs and white flowers. The palate froths with pear juice flavour.*	£8.70 BNK/FRW

☆ QUARTESE NV, RUGGERI **Veneto** – *Persistent bubbles. Apple cinnamon flavours and scents. Dry, refreshing, and enjoyable.*	£9.20 V&C/ENO

SEAL OF APPROVAL
VENETO + NORTHEAST SPARKLING

☆ GANCIA PINOT DI PINOT NV, GANCIA **Trentino-Alto Adige** – *Textured and soft. Green and white fruit flavours.*	£6.00 FXT
☆ GANCIA PROSECCO NV, GANCIA **Veneto** – *Vibrant citrus and pear flavours. Almond hints.*	£6.00 UNW
☆ VESPAIOLO FRIZZANTE DEL VENETO NV, B BARTOLOMEO DA BREGANZE **Veneto** – *Vespe, or wasps, are attracted to these honeyed, aromatic sweet grapes - hence their name, Vespaiolo.*	£6.00 LAI
☆ PROSECCO DI VALDOBBIADENE SPUMANTE EXTRA DRY NV, LA GIOIOSA **Veneto** – *Bitter almond, pear drops, and sweet flowers.*	£7.00 TOS

GOLD
VENETO + NORTHEAST SWEET

☆ VIGNETI DI MORON RECIOTO DELLA VALPOLICELLA DOMINI VENETI 2003, CANTINA VALPOLICELLA NEGRAR **Veneto** – *Sweet sundried red cherries and nutmeg. Red stone fruit and sultanas fill the mouth.*	£15.00 WRK

TROPHY
TUSCANY + CENTRAL WHITE

☆ LE VELE VERDICCHIO DEI CASTELLI DI JESI CLASSICO 2004, MONCARO **The Marches** – *Impeccably balanced with grass, melon, and hyacinth aromas. Clean palate with lovely white fruit purity and fine mineral structure.*	£6.90 EUW/THS NYW

GOLD
TUSCANY + CENTRAL WHITE

☆ VERDE DI CA' RUPTAE VERDICCHIO DEI CASTELLI DI JESI CLASSICO 2003, MONCARO THE MARCHES – *Notes of grass, lemon, and almond. A fine balance of ripe white fruit and piercing mineral acidity.*	£10.00 EUW

SILVER
TUSCANY + CENTRAL WHITE

☆ SAUVIGNON DELL'EMILIA 2004, AZIENDA AGRICOLA BASSI EMILIA ROMAGNA – *Crisp, clear, and aromatic, with a fragrance of freesia, candied citrus, and honey. Apple and gooseberry flavours.*	£7.50 FWI
VERNACCIA DI SAN GIMIGNANO FIORE 2003, MONTENIDOLI TUSCANY – *Powdered minerals and lemons. Expressive, herbal palate, with an oily texture and restrained, medium-bodied flesh.*	£10.00 FLY
TRALIVIO VERDICCHO DEI CASTELLI DI JESI CLASSICO 2003, SARTARELLI THE MARCHES – *Almond blossom, crisp apple fruit, and a light nutty aftertaste make this wine stand out. Classic Verdicchio.*	£10.50 ATM
VERDICCHIO DEI CASTELLI DI JESI CLASSICO CONTRADA BALCIANA 2003, SARTARELLI THE MARCHES – *Refreshing lemon and lime flavours. Although this wine is light-bodied, it still has a substantial presence.*	£19.00 ATM

BRONZE
TUSCANY + CENTRAL WHITE

VILLA MASETTI PINOT GRIGIO 2004, TENIMENTI ASSOCIATI UMBRIA – *Greengages, lime zest, and ripe lemons grace this refreshing, light-bodied wine. Just the thing with white fish dishes.*	£5.50 LAI
BARBI ARCHE ORVIETO 2004, BARBI UMBRIA – *Delicate minerality, a handful of flowers and marzipan. The palate has fresh pear drop and nutmeg flavours.*	£10.00 PLB

NOVALI VERDICCHIO DEI CASTELLI DI JESI CLASSICO RISERVA 2001, MONCARO **The Marches** – *Aromas of orange blossom and almonds. Vibrant fruit and subtle creaminess. Long elegant finish.*	**£10.00** EUW/NYW

TROPHY
TUSCANY + CENTRAL RED

VILLA CAFAGGIO SAN MARTINO 2001, BASILICA CAFAGGIO **Tuscany** – *The talented Stefano Farkas and team have created a graceful, elegant, chocolatey Chianti. Fine aromatics. Excellent balance.*	**£28.00** HWL/VLW

GOLD
TUSCANY + CENTRAL RED

☆ SOVESTRO ROSSO DI SAN GIMIGNANO 2003, BARONCINI **Tuscany** – *Uplifted, perfumed floral notes. Red stone fruits, tobacco, wet earth, and prunes. Very long, with notes of smoke.*	**£7.60** LAI
☆ AMARASCO 2003, PRINCIPE PALLAVICINI **Lazio** – *Appassimento Cesanese grapes. Honey, fruitcake, and rose petal scents rise from this unctuous, intoxicating wine.*	**£8.00** THI
☆ BASILICA CAFAGGIO CHIANTI CLASSICO 2003, BASILICA CAFAGGIO **Tuscany** – *The bouquet sings with plums and juniper. Packed with mouthwatering cherries, tree bark and earth.*	**£10.50** M&S/VLW
CASTELLO DI FONTERUTOLI CHIANTI CLASSICO 2003, FONTERUTOLI **Tuscany** – *Black cherries, undergrowth, roast coffee beans, hazelnuts, and charred wood. Pine and cypress notes.*	**£16.90** FHM/V&C ENO/NYW P&S/VLW
AVVOLTORE 2001, MORIS FARMS **Tuscany** – *Ink, tar, and blackberries; coffee, bark, and leather. Harmonious, balanced, and finely knit. Fine cherry flavours.*	**£23.40** C&B/JNW
PELAGO MARCHE ROSSO 2001, UMANI RONCHI **The Marches** – *Cocoa powder, toast, pepper, and clove. Dense leather, espresso, tobacco, and plums. Stylish.*	**£26.10** V&C/ICL ENO/VLW

VIGNA DEL SORBO CHIANTI CLASSICO RISERVA 2001, FONTODI Tuscany – *Game, leather, smoke, blueberries, cherries, charred wood, and steak characteristics.*	**£28.60** POR/V&C BEN/FLY LIB/VLW
NERONE ROSSO CONERO RISERVA 2001, MONCARO The Marches – *Sun-warmed ripe red cherry fruit. Toasted almonds, coal, bay leaves, toast, vanilla, and minerals. Powerful and warming.*	**£29.50** EUW/NYW

SILVER
TUSCANY + CENTRAL RED

☆ SOLO SHIRAZ 2003, CANTINA SAN MARCO Lazio – *Deep, deep, fathoms deep. Sweet and sour, plummy and spicy; the meaty textured fruit finishes on a long dry note.*	**£4.80** MCT
☆ PICCOLO DEMONIO SANGIOVESE 2003, TENUTE DE ANGELIS The Marches – *Ripe and dry, with a deep, youthful well of lively blackberry fruit, cloves, cardamom pods and pine.*	**£6.00** VGN
☆ MONTEPULCIANO D'ABRUZZO RUBINO 2002, CANTINA TOLLO Abruzzi – *Clear, deep ruby-purple. Crunchy blackcurrant fruit, scents of tea leaves and ink, and a youthful, brooding finish.*	**£7.00** RAV
JORIO 2002, UMANI RONCHI Abruzzi – *Inky black vine fruit and silky oak nose. Fresh acidity adds lift to the polished, full, youthful palate. Long.*	**£9.00** ENO/VLW
CHIANTI CLASSICO CONTESSA DI RADDA 2002, GEOGRAFICO Tuscany – *Morello cherries, red plums, animal, and haystack characteristics parade across this complex, persistent wine.*	**£10.20** AFI
CHIANTI CLASSICO CASTELLO DI QUERCETO RISERVA 2000, CASTELLO DI QUERCETO Tuscany – *Raspberry red. Stylish allspice, bay leaves, and wild herbs nose. Attractive bitter cherry flavours and taut tannins.*	**£10.30** COE
SAVIGNOLA PAOLINA CHIANTI CLASSICO 2003, SAVIGNOLA PAOLINA Tuscany – *Pronounced herby intensity. Charred wood, cherries, prunes, marjoram, and warm earth. Very fine.*	**£11.00** SKB

VALDIFALCO 2003, LOACKER Tuscany – *Raspberry compote, cherry cola, cinnamon, and cloves scent the nose. The palate is supple and long.*	**£11.00** GRT
MORELLINO DI SCANSANO LOHSA 2003, POLIZIANO Tuscany – *Savoury notes of the barnyard. Youthful cassis nose. Earth, sweet coconut, strawberries, and nutmeg. Long and vivid.*	**£11.70** ICL/ENO
CHIANTI CLASSICO SELVE SCURE 2001, CAGGIO Tuscany – *Spicy, clear, and deep, with an Assam tea nose and a fine-grained palate of cherry fruit. Minerals and cedar.*	**£12.50** TWL
PIOCAIA SAN FABIANO 2001, SAN FABIANO Tuscany – *Liquorice, tobacco, nutmeg, and cinnamon. Plenty of redcurrant and blueberry fruit. Smoothly textured and herbal.*	**£13.00** AVB
ROSSO DI MONTALCINO 2003, TENUTA IL POGGIONE Tuscany – *Elegant, firm, and long, with a clear, soft attack of sultanas, blackberries, and wild herbs. Balanced and structured.*	**£14.00** ENO
LIANO SANGIOVESE CABERNET SAUVIGNON 2002, UMBERTO CESARI Emilia Romagna – *Leather, pine cones, and wild game scent this wine. Savoury coffee oak and moist earth notes. Black cherry flavours.*	**£16.00** AVB
ROSSO DI MONTALCINO 2003, POGGIO SAN POLO Tuscany – *Dried fruit, stony minerals, and soft sultry oak. Coffee, blackberries, liquorice, and spice. Ripe and persistent.*	**£16.40** CCS/BEN FLY/LIB VLW
VILLA CAFAGGIO CHIANTI CLASSICO RISERVA 2001, BASILICA CAFAGGIO Tuscany – *Blackcurrants, mulling spices, pine needles, stewed prunes, and black plums are all evident.*	**£16.50** HWL/VLW
VINO NOBILE DI MONTEPULCIANO 2002, AZIENDA AGRICOLA POLIZIANO Tuscany – *Lavish Morello cherries, mocha, roast herbs, and cinnamon. Persistent and stylish.*	**£16.60** V&C/ENO NYW
SANTO IPPOLITO 2002, CANTINE LEONARDO Tuscany – *Juicy, ripe, and elegant. Sweet oak and plum fruit nose. Alluring red and black stone fruit.*	**£19.70** CCS/FLY LIB/VLW

VINO NOBILE DI MONTEPULCIANO SIMPOSIO 2001, TENIMENTI ANGELINI TUSCANY – *Tea leaf, bonfire, and creosote aromas. Mature black cherries on nose and palate. Chocolate oak smoothness.*	**£21.00** H&H
MONTIANO 2001, FALESCO UMBRIA – *An attack of bright, full, cedary raspberry jam. Peppery, integrated, and soft.*	**£23.00** BWC
BRUNELLO DI MONTALCINO 2000, POGGIARELLINO TUSCANY – *Amber-hued, mature, aromatic, and old school, with clear tobacco and fruitcake aromas. Crunchy, savoury fruit.*	**£25.00** SKB
VIGNETO RANCIA CHIANTI CLASSICO RISERVA 2001, FELSINA TUSCANY – *Cherry stones, minerals, plums, and a tangle of undergrowth. Some evolution is apparent. Austere, elegant, and polished.*	**£27.00** POR/LIB

BRONZE
TUSCANY + CENTRAL RED

CONVIVIO MONTEPULCIANO D'ABRUZZO 2003, ADRIA VINI ABRUZZI – *A supple red with good fruit flavours, plenty of tannins and a swish of acidity all in balance.*	**£5.30** MDN/ICL
IL FAGIANO DUE NV, BOVE ABRUZZI – *A cheerful red, with juicy cherry fruit, fresh acidity, and ripe, integrated tannins in all the right places.*	**£5.50** AVB
MONTEPULCIANO D'ABRUZZO 2004, CASA GIRELLI ABRUZZI – *This crisp red is rounded out by a milk chocolate undertone and a long, sweetly ripe finish.*	**£5.80** TPE
SANGIOVESE DI ROMAGNA 2002, UMBERTO CESARI EMILIA ROMAGNA – *Attractive sweet vanilla and red stone fruit. Crisp, mouthwatering, and very fresh. Brisk tannins.*	**£6.00** AVB
SENSI CHIANTI RISERVA 2001, FRATELLI SENSI TUSCANY – *Mature, with figgy notes, chocolate, and lean raspberry fruit. A gracefully ageing Chianti.*	**£6.50** CTL

SAN FABIANO CHIANTI 2003, SAN FABIANO Tuscany – *Dense and smoky. The sultry palate has fresh red stone fruit and rich chocolate flavours.*	**£7.00** AVB
SERRANO ROSSO CONERO 2004, UMANI RONCHI **The Marches** – *Bright, fresh, medium-bodied red cherry flesh and sweetly fragrant floral notes. Balanced and refreshing.*	**£7.00** ENO
SOMERFIELD CHIANTI CLASSICO VILLA PRIMAVERA 2000, GRUPPO ITALIANO VINI Tuscany – *A pleasing Chianti with plenty of red cherry fruit, firm woody tannins, and fresh acidity.*	**£7.00** SMF
CHIANTI CLASSICO CASTELGREVE L'ESSENZIALE 2003, CASTELLI DEL GREVEPESA Tuscany – *Fresh and youthful with great cherry flavours. The integrated tannin structure is in good harmony with the fruit.*	**£7.80** CTL
MONTEPULCIANO D'ABRUZZO BUCARO 2003, VOLPI **Abruzzi** – *This wine is reminiscent of cherry pie, its red fruit and vanilla oak notes in harmony.*	**£8.00** VER
VITIANO 2003, FALESCO Umbria – *Mulberry, plum, and bittersweet chocolate flavours. The nose is herbaceous with inkwell aromas.*	**£8.00** BWC
GEOGRAFICO CHIANTI CLASSICO 2003, GEOGRAFICO Tuscany – *Great personality and quality. Liquorice, rubber, and dark fruit flavours lifted by a slick of acidity.*	**£8.70** AFI
LACRIMA DI MORRO D'ALBA 2004, MONTE SCHIAVO **The Marches** – *Beautifully rustic with sweet herbs underpinned by earthy aromas. Rich and wonderfully pleasing.*	**£9.00** BWC
ROSSO DI MONTEPULCIANO 2004, POLIZIANO Tuscany – *The vivid black cherry fruit is supported by firm, fine-grained tannins and sprinkled with coaldust.*	**£9.60** V&C/JSM ENO/NYW
CIMERIO ROSSO CONERO RISERVA 2002, MONCARO **The Marches** – *Ripe, concentrated, weighty, and structured. The inky bramble fruit has silky tannins and delicate vanilla spice.*	**£10.00** EUW

ORNELLAIA LE VOLTE 2003, TENUTA DELL'ORNELLAIA Tuscany – *Real finesse on the nose and palate of this wine. Crisp and fragrant with a long finish.*	**£10.00** JAR
CAMPO CENI 2003, BARONE RICASOLI Tuscany – *Black tea, strawberry jam, and buttered burnt toast make this wine a lip-smacking delight.*	**£10.50** FLA/ENO
PESANO MERLOT 2003, FALESCO Umbria – *Powerful yet austere, with herbal nuances on the nose and a mouthful of little black plums.*	**£10.50** BWC
VILLA CAFAGGIO CHIANTI CLASSICO 2003, BASILICA CAFAGGIO Tuscany – *Fruit, tar, and liquorice on the nose and palate, with an underpinning of assertive tannins. One to watch.*	**£11.10** TPE/VLW
CHIANTI RISERVA 2002, CANTINE LEONARDO Tuscany – *A warm and wooded wine with notes of Darjeeling tea, rich black cherries, and refreshing acidity.*	**£11.40** POR/CCS FLY/LIB VLW
CHIANTI CLASSICO RISERVA MONTEGIACHI 2001, GEOGRAFICO Tuscany – *One to drink this holiday. Lovely balance has been achieved between silky red fruit and robust tannins.*	**£12.30** AFI
ROSSO DI MONTALCINO 2003, CASTIGLION DEL BOSCO Tuscany – *Excellent fruit driven nose with hints of allspice. Good weighty palate with cooked fruit tones. Fine grip.*	**£12.50** MDN
VINO NOBILE DI MONTEPULCIANO CERRAIA 2002, GEOGRAFICO Tuscany – *Full bodied with warm fruit and violet overtones. Oak notes offset the acidity and deep ripe fruit.*	**£13.30** AFI
CAMPO DELLE MURA ROSSO PICENO SUPERIORE 2002, MONCARO The Marches – *A real Southern wine with heaps of sun ripened fruit flavours and a warm finish.*	**£14.00** EUW
CHIANTI CLASSICO IL PICCHIO RISERVA 2000, CASTELLO DI QUERCETO Tuscany – *Deeply coloured, with a textured mouthfeel, and a developed palate of cherries and leather.*	**£14.00** COE

GROSSO AGONTANO ROSSO CONERO 2001, GAROFOLI **THE MARCHES** – *Espresso, roast herbs, autumn leaves, and lush blackberry fruit. Rich and mature.*	**£14.50** HOH
VIGNETI DEL PARCO ROSSO CONERO RISERVA 2001, MONCARO THE MARCHES – *Youthful, with a linear palate of tight bramble berries and spice. Full toasty tannins support the fruit.*	**£15.00** EUW
BROLIO CHIANTI CLASSICO 2003, BARONE RICASOLI TUSCANY – *Fresh clean fruit with an edge of spiciness and a hint of oak which rounds off the palate.*	**£16.10** V&C/EDC FLA/ENO
SAN ZIO 2002, CANTINE LEONARDO TUSCANY – *Toasty, vanilla oak in happy juxtaposition with plummy fruit and crisp acidity. A tasty wine to savour.*	**£17.00** V&C/CCS FLY/LIB VLW
NENFRO 2003, MOTTURA LAZIO – *Warm damsons and hints of violets feature on the bouquet. The palate is young, ripe, and plummy.*	**£18.00** VIN
FRABUSCO 2002, TENUTA CORINI UMBRIA – *Attractive cherry, raspberry, and plum flavours with a creamy, melting vanilla ice cream finish.*	**£20.00** FWI
TENIMENTI ANGELINI BRUNELLO DI MONTALCINO 2000, TENIMENTI ANGELINI TUSCANY – *Black cherries, bittersweet chocolate, cedar, vanilla and tar characteristics. Complex and persistent.*	**£20.00** H&H
BRUNELLO DI MONTALCINO 2000, CASTIGLION DEL BOSCO TUSCANY – *Ruby red. Mature notes are creeping in to the fresh, charged, focused cherries, and chocolate palate.*	**£22.00** MDN
MONTE SCHIAVO ADEODATO 2002, MONTE SCHIAVO THE MARCHES – *Firm red cherry and cassis flavours entwine with dark wood, chocolate, and earthy mineral aromas.*	**£22.00** BWC
VILLA DI CORSANO 2001, CANTINA DI MONTALCINO TUSCANY – *Very rich colour and complex nose. Creamy palate with herbs, spice, and floral notes. Still developing.*	**£23.00** LIB

CA'MARCANDA MAGARI 2002, GAJA Tuscany – *Creamy, ripe and smoky, with delicate cherry flavours of some complexity. Well structured and long.*	£23.50
	JAR

BRUNELLO DI MONTALCINO 2000, COLDI SOLE Tuscany – *Cedary, its nose reminiscent of claret. Vinous and polished, with a turbo-charged Morello cherry profile.*	£27.00
	MON

VILLA CAFAGGIO CORTACCIO 2001, BASILICA CAFAGGIO Tuscany – *Modern and stylish. Blackcurrant flavours entwine with woody tannins. Structured.*	£28.00
	HOT/VLW

FLACCIANELLO DELLA PIEVE 2001, FONTODI Tuscany – *A classy wine with smooth chocolate and blackcurrant flavours. Very dense and powerful.*	£33.90
	WIDELY AVAILABLE

BRUNELLO DI MONTALCINO 2000, POGGIO SAN POLO Tuscany – *Fresh, tight-knit, and modern, with lots of cherry flavours and spice notes. Juicy, firm, and attractive.*	£36.30
	WIDELY AVAILABLE

SEAL OF APPROVAL
TUSCANY + CENTRAL RED

☆ COLLEZIONE ITALIANA MONTEPULCIANO D'ABRUZZO 2003, CASA GIRELLI Abruzzi – *Prune scents enhance sweet cherry flavours.*	£2.80
	ALD

☆ MONTUPLCIANO D'ABRUZZO ROSSO 2003, FRATELLI MARTINI Abruzzi – *Black cherries flavour this robust wine.*	£3.60
	MCT

BRONZE
TUSCANY + CENTRAL SPARKLING

☆ VIGNETO ENRICO CIALDINI 2004, CANTINE CHIARLI & FIGLI Emilia Romagna – *Ruby red with foaming froth, rigid structure and soft blackberry and raspberry fruit flavours.*	£10.00
	V&C/ENO

SILVER
TUSCANY + CENTRAL SWEET

TORDIRITA VERDICCHIO DEI CASTELLI DI JESI PASSITO 2002, MONCARO THE MARCHES – *Lemon blossom, honey, roast nuts, and rich greengage fruit. White pepper and mineral hints. Long.*	**£30.00** EUW

SEAL OF APPROVAL
TUSCANY + CENTRAL FORTIFIED

☆ BARONA BIANCO NV, WSE REGIONAL BLEND – *Freshly picked pears and talc elements.*	**£3.30** MHV
☆ BARONA ROSSO NV, WSE REGIONAL BLEND – *Golden grapefruit flavours. Nutty hints.*	**£3.30** MHV

GOLD
SOUTH + THE ISLANDS WHITE

☆ SANNIO FALANGHINA 2004, VESEVO CAMPANIA – *Almighty Vesuvius lends rich minerality to this highly aromatic, exotic wine, alive with guava and grass.*	**£8.00** WIDELY AVAILABLE

SILVER
SOUTH + THE ISLANDS WHITE

☆ INYCON CHARDONNAY 2004, SETTESOLI SICILY – *A bouquet of perfumed lemon flowers. The palate has crystallised ginger and cocktail citrus fruits flavour.*	**£4.70** TOS/JSM ENO

BRONZE
SOUTH + THE ISLANDS WHITE

☆ D'ISTINTO CATARRATTO CHARDONNAY 2003, CALATRASI Sicily – *Brisk chopped almond notes mingle with fresh lemon zest and grapefruit. Acacia blossom fragrance. Structured.*	£4.50 ECA
☆ FIORILE GRENANICO 2004, CARLO PELLEGRINO Sicily – *Hints of chalky minerals score the fleshy pear and lemon fruit palate. Mouthfulling, textured, and long.*	£5.00 AVB
D'ISTINTO CHARDONNAY 2003, CALATRASI Sicily – *Intriguing capsicum and rosemary scents. Very ripe, with an intense attack of lemons and oranges.*	£6.00 ECA
TERRE DI GINESTRA CATARRATTO 2003, CALATRASI Sicily – *Cashew, lemon, grapefruit, and ripe pineapple aromas and flavours. Sun-warmed and satisfying.*	£7.60 MCT
VESEVO GRECO DI TUFO 2004, VESEVO Campania – *Robust, vivid, and full. Intense ripe lemon, mandarin orange, crushed pumice stone, and red honeysuckle characteristics.*	£10.10 WIDELY AVAILABLE
RADICI FIANO DI AVELLINO 2003, MASTROBERARDINO Campania – *Delicate flowers and intense minerals scent the nose. The palate has sturdy honeyed citrus flavours.*	£11.00 BWC

GOLD
SOUTH + THE ISLANDS RED

☆ VIRTUOSO SYRAH SICILIA 2002, CASA GIRELLI Sicily – *Sweetly perfumed with blueberry jam, quince, and leather. Massive fruit concentration, big tannins, and sweet vanilla oak.*	£10.00 VLW

SILVER
SOUTH + THE ISLANDS RED

★ PRIMITIVO SALENTO 2003, CANTINE DUE PALME **PUGLIA** – *Brooding red strawberry and loganberry nose. Deep, complex blackberry fruit and a plethora of cedary tannins.*	£6.00 RDS
☆ SQUINZANO ROSSO 2003, CANTINE DUE PALME **PUGLIA** – *Very sweet, fully ripe blackberries, coal, and prune scents. The palate is muscular, with toast and cinnamon bark notes.*	£6.00 L&T
☆ LUSIO NERO D'AVOLA 2003, VULCANIA **SICILY** – *Truffles, bittersweet chocolate, persimmons, and blackberries. Toast, sweet liquorice, and vanilla. Meaty, yet elegant.*	£7.00 LIB
TERRAGNOLO PRIMITIVO SALENTO 2001, APOLLONIO **PUGLIA** – *Strawberry, graphite, ink, and undergrowth scents. Packed with glossy red stone fruit and creosote undercurrents.*	£8.10 TNG/OCM CCS/JSM
SELVAROSSA SALICE SALENTINO ROSSO RISERVA 2001, CANTINE DUE PALME **PUGLIA** – *Violet-black. Roast nuts, baked plums, minerals, and flowers. Big, port-like, and weighty. Earthy and spicy.*	£8.50 CTL/V&C
VIRTUOSO PRIMITIVO PUGLIA 2003, CASA GIRELLI **PUGLIA** – *Tobacco, tea leaves, cherries, and freshly ground pepper. Supported by a powerful tannic backbone.*	£10.00 ODD/VLW
AVULISI NERO D'AVOLA SICILIA 2003, SANTA TRESA **SICILY** – *Madagascar vanilla and coconut nose. The black cherry palate is intense, balanced, and full.*	£10.50 AMP/VLW
PIERRE DELLE VIGNE 2000, BOTROMAGNO **PUGLIA** – *Dark chocolate, charred wood, cloves, and sultanas. Smoky, savoury cherries and cranberries. Grippy and structured.*	£10.50 ENO
DIVOTO COPERTINO 2000, APOLLONIO **PUGLIA** – *Highly spiced and rich. Big, its sweetly ripe fruit possessing a bracing mineral backbone.*	£12.40 TNG/OCM CCS

ALGHERO ROSSO CAGNULARI 2003, SANTA MARIA LA PALMA **Sardinia** – *Dry, highly original, delicately spiced red with a medium-full body, vanilla and liquorice hints and a long finish.*	**£13.50** MON
IL GRAVELLO 2001, LIBRANDI **Calabria** – *Blackcurrants, sweet oak, and crushed bay leaves. Rich, fresh, and long. Littered with tobacco leaf tannins.*	**£18.80** V&C/EDC ENO
VESEVO TAURASI 2000, VESEVO **Campania** – *Rich, spicy, and aromatic, with soft, mature strawberry and raspberry flavours and perfume of violets.*	**£20.20** CCS/FLY ICL/LIB

B R O N Z E
SOUTH + THE ISLANDS RED

☆ TENUTE AL SOLE NEGROAMARO 2003, CANTINE DUE PALME **Puglia** – *Sturdy tannins and well ripened black fruit are balanced with refreshing acidity on the finish.*	**£4.50** CTL
☆ INYCON MERLOT 2004, SETTESOLI **Sicily** – *Beautiful crimson red colour. Intense ripe sugar plum flavours line the palate.*	**£4.70** TOS/ENO
☆ ANCORA BENEVENTANO ROSSO 2003, ADRIA VINI **Campania** – *A well balanced wine with prominent acidity that is well matched with crunchy cranberry and red apple fruit.*	**£4.90** MDN/DEF
☆ BRINDISI ROSSO 2003, CANTINE DUE PALME **Puglia** – *Robust flavours, sturdy tannins, and balanced acidity combine in this masculine, pleasing wine.*	**£5.00** CTL
☆ TERRANTO PRIMITIVO 2003, CANTINE DUE PALME **Puglia** – *Autumnal forest fruits, lilacs, and pepper on the nose. The palate is dense and flavourful, with lingering flavours.*	**£5.00** CTL
VILLA TONINO NERO D'AVOLA 2003, VILLA TONINO **Sicily** – *Heaps of cherry fruit, balanced tannins, and refreshing acidity. Drinking well now.*	**£5.50** AWO/FLY LIB/NYW

MARKS & SPENCER MANDORLA SYRAH 2003, MGM **SICILY** – *Sweet plum and leather scents make way for smoothly textured black fruit. Balanced and clean.*	£6.00 WST
SALICE SALENTINO ROSSO 2003, CANTINE DUE PALME **PUGLIA** – *Drying tannins. The wood influence is softened by ripe summer fruit with a sun-kissed finish.*	£6.00 UNS
VIGNA FLAMINIO ROSSO BRINDISI 2001, AGRICOLE VALLONE **PUGLIA** – *Black cherries, hay, fragrant flowers, and earth scent and flavour this full-bodied wine.*	£6.00 FHM/TRO MDN/WRK DEF
VARIUS SALENTO 2002, CÀNTELE **PUGLIA** – *The tarry, full flavoured wine has light cassis and black cherry flavours galore. Characterful and dark.*	£7.00 WAV
AMATIVO SALENTO 2001, CÀNTELE **PUGLIA** – *Tertiary aromas of leather and tobacco are evident on this maturing wine. Flavours of red and black berries.*	£8.00 WAV
BENEVENTANO AGLIANICO 2004, VESEVO **CAMPANIA** – *Deep red cherry flavours. The palate is juicy, concentrated, and supple, with lifted herbal notes. Long.*	£8.00 V&C/CCS FLY/ICL WRK
TERESA MANARA ROSSO SALENTO 2002, CÀNTELE **PUGLIA** – *This powerful beast blackens the teeth but its juicy fruit and spicy undertone makes it all worthwhile.*	£8.00 WAV
CERASUOLO DI VITTORIA 2004, SANTA TRESA **SICILY** – *Attractive sweet rose blossom, violet, and cherry nose. Mouthfilling, the red fruity flesh is buttressed by tannins.*	£8.50 HWL/VLW
SEGRETA ROSSO 2004, PLANETA **SICILY** – *Earth, cinnamon, ripe sweet red damsons, and blueberries. Balanced, youthful, and very fresh.*	£8.60 V&C/EDC JNW/DEF ENO/VLW
SELVAROSSA SALICE SALENTINO ROSSO RISERVA 2001, CANTINE DUE PALME **PUGLIA** – *Ripe, mature, and packed with flavour. A full-bodied, structured wine with red and black berry flavours.*	£8.80 L&T

SALICE SALENTINO RISERVA 2001, TAURINO Puglia – *Full-bodied wine with a deep colour, vigorous dark fruit, and plenty of tannins and acidity.*	£9.50 CAB
ALLORA PRIMITIVO 2003, CALATRASI Puglia – *A rustic Gypsy wine with hedgerow fruit and herbs in an exuberant mix. Perfect with rabbit stew.*	£10.00 WPR
CARATO VENUSIO AGLIANICO DEL VULTURE 2001, CANTINA DI VENOSA Basilicata – *An intriguing aroma of melting tarmac and sweet roses entices the taster. Robust bittersweet palate.*	£10.00 WAV
RADICI TAURASI 2001, MASTROBERARDINO Campania – *Deep, bittersweet chocolate, violet, and prune aromas. The black and red vine fruits are balanced with savoury appeal.*	£19.00 BWC

SILVER
SOUTH + THE ISLANDS SWEET

GRAVISANO 2000, BOTROMAGNO Puglia – *Rich and sticky, with a heady beeswax and roast nut nose. Honeydew melon and pretty notes of ginger and nutmeg.*	£16.00 ENO

GOLD
SOUTH + THE ISLANDS FORTIFIED

☆ MARSALA SUPERIORE SECCO NV, CARLO PELLEGRINO Sicily – *Roast almonds, barley sugar, and quince nose. Golden apples, raisins, and burnt sugar scored by tree bark tannins.*	£8.00 AVB

SILVER
SOUTH + THE ISLANDS FORTIFIED

★ MARSALA SUPERIORE GARIBALDI DOLCE NV, CARLO PELLEGRINO Sicily – *Pungent creosote, lemon, and hay aromas. The palate is crammed with tangy citrus, walnuts, coffee, and brown sugar.*	£7.00 TRO

NEW ZEALAND

It is a curious fact that we are now happy to spend more on a bottle of New Zealand wine than on one from anywhere else. These – relatively – high prices are justified by the quality of the Kiwi wines. All of the wines listed here won medals, including no fewer than twelve golds. Interestingly, while most of the top awards went to the Sauvignon Blanc, the variety with which New Zealand is most closely associated, recognition was also given to Chardonnay, Riesling, Pinot Noir, and Syrah. Of the fifty-eight red, white, and rosé gold and silver-medal winning wines, forty-one were sealed with screwcaps. Nowhere has embraced these closures with greater enthusiasm.

TROPHY
NEW ZEALAND WHITE

★ SILENI CELLAR SELECTION SAUVIGNON BLANC 2004, SILENI ESTATES MARLBOROUGH – *Bright young gooseberries scent the nose. The palate is fresh, with crystal-clear green berries, minerals, and white orchard blossom.*	**£9.40** NZH/RSS

GOLD
NEW ZEALAND WHITE

☆ JACKSON ESTATE SAUVIGNON BLANC 2004, JACKSON ESTATE MARLBOROUGH – *Grass, passion-fruit, and understated mango dance on the tropical palate, whilst fine minerals and flowers scent the nose.*	**£9.20** NZH/MW W TAN/JSM
☆ MUD HOUSE SAUVIGNON BLANC 2004, MUD HOUSE WINE COMPANY MARLBOROUGH – *A bright gooseberry and elderflower nose. Beautifully focused, with sharp fruit underpinned by a fine line of mineral acidity.*	**£9.50** WIDELY AVAILABLE
☆ THE LODGE CHARDONNAY 2004, SILENI ESTATES HAWKE'S BAY – *The palate is filled with bright, ripe, juicy citrus which integrates beautifully with sweet vanilla pod and nutmeg flavours imparted by silky oak. Powerfully flavoured.*	**£12.00** NZH/RSS

CABLE BAY CHARDONNAY 2002, CABLE BAY **AUCKLAND** – *Heavy, green-gold flesh on a framework* *of balanced acidity. Tangy mouthwatering lemon, starfruit,* *and artichoke heart flavours.*	**£13.20** TNG/NZH RAV/NYW SWS
GIMBLETT ROAD CHARDONNAY 2002, TRINITY HILL **HAWKE'S BAY** – *Golden pear, pineapple, and lemon fruit scored* *with clove, cinnamon, and nutmeg. A weighty, concentrated,* *sumptuous wine.*	**£15.00** NZH

SILVER
NEW ZEALAND WHITE

☆ MATUA VALLEY MARLBOROUGH SAUVIGNON BLANC 2004, MATUA VALLEY **MARLBOROUGH** – *A* *herbaceous nose with mange-tout perfumes. Soft palate* *with baked apples and some exotic fruit.*	**£7.00** TOS
☆ SHINGLE PEAK MARLBOROUGH SAUVIGNON BLANC 2004, MATUA VALLEY **MARLBOROUGH** – *An intense* *nose of green pepper and spice. Concentrated and fresh, with* *honey and mineral notes.*	**£7.00** JSM
SHINGLE PEAK SAUVIGNON BLANC 2004, MATUA VALLEY **MARLBOROUGH** – *Fresh pea pods, lemon zest,* *and kaffir lime leaves on nose and palate. Exotic, focused,* *and bursting with flavour.*	**£7.00** WFB
☆ STONELEIGH CHARDONNAY 2003, STONELEIGH **MARLBOROUGH** – *Very ripe, clear, and full of perfumed Sicilian* *lemon fruit. Delightful toasty oak and orange liqueur aromas.*	**£7.00** NZH
☆ STONELEIGH RIESLING 2003, STONELEIGH **MARLBOROUGH** – *Fresh pear, lime, and lemon flavours spring* *from the palate. The nose has delicate floral and petrol notes.*	**£7.00** NZH
☆ VIDAL ESTATE MARLBOROUGH SAUVIGNON BLANC 2004, VIDAL ESTATE **MARLBOROUGH** – *Full-bodied* *and long with abundant asparagus, citrus, and gooseberry* *flavours. A good mouth-filling wine with satisfying length.*	**£7.50** NZH/THS
AWATERE MARLBOROUGH SAUVIGNON BLANC 2004, TOHU WINES **MARLBOROUGH** – *Intense, crisp, lemon, and lime* *fruit on the nose, these flavours really come into their own on* *the palate.*	**£8.00** NDJ

DELEGAT'S RESERVE CHARDONNAY 2004, DELEGAT'S WINE ESTATE HAWKE'S BAY – *Packed with fresh pineapple and apple fruit. Intense, creamy, and nutty, with good depth and breadth.*	**£8.00** NZH
TE KAIRANGA RESERVE CHARDONNAY 2003, TE KAIRANGA WINES WAIRARAPA – *Old world elegance and admirable restraint, with delicate buttery hints and vivid yet balanced lemon fruit.*	**£8.00** NZH
SOUTHBANK ESTATE THE TERRACES SAUVIGNON BLANC 2004, SOUTHBANK ESTATE MARLBOROUGH – *Fresh with asparagus, Granny Smith apples, and grass notes, with a refreshing seam of acidity.*	**£8.20** NEC/WPR TNG/HAC NYW
MONTANA RESERVE GEWURZTRAMINER 2004, MONTANA GISBORNE – *Vivid lychee, white rose, and pear nose. A creamy palate, its ripe citrus and peach flavours smooth and soft.*	**£8.30** BNK/NZH RAV/THS
VILLA MARIA PRIVATE BIN GEWURZTRAMINER 2004, VILLA MARIA EAST COAST – *Inviting peach and ginger aromas rise from the classic nose. Delicately perfumed rose petals and stone fruits.*	**£8.50** NZH/WDI
CABLE BAY SAUVIGNON BLANC 2004, CABLE BAY MARLBOROUGH – *A youthful, spicy nose with light and subtle melon and gooseberry fruits. Fresh sherbet fruit and zingy acidity.*	**£8.80** TPE/TNG NZH/RSV RAV/SWS
MUD HOUSE WHITE SWAN RESERVE SAUVIGNON BLANC 2004, MUD HOUSE MARLBOROUGH – *A fresh apple, gooseberry, mineral style with a stoney, greenfruit nose and palate. Rounded and ripe.*	**£9.00** JNW
TE ARAI CHENIN BLANC 2004, THE MILLTON VINEYARDS GISBORNE – *Big and bursting with plums, golden apples, nettles, and spice. An aromatic, complex beauty.*	**£9.00** VER
TOHU MARLBOROUGH SAUVIGNON BLANC 2004, TOHU WINES MARLBOROUGH – *Green, crisp gooseberry fruit. A touch floral on the palate matched with crisp acidity, a firm body.*	**£9.00** HPW/NZH
WAIPARA WEST RIESLING 2002, TUTTON SIENKO & HILL CANTERBURY – *Pronounced mineral notes grace the lime juice and orchard blossom nose. Richly textured and filled with green apple flavours.*	**£9.00** WAW

SPY VALLEY GEWURZTRAMINER 2004, SPY VALLEY WINES **Marlborough** – *Rose petals, nutmeg, and cinnamon spice. The rich white and yellow fruit palate has a welcome edge of fresh acidity.*	**£9.50** BNK/CCS FLY
MARLBOROUGH SAUVIGNON BLANC 2004, WAIPARA HILLS **Marlborough** – *Plenty of gooseberry and melon fruit, with the addition of Granny Smith apple tartness and good length.*	**£9.70** NZH/TNI OZW
THE STONES SAUVIGNON BLANC 2004, CAIRNBRAE **Marlborough** – *Pungent grass and gooseberry nose and palate. A touch of sweetness rounds out the crisp acidity.*	**£10.00** TNG/NYW
DRYLANDS MARLBOROUGH SAUVIGNON BLANC 2004, DRYLANDS **Marlborough** – *The palate is full of rounded apple and gooseberry flavours. Very creamy, luscious, and long.*	**£10.20** NZH/MW W
HUNTERS RIESLING 2004, HUNTERS WINES **Marlborough** – *Honeysuckle and white fruit nose. An elegant palate of lush peach, green apple, and pear fruit.*	**£10.20** BNK/NZH LAY/NYW
MARLBOROUGH DRY RIESLING 2004, WAIPARA HILLS **Marlborough** – *Complex aromas of apricots, lychees, spicebox, lush baked apples, and honey scent the nose.*	**£10.30** NZH/OZW
SEIFRIED ESTATE CHARDONNAY 2004, SEIFRIED ESTATE **Nelson** – *Soft vanilla and spice scents mingle with pears. The white and yellow summer fruit palate is opulent and attractive.*	**£11.00** CRI
STONE CREEK MARLBOROUGH SAUVIGNON BLANC 2004, MORTON ESTATE **Marlborough** – *Less pungent than some with a gooseberry fruit character, fresh acidity, and a herbaceous character to the palate.*	**£11.50** NZH
HIGHFIELD SAUVIGNON BLANC 2004, HIGHFIELD ESTATE **Marlborough** – *Pretty gooseberry, greengage, lemon and lime flavours. The nose has fresh flowers, minerals, and nettles.*	**£11.60** NZH/BBO
SILENI THE LODGE CHARDONNAY 2002, SILENI ESATES **Hawke's Bay** – *Toast, perfumed lemons, spring blossom, and lees scent the nose. The palate is lush, weighty, and full.*	**£12.00** NZH/RSS

CRAGGY RANGE SAUVIGNON BLANC 2004, BOUTINOT **MARLBOROUGH** – *Gooseberry and passion-fruit on the nose and palate, with floral notes on the finish.*	**£12.10** NZH/ICL P&S

B R O N Z E
NEW ZEALAND WHITE

VILLA MARIA PRIVATE BIN EAST COAST CHARDONNAY 2004, VILLA MARIA EAST COAST – *Bright green-gold. Creamy lemon tart flavours and aromas of jasmine and vanilla pod. Hints of resin.*	**£5.70** BGN/NZH DEF
CO-OP EXPLORERS VINEYARD UNOAKED CHARDONNAY 2004, SAINT CLAIR ESTATE WINERY MARLBOROUGH – *Green-yellow, with all the brightness of youth. Clean, fresh, and zingy, with perfumed lemon fruit.*	**£6.50** CWS
VILLA MARIA PRIVATE BIN CHARDONNAY 2004, VILLA MARIA GISBORNE – *Ripe, with grapefruit pith flavours. Integrated and silky. Long, lavish, and full. Buttery hints.*	**£6.50** BGN/NZH WDI/THS
MONTANA SAUVIGNON BLANC 2004, MONTANA MARLBOROUGH – *A pronounced, herbaceous nose with good fruit character on the palate off-set by a subtle cut grass flavour.*	**£6.70** WIDELY AVAILABLE
OYSTER BAY CHARDONNAY 2004, OYSTER BAY WINES MARLBOROUGH – *Soft peach and pear fruit flavours tinged with vanilla. The oak enhances rather than masks the fruit.*	**£7.00** NZH/MW W JSM
SPY VALLEY SAUVIGNON BLANC 2004, SPY VALLEY WINES MARLBOROUGH – *Crunchy, freshly shelled pea flavours and scents. Brisk acidity. Scents of thyme.*	**£7.00** BWL
VILLA MARIA PRIVATE BIN RIESLING 2004, VILLA MARIA MARLBOROUGH – *Crunchy green apple and peach kernel flavours are cut by lime juice acidity. Leafy, creamy, and fleshy.*	**£7.30** BGN/NZH MWW/WD I THS/DEF
BABICH MARLBOROUGH SAUVIGNON BLANC 2004, BABICH MARLBOROUGH – *A pronounced herbaceous nose with crisp acidity on the palate and a crunchy, juicy red apple finish.*	**£7.40** PFC/NZH RSV/CNL WDI/HAC

SACRED HILL BARREL FERMENTED CHARDONNAY 2004, SACRED HILL **Hawke's Bay** – *Vanilla, butterscotch, pineapple, and papaya nose. Flavours of tarte tatin feature on the warming palate.*	£7.50 NZH
VIDAL ESTATE RIESLING 2004, VIDAL ESTATE **Marlborough** – *Pale straw coloured. A honeyed nose with some mineral character and a crisp fresh palate.*	£7.70 FHM/NZH
MONTANA RESERVE SAUVIGNON BLANC 2004, MONTANA **Marlborough** – *Crisp and zesty character, with a toasty note and supple ripe fruit. A good balance of acidity and complexity.*	£7.90 BNK/NZH RAV/JSM
GIBBSTON VALLEY RESERVE CHARDONNAY 2003, GIBBSTON VALLEY WINES **Central Otago** – *Buttery and rich, with ripe cantaloupe flavours and fresh juicy acidity. Long and spicy, with pear skin structure.*	£8.00 NZH
GIBBSTON VALLEY RESERVE CHARDONNAY 2004, GIBBSTON VALLEY WINES **Central Otago** – *A nose of pulverised spices and vanilla pods, and a palate of fresh lemonade flavours.*	£8.00 NZH
MONTANA RESERVE RIESLING 2003, MONTANA **Marlborough** – *Crunchy ripe apples, pears, pineapples, and fresh lemon flavours. Honeysuckle and pure, limpid lime fruit scents.*	£8.00 NZH
VIDAL ESTATES NATURAL FERMENT CHARDONNAY 2004, VIDAL ESTATE **hawke's Bay** – *Bright gold. Ripe, fruit-driven nose. The palate has plenty of characterful lemons and butterscotch. The finish is rich.*	£8.00 NZH
VILLA MARIA PRIVATE BIN PINOT GRIS 2004, VILLA MARIA **Marlborough** – *Luxuriant apricot and pineapple flavours permeate the palate of luscious, off-dry fruit. Enjoy with fragrant fish dishes.*	£8.00 NZH
WITHER HILLS SAUVIGNON BLANC 2004, WITHER HILLS **Marlborough** – *A sweet and fragrant nose. This sweetness is off-set by crisp acidity leading to a long finish.*	£8.40 ESL/NZH CHN/WSO VLW
GROVE MILL RIESLING 2004, GROVE MILL **Marlborough** – *Linear and vibrant, with lychee and lime zest aromas and a candlewax-textured palate of greengages and rapier acidity.*	£8.70 ESL/NZH

ESK VALLEY BLACK LABEL CHARDONNAY 2004, ESK VALLEY **Hawke's Bay** – *Round and complex, with vanilla beans and fresh lemon fruit. Lively and crisp, yet creamy.*	**£8.80** FHM/NZH FLA
GOLDWATER NEW DOG SAUVIGNON BLANC 2004, GOLDWATER ESTATE **Marlborough** – *A zingy and zesty nose and palate with a touch of sweetness which gives a good mouthfeel to this well-balanced wine.*	**£8.80** NZH/MWW NYW
SHERWOOD ESTATE RIESLING 2004, SHERWOOD ESTATE **Canterbury** – *A robust Riesling with petrol aromas, lime acidity, a viscous mouthfeel, and a long, luscious finish.*	**£9.00** NZH/CCS NYW
WAIPARA WEST SAUVIGNON BLANC 2004, TUTTON SIENKO & HILL **Canterbury** – *A young fresh and grassy style with a pungent nose and a crisp palate. Ideal with fish.*	**£9.00** WAW
GLAZEBROOK SAUVIGNON BLANC 2004, NGATARAWA WINES **Hawke's Bay** – *Vivid pea pod, nettle, freshly cut grass, and gooseberry aromas and flavours. Fine acidity and delicate herb nuances.*	**£9.10** NZH/RSV CCS/WRW
KIM CRAWFORD DRY RIESLING 2004, KIM CRAWFORD **Marlborough** – *A lovely floral and summer meadow aroma. Elegant palate with good complexity and finesse on the finish.*	**£9.10** WIDELY AVAILABLE
ESK VALLEY SAUVIGNON BLANC 2004, ESK VALLEY **South Island** – *A good intense aroma with an earthy mineral style to the spicy palate. Good length and balance of acidity.*	**£9.20** NZH/LAI
KIM CRAWFORD PINOT GRIS 2004, KIM CRAWFORD **Marlborough** – *Textured lime cordial fruit scented with white pepper and kaffir lime leaves. Vibrant and long.*	**£9.20** WIDELY AVAILABLE
VILLA MARIA RESERVE CHARDONNAY 2003, VILLA MARIA **Marlborough** – *Pale lemon yellow. Spice powder and peaches on the nose. Elegant, medium-bodied palate of green apple fruit.*	**£9.20** NZH/HAC
MARLBOROUGH RIESLING 2003, BABICH **Marlborough** – *The colour has green hints, the nose a rich honeysuckle perfume, and the palate mouthwatering honey and lime flavours.*	**£9.50** PFC/NZH WDI/HAC

SPY VALLEY PINOT GRIS 2004, SPY VALLEY WINES MARLBOROUGH – *A lively nose with hints of spice, while apples and pears fill out the palate.*	**£9.50** BNK/CCS FLY
FRAMINGHAM MARLBOROUGH SAUVIGNON BLANC 2004, FRAMINGHAM MARLBOROUGH – *An elegant and aromatic nose with a crisp, elegant palate. A lighter style perfect to drink without food.*	**£9.60** TNG/NZH
FRAMINGHAM MARLBOROUGH CLASSIC RIESLING 2004, FRAMINGHAM WINE COMPANY MARLBOROUGH – *Grapefruit, honeysuckle, orange peel, and grass aromas. This green-gold wine has dense honeydew melon and lemon flavours.*	**£9.70** TNG/NZH
CAIRNBRAE OLD RIVER RIESLING 2003, CAIRNBRAE VINEYARDS MARLBOROUGH – *Fabulous diesel aromas on the nose, reminiscent of the No 36 bus. A true Riesling that will please the connoisseur.*	**£9.80** TNG
OLD RIVER RIESLING 2004, CAIRNBRAE VINEYARDS MARLBOROUGH – *Ripe Cox's Orange Pippin apple nose. The palate has generous floral tones and a long finish.*	**£9.80** TNG
BLIND RIVER SAUVIGNON BLANC 2004, BLIND RIVER WINES MARLBOROUGH – *A tight nose leads to a good spritz of citrus fruit on the palate. Straightforward, attractive style.*	**£10.00** ODD
JUDD ESTATE CHARDONNAY 2003, MATUA VALLEY GISBORNE – *Ripe, creamy, balanced, and attractive, with a warm nose and palate of ruby grapefruit and lime.*	**£10.00** WFB/NYW
MATUA VALLEY PARETAI SAUVIGNON BLANC 2004, MATUA VALLEY MARLBOROUGH – *An assertive nose filled with asparagus notes. The palate is very full and ripe with lovely fresh acidity.*	**£10.00** WFB
MONTANA TERROIR SERIES CONDERS FORREST SAUVIGNON BLANC 2004, MONTANA MARLBOROUGH – *A pronounced nettle and herb character is matched with lively acidity, good intensity, and a rounded, crisp finish.*	**£10.00** AD1
STONELEIGH RAPAURA SERIES SAUVIGNON BLANC 2004, STONELEIGH MARLBOROUGH – *A fresh and grassy style. Very pleasant, light, easy drinking wine, perfect for summer evenings.*	**£10.00** AD1

TERROIR SERIES FESTIVAL BLOCK SAUVIGNON BLANC 2004, MONTANA Marlborough – *Bright gooseberry flavours. Fresh floral aromas. Lime cordial acidity and hints of gravelly minerals.*	**£10.00** AD1
VILLA MARIA RESERVE WAIRAU VALLEY SAUVIGNON BLANC 2004, VILLA MARIA Marlborough – *Elegant ripe wine in a light style with lovely citrus, gooseberry fruit. Good balance and length.*	**£10.70** V&C/EDC NZH/NYW
LAWSONS DRY HILLS GEWURZTRAMINER 2004, LAWSON'S DRY HILLS Marlborough – *Saturated with tropical mangosteen, white peach, and key lime flavours. Aromas of pink roses and white pepper.*	**£11.00** NEC/V&C NZH/NYW P&S
CLIFFORD BAY SAUVIGNON BLANC 2004, CLIFFORD BAY ESTATE Marlborough – *Fresh, clean, aromatic nose. Cut grass and mineral notes bring a layered complexity to the fresh palate.*	**£11.50** TNG/NZH
VILLA MARIA RESERVE CLIFFORD BAY SAUVIGNON BLANC 2004, VILLA MARIA Marlborough – *Good fruit on the nose, clearly made from well-ripened grapes. Juicy with good balance and length.*	**£12.00** ODD
CARRICK PINOT GRIS 2004, CARRICK WINES Central Otago – *White fruit glides across the palate, which is mouthcoating and spiked with white pepper.*	**£12.50** NZH/DEF VLW
VILLA MARIA SINGLE VINEYARD KELTERN CHARDONNAY 2003, VILLA MARIA Hawke's Bay – *Golden apples and warm honey nose. Soft fruit, intense oak, and creamy vanilla. Balanced, toasty, and zippy.*	**£13.00** WIM
VILLA MARIA SINGLE VINEYARD WALDRON CHARDONNAY 2003, VILLA MARIA Wairau Valley – *Elegant and light, yet saturated with citrus and white peach fruit. Should age beautifully for several years.*	**£13.00** WIM
GIBBSTON VALLEY CENTRAL OTAGO RIESLING 2004, GIBBSTON VALLEY WINES Central Otago – *Lime cordial, may flower, pear juice, and lemonade flavours. The textured flesh is seared by acidity.*	**£17.00** P&S

TROPHY
NEW ZEALAND RED

☆ DOCTORS CREEK PINOT NOIR 2003, SAINT CLAIR **MARLBOROUGH** – *The fruit is ripe and soft, with fine-grained tannins. Cherry liqueur, strawberry sorbet, and cinnamon spice flavours and scents.*	**£12.40** NFW/NZH NYW/VLW

GOLD
NEW ZEALAND RED

☆ WILD ROCK PINOT NOIR 2004, CAPRICORN WINE **WAIRARAPA** – *Vivid wild thyme and forest floor scents. Ripe strawberries dance on the textured and firmly structured palate.*	**£9.00** CPR/NZH OCM/ICL DEF/NYW
☆ VIDAL ESTATE SYRAH 2003, VIDAL ESTATE **HAWKE'S BAY** – *Blackberry scented wine showing complex notes of smoke, spice, and leather on the nose. The palate is structured with fine tannins and sweet oak supporting juicy black fruit.*	**£10.50** FHM/NZH
MONTANA ESTATES TERRACES 2003, MONTANA **MARLBOROUGH** – *Delicious scents of menthol, earth, and game. Soft cherry fruit enlivened by fine acidity and a finish with hints of game.*	**£13.00** NZH
WITHER HILLS PINOT NOIR 2003, WITHER HILLS **MARLBOROUGH** – *Aromas of summer fruits, vanilla, and tobacco. An elegant blend of red cherries, mocha, sage, and tamarind.*	**£15.10** ESL/NZH MWW/CH N VLW
VILLA MARIA RESERVE MERLOT 2002, VILLA MARIA **HAWKE'S BAY** – *Silky plum and blackberry fruit, leathery notes, and fine-grained tannins. Notes of espresso and flowers enliven the nose.*	**£16.00** CEB/NZH NYW
CLIFFORD BAY SINGLE VINEYARD PINOT NOIR 2003, CLIFFORD BAY ESTATE **MARLBOROUGH** – *Dark, brooding cherry fruit, espresso, and lifted herbal hints. Toasty oak swathes the palate of plum strawberries.*	**£17.50** TNG/NZH
MOUNT DIFFICULTY CENTRAL OTAGO PINOT NOIR 2003, MOUNT DIFFICULTY WINES **CENTRAL OTAGO** – *Stunning ginger, cinnamon, and nutmeg spice, hints of tree bark, minerals, and violets. The palate drips with fresh red cherry juice.*	**£20.30** WIDELY AVAILABLE

SILVER
NEW ZEALAND RED

MATUA VALLEY MARLBOROUGH PINOT NOIR 2004, MATUA VALLEY **Marlborough** – *An intense melange of strawberries, cinnamon, and flowers. Firm, balanced acidity and a hint of the farmyard.*	**£8.00** WFB
SHINGLE PEAK PINOT NOIR 2004, MATUA VALLEY **Marlborough** – *Strawberry jam flavours and supple, balanced tannins. Flecks of crushed black peppercorn, creamy texture, and earthy scents.*	**£8.00** WFB
BABICH WINEMAKERS RESERVE SYRAH 2002, BABICH **Hawke's Bay** – *Nutty and elegant, displaying pepper and jam with ripe, firm tannins. The texture is almost milky in character.*	**£8.70** PFC/NZH WDI/HAC
FAIRLEIGH ESTATE PINOT NOIR 2003, WITHER HILLS **Marlborough** – *Notes of tea leaves, cinnamon spice, and cherries meld on the firm, broad palate. Exceptionally well made.*	**£10.00** MWW
SPY VALLEY PINOT NOIR 2003, SPY VALLEY WINES **Marlborough** – *Sweet oak, raspberries, and violets. The palate is a layered array of spices, vanilla, smoke, black cherries, and toast.*	**£11.10** WIDELY AVAILABLE
VAVASOUR PINOT NOIR 2003, VAVASOUR **Marlborough** – *Redcurrant jelly and raspberry compôte. Fresh acidity balances the richness of the lavish fruit.*	**£12.00** C&B
ALLAN SCOTT PINOT NOIR 2003, ALLAN SCOTT WINES **Marlborough** – *Impeccably made, with vibrant blueberry, chocolate, coffee, and game aromas and flavours.*	**£12.50** NZH/CCS FLA
PALLISER ESTATE PINOT NOIR 2003, PALLISER ESTATE **Martinborough** – *Ripe and bright, with bountiful blackcurrant and raspberry fruit flavours and scents. A dark spicy wine with real appeal.*	**£13.00** TNG/NZH
RESERVE DECLARATION 2002, CJ PASK WINERY **Hawke's Bay** – *Gravel, spearmint, earth, roast herbs, and caramel on the nose. The palate is laden with ripe damson fruit.*	**£15.00** POR

VILLA MARIA RESERVE CABERNET SAUVIGNON MERLOT 2002, VILLA MARIA REGIONAL BLEND – *A velvet glassful of black cherries and caramel, its toasty nose complementing the lush, heady fruit.*	**£15.20** NZH/WDI
GRAVITAS PINOT NOIR 2004, GRAVITAS MARLBOROUGH – *Gently spicy cinnamon nose. The fresh palate has supple raspberry fruit flavours and a long, resounding finish.*	**£15.40** NZH/JNW OWL/P&S
TRINITY HILL GIMBLETT ROAD SYRAH 2001, TRINITY HILL HAWKE'S BAY – *Deep plum, cassis, herb, and vanilla aromas. A ripe attack of summer fruits with a burst of refreshing acidity.*	**£16.50** NZH
VILLA MARIA SINGLE VINEYARD TAYLORS PASS PINOT NOIR 2003, VILLA MARIA MARLBOROUGH – *Classic barnyard and floral aromas. The palate is balanced, integrated, and polished, with a pronounced flavour of strawberries.*	**£17.00** NZH/NYW
ESK VALLEY RESERVE MERLOT CABERNET SAUVIGNON MALBEC 2002, ESK VALLEY HAWKE'S BAY – *Finely-knit blackcurrants, raspberries, and spice. Dark and brooding and exhibits excellent fruit/oak balance.*	**£17.10** FHM/NZH FLA/NYW
TE KAIRANGA RESERVE PINOT NOIR 2003, TE KAIRANGA WINES MARTINBOROUGH – *Enticing cranberry and strawberry bouquet full of earth and flowers. The palate is saturated with ripe fruit.*	**£19.00** NZH
CARRICK PINOT NOIR 2003, CARRICK WINES CENTRAL OTAGO – *Youthful yet restrained, with a nose of deep, chocolate-laced mulberry fruit. Mushrooms, coffee, and plums on the palate.*	**£19.80** NZH/DEF VLW
CARRICK PINOT NOIR 2002, CARRICK WINES CENTRAL OTAGO – *Dark and full-bodied, its nose packed with black cherries and strawberries. Chocolate nuances grace the young, soft, juicy palate.*	**£20.20** NZH/P&S VLW
MOUNT DIFFICULTY SINGLE VINEYARD TARGET GULLY PINOT NOIR 2003, MOUNT DIFFICULTY CENTRAL OTAGO – *A heady nose of undergrowth, blueberries, and crushed leaves. Concentrated, fine, and balanced cherry flavours.*	**£27.80** NZH/MDW VLW

BRONZE
NEW ZEALAND RED

RESERVE CABERNET SAUVIGNON MERLOT 2004, DELEGAT'S WINE ESTATE HAWKE'S BAY – *Harmonious, gentle, ripe, and long, this beauty has lots of spice and plenty of bramble flavour.*	£8.00 MWW
SILENI ESTATES SELECTION THE TRIANGLE MERLOT 2002, SILENI ESTATES HAWKE'S BAY – *This powerful blend has leather, stone, blackberry, and flower aromas and flavours. Round and balanced.*	£8.00 RSS
STONELEIGH PINOT NOIR 2003, STONELEIGH MARLBOROUGH – *Ripe wild strawberry flavours. Scents of hot stone after summer rain. Ripe. Balanced.*	£8.00 AD1
STONELEIGH PINOT NOIR MARLBOROUGH 2003, STONELEIGH MARLBOROUGH – *Savoury notes meld with sweet bay leaves, marjoram, and dill. The palate is filled with chocolate covered cherries.*	£8.00 NZH
MONTANA PINOT NOIR 2004, MONTANA MARLBOROUGH – *A flush of redcurrants and cranberries on the palate and a nose of chocolate, cherries, and liquorice.*	£8.20 ESL/NZH
THE TERRACES MERLOT CABERNET 2002, SOUTHBANK ESTATE HAWKE'S BAY – *Developed and ready for drinking now, this wine is elegant and firm, with black cherry flavours and scents.*	£9.10 NEC/TNG
MONTANA RESERVE PINOT NOIR 2003, MONTANA MARLBOROUGH – *Pine cones and alpine strawberries on the nose. Black cherries, leaves, and dry earth on the palate.*	£9.90 TOS/NZH RAV
OYSTER BAY PINOT NOIR 2004, OYSTER BAY MARLBOROUGH – *Subtly spicy, with delicious liquorice hints and a full-bodied palate of red and black vine fruits.*	£9.90 NZH/MW W
MATUA VALLEY WAIRARAPA PINOT NOIR 2003, MATUA VALLEY WAIRARAPA – *Delicious strawberries, loam, leaves, and flowers on nose and palate. Balanced and long.*	£10.00 WFB

THE CROSSINGS ESTATE PINOT NOIR 2004, THE CROSSINGS Marlborough – *Light and lifted, with lavender and marjoram notes hovering over the succulent raspberry fruit.*	£10.00 HBJ
WAIMEA ESTATES NELSON PINOT NOIR 2003, WAIMEA ESTATES Nelson – *Rich, deep, and laden with strawberry compôte flavours, this is structured, flowery, savoury Pinot at its most typical.*	£10.00 MWW
WEST BROOK PINOT NOIR 2004, WEST BROOK WINERY Marlborough – *This burgundian Kiwi boasts undergrowth, minerals, soft yet vivid raspberry fruit, and a powerful finish.*	£10.00 GRT
ESK VALLEY BLACK LABEL 2003, ESK VALLEY Hawke's Bay – *Expressive youthful blackberries and spice on the nose and palate. Medium-bodied. Elegant.*	£10.70 NZH/FLA
STONELEIGH RAPAURA SERIES PINOT NOIR 2003, STONELEIGH Marlborough – *Delicate and long, with admirable understatement and finesse, this pleasing wine is packed with cherry compôte character.*	£11.00 AD1
TRINITY HILL HAWKE'S BAY 2002, TRINITY HILL Hawke's Bay – *Balanced, polished, and harmonious, with lots of redcurrant, cherry, and vanilla flavours and scents.*	£11.00 NZH
DRYLANDS MERLOT 2003, DRYLANDS Marlborough – *Big, plump, and ripe. Prunes and damsons saturate the nose and palate. Sweet coconut oak. Very pretty.*	£11.50 NZH
GLAZEBROOK MERLOT 2002, NGATARAWA WINES Hawke's Bay – *Rich, round cherry fruit flavours of good concentration. Generously oaked, with a long dry finish.*	£11.70 NZH/CCS WRW
HUNTERS PINOT NOIR 2003, HUNTERS Marlborough – *Vibrant cherry flavours. A tipple of gravity and beauty. In the words of one judge: "This wine really sings."*	£11.70 POR/CEB BNK/NZH BEN/LAY
VAVASOUR PINOT NOIR 2003, VAVASOUR Marlborough – *Dense summer fruit compôte balanced by cleansing acidity and firm, fine tannins. Good balance.*	£12.00 C&B

CANTERBURY MARLBOROUGH PINOT NOIR 2003, WAIPARA HILLS Marlborough – *Prunes and blueberries vie for attention. The bright, ripe palate is integrated, balanced, and long.*	**£12.40** NZH/OZW
CLEARWATER PINOT NOIR 2002, SHERWOOD ESTATE Marlborough – *Fresh summer fruit flavours are fleshed out by earth, cedar, and currant leaf aromas.*	**£12.50** NZH/CCS
SEIFRIED ESTATE WINEMAKERS COLLECTION 2004, SEIFRIED ESTATE Nelson – *Sweet violet and slinky coconut oak nose. The toothsome palate is crammed with kirsch and buttressed by ripe tannins.*	**£13.00** CRI
SILENI ESTATE SELECTION MERLOT CABERNET 2000, SILENI ESTATES Hawke's Bay – *Well-balanced and ripe, with grippy black cherry flavours. Youthful. Luxuriant tobacco leaf notes.*	**£13.30** NZH/RSS WOC
MOUNT RILEY PINOT NOIR 2004, MOUNT RILEY Marlborough – *Ripe, youthful, and focused, its sunny strawberry flavours lifted by herbal notes.*	**£13.50** PAT
NEWTON FORREST CORNERSTONE CABERNET MERLOT MALBEC 2002, FORREST ESTATE WINERY Hawke's Bay – *Cherries, nutmeg, clove, and cinnamon dance on the nose. The palate is dense, deep, and very young.*	**£13.50** NZH/ADN JNW
SAINT CLAIR RAPAURA RESERVE MERLOT 2002, SAINT CLAIR Marlborough – *Plums, cocoa powder, earth, and mint. Displaying evolution, yet fresh. Long.*	**£13.50** CEB/NFW NZH
HATTER'S HILL MARLBOROUGH PINOT NOIR 2004, DELTA WINE COMPANY Marlborough – *Fresh red berries and cream. Round, smooth, and sustained by a backbone of leafy tannins.*	**£14.00** LIB
SAINT CLAIR OMAKA RESERVE PINOT NOIR 2002, SAINT CLAIR Marlborough – *Medium-bodied, its crisp cranberry fruit nose and palate balanced, long and scattered with leather and spice.*	**£14.70** NFW/NZH
MATUA ARARIMU MERLOT SYRAH CABERNET SAUVIGNON 2002, MATUA VALLEY Hawke's Bay – *Minty overtones. The palate is packed with raspberry fruit and forest floor notes, with a soft finish.*	**£15.00** WFB

RESERVE MERLOT 2002, CJ PASK WINERY HAWKE'S BAY – *There's a good future in store for this whippersnapper. Fresh, sweetly ripe spiced plum flavours galore.*	£15.00 POR
VIDAL RESERVE MERLOT CABERNET SAUVIGNON 2000, VIDAL ESTATE HAWKE'S BAY – *Firm, brooding, and tight-knit, its glossy blackberry and damson fruit suspended in a web of firm tannins.*	£15.00 WIM
WAIPARA WEST PINOT NOIR 2003, TUTTON SIENKO & HILL CANTERBURY – *Crushed redcurrant flavours. Strawberry pip tannins. Tree bark and undergrowth overtones.*	£15.00 WAW
NAUTILUS ESTATE MARLBOROUGH PINOT NOIR 2003, NAUTILUS ESTATE MARLBOROUGH – *Cherries and wine gums on the nose. The palate sports chocolate oak and intense red summer fruits.*	£16.50 NZH/MWW
WOOING TREE PINOT NOIR 2003, WOOING TREE VINEYARD CENTRAL OTAGO – *Restrained, complex nose. The palate has rather intense black plums and redcurrants. Youthful. Tinged with vanilla.*	£17.00 NZH
GIBBSTON VALLEY CENTRAL OTAGO PINOT NOIR 2004, GIBBSTON VALLEY WINES CENTRAL OTAGO – *Soft cherry fruit perfumes the nose. Firmly structured, with fresh acidity and lively, lush red fruit flavours.*	£18.00 P&S

SILVER
NEW ZEALAND ROSÉ

VILLA MARIA PRIVATE BIN MERLOT MALBEC ROSÉ 2004, VILLA MARIA HAWKE'S BAY – *Fresh red plums, blueberries, strawberries, coconut and hints of mint whirl together on the nose and palate.*	£8.00 NZH/NYW

BRONZE
NEW ZEALAND SPARKLING

☆ **LINDAUER BRUT NV, LINDAUER** MARLBOROUGH – *Deep, bright tawny gold colour. Lively mousse rises from the palate of invigorating pineapples, pears, and strawberries.*	£8.00 WIDELY AVAILABLE

NORTH AMERICA + CANADA

It is a sad fact that, while California produces some of the very finest wines in the world, most come with price tags that not only deny them value for money awards, but also keep them off the shelves of British shops. We drink a lot of California wine, but unfortunately, most of it is undemanding, branded stuff that would not warrant a seal of approval. The wines on these pages are the exceptions to both rules; they're very good and great wines at fair prices, including several examples of the under-appreciated Petite Sirah, a variety that is quite unrelated to the Syrah but, in the right hands can be of similar quality and interest.

GOLD
CALIFORNIA WHITE

ARROYO VISTA CHARDONNAY 2002, J LOHR **California** – *Finely knit and densely packed with toasted nuts, melted butter, and perfumed Sicilian lemons.*	£17.70 ENO/NYW
ROBERT MONDAVI RESERVE FUMÉ BLANC 2001, ROBERT MONDAVI **California** – *Smoky wine showing rich citrus, gooseberry, and oak toast on the nose. Ripe fruit married to fine mineral acidity.*	£18.00 CNT

SILVER
CALIFORNIA WHITE

KENDALL JACKSON VINTNERS RESERVE CHARDONNAY 2003, KENDALL JACKSON ESTATES **California** – *Roast mixed nuts, melted butter, and ruby grapefruit pith. The palate displays coconut oak and ginger spice.*	£9.00 SAF
BOGLE CHARDONNAY 2002, BOGLE VINEYARDS **California** – *Lively and vibrant, with delightful zesty lime marmalade overtones. Smoky and elegant.*	£9.20 GRT/DEF

BONTERRA ROUSSANNE 2004, BONTERRA VINEYARDS CALIFORNIA – *Waxy ripe apricots matched with sweet ripe grapes and nectarines on the palate. A honeyed, viscous, rich wine.*	**£10.00** VER
E & J GALLO SINGLE VINEYARD LAGUNA RANCH CHARDONNAY 2003, ERNEST & JULIO GALLO CALIFORNIA – *Aromas of toasty oak married to evolved citrus. Elegant, supple, light-bodied citrus fruit flavours.*	**£14.00** E&J
HYDE VINEYARD CHARDONNAY 2001, RAMEY WINE CELLARS CALIFORNIA – *The nose is very inviting, with lively green apple and lemon blossom scents, with sweet tropical yellow mango notes.*	**£43.00** BBR

B R O N Z E
CALIFORNIA WHITE

☆ **E & J GALLO SIERRA VALLEY CHARDONNAY 2003, ERNEST & JULIO GALLO** CALIFORNIA – *Lemon and green apple fruit nose. Refined, restrained, and refreshing, with lemon peel, honeysuckle, and melon flavours.*	**£5.00** BGN/TOS E&J/JSM NTD
BLOSSOM HILL RESERVE CHARDONNAY 2002, BLOSSOM HILL CALIFORNIA – *Fresh lime and hints of papaya. The palate has a honeyed quality, with vanilla pod elements.*	**£5.70** BGN/PFC TOS/JSM
ESSER CELLARS CHARDONNAY 2003, ESSER CELLARS CALIFORNIA – *Diamond-bright pale gold. Creamy, spicy nose; the palate has pear and apple pie flavours. Elegant and delicate.*	**£6.00** CWS
STONE CELLARS CHARDONNAY 2003, BERINGER VINEYARDS CALIFORNIA – *Smoky, spicy, and buttery, with seductive pear tartlet and cinnamon aromas. The palate is crunchy and youthful.*	**£6.50** WFB
COLLAGE SEMILLON CHARDONNAY 2004, KENDALL JACKSON CALIFORNIA – *White flowers, honey, lime and peaches. The palate is equally complex with crisp acidity and fair length.*	**£7.00** SOM
FETZER VALLEY OAKS CHARDONNAY 2004, FETZER VINEYARDS CALIFORNIA – *Youthful pear drop aromas. Hints of cream soften the grapefruit zest palate. White flower and passion, fruit notes.*	**£7.00** BRF

FOUNDERS ESTATE CHARDONNAY 2003, BERINGER VINEYARDS CALIFORNIA – *Smoky, mineral nose. The palate is balanced and unctuous, its soft pear fruit complemented by gentle oak.*	£8.00 WFB
BONTERRA VIOGNIER 2003, BONTERRA VINEYARDS CALIFORNIA – *Blossomy and perfumed with loads of ripe apricot fruit, smooth velvety texture with balanced and refreshing acidity.*	£10.00 VER/CTC
SIMI CHARDONNAY 2003, SIMI CALIFORNIA – *Deep lemony flavours etched with notes of gooseberry and grass. Toast and vanilla notes.*	£12.00 FTH
E & J GALLO NORTHERN SONOMA ESTATE CHARDONNAY 2000, ERNEST & JULIO GALLO CALIFORNIA – *Bags of sweetly ripe sunny lemon and lime fruit. Notes of vanilla pod and clove scent the nose.*	£33.40 HBJ/E&J

SEAL OF APPROVAL
CALIFORNIA WHITE

☆ CORBETT CANYON CHARDONNAY 2003, THE WINE GROUP CALIFORNIA – *Fresh pear juice flavours and white flower scents.*	£4.00 TGP
☆ CROWS LANDING CHARDONNAY 2003, KINGSLAND WINES & SPIRITS CALIFORNIA – *Fresh toast and lemon blossom characteristics.*	£4.00 CWS
☆ GRAY FOX CHARDONNAY 2003, THE WINE GROUP CALIFORNIA – *Sweet vanilla, peach, pear, and lemon flavours.*	£4.00 JSM

TROPHY
CALIFORNIA RED

☆ HAHN ESTATES CABERNET SAUVIGNON 2003, HAHN ESTATES CALIFORNIA – *This wine is crammed with blueberries, Havana cigars, vanilla beans, and prunes.*	£9.00 PAT

GOLD
CALIFORNIA RED

☆ CONCANNON SELECTED VINEYARDS PETITE SIRAH 2003, CONCANNON CALIFORNIA – *Restrained bouquet of smoke and red stone fruit. Plenty of spice, soft tannins, and delicious plump raisin flavours.*	£8.00 TGP
QUINTESSA 1997, QUINTESSA CALIFORNIA – *Optimally ripe redcurrant fruit, fine tannins, bright acidity, and an exquisitely long finish. Genuinely profound and gracefully harmonious.*	£67.00 BBR
RIDGE MONTE BELLO 1997, RIDGE CALIFORNIA – *Roasted herb, blackcurrant jelly and smoke aromas. Masses of silky cassis and just the right amount of sweet oak.*	£89.50 BBR/CCS

SILVER
CALIFORNIA RED

☆ PARDUCCI PETITE SIRAH 2001, PARDUCCI WINE CELLARS CALIFORNIA – *Dark, with a bouquet of flowers, toast, mint, and blackcurrants. This is rich, vibrant, smoky wine, with raisin hints.*	£7.50 PAT
☆ PARDUCCI ZINFANDEL 2001, PARDUCCI WINE CELLARS CALIFORNIA – *Loganberries, raisins, and spice. The palate is richly fruited, warming, peppery, and textured, with a lick of smoke.*	£7.50 PAT
HAHN ESTATES SYRAH 2003, HAHN ESTATES CALIFORNIA – *Rich and deep in colour with a big, bold oaked nose. Prepare yourself for juicy ripe fruit with lingering taste.*	£9.00 PAT/WSO
ARTEZIN ZINFANDEL 2002, ARTEZIN WINES CALIFORNIA – *Smooth, forward cherry fruit and sweet vanilla. Soft yet firm, its yielding flesh draped over taut tannins.*	£10.00 PLE
LA CREMA SONOMA COAST PINOT NOIR 2003, LA CREMA CALIFORNIA – *The rich cherry flesh is bolstered by fresh cleansing acidity. A pretty, slightly savoury perfume of spices.*	£12.00 JSM

FETZER PRIVATE COLLECTION PINOT NOIR 2000, FETZER VINEYARDS CALIFORNIA – *Unctuous prune and fig fruit. The palate has more of the same, with an elegant, tastefully oaked, pippy finish.*	£17.00 BRF
ROBERT MONDAVI NAPA VALLEY PINOT NOIR 2002, ROBERT MONDAVI CALIFORNIA – *Sensual red cherry, coffee, and raspberry leaf nose. Bright summer fruits, firm tannins, balanced acidity, and a long finish.*	£18.00 CNT
SEGHESIO OLD VINE ZINFANDEL 2003, SEGHESIO CALIFORNIA – *Liquorice whips, cinnamon, and currant leaves decorate the bouquet. Deep, dark cherry, wild herb, and smoke flavours.*	£23.40 WIDELY AVAILABLE
SEGHESIO CORTINA ZINFANDEL 2003, SEGHESIO CALIFORNIA – *Satin-smooth, liberally spiced, and lavishly fruited. Bags of dried cherries, rich oak, and vibrant acidity.*	£23.60 V&C/CCS FLY/LIB P&S/VLW
CRISTINA PINOT NOIR 2002, MARIMAR TORRES CALIFORNIA – *Smoke, raspberry jam, and dried rosemary aromas. The palate features fine, firm tannins and a warming finish.*	£28.00 JEF
CAIN FIVE 1998, CAIN CELLARS CALIFORNIA – *Scents and flavours of liquorice, grilled meats, red apples, and Christmas spices. Mature, focused, and exotic.*	£42.00 J&B

BRONZE
CALIFORNIA RED

☆ E & J GALLO SIERRA VALLEY SHIRAZ 2003, ERNEST & JULIO GALLO CALIFORNIA – *Concentrated black fruit and berry nose, matching the sweet entrance on the tongue. Deep colour and a great length and depth make this a yummy shiraz.*	£4.70 E&J
☆ THE BOULDERS PETITE SIRAH 2003, KINGSLAND WINES SPIRITS CALIFORNIA – *Liquorice, black pepper, and tobacco nose. Bold and spicy, with generous redcurrant fruit and hints of undergrowth.*	£5.00 CWS
ESSER CELLARS CABERNET SAUVIGNON 2003, ESSER CELLARS CALIFORNIA – *Expressive red stone fruit compôte nose and palate. Youthful, soft, and medium-bodied.*	£6.00 CWS

CALIFORNIA OLD VINE ZINFANDEL 2003, DELICATO FAMILY VINEYARDS CALIFORNIA – *Rich mocha with liquorice, blackberry, and pepper aroma. Full-bodied, succulent flavours of sweet berry-jam fruit and soft tannin finish.*	£6.70 ESL
RAVENSWOOD LODI ZINFANDEL 2002, RAVENSWOOD CALIFORNIA – *Spicy and jammy with hedonistic blackberries and plums, a real mouthful of fruit and spice with seductive tannins.*	£7.20 NEC/BNK TOS/JSM WSO
FOUNDERS ESTATE ZINFANDEL 2002, BERINGER VINEYARDS CALIFORNIA – *Lively and robust, this has rich dark fruits and warm spice. Well balanced with ripe tannin.*	£8.00 WFB
RAVENSWOOD SONOMA ZINFANDEL 2001, RAVENSWOOD CALIFORNIA – *Dark fruits and spicy black pepper. The wine is full-bodied and rich with loads of enticing firm tannins.*	£8.30 TOS/WSO
BONTERRA CABERNET SAUVIGNON 2001, BONTERRA VINEYARDS CALIFORNIA – *The spiced dark fruit flavours of this wine are restrained. Good balance between cassis fruit and fresh acidity.*	£9.00 VER
FETZER BARREL SELECT ZINFANDEL 2003, FETZER VINEYARDS CALIFORNIA – *Deep ruby colour, aromas of black pepper and spice, showing dark berry flavours and creamy vanilla.*	£9.00 BRF
FOUNDERS ESTATE CABERNET SAUVIGNON 2002, BERINGER VINEYARDS CALIFORNIA – *Ruby purple, with lots of pigmented legs. Pronounced green pepper, spice, leather, and blackcurrant nose and palate.*	£9.00 WFB
MORRO BAY CABERNET 2002, MORRO BAY CALIFORNIA – *Highly coloured, with generous cedary tannins, spicy blackcurrant fruit, very firm structure, and fine acidity.*	£9.00 EHL
PAINTER BRIDGE ZINFANDEL 2002, J LOHR CALIFORNIA – *Jammy raspberry and cherry with black tea spice. Warm and supple with soft tannin and lengthy richness of flavour.*	£9.50 ENO
E & J GALLO COASTAL VINEYARDS CABERNET SAUVIGNON 2002, ERNEST & JULIO GALLO CALIFORNIA – *Kirsch, cinnamon, and blackberry preserve flavour in this powerhouse. Ripe, fresh, and firm.*	£10.00 TOS/E&J

TRINCHERO FAMILY CABERNET SAUVIGNON 2002, TRINCHERO FAMILY ESTATES CALIFORNIA – *Youthful yet super-ripe, possesing fine cassis intensity, fresh acidity, and a long, harmonious finish.*	**£10.00** PLB
OLD VINE ZINFANDEL 2003, BOGLE VINEYARDS CALIFORNIA – *Deep, ruby colour, and generous, jammy fruit aromas. Blackberry and clove meld with warm spicy, peppery finish.*	**£10.80** DEF/NYW
E & J GALLO SINGLE VINEYARD BARRELLI CREEK ZINFANDEL 1999, ERNEST & JULIO GALLO CALIFORNIA – *Smooth mouth-watering blueberry fruit with hints of smokiness. An intense melange of fruit and spice with complex character.*	**£15.00** E&J
SIMI CABERNET SAUVIGNON 2001, SIMI CALIFORNIA – *Developed, its sweetly ripe red fruit flavours balanced by softening tannins. A crowd pleaser.*	**£15.00** FTH
FETZER PRIVATE COLLECTION CABERNET SAUVIGNON 2000, FETZER VINEYARDS CALIFORNIA – *Powerfully intense, ripe, and very spicy, its summer fruit flavours supported by brisk tannins.*	**£17.00** BRF
ROCKING HORSE ZINFANDEL 2000, ROCKING HORSE CALIFORNIA – *Deep blueberry and vanilla flavours. Aromas of lilacs, toast, and spearmint. Textured and persistent.*	**£18.00** ODD
ROCKING HORSE GARVEY MERLOT 1999, ROCKING HORSE CALIFORNIA – *Plums, cherries, chocolate, and toast notes. Aromas of vanilla and flowers and gravel. Long.*	**£19.00** ODD
MAIN STREET CABERNET SAUVIGNON 2000, TRINCHERO FAMILY ESTATES CALIFORNIA – *Ripe blackcurrant and cherry flavours. Aromas of vanilla beans and red honeysuckle. Vibrant and long.*	**£25.00** PLB
MONTEVINA TDO ZINFANDEL 2002, TRINCHERO FAMILY ESTATES CALIFORNIA – *A sweet aroma of blackberries, liquorice, and pepper with well-integrated tannin, jammy fruits, and warm lifting finish.*	**£25.00** PLB
ROBERT MONDAVI RESERVE PINOT NOIR 2000, ROBERT MONDAVI CALIFORNIA – *Soft strawberry flavours, cinnamon spice and autumn leaves on nose and palate. Layered and long.*	**£25.00** CNT

MOUNT VEEDER CABERNET SAUVIGNON 2001, MOUNT VEEDER CALIFORNIA – *The blackcurrant fruit is dusted with soft tannins. Developed. This wine should be enjoyed now.*	**£26.00** CNT
DOMAINE CARNEROS FAMOUS GATE PINOT NOIR 2001, DOMAINE CARNEROS CALIFORNIA – *Soft, warm raspberry fruit. Leafy notes and barnyard elements complete the picture. Unmistakably Pinot.*	**£30.00** POR
E&J GALLO NORTHERN SONOMA CABERNET SAUVIGNON 1998, ERNEST & JULIO GALLO CALIFORNIA – *Tight blackberry fruit and vanilla pod flavours. Round, medium-bodied, crisp, and clear.*	**£30.00** SEL
SIMI RESERVE CABERNET SAUVIGNON 2000, SIMI CALIFORNIA – *Ripe, rich crimson colour. Damsons and strawberries flavour the balanced palate.*	**£50.00** FTH

SEAL OF APPROVAL
CALIFORNIA RED

☆ CORBETT CANYON RUBY CABERNET 2003, THE WINE GROUP CALIFORNIA – *Ripe, fresh redcurrants, cassis, and cherries.*	**£4.00** TOS
☆ GRAY FOX CABERNET SAUVIGNON 2002, THE WINE GROUP CALIFORNIA – *Dusty tannins underscore fresh summer fruit.*	**£4.00** JSM
☆ GRAY FOX MERLOT 2002, THE WINE GROUP CALIFORNIA – *Sweetly ripe and laced with vanilla aromas.*	**£4.00** TGP

BRONZE
CALIFORNIA ROSÉ

VALLEY OAKS SYRAH ROSÉ 2004, FETZER VINEYARDS CALIFORNIA – *Intense blueberry, plum, violet, and even clove elements. Full-bodied, yet fresh, and harmonious.*	**£6.20** BGN/BNK JSM/THS NTD

SILVER
CALIFORNIA SPARKLING

QUARTET NV, ROEDERER ESTATE California – *Notes of mushroom, white currant, citrus, and brioche on nose and palate.*	£15.70 FHM/POR MWW/WR K VLW
DOMAINE CARNEROS BRUT 2000, DOMAINE CARNEROS California – *Pretty floral aromas rise from the nose. The mousse is vigorous, lifting the grapefruit and lees flavours.*	£17.00 HMA/NYW

BRONZE
CALIFORNIA SPARKLING

LE RÊVE BLANC DE BLANCS 1996, DOMAINE CARNEROS California – *Fine bubbles with passion-fruit and floral notes of honeysuckle. A toasty vanilla cream and citrus palate.*	£26.50 POR/NYW

BRONZE
CALIFORNIA FORTIFIED

ELYSIUM 2004, QUADY WINES California – *Fiery raisin, rose petal, honey, and grape scents and flavours. Luscious, mouthcoating, and very long.*	£9.40 WIDELY AVAILABLE

BRONZE
PACIFIC NORTHWEST WHITE

RED HILLS ESTATE CHARDONNAY 2001, DOMAINE DROUHIN Oregon – *Nutmeg and clove aromas accent the creamy banana and pineapple cake flavours. Textured, tropical, and bright.*	£20.50 BBR

GOLD
CANADIAN SWEET

OAK AGED VIDAL ICEWINE 2003, INNISKILLIN	£44.50
ONTARIO – *Herbs, flowers and honey scent the nose. Tropical mango, guava, toast, marmalade, quince, and apricot palate.*	FHM

PORTUGAL

A country that is certainly on its way up the charts, Portugal is proving that its medal-winning team is no longer, as it once was, exclusively made up of ports and Madeiras. Now, there are fascinating unfortified wines made from traditional local grapes like the Touriga Nacional and newcomers such as the Chardonnay and Cabernet Sauvignon. The transformation of Portugal's vinous fortunes has been wrought by a new generation of winemakers, both Portuguese and from Australia, who have learned how to temper the often intense heat of regions such as the Douro valley, and to extract flavour from the grapes without the harsh tannins that were once a Portuguese hallmark.

TROPHY
MADEIRA

☆ COSSART COLHEITA MALMSEY 1998, MADEIRA WINE COMPANY **Madeira** – *Glowing tawny colour. Demerara sugar, golden syrup, clove bud, and tobacco scents and flavours. Opulent, long, and fine.*	**£12.00** JEF

GOLD
MADEIRA

☆ COSSART COLHEITA MALMSEY 1994, MADEIRA WINE COMPANY **Madeira** – *Roast hazelnut, toast, and pear blossom nose. Ripe mandarin orange and Granny Smith apple flavours.*	**£9.00** JEF
☆ COSSART COLHEITA BUAL 1995, MADEIRA WINE COMPANY **Madeira** – *Juicy peaches, soft apricots, candied lemons, and walnuts. Deepest chocolate brown and freshest lemon zest acidity.*	**£12.00** JEF
☆ COSSART COLHEITA VERDELHO 1995, MADEIRA WINE COMPANY **Madeira** – *Golden apples and green plums with a poignant bittersweet nuance. Richly spiced, dense, and minerally.*	**£13.00** JEF

COSSART BUAL 1969, MADEIRA WINE COMPANY **MADEIRA** – *Coconut, marshmallow, liquorice, flowers, and caramel. A captivating Bual with a sensual quality.*	**£130.00** JEF
BLANDY'S TERRANTEZ 1975, MADEIRA WINE COMPANY MADEIRA – *Made from noble Terrantez. Ripe satsumas and orange zest nose. Honeycomb, flowers, minerals, and herbs.*	**£150.00** JEF

SILVER
MADEIRA

MALVASIA CASCO 18A MADEIRA 1994, VINHOS BARBEITO MADEIRA – *Lemony palate chock full of roast hazelnuts, walnuts, demerara sugar, and spice. Elegant, intense, and long.*	**£18.00** WPR
SERCIAL 10 YEAR OLD RESERVE MADEIRA NV, VINHOS BARBEITO MADEIRA – *The inviting nose has rich freshly ground coffee bean aromas and roasted nuts. Complex caramel and sweet honey flavours.*	**£20.30** WPR/TNI FLY/DEF
15 YEAR OLD MALMSEY MADEIRA NV, BLANDY'S MADEIRA – *Rich caramel and fig scents mingle with coffee and toasted nuts. The palate is laden with Christmas cake flavours.*	**£25.00** LAI
BLANDY'S BUAL 64 MADEIRA 1964, MADEIRA WINE COMPANY MADEIRA – *Amber-chestnut brown. Rich toffee and caramel notes. Aniseed elements and savoury white flesh.*	**£100.00** JEF

BRONZE
MADEIRA

☆ **BLANDY'S ALVADA NV, MADEIRA WINE COMPANY** **MADEIRA** – *Deep marmalade colour. Hints of creosote enrich the flavours of caramelly citrus. Notes of spice and smoke.*	**£9.50** POR/JEF
VERMAR RESERVA MADEIRA NV, VINHOS BARBEITO **MADEIRA** – *Caramel, raisins, and toffee scent and flavour this medium-sweet Madeira. A fresh tingle of acidity lifts the rich fruit.*	**£10.10** WPR/TNI FLY

BLANDY'S HARVEST 1998, MADEIRA WINE COMPANY **MADEIRA** – *Smoky, leathery and packed with raisins, this is lush, deep Madeira perfumed with flowers and roast nuts.*	**£10.80** JEF/JSM
COSSART COLHEITA SERCIAL 1988, MADEIRA WINE COMPANY **MADEIRA** – *Light-bodied and refreshing, with caramelised citrus flavour and aromas. Serve well chilled for an elegant treat.*	**£13.00** JEF

TROPHY
PORT

OFFLEY VINTAGE PORT 2003, SOGRAPE **DOURO** – *Bell heather and bay leaf aromas. Fiery yet tempered with coffee, cream, and treacle. Lush, concentrated and long.*	**£.00** NOT AVAILABLE IN THE UK
☆ SMITH WOODHOUSE BOTTLE MATURED LBV PORT 1994, SMITH WOODHOUSE **DOURO** – *Sweet and vibrant with rich plum, spice, and fruitcake aromas. Lush fruit, intense sweetness, and good acidity.*	**£14.00** JEF
QUINTA DE RORIZ VINTAGE 2000, QUINTA DE RORIZ **DOURO** – *Cherries, cloves, and inkwell. Leather, spices, redcurrants, and mulberries. Fresh, inky, and youthful. Refined and radiant.*	**£33.80** POR/JEF FLY
GRAHAM'S 30 YEAR OLD TAWNY PORT NV, W&J GRAHAM **DOURO** – *Complex marmalade, burnt sugar, and spice aromas. Harmonious fruit flavours married to fine structure and acidity.*	**£40.00** JEF

GOLD
PORT

☆ RAMOS PINTO LBV 2000, ADRIANO RAMOS PINTO **DOURO** – *Intensely sweet with baked prune, cherry, and fruitcake aromas. The palate has blackfruit flavours and power, opulence, and harmony.*	**£12.40** A&A/WPR BBO/VLW
☆ DOW'S CRUSTED PORT BOTTLED 1999 NV, DOW'S **DOURO** – *Sweet, juicy, dense, and warm, with coffee, chocolate, raspberries, pencil lead, dark plums, smoke, and a long finish.*	**£13.20** TOS/JEF JSM

☆ CROFT QUINTA DE ROÊDA 1995, THE FLADGATE PARTNERSHIP **Douro** – *Raspberries, roasted coffee beans, liquorice whips, graphite, and nougat nose. Dried cherries, toasted hazelnuts, and Victoria plums.*	**£14.50** BNK/MW W
☆ CASAL DOS JORDOES PORT 10 ANOS NV, PINTO **Douro** – *Chestnut coloured. Balanced, elegant, and complex. Roast nuts, black cherries, chocolate, and flowers. Organic.*	**£15.00** VER
☆ PORTAL LBV PORT 2000, QUINTA DO PORTAL **Douro** – *Plum cake, clove, and tar aromas. Lovely sweetness balanced by supple tannins and good acidity.*	**£15.70** ESL/CHN
DOW'S QUINTA DO BOMFIM VINTAGE PORT 1996, SILVA & COSENS **Douro** – *Raisins, ripe blackberries, spice, and earth. Sun-warmed blueberry and prune flesh supported by firm tannins.*	**£20.80** TOS/JEF TAN/JSM
SILVAL 2000, QUINTA DO NOVAL **Douro** – *Exotically flavoured, its grainy tannins supporting blueberry, cherry, and mineral flavours. Chocolate and cinnamon scents.*	**£26.00** WPR
GRAHAM'S 20 YEAR OLD TAWNY NV, W&J GRAHAM **Douro** – *Sea air, espresso, mandarin oranges, and cocoa powder. Signs of evolution. Ample apricot flesh and fruitcake spiciness.*	**£26.80** TOS/JEF JSM
FERREIRA VINTAGE PORT 2003, SOGRAPE **Douro** – *Intense, lifted baked plum and bittersweet chocolate aromas. Enormous, concentrated attack of chocolate covered cherries.*	**£30.00** BWC
TAYLOR'S 20 YEAR OLD TAWNY PORT NV, THE FLADGATE PARTNERSHIP **Douro** – *Sophisticated tea-amber colour. Taut tannins delicately cushion the polished favours and scents of figs and hazelnuts.*	**£31.70** POR/TNG MWW/BE N JSM
DOW'S 30 YEAR OLD TAWNY PORT NV, SILVA & COSENS **Douro** – *Rich nuts, raisins, and spice. Perfectly integrated, amazing depth, and fresh acidity. Concentrated, harmonious, and long.*	**£35.00** JEF
DOW'S VINTAGE PORT 80, DOW'S **Douro** – *Deep fruitcake, pepper, and cinnamon notes. Blackcurrant fruit. Voluptuous, savoury palate with hints of meat and leather.*	**£35.00** JEF

QUINTA DO BOM RETIRO 20 YEAR OLD PORT NV, **ADRIANO RAMOS PINTO** Douro – *Caramel, molasses, and burnt sugar flavours. Flowery notes, raisins, toffee, and powdered minerals. Lively, complex, and long.*	**£36.00** BEN/VLW
QUINTA DO VESUVIO VINTAGE PORT 2001, **SYMINGTON** Douro – *Lush wine with plumcake, spice, and blueberry aromas. Perfect integration of succulent black fruit, grape spirit, and fine tannins.*	**£36.60** JEF/JSM
KROHN COLHEITA PORT 1967, WIESE & KROHN **Douro** – *A nose of fig, burnt sugar, and spice. Well-integrated grape spirit married to rich evolved fruit and fresh acidity.*	**£50.00** MDN
TAYLOR'S VINTAGE PORT 1985, THE FLADGATE PAPRTNERSHIP **Douro** – *Clear, ripe fruitcake nose. Luscious flavours of figs, espresso, plums, raisins, spicy blackberries, and dark chocolate.*	**£57.50** JSM/DEF
FONSECA VINTAGE PORT 1985, THE FLADGATE PARTNERSHIP **Douro** – *Fig, leather, prune, and baked blackcurrant bouquet. Palate of kirsch, crushed black pepper, and fruitcake.*	**£60.00** MZC

SILVER
PORT

★ CROFT DISTINCTION PORT NV, THE FLADGATE PARTNERSHIP **Douro** – *Mouthcoating strawberry and cherry fruit with floral notes. Fiery and long. Hints of bonfire smoke.*	**£9.00** SMF
★ DOW'S LBV PORT NV, DOW'S **Douro** – *Mature, with an unusual palate of pepper, strawberry jam, and blackcurrants. Prune and chocolate richness.*	**£9.40** TOS/JEF JSM
☆ WARRE'S OTIMA 10 YEAR OLD TAWNY PORT NV, WARRE & CO **Douro** – *Ginger, dried figs, dates, and raisins. The palate is very sweet, with a tingle of acidity and a tannic edge.*	**£9.90** TOS/JEF JSM/NYW
☆ NOVAL TRADITIONAL LBV PORT 1998, QUINTA DO NOVAL **Douro** – *Spices, flowers, and savoury prunes populate the richly fruited, savoury palate. Deep, brooding, and sweetly ripe.*	**£10.90** WIDELY AVAILABLE

☆ SAINSBURY'S 10 YEAR OLD TAWNY PORT NV, SAINSBURY'S Douro – *Honey, walnuts, and mandarin oranges. Sweet, concentrated apricot and marmalade flavours with a sprinkling of cinnamon.*	£11.00 JSM
☆ FONSECA LBV PORT 2000, THE FLADGATE PARTNERSHIP Douro – *Ripe, intense, and very fresh, with a mouthful of fresh plump raisins and blackcurrants. Fine acidity.*	£11.30 MWW/BEN
☆ QUINTA DO CRASTO LBV PORT 1999, QUINTA DO CRASTO Douro – *Sultry deep red and black vine fruits. Pretty lilacs and fresh herbs. Good acidity, balance, and fine length.*	£12.20 ADN/ENO
☆ GRAHAM'S CRUSTED PORT BOTTLED 2000 NV, W&J GRAHAM Douro – *Understated soft vine fruits, smoke, dark chocolate, blueberries, and stewed plums. Plump, rich, fine, and long.*	£13.50 JEF
☆ NIEPOORT LBV PORT 1999, NIEPOORT VINHOS Douro – *Juicy black cherry, spice, and raisin flavours. Intense and warming. Long, with a touch of herbs on the nose.*	£14.20 FHM/NEC WPR/TAN FLY/P&S
DOW'S 10 YEAR OLD TAWNY PORT NV, SILVA & COSENS Douro – *Reddish chestnut brown. Integrated and luscious, with candied cherries, marmalade, and treacle. Aromatic and long.*	£15.40 TOS/JEF
QUINTA DO VALLADO 10 YEAR OLD PORT NV, QUINTA DO VALLADO Douro – *Delicate, with restrained mulling spices, toffee, and caramel on nose and palate. Deep brown, lusciously sweet, and rich.*	£17.00 BWL
WARRE'S OTIMA 20 YEAR OLD TAWNY PORT NV, WARRE & CO Douro – *Liquorice, burnt rubber, honey-coated nuts, and marmalade. Sweet, smoky, mellow, and attractive. Long finish.*	£20.00 JEF/JSM
NIEPOORT 10 YEAR OLD TAWNY PORT NV, NIEPOORT VINHOS Douro – *Bitter oranges, caramel, roast nuts, and toffee. Red-hued mahogany nectar with very good balance. Elegant and long.*	£20.40 FHM/NEC WPR/FLY DEF
MAJARA VINTAGE PORT 2000, PINTO Douro – *Raspberries, minerals, aniseed, and clove buds. The palate has plenty of elegant ripe blackberry fruit and soft tannins.*	£21.00 VER

SMITH WOODHOUSE MADALENA VINTAGE PORT 1995, SMITH WOODHOUSE **Douro** – *Balanced, smoothly textured, sweet, and very long. Crushed strawberry flavours melt into firm tannins. White pepper and tar.*	**£21.00** JEF
DELAFORCE CURIOUS AND ANCIENT 20 YEAR OLD TAWNY PORT NV, THE FLADGATE PARTNERSHIP **Douro** – *Coffee, chocolate, hazelnuts, smoke, and walnuts galore. Mellow, ripe and intense, with good definition and poise.*	**£23.00** POR
FONSECA PANASCAL VINTAGE PORT 1996, THE FLADGATE PARTNERSHIP **Douro** – *Strong, youthful, round, and very attractive, with ground spices, tobacco leaves, and black liquorice. Firm yet integrated, and very long.*	**£23.00** TNG
TAYLOR'S QUINTA DE VARGELLAS VINTAGE PORT 1996, THE FLADGATE PARTNERSHIP **Douro** – *Complex and peppery, with a powerful structure and excellent richness and depth.*	**£23.00** POR/BNK TOS/MWW TAN/JSM
GRAHAM'S MALVEDOS VINTAGE PORT 1996, W&J GRAHAM **Douro** – *Alpine strawberries, toasted mixed nuts, moist fruitcake, and stewed prunes. Sweet yet flushed with acidity. In its prime.*	**£24.70** FHM/JEF TAN/JSM
PINTO VINTAGE PORT 2003, ADRIANO RAMOS PINTO **Douro** – *Inky, blood-red ruby. Violets and liquorice scent the nose. Long and complex, with summer fruit flavours.*	**£25.00** VLW
PORTO POÇAS VINTAGE PORT 2002, MANUEL D POÇAS JUNIOR **Douro** – *Ruby-purple. Ripe, figgy aromas. The rich palate of summer fruit pudding is laced with freshly brewed coffee.*	**£28.00** HOT
DOW'S QUINTA DA SENHORA DA RIBEIRA VINTAGE PORT 2001, SILVA & COSENS **Douro** – *This aristocratic wine shows excellent promise. Crammed with juicy ripe blackberries and redcurrants. Polished and long.*	**£30.00** JEF
SANDEMAN VINTAGE PORT 2003, SOGRAPE **Douro** – *Medium-bodied, sweetly fiery, and lifted. Packed with plump strawberries, asphalt, and inkwell. Virtually opaque.*	**£30.00** SGL
SMITH WOODHOUSE VINTAGE PORT 1994, SMITH WOODHOUSE **Douro** – *Complex, balanced, and elegant. Pure, sweet raspberry flavours on the liberally spiced nose and palate.*	**£30.00** JEF

CROFT VINTAGE PORT 1977, CROFT Douro – *Ruby-amber hue. A fantastic array of spicewood, smoke, toasted hazelnuts, figs, coffee, and raspberries.*	**£40.00** BNK
NIEPOORT 20 YEAR OLD TAWNY PORT NV, NIEPOORT VINHOS Douro – *Very spicy, with cloves, cardamom, cherries, raspberries, roses, and undergrowth. Rotund and finely textured.*	**£41.20** WPR/FLY DEF
QUINTA DO VESUVIO VINTAGE PORT 2000, SYMINGTON'S Douro – *Inky ripe loganberry and blueberry fruits. Scented with white pepper and chocolate covered ginger.*	**£42.20** POR/CNL JEF/FLY
TAYLOR'S 30 YEAR OLD TAWNY PORT NV, THE FLADGATE PARTNERSHIP Douro – *Dried nectarines and cherries, apricots, and marmalade. Smoky tones perfume the nose. Seriously rich with a neverending finish.*	**£45.00** TNG
NOVAL 40 YEAR OLD TAWNY PORT NV, QUINTA DO NOVAL Douro – *Coffee and caramel richness. Dotted with nutty scents and flavours and lifted by plenty of warming alcohol.*	**£69.50** WRW
ROZES 40 YEARS OLD PORT NV, VRANKEN POMMERY MONOPOLE Douro – *Orange peel, coffee, nuts, and minerals. A fine tingle of acidity sustains the finish.*	**£80.00** PFC

BRONZE
PORT

☆ **REGIMENTAL FINE TAWNY PORT NV, SILVA & COSENS Douro** – *A baked fruit nose leads to a smooth palate with toasty, spiced notes and amber honeyed fruit.*	**£6.00** BNK
☆ **ANDRESEN LBV 2000, J. H. ANDRESEN Douro** – *An evolved tawny colour. Medium weight, with blackcherry and black chocolate flavours. Fair quality.*	**£8.00** LAI
☆ **TAYLOR'S FIRST ESTATE PORT NV, THE FLADGATE PARTNERSHIP Douro** – *Classic port flavours: robust fruit, good acidity, and tannins with balanced alcohol.*	**£8.00** TOS/MWW JSM

☆ WR LATE BOTTLED VINTAGE PORT 1999, JOHN E FELLS & SONS LTD **Douro** – *Subdued and stylish, with elegant cooked fruit and raisin scents and flavours. Good structure.*	**£8.50** WTS
☆ FONSECA BIN 27 PORT NV, THE FLADGATE PARTNERSHIP **Douro** – *Toasted nose and rich plum cake palate. Well balanced tannins and a warm, round finish.*	**£9.00** FHM/NYW VLW
☆ PORTO POÇAS LBV 1999, MANUEL D POÇAS JUNIOR VINHOS **Douro** – *Intense black cherry fruit and smoky oak on the nose. Sweet, grippy tannins, fresh acidity, and good balance.*	**£9.70** HOT
☆ COCKBURN'S VINTAGE PORT 2000, COCKBURN'S **Douro** – *Inky red. Ripe nose and full-bodied palate of blackcurrants and dates. Complex, powerful, and ageworthy.*	**£9.90** TOS/JSM
☆ GRAHAM'S LBV 2000, W&J GRAHAM **Douro** – *An earthy nose with a sweet palate. The alcohol is balanced, with liquorice flavours and sweetness. A soft finish.*	**£10.00** TOS/JEF WAW/JSM
TAYLOR'S LBV PORT 2000, THE FLADGATE PARTNERSHIP **Douro** – *An accessible red fruit nose leads to a well-balanced red fruit and milk chocolate palate. Balanced.*	**£10.20** TPE/TNG TOS/MWW JSM/WOC
GRAHAM'S LBV 1999, W&J GRAHAM **Douro** – *A spicy, sweet, smooth wine, which shows some evolution and has a good balance between spirit and fruit.*	**£10.40** WIDELY AVAILABLE
FONSECA 10 YEAR OLD TAWNY PORT NV, THE FLADGATE PARTNERSHIP **Douro** – *A clean and nutty nose with a soft cinder, toffee, caramel palate. Finishes on a fresh long note.*	**£11.00** BEN
TESCO FINEST 10 YEAR OLD TAWNY PORT NV, SYMINGTON **Douro** – *The nose is marked by barrel-scent and ground nuts. The palate has citrus flavours with complex dried fruits.*	**£11.00** TOS
CHURCHILL'S LBV PORT 1999, CHURCHILL GRAHAM **Douro** – *Pretty lilac and spice bouquet. Very sweet and juicy with good freshness and fine tannins.*	**£11.40** FHM/CCS RAV/NYW

CALEM LBV PORT 2000, AA CALEM Douro – *A deep and spicy nose with cloves and liquorice aromas. Raisins and blackberries combine on the structured palate.*	**£12.00** CRI
GRAHAM'S SIX GRAPES NV, W&J GRAHAM Douro – *Dark with a redcurrant and forest fruit nose and palate. Spiced wood.*	**£12.00** JEF
DOW'S CRUSTED PORT BOTTLED 2000 NV, SILVA & COSENS Douro – *Black, spiced fruit with a savoury edge. Rich and persistent with an acidic lift on the finish.*	**£13.20** TOS/JEF JSM
MARTINEZ UNFILTERED LBV PORT 2000, COCKBURN SMITHES Douro – *An evolved wine with well integrated sweet plum flavours and soft spice notes on the palate.*	**£13.50** CNL
DELAFORCE QUINTA DA CORTE PORT 1987, THE FLADGATE PARTNERSHIP Douro – *The nose is restrained but the palate contrasts this with good intense fruit and a long finish.*	**£14.00** POR
ROZES 10 YEAR OLD INFANTA ISABEL NV, VRANKEN POMMERY MONOPOLE Douro – *Good balanced nutty honey flavour. Slightly vegetal and spicy with low acidity. A pleasing port.*	**£14.00** PFC
GRAHAM'S CRUSTED BOTTLED 1999 NV, W&J GRAHAM Douro – *An opaque colour with spiced, dense plums on the nose. Medicinal liquorice and tar flavours lead to a long finish.*	**£14.10** ESL/JEF
ANDRESEN PORTO COLHEITA 1995, J. H. ANDRESEN Douro – *A plump palate with lots of sweet black fruit, off-set by fine tannins and acidity.*	**£16.20** LAI
TAYLOR'S 10 YEAR OLD TAWNY PORT NV, THE FLADGATE PARTNERSHIP Douro – *Fresh, vibrant fruit on the nose and palate. Fair concentration, matched with good tannins and acidity.*	**£17.10** POR/TPE TOS/MWW BEN/JSM
QUINTA DE ERVAMOIRA 10 YEAR OLD PORT NV, ADRIANO RAMOS PINTO Douro – *Hazelnut, orange, and mint aromas on the nose. The palate is thick and flavoursome and concentrated.*	**£19.30** WPR/TPE BBO/BEN DEF/VLW

FONSECA GUIMARAENS VINTAGE PORT 1987, THE FLADGATE PARTNERSHIP Douro – *Baked leathery fruits. The palate is intense and full-bodied with black pepper and dark fruits.*	**£19.50** FHM/POR JSM
QUINTA VALE DO MARIA VINTAGE PORT 2002, JOSÉ MARIA FONSECA & VAN ZELLER Douro – *Balsamic vinegar nose. Floral and attractive. Good fruit, powerful structure, and long finish.*	**£19.50** LAI
DOW'S 20 YEAR OLD TAWNY PORT NV, SILVA & COSENS Douro – *A caramel aroma entices on to a seriously nutty, good, and juicy palate with a long finish.*	**£21.70** JEF/JSM
WARRE'S QUINTA DA CAVADINHA VINTAGE 1995, WARRE & CO Douro – *A fine fruit nose with a thick and sweet palate. Very classic with a chewy, meaty finish.*	**£21.70** FHM/JEF
PORTO POÇAS COLHEITA VINTAGE 1986, MANUEL D POÇAS JUNIOR VINHOS Douro – *A coppery brown colour with a classic oxidised nose. Nutty, smoky palate. Very long and rich.*	**£25.50** HOT
CALEM VINTAGE PORT 2002, AA CALEM Douro – *Luscious black fruit and dried leaves on the nose and palate. A smooth wine with a long finish.*	**£32.00** CRI
QUINTA DO NOVAL COLHEITA 1974, QUINTA DO NOVAL Douro – *Delicate and round. Nutty oak richness. Not as intense as some, but in possession of great elegance.*	**£32.00** WPR
PORTO POÇAS VINTAGE 2001, MANUEL D POÇAS JUNIOR VINHOS Douro – *Creamy blackberry fruit palate, with chocolate and mocha notes. Huge concentration and dusty tannins.*	**£33.80** HOT
NOVAL 20 YEAR OLD TAWNY NV, QUINTA DO NOVAL Douro – *Powerful caramel flavours. The palate is sweet and fresh with raisined depths and a long finish.*	**£34.80** TPE/TAN WRW
"QUINTA DO VALLADO" 20 YEAR OLD NV, QUINTA DO VALLADO SCC. AGRICOLA LDA. Douro – *Dark brown, with a rich molasses nose and luscious burnt sugar flavours. A classic.*	**£35.00** BWL

MARTINEZ VINTAGE PORT 2000, COCKBURN SMITHES & CIA SA Douro – *A deeply coloured port showing age on its ripe strawberry fruit. Ready to drink this festive season.*	£36.00 CNL
GRAHAM'S VINTAGE PORT 1980, W&J GRAHAM Douro – *A chocolate, spice, and pepper nose. Stewed fruit and meat on the palate. Mid-weight and a fair length.*	£42.80 JEF/TAN

SEAL OF APPROVAL
PORT

☆ CO-OP RUBY PORT NV, SMITH WOODHOUSE Douro – *Ripe summer fruit flavours. Cinnamon spice.*	£5.50 CWS
☆ PORTO DO POÇAS RUBY PORT NV, MANUEL D POÇAS JUNIOR-VINHOS Douro – *Raspberry flavours commingle with earthy spice.*	£6.90 HOT
☆ WAITROSE SPECIAL RESERVE PORT NV, JOHN E FELLS & SONS Douro – *Fresh strawberry flavours. Leafy depths.*	£7.50 WTS

SILVER
PORTUGUESE WHITE

☆ BELA FONTE BICAL 2004, DFJ VINHOS Beiras – *Fresh citrus flavours. A flush of acidity and hints of white flowers. Luxuriant fruit.*	£5.00 D&F

BRONZE
PORTUGUESE WHITE

CASA DO LAGO WHITE 2004, DFJ VINHOS Estremadura – *Warm orange blossom notes, honeyed apple flavours, and lively acidity. Fresh and long.*	£5.50 D&F

ESPORÃO MONTE VELHO WHITE 2004, ESPORÃO **ALENTEJO** – *A peachy aromatic perfume is fleshed out on the palate with an oily mouthfeel and a lime bite.*	**£5.70** FHM/POR JEF/WRW
GRAND' ARTE CHARDONNAY 2003, DFJ VINHOS **ESTREMADURA** – *Lifted nose of fresh, delicate peaches and wildflowers. Warm honey and citrus palate.*	**£6.00** D&F
CASTELLO D'ALBA 2003, VINHOS DOURO SUPERIOR **DOURO** – *A warm nose with an old fashioned thick cut marmalade scent. Fine acidity keeps the richness in balance.*	**£7.00** WPR
COVELA SELECCIONDA 2003, QUINTA DO COVELA **DOURO** – *The nose has a mineral aspect and a tang of salty sea air. Delicious toast and grapefruit. Characterful.*	**£13.30** C&B
REDOMA BRANCO 2003, NIEPORT VINHOS DOURO – *One of Portugal's most exemplary whites, barrel fermented in Francois Frères oak. Pear juice, cream, and mineral flavours.*	**£18.30** WPR/FLY

S E A L   O F   A P P R O V A L
PORTUGUESE WHITE

☆ **CORETO 2004, DFJ VINHOS ESTREMADURA** – *Bruised apples, cashews, and fresh raisins.*	**£4.00** D&F
☆ **FIUZA CHARDONNAY 2004, " FIUZA & BRIGHT"** **RIBATEJO** – *Refreshing buttery notes with some attractive stone fruit flavours.*	**£4.00** CWS

T R O P H Y
PORTUGUESE RED

MALHADINHA 2003, HERDADE DA MALHADINHA **NOVA ALENTEJO** – *Ripe cherries, leather, and prunes. Deep and spiked with black pepper. Huge, aromatic, and virtually black.*	**£.00** NOT AVAILABLE IN THE UK

QUINTA DO VALLADO RESERVA 2003, QUINTA DO VALLADO **Douro** – *Pungent prune, damson, and baked earth. Tannins are muscular but well-integrated and the use of oak is deft.*	**£16.50** BWL/NYW
CORTES DE CIMA TOURIGA NACIONAL 2003, CORTES DE CIMA **Alentejo** – *Baked earth, prune, blackberry, and spice notes. Fine tannins and a judicious use of new oak.*	**£19.00** ADN

GOLD
PORTUGUESE RED

☆ TESCO FINEST TOURIGA NACIONAL 2003, TESCO **Regional Blend** – *Deeply spiced wine with rich baked plum, earth, and spice aromas. The palate shows concentrated, leathery black fruit.*	**£6.00** TOS
☆ QUINTA DO VALLADO 2003, QUINTA DO VALLADO **Douro** – *Baked fruit, spice, and earth aromas. Supple with ripe fruit, fine tannins, and a touch of sweet oak.*	**£8.20** BWL/NYW
CARM RESERVA 2001, CARM **Douro** – *Mature tannins and concentrated chocolate and plum pudding flavours. Flowers, blackberries, and leather. Lively and persistent.*	**£13.00** REY
RESERVA RED 2003, QUINTA DE LA ROSA **Douro** – *Dark cerise. Intensely ripe, lifted aromas of tar, flowers, strawberries, toast, and vanilla. Pie flavours, hints of roses, and mint.*	**£15.70** CCS/QDR FLY
LA RESERVA 2001, QUINTA DE LA ROSA **Douro** – *Deep plum, spice, and savoury aromas. Rich black fruit, harmonious tannins, and some sweet new oak.*	**£19.60** BBR/BEN NYW
PASSADOURO RESERVA 2003, QUINTA DO PASSADOURO **Douro** – *Powerfully spiced with damson and prune aromas. Ripe black fruit, a firm tannic structure, and nicely judged oak.*	**£20.80** FLY/RWD
ESPORÃO GARRAFEIRA 2001, ESPORÃO **Alentejo** – *Solid wine with fabulous inky depth. Chunky, ripe black fruits married to firm tannins and well-judged oak.*	**£22.00** JEF/NYW

T DA TERRUGEM 2001, CAVES ALIANCA **A**LENTEJO – *Flowers, fresh redcurrants, and hints of tobacco. A tang of acidity lifts the richness of the palate.*	**£32.00** MDN/NYW

SILVER
PORTUGUESE RED

QUINTA DO CRASTO DOURO RED 2003, QUINTA DO CRASTO **D**OURO – *Ripe blackberries fill the perfumed, persistent palate. Exuberant herbs and spice. Soft, young, intense, complex, and rich.*	**£7.40** ADN/TNI ENO/NYW
RESERVA DÃO 2000, SOGRAPE **D**ÃO – *Graphite, tobacco, violets, and raspberries scent the nose. Flavours of soft vine fruits ravished by fresh acidity.*	**£8.00** MWW
QUINTA DO COA 2003, CARM **D**OURO – *Fresh cassis flavours. Pure, smooth, and persistent, this medium-firm wine has flowers and herbs.*	**£8.20** POR/RSV FLA/BBL
ESPORÃO RESERVA 2002, ESPORÃO **A**LENTEJO – *Currants, blackberries, and strawberries. Fine equilibrium of acidity, fruit, and wood. Scents of coconut.*	**£9.60** FHM/POR JEF
ESPORÃO ARAGONES 2003, ESPORÃO **A**LENTEJO – *Bright and very juicy, with loads of fresh raspberry fruit. Sweet, soft, round, and deep, with smoky overtones.*	**£10.00** JEF
DUAS QUINTAS RED RESERVE 2000, ADRIANO RAMOS PINTO VINHOS **D**OURO – *Attractive strawberry and white pepper notes. Firm, fine, and long, with perfumed cherry fruit.*	**£12.50** FHM/WPR MWW/BBO VLW
QUINTA VALE DO MARIA DOURO RED 2002, JOSÉ MARIA FONSECA & VAN ZELLER **D**OURO – *Intense, rich, vibrant, and perfumed, with excellent integration fruit and wood integration. High extract. Long.*	**£13.00** LAI
QUINTA DOS QUATRO VENTOS 2001, CAVES ALIANCA **D**OURO – *Ripe, with sweet berry flavours and savoury notes of balsamic vinegar. Earl Grey scents and a long, muscular finish.*	**£13.60** V&C/MDN NYW

QUINTA DO PORTAL GRANDE RESERVA 2001, QUINTA DO PORTAL **Douro** – *Bright ruby-garnet colour. Some evolution is present. An edge of smoke, coffee, and spice. Smooth and balanced.*	£20.00 CHN/VLW
TERRA DO ZAMBUJEIRO 2001, QUINTA DO ZAMBUJEIRO **Alentejo** – *Chunky chocolate and red cherry flavours. Spice and menthol notes add interest. Long, integrated, and very appealing.*	£24.50 FLY
VINHA BAROSSA 1998, LUIS PATO **Beiras** – *Opaque violet. Barnyard, garrigue, dark fruits, and undergrowth. The fresh flavours are buttressed by chewy tannins.*	£25.00 L&S
QUINTA DO VALE MEAO 2002, FJ OLAZABAL & FILHOS **Douro** – *Inky, restrained, and toasty. Upfront ripe blackcurrant fruit underscored by brisk bark tannins. Silky and exuberant.*	£29.00 WPR

B R O N Z E
PORTUGUESE RED

☆ PREMIUM PORTUGUESE RED 2003, JP VINHOS **Alentejo** – *Leather, spice, and fresh strawberry fruit. Firm, mouthwatering and ripe.*	£4.00 JSM
SERRA DE AZEITAO 2004, JP VINHOS **Terras do Sado** – *Smoke, bark, flowers, and chocolate wind round black cherry and strawberry fruit.*	£4.50 EHL
☆ FIUZA PREMIUM 2003, FIUZA & BRIGHT **Ribatejo** – *Red plums, cherries, and blackcurrants flavour this wine. Hints of warming Christmas spice.*	£5.00 CWS
MEIA PIPA 2001, JP VINHOS **Terras do Sado** – *Cassis, cherries, strawberries, and hedgerow flowers scent the nose and flavour the palate.*	£5.00 EHL
CASA DO LAGO 2004, DFJ VINHOS **Ribatejo** – *Perfumed with hints of caramel. The palate has a great burst of curranty fruit and a firm finish.*	£5.40 TPE

DFJ TOURIGA NACIONAL TOURIGA FRANCA 2003, DFJ VINHOS ESTREMADURA – *Good colour and clear firm bouquet. The palate has a soft, minty flavour with ripe fruit and harmonious tannins.*	**£6.00** TOS
MANTA PRETA 2003, DFJ VINHOS ESTREMADURA – *A well-defined, chewy wine with strong strawberry flavours, balanced acidity, and ripe, soft tannins.*	**£6.00** D&F
QUINTA DAS SETENCOSTAS 2004, CASA SANTOS LIMA ESTREMADURA – *A spicy, warm, refreshing red with perfectly ripe fruit and a long, mouthwatering strawberry finish.*	**£6.00** ENO
MONTE ALENTEJANO 2004, DFJ VINHOS ALENTEJO – *A very deep colour. Bags of ripe, spicy, juicy fruit on the nose and palate. Brisk, well-defined finish.*	**£7.00** JSM
VALTORTO 2003, WIESE & KROHN DOURO – *Elegant wine, very balanced with fine tannins.*	**£7.00** AVB
ALTANO RESERVA 2001, SILVA & COSENS DOURO – *A crimson colour, with inky black cherries on the nose. Intense, dense, and very long, with complex sooty tannins.*	**£7.50** POR/JEF
RESERVA ALENTEJO 2002, SOGRAPE ALENTEJO – *Bitter cherry aromas lead to a smoky bramble fruit palate with a tannic edge.*	**£8.00** MWW
VIDA NOVA 2004, ADEGA DO CANTOR ALGARVE – *An inky purple colour with a bramble nose and palate. Good tannins. Liquorice finish. Very fresh still.*	**£8.20** JEF/JSM
GRAND' ARTE TOURIGA NACIONAL 2003, DFJ VINHOS ESTREMADURA – *Both the nose and palate are in a warm and plummy style, integrated, soft, and harmonious.*	**£9.50** RAV/FLA NYW
ESPORÃO ALICANTE BOUSCHET 2003, ESPORÃO ALENTEJO – *Lots of tannins and juicy fruit on the palate, but as these are well-balanced this is a satisfying wine.*	**£10.00** JEF

ESPORÃO TOURIGA NACIONAL 2003, ESPORÃO **ALENTEJO** – *Caramel, spice, and rose perfume. Good tannins on the palate with a persistent finish.*	**£10.00** JEF
DOURO TINTO 2003, QUINTA DE LA ROSA **DOURO** – *Pretty cherry fruit with fine wood and herb notes. Medium weight. Flavourful and long.*	**£10.30** RSV/CCS BEN/FLY DEF/FRW
CURVA RESERVA TINTO 2002, AA CALEM **DOURO** – *Smoky dark chocolate and black cherries. A dry crisp palate with fine crunchy tannins and black pepper notes.*	**£11.00** CRI
QUINTA DE RORIZ RESERVA 2001, QUINTA DE RORIZ **DOURO** – *Youthful with peppery fruit, plenty of tannins, acidity, and alcohol. Additional cellaring will benefit this wine.*	**£12.00** FHM/JEF WSO
DUAS QUINTAS TINTO RESERVA 2001, ADRIANO RAMOS PINTO **DOURO** – *Rich loganberry perfumed nose. Complex palate with forest fruits and chocolate. Great length.*	**£14.80** FHM/POR MWW/BB O VLW
QUINTA DO PORTAL TOURIGA NACIONAL 2001, QUINTA DO PORTAL **DOURO** – *A soft attack of prunes, morello cherries, blackcurrants, and savoury oak. Long, sweet finish.*	**£17.00** CHN/VLW
REGUENGOS GARRAFEIRA DOS SOCIOS 2000, CARMIM **ALENTEJO** – *An evolved nose leads to a juicy blackberry and currant fruit palate with strong grippy tannins.*	**£18.00** PPW
QUINTA DE MACEDOS 2001, PAUL REYNOLDS LDA **DOURO** – *Complex, with powerful blackberry fruit and heavy tannins. More time in cellar would benefit this densely flavoured wine.*	**£18.40** FHM/FLY BBL
REDOMA 2001, NIEPOORT VINHOS **DOURO** – *Blackberry flavoured palate with well-integrated tannins and plenty of fruit on the firm finish.*	**£24.20** FHM/WPR TNI/FLY DEF/P&S
VINHA PAN 2001, LUIS PATO **BAIRRADA** – *Forest fruit nose. Very dry with herb and eucalyptus notes. Long finish.*	**£25.00** L&S

PASSADOURO 2000.00, "QUINTA DO PASSADOURO, SOC. AGRÌCOLA LDA." **Douro** – *Mature wood aromas. Straightforward black plummy fruits with some clove and cinnamon flavours.*	**£35.30** WPR/FLY RWD

SEAL OF APPROVAL
PORTUGUESE RED

☆ FIUZA CABERNET SAUVIGNON 2003, FIUZA & BRIGHT **Ribatejo** – *Deep blackcurrant and tobacco character.*	**£4.00** CWS

Gold medals have scored the equivalent of at least 18.5/20 (or 95/100) and are exceptional. Silver has scored over 17/20 (or 90/100), bronze over 15.5/20 (or 85/100), and seals of approval over 14/20 (or 80/100).
☆ particularly good value
★ truly great value

For stockist codes turn to page 317. For regularly updated information about stockists and the International Wine Challenge, visit wineint.com. For a full glossary of wine terms and a complete free wine course, visit robertjoseph-onwine.com

REST OF THE WORLD

After initially attempting to make mock-Germanic, semi-sweet whites. England's winemakers are now producing medalworthy dry whites and gaining genuine global respect for the quality of their sparkling wines. In retrospect, the potential to produce world-class fizz should have occurred to Britain's producers rather earlier. After all, the climate and the chalky soil are very similar to those of Champagne, a Northern French region with no history of making great still white wine.

BRONZE
REST OF THE WORLD WHITE

SURREY GOLD 2004, DENBIES WINE ESTATE SURREY, ENGLAND – *Aromatic, with restrained spicebox aromas on the nose. Plenty of medium-dry white peach and apple flavours.*	**£6.30** DBS/JSM ENG/EWC
CHAPEL DOWN ORTEGA 2003, CHAPEL DOWN KENT, ENGLAND – *Youthful with a verdant, fresh, and balanced palate. A very drinkable wine with a zesty, refreshing finish.*	**£7.50** BNK
BACCHUS DRY 2004, CAMEL VALLEY CORNWALL, ENGLAND – *An attractive grassy, aromatic nose with a lovely mix of off-dry Conference pear, nettles, and high acidity.*	**£9.00** CVV
CHAPEL DOWN BACCHUS RESERVE 2003, CHAPEL DOWN KENT, ENGLAND – *Sophisticated, textured, and aromatic, with nettles, green strawberries, and blackthorn flowers. Fresh and long.*	**£9.80** BNK/P&S
CHAPEL DOWN PINOT BLANC 2002, CHAPEL DOWN KENT, ENGLAND – *Textured whitecurrant and greengage flavours are seared by fresh acidity. Balanced, fragrant, and light-bodied.*	**£10.00** ENG

BRONZE
REST OF THE WORLD RED

BOUZA TEMPRANILLO TANNAT 2004, BODEGA BOUZA CANELONES, URUGUAY – *Soft strawberry fruit mingles with blackberries and prunes. Grilled meat nuances. Full and fragrant.*	£10.00 GRT
CUVÉE 3ÈME MILLÉNAIRE 2003, CHÂTEAU KSARA BEKAA VALLEY, LEBANON – *Deep, soulful, and piled high with summer fruits. Aromatic spice and chocolate aromas.*	£20.00 CAB

BRONZE
REST OF THE WORLD ROSÉ

PLUMPTON ESTATE ROSÉ 2004, PLUMPTON ESTATE EAST SUSSEX, ENGLAND – *Fragrant, its red cherry aromas and flavours tinged with pretty floral and deep herbal overtones.*	£6.00 CCS

GOLD
REST OF THE WORLD SPARKLING

☆ **CAMEL VALLEY BRUT 2001, CAMEL VALLEY** CORNWALL, ENGLAND – *Yeast mingles with greengages, whitecurrants, and Conference pears on the nose. Fine, slow-rising mousse and balanced acidity.*	£18.20 CVV/ENG EWC

SILVER
REST OF THE WORLD SPARKLING

MERRET GROSVENOR BLANC DE BLANC 2001, RIDGEVIEW SUSSEX, ENGLAND – *Elegant key lime, pear, and apple flavours. Pure, pretty scents of lemons and acacia blossom.*	£23.70 RVE/ENG EWC

B R O N Z E
REST OF THE WORLD SPARKLING

☆ CHAPEL DOWN BRUT NV, CHAPEL DOWN KENT, ENGLAND – *Peach, nettle, and rhubarb flavours.*	**£10.00** BGN/BNK
CHAPEL DOWN PINOT RESERVE 2001, CHAPEL DOWN KENT, ENGLAND – *This pretty, textured wine fairly bursts with whitecurrants, elderflowers, and pears.*	**£18.00** ENG

S E A L   O F   A P P R O V A L
REST OF THE WORLD FORTIFIED

☆ KINGS OAK PALE CREAM FORTIFIED BRITISH WINE NON VINTAGE, CONSTELLATION REGIONAL BLEND – *Richly sweet. Caramel and chocolate flavours.*	**£3.00** MHV
☆ KINGS OAK GINGER FORTIFIED BRITISH WINE NON VINTAGE, CONSTELLATION REGIONAL BLEND – *Freshly ground ginger aromas and flavours.*	**£3.10** MHV

FOR STOCKIST CODES turn to page 317. For regularly updated information about stockists and the International Wine Challenge, visit wineint.com. For a full glossary of wine terms and a complete free wine course, visit robertjoseph-onwine.com

SOUTH AFRICA

The first New World country to gain a name for the quality of its wines, South Africa allowed itself to be overtaken by Australia, New Zealand, and the Americas during the years of isolation. Today, a younger generation of winemakers is exploring new regions and more modern methods to produce Sauvignon Blancs good enough to beat the Kiwis and Shirazes that compete with both Australia and France. Look out, too, for examples of the Chenin Blanc, a variety that has long been a speciality in the Cape, and of course well-handled examples of the Pinotage, a South African invention grown almost nowhere else.

SILVER
SOUTH AFRICAN WHITE

☆ ORACLE SAUVIGNON BLANC 2004, DISTELL **STELLENBOSCH** – *Pungent green pepper and asparagus. Very crisp and spicy, with chalky minerality offsetting the sweet fruit.*	**£5.00** DTE
☆ THANDI CHARDONNAY 2004, OMNIA WINES **ELGIN** – *Restrained, youthful aromas of toast and pear. The palate is packed with jackfruit, melons, and apples.*	**£6.30** BGN/TOS OMN
GROOTE POST SAUVIGNON BLANC 2004, GROOTE POST **SWARTLAND** – *Subtle mix of herbs and mangoes. Flavoursome and packed with tropical fruit. Good balance between fruit and acidity.*	**£8.10** SAO/NZH WDI/HAC
ZEVENWACHT TIN MINE WHITE 2004, ZEVENWACHT ESTATE **COASTAL** – *Grassy, aromatic nose. Lush tropical fruit and good acidity keeping the balance poised on a knife-edge. A concentrated, polished wine.*	**£8.30** SAO
SAXENBURG PRIVATE COLLECTION SAUVIGNON BLANC 2004, SAXENBURG WINES **STELLENBOSCH** – *Grassy aromas on the nose with undertones of ripe melon. A jucy wine with a luscious finish.*	**£8.50** SAO/DEF

STELLENBOSCH CHARDONNAY 2003, NEIL ELLIS **Stellenbosch** – *White pepper powder and tobacco leaf nose. The palate has poached pear flavours and is admirably balanced.*	**£9.50** TOS/VLW
RUSTENBERG CHARDONNAY STELLENBOSCH 2003, RUSTENBERG ESTATE **Stellenbosch** – *Golden green, with pale persistent legs. Tropical pineapple aromas and intense flavours of butterscotch and lychees. Long and polished.*	**£10.90** SAO/FLA
GLEN CARLOU CHARDONNAY RESERVE 2004, GLEN CARLOU **Paarl** – *Ripe and buttery. The palate is a big, weighty mouthful of melon, butterscotch, and toast. Long and spicy.*	**£12.00** SAO

BRONZE
SOUTH AFRICAN WHITE

☆ DOUGLAS GREEN CHENIN BLANC 2004, DOUGLAS GREEN BELLINGHAM **Western Cape** – *Pineapple and acacia honey flavours drench the palate. Warm late harvest notes on the nose.*	**£4.50** TOS
☆ NIEL JOUBERT SAUVIGNON BLANC 2004, NIEL JOUBERT **Stellenbosch** – *Complex nose with fresh floral and zesty aromas. Ripe fruits linger on the palate for a balanced finish.*	**£4.70** POR/VNO
NIEL JOUBERT CHARDONNAY 2004, NIEL JOUBERT **Stellenbosch** – *Bright pale yellow. Very ripe, powerful flavours of melons and peaches with creamy vanilla undertones.*	**£5.20** ESL/VNO
BARREL FERMENTED CHENIN BLANC 2004, KLEINE ZALZE **Stellenbosch** – *A plethora of freshly squeezed lemons, green plums, honey and toast scents and flavours this delicious Chenin.*	**£5.30** MCT
MARTHINUS CHARDONNAY 2004, BOVLEI **Coastal** – *Fresh ripe apple nose. Hints of cinnamon toast and flavours of rhubarb crumble and custard.*	**£6.00** LAI
SAINSBURY'S CLASSIC SELECTION SOUTH AFRICAN CHARDONNAY 2003, VERGELEGEN **Western Cape** – *Gently oaked, with soft pineapple and butter scents. The golden citrus fruit palate is richly spiced.*	**£6.00** JSM

ZONNEBLOEM CHARDONNAY 2003, DISTELL **WESTERN CAPE** – *Floral notes perfume the nose. Herbal tones streak through the creamy palate of peach fruit and powdered oats.*	**£6.20** FHM/HBJ SAO/DTE
GRAHAM BECK CHARDONNAY VIOGNIER 2004, GRAHAM BECK WINES WESTERN CAPE – *Apricot and peach fruit, creamy nose, round body, and lifted floral notes. Warm and buttery. Soft.*	**£7.00** TOS/CCS FLY
RIVERS EDGE CHARDONNAY 2004, WELTEVREDE ROBERTSON – *Fresh and full. The deep gold colour is complemented by a bouquet and palate of limes and guavas.*	**£7.00** SAO
THANDI CHARDONNAY 2004, OMNIA WINES ELGIN – *Very brisk acidity lifts this youthful, creamy, gently oaked wine. Racy apple peel flavours.*	**£7.00** TOS/OMN
KEN FORRESTER CHENIN BLANC 2004, KEN FORRESTER STELLENBOSCH – *Fresh waxy lemons, lime zest, sweet honeysuckle, and mandarin orange flavours and scents. Zesty acidity.*	**£7.20** WPR/JSM
SIMONSIG CHARDONNAY 2003, SIMONSIG STELLENBOSCH – *Lemon meringue pie, creamy oak, and ripe pineapple. Buttery yet fresh, and remarkably persistent.*	**£7.20** SAO/CRI BBO
CHARDONNAY PRESTIGE CUVÉE 2004, BON COURAGE ESTATE BREEDE RIVER VALLEY – *Saturated with butterscotch and orange blossom essence. Lush, gratifying, and round.*	**£7.50** SAO
DE WETSHOF LESCA CHARDONNAY 2004, DANIE DE WET BREEDE RIVER VALLEY – *Youthful, with a smoky nose and soft peach and apricot fruit flavours. Well balanced and persistent.*	**£7.50** SAO/MWW RSS/VLW
UITKYK SAUVIGNON BLANC 2004, UITKYK STELLENBOSCH – *A fresh, aromatic, and grassy Sauvignon Blanc with a fruit-driven palate and long finish.*	**£7.60** FHM/HBJ SAO
JOOSTENBERG CHENIN BLANC 2004, JOOSTENBERG COASTAL – *Soft lanolin notes smooth out the fresh, floral palate of tropical white fruit salad flavours. Musky scents.*	**£7.70** BBR/CCS

CHARDONNAY RESERVE 2004, PERDEBERG CELLARS **Paarl** – *Clear ripe white melon aromas. Creamy flavours of soft oak and orchard fruits. Restrained tropical elements.*	£8.00 VNO
FORT SIMON CHARDONNAY 2004, AFRICAN PRIDE WINES Stellenbosch – *Oranges and limes scent the nose. The body is full of weighty, structured apricot fruit. Smoky notes.*	£8.00 D&D
JORDAN SAUVIGNON BLANC 2004, JORDAN ESTATE **Stellenbosch** – *The nose is light and floral. The palate is zippy with a ripe citrus attack and persistent finish.*	£8.10 SAO/FLY WRW
RAATS CHENIN BLANC 2004, RAATS FAMILY WINE **Stellenbosch** – *Buttery, round and full-bodied, this Chenin has lanolin notes, Sicilian lemon flavours, and warm spice bazaar scents.*	£8.70 ORB/DEF
LADY ANNE BARNARD 2003, AFRICAN PRIDE WINES **Stellenbosch** – *Big and lush, with loads of ripe guava and honeydew melon flavours. Tropical and rich.*	£9.00 D&D
PLACE OF ROCKS CHARDONNAY 2002, WELTEVREDE **Robertson** – *Burnished gold colour. Creamy yet fresh, with a fat, round palate of lemons and starfruit.*	£9.00 HOH
BARREL FERMENTED CHARDONNAY 2003, MULDERBOSCH VINEYARDS Stellenbosch – *Pronounced peaches and cream nose. Balanced and medium-bodied, with white stone fruit and sweet oak flavours.*	£9.70 NZH/VLW
CELLAR DOOR CHENIN BLANC 2004, VILLIERA **Western Cape** – *Spring blossom, fresh lemons, and aromatic beeswax flavour this buttery beauty. Hints of vanilla add softness.*	£10.00 WST
FROSTLINE CHARDONNAY 2004, FLAGSTONE **Prince Albert** – *Elegant pineapple flavours. Taut herbal aromas and savoury bready notes. Clear, long, and fresh.*	£10.00 ORB/DEF
BOSCHENDAL CHARDONNAY RESERVE 2004, BOSCHENDAL Paarl – *Lemons, green apples, runny honey, and juicy pineapples flavour this rich, buttery, mouthcoating Chardonnay.*	£10.10 SAO/EDC

FROSTLINE RIESLING 2004, FLAGSTONE	**£10.50**
PRINCE ALBERT – *Big yet sophisticated, with a fresh, light-bodied palate. Pronounced crisp green apple flavours. Textured.*	ORB/DEF
RIJK'S PRIVATE CELLAR CHARDONNAY 2003, RIJK'S PRIVATE CELLAR **TULBAGH** – *Buttered toast and smoke. A sophisticate with leesy burgundian character and radiant lemon flavours.*	**£11.00** CHN
VERGELEGEN SAUVIGNON BLANC RESERVE 2004, VERGELEGEN **STELLENBOSCH** – *Heaps of asparagus notes on the nose, followed by a soft, almost creamy palate with a long streak of acidity.*	**£12.70** FHM/SAO WPR/CNL NYW/P&S
JEAN LE LONG SAUVIGNON BLANC 2004, BOSCHENDAL **PAARL** – *Soft nettle and white peach aromas meld with flavours of pea pods and gooseberries. Ripe, linear, and focused.*	**£14.50** FHM/SAO
JORDAN NINE YARDS CHARDONNAY 2003, JORDAN ESTATE **STELLENBOSCH** – *Deep, elegant gold. Toast and spicebox scents. Ripe, with plenty of grapefruit and a long buttery finish.*	**£16.80** FHM/HPW SAO/FLY WRW/NY W
FMC 2003, KEN FORRESTER WINES **STELLENBOSCH** – *Fresh waxy lemon, elderflower, and honeycomb scents rise from the glass. Mineral-infused pear flavours pour from the palate.*	**£18.70** WPR/THI
DE WETSHOF BATELEUR CHARDONNAY 2003, DANIE DE WET **BREEDE RIVER VALLEY** – *The peachy nose is subtly spiced. Creamy attack of classy vanilla beans and pears.*	**£23.30** SAO/RSS VLW

SEAL OF APPROVAL
SOUTH AFRICAN WHITE

☆ TABLE MOUNTAIN CHENIN BLANC 2004, DISTELL **WESTERN CAPE** – *Mayflowers, elderflowers, and sweet citrus.*	**£3.00** DTE
☆ CO-OP CAPE OAK AGED CHENIN BLANC 2004, STELLENBOSCH VINEYARDS **WESTERN CAPE** – *Round apple flavours. Floral perfume.*	**£4.00** CWS

☆ ELEPHANT WALK CHENIN BLANC COLOMBARD 2004, GROOT EILAND Regional blend – *Crunchy white fruit flavours and lychee scents.*	£4.00 MYL
☆ GOIYA CHARDONNAY SAUVIGNON 2004, WESTCORP INTERNATIONAL Olifantsriver – *Intense flavours of peach and pineapple.*	£4.00 BGN/TOS
☆ KATHENBERG CHARDONNAY 2004, WINECORP Western Cape – *Bright gold. Pineapple and spice flavours.*	£4.00 WRT
☆ NIEL JOUBERT CHENIN BLANC 2004, NIEL JOUBERT Stellenbosch – *Fresh flowers and crunchy green apples galore.*	£4.00 VNO
☆ OBIKWA CAPE WHITE 2004, DISTELL Western Cape – *Fresh floral scents and flavours of ripe pear.*	£4.00 DTE

TROPHY
SOUTH AFRICAN RED

☆ DIEMERSFONTEIN CARPE DIEM PINOTAGE 2003, DIEMERSFONTEIN Paarl – *Delicious blueberry, rhubarb, and tar perfume. Lush berry fruit with supple tannins and sweet vanilla oak.*	£10.00 THI

GOLD
SOUTH AFRICAN RED

☆ LORD NEETHLING LAURENTIUS 1999, NEETHLINGSHOF Stellenbosch – *Restrained and elegant with fragrant blackberry, grass, and cedar aromas. Layered ripe fruit, sweet tannins and new oak.*	£10.00 HBJ
☆ PLAISIR DE MERLE MERLOT 2002, PLAISIR DE MERLE Stellenbosch – *Ripe cherries, black plums, forest floor, and summer rain scents and flavours. A round, full-bodied wine of exceptional quality.*	£12.00 FHM

RIJK'S PRIVATE CELLAR PINOTAGE 2002, RIJK'S PRIVATE CELLAR TULBAGH – *Succulent blackberry, tomato, and tar aromas. The thick palate shows rich fruit, balanced tannins, and well-judged oak.*	**£15.00** CHN
ENGELBRECHT ELS 2003, ENGELBRECHT ELS STELLENBOSCH – *Complex berry fruits, smoke, and violet perfume. Lush, sweet fruit with a sturdy yet supple tannic framework.*	**£20.50** SCK/CCS LEA/NYW

SILVER
SOUTH AFRICAN RED

BOSCHENDAL CHARDONNAY 2004, BOSCHENDAL PAARL – *Golden raisin and pear drop nose. Flavours of lemons, crème brulee, flowers, and powdered minerals. Long and rich.*	**£7.60** SAO/EDC FLA
BOSCHENDAL CABERNET SAUVIGNON 2002, BOSCHENDAL PAARL – *Elegant notes of cedar grace the nose. Some evolution showing on the smooth palate, which displays excellent balance.*	**£7.90** SAO/TPE EDC
GUARDIAN PEAK FRONTIER 2003, ENGELBRECHT ELS VINEYARDS STELLENBOSCH – *Bright, fresh redcurrant, herb, and stone nose. The palate is fruited and supported by a fine-grained tannic backbone.*	**£8.00** SAO/SCK CCS
INDALO PINOTAGE 2003, SWARTLAND WINERY SWARTLAND – *Cherries, raspberries, chocolate, balsamico, and coal elements. Creamy, with youth on its side. Coconut notes.*	**£8.00** RSS
UITKYK CARBERNET SAUVIGNON 2001, UITKYK STELLENBOSCH – *Full of blackcurrants, toast, bonfire scents, and forest floor echoes. Earthy yet polished.*	**£9.10** HBJ/SAO
ALLESVERLOREN TINTA BAROCCA 2003, ALLESVERLOREN STELLENBOSCH – *Sweet, juicy ripe blackberries, redcurrants, and cranberries. Herbal notes, scents of tar, smoke, and earth perfume the nose.*	**£9.20** FHM/SAO POR/ICL
BOSCHENDAL SYRAH 2001, BOSCHENDAL PAARL – *Rustic, earthy notes of the barnyard, with fresh, lifted menthol aromas, and piles of bright red cherry fruit.*	**£9.20** SAO/EDC

GRAHAM BECK MERLOT 2003, GRAHAM BECK WINES **WESTERN CAPE** – *A full palate of satiny plum and prune fruit, firm oak, and spice. Structured and integrated. Velvety red colour.*	**£9.30** SAO/CCS FLY
JORDAN MERLOT 2002, JORDAN **STELLENBOSCH** – *Maquis and red damsons rise from the glass. Flavours of redcurrants, apple skin, and leather line the palate. Smoky undertones.*	**£9.70** SAO/FLY WRW
CARPE DIEM CABERNET SAUVIGNON 2003, DIEMERSFONTEIN WINE **PAARL** – *Cigar box, red plum, and vanilla aromas. Flavours of blackcurrants, toast and crumpled leaves on the balanced palate.*	**£10.00** THI
DEVON CREST 2001, MARTIN MEINERT WINES **STELLENBOSCH** – *A mouthful of red and black vine fruits, cinnamon, cocoa powder, and tarmac. Scents of wild herbs and smoke.*	**£10.00** GRT
HORSE MOUNTAIN SHIRAZ 2004, HORSE MOUNTAIN **PAARL** – *Deep, rich, and masculine, its aromatic leather and cigar smoke notes mixing freely with raspberry pip flavours. Long.*	**£10.00** SAO
KLEIN CONSTANTIA MARLBROOK 2000, KLEIN CONSTANTIA **CONSTANTIA** – *Copious quantities of sun-warmed red berries. This classic is invitingly full, with soft tannins and fresh acidity.*	**£10.30** WIDELY AVAILABLE
KAAPZICHT ESTATE CABERNET SAUVIGNON 2001, KAAPZICHT ESTATE **STELLENBOSCH** – *Tarmac, toast, currants, and leaves scent the nose of this powerful wine. Cinnamon and blackberries grace the palate.*	**£10.80** SAO/SCK CCS
JOHN X MERRIMAN 2002, RUSTENBERG ESTATE **STELLENBOSCH** – *Exotic Patchouli and prunes with fresh blackberries on the nose. Flavourful raspberries and coconut line the integrated palate.*	**£11.10** WIDELY AVAILABLE
CEDERBERG SHIRAZ 2003, CEDERBERG **OLIFANTSRIVER** – *Heady scents of burning scrub, Indian peppercorns, earth, and blackberry compôte. Lively plum, and sweet oak flavours.*	**£11.50** H&H
LORD NEETHLING CABERNET FRANC 2002, NEETHLINGSHOF **STELLENBOSCH** – *Red stone fruits and exotic spices. Patchouli, vanilla, coconut, and chocolate add dimensionality to the fresh, juicy flavours.*	**£11.50** FHM/HBJ SAO

GLEN CARLOU GRAND CLASSIQUE 2002, GLEN CARLOU PAARL – *Clear, focused currant flavours and delicate herbal tones on the palate. The nose has lifted floral aromas.*	£12.00 SAO
HIDDEN VALLEY CABERNET SAUVIGNON 2000, HIDDEN VALLEY WINES STELLENBOSCH – *Granite, black cherries, flowers, and bay leaves. Packed with redcurrants, plums, and delicate notes of vanilla.*	£12.00 GRT
WARWICK CABERNET FRANC 2002, WARWICK WINE ESTATE STELLENBOSCH – *Deep, complex, and brooding, its sophisticated, mellow oak accentuating the beautiful blueberry, spice, and roast herb palate.*	£12.30 FLY/WDI HAC
SAXENBURG PRIVATE COLLECTION CABERNET SAUVIGNON 2001, SAXENBURG WINES STELLENBOSCH – *Inviting brick red colour displays signs of evolution. Nettles rise from the nose, blackcurrants linger on the palate.*	£12.50 MOR
LE BONHEUR CABERNET 2000, LE BONHEUR STELLENBOSCH – *Exotic aromas of sandalwood, Moroccan mint, and eucalyptus. The palate sports capsicum, prunes, and cassis.*	£14.00 SAO
RIDGEBACK SHIRAZ 2002, RIDGEBACK WINES PAARL – *Smoking tarmac on a hot summer's day and plenty of blackberries fill the nose of this many-faceted wine.*	£16.00 SAO
GRAHAM BECK THE JOSHUA 2002, GRAHAM BECK WINES COASTAL – *Deep colour. Cassis, apricot kernel, tree bark, clove, and jasmine scents. Balanced, soft, mellow, and long.*	£16.30 CCS/FLY
ERNIE ELS 2002, ENGELBRECHT ELS VINEYARDS STELLENBOSCH – *Huge quantities of currants meld into cedary tannins and minerals. One to cellar for some time.*	£40.00 SAO/SCK CCS/NYW

B R O N Z E
SOUTH AFRICAN RED

☆ CATHEDRAL CELLAR CABERNET SAUVIGNON 2000, KWV WESTERN CAPE – *Rich, fruit with distinct Cabernet nose. The palate shows delightful blackberry jam etched with vanilla.*	£5.00 NTD

☆ FOOTPRINT SHIRAZ 2004, AFRICAN PRIDE WINES WESTERN CAPE – *Bold blackberry flavours mingle with scents of suede and grilled meats. Balanced, fresh, and medium-bodied.*	£5.00 D&D
☆ PETIT PINOTAGE 2004, KEN FORRESTER WINES STELLENBOSCH – *Sweetly ripe summer fruit pudding flavours mingle with cracked black pepper and tarmac on nose and palate.*	£5.00 THI
☆ TESCO FINEST SOUTH AFRICAN PINOTAGE RESERVE 2003, TESCO – *Robust, full-bodied, and packed with red and black berries. This wine would be fantastic with grilled lamb or beef stew.*	£5.00 TOS
TWO OCEANS SHIRAZ 2003, DISTELL WESTERN CAPE – *Sweetly ripe, youthful, and fresh, with a deep purplish colour, flavours of sloes, and scents of wildflowers.*	£5.30 SAO/DTE PFC
SPIER INSPIRE MERLOT 2003, SPIER WESTERN CAPE – *Intense bramble fruit nose. The palate is a meaty affair with mown hay and cinder-strewn cherries.*	£6.00 PLB
GRAHAM BECK PINNO 2004, GRAHAM BECK WINES WESTERN CAPE – *Fresh hedgerow fruit, currant leaf, grilled meat, and sweet cherry tomato flavours.*	£6.50 SAO/TOS CCS/FLA FLY
KUMALA RESERVE SHIRAZ 2003, ORIGIN WINE WESTERN CAPE – *Rich, concentrated, and intense, with bright ripe blackberries, saddle leather, and savoury strawberry flavours.*	£6.50 BGN/THS
CATHEDRAL CELLAR MERLOT 2001, KWV WESTERN CAPE – *Tangy famyard and burnt rubber aromas on the nose, and a palate of raisined, smoky fruit. Long.*	£6.60 ECA/NTD
FAIRVIEW GOATS DO ROAM IN VILLAGES 2003, WINES OF CHARLES BACK WESTERN CAPE – *An attractive blend, with fresh mulberries, tar, peaches, and tobacco in abundance.*	£6.60 TOS
ASDA EXTRA SPECIAL STELLENBOSCH PINOTAGE 2003, FRANS SMIT FOR STELLENBOSCH STELLENBOSCH – *Fleshy red summer berries stud the robust, medium-full palate. This inky, savoury Pinotage has heady tarry aromas.*	£7.00 ASD

BOSCHENDAL CABERNET SAUVIGNON 2002, **BOSCHENDAL** PAARL – *A well-crafted, integrated wine. Kirsch, tobacco, smoke, and toast characteristics.*	**£7.60** SWG
VERGELEGEN MILL RACE 2002, VERGELEGEN **STELLENBOSCH** – *The fresh damson fruit has delicious soot and chocolate overtones. Structured and long.*	**£7.80** WIDELY AVAILABLE
CLOS MALVERNE PINOTAGE 2001, CLOS MALVERNE **STELLENBOSCH** – *Mouthwatering strawberry and red cherry flavours mix with loam and stony minerals on this focused, flavour-packed wine.*	**£7.90** FHM/CPR NEC/RSV CNL/WRK
RIETVALLEI ESTATE CABERNET SAUVIGNON 2002, **RIETVALLEI ESTATE** ROBERTSON – *Dark purple, youthful oak, currant fruit, clear minty aromas, and a long finish.*	**£8.00** RWA
FAIRVIEW GOAT ROTI 2003, WINES OF CHARLES **BACK** WESTERN CAPE – *Spicy, lively, elegant, and structured, with leather, hedgerow fruit, vanilla, and cinnamon. Balanced and long.*	**£9.00** MWW
FAIRVIEW PINOTAGE VIOGNIER 2003, WINES OF **CHARLES BACK** COASTAL – *Sweet hints of peaches grace the nose. Deep blackberry flavours laced with vanilla beans. Long and balanced.*	**£9.00** CCS/FLY DEF/LIB
KLEIN CONSTANTIA CABERNET SAUVIGNON 2000, **KLEIN CONSTANTIA** CONSTANTIA – *Gunsmoke, capsicum, and fresh plum scents and flavours. Ripe, robust and ready to drink.*	**£9.00** SWG
FAIRVIEW SMV 2002, WINES OF CHARLES BACK COASTAL – *Garrigue notes scent the toasty blackberry nose. Fresh, bright plums, spices, and smoke flavour the tasty palate.*	**£9.20** CCS/FLY WRK/DEF LIB
BEAUMONT PINOTAGE 2003, BEAUMONT WINES WALKER BAY – *Tarmac, red honeysuckle, savoury red cherries, and bonfire smoke scents. Rich, robust, and firmly structured.*	**£9.30** FTH
RIETVALLEI ESTATE SHIRAZ 2003, RIETVALLEI ESTATE ROBERTSON – *Glossy coal, perfumed flowers, smoky bacon, and sweet raspberries pour from this wine. Dense and long.*	**£9.50** RWA

GRAHAM BECK THE WILLIAM 2001, GRAHAM BECK WINES Coastal – *Clear black fruit aromas and flavours. Spiked with fresh mint and pine needle characteristics.*	**£9.80** SAO/CCS FLY
AGOSTINELLI BARBERA 2004, WINES OF CHARLES BACK Swartland – *Inky, juicy, and very fresh – true to its viticultural roots, this cherry-laden beauty would make an excellent food wine.*	**£9.90** CCS/FLY LIB
CLOOF PINOTAGE 2002, CLOOF WINES Coastal – *Black cherry, blackberry, and leather scents and flavours. The palate is etched with cleansing acidity. Long.*	**£10.00** BWC
EIKENDAL CLASSIQUE 2001, EIKENDAL VINEYARDS Western Cape – *A soft mountful of juicy currant fruit and hints of spicebox and vanilla on the nose.*	**£10.00** VNO
GOLDEN TRIANGLE PINOTAGE 2003, STELLENZICHT Stellenbosch – *Youthful yet starting to evolve, this rich Pinotage has deep tar and redcurrant flavours on its broad, powerful palate.*	**£10.00** SAO
PINOTAGE RESERVE SELECTION 2003, BEYERSKLOOF Stellenbosch – *Sophisticated, sleek, and finely crafted, with piles of red and blue berries and liberal lashings of sweet oak.*	**£10.00** RSS
THE BERRIO CABERNET SAUVIGNON 2003, FLAGSTONE Western Cape – *Cassis, strawberries, charcoal, and herbs scent and flavour the palate. Chocolate notes.*	**£10.00** ODD
JORDAN CABERNET SAUVIGNON 2002, JORDAN ESTATE Stellenbosch – *Intense cassis and mineral aromas and flavours. Hints of charred wood. Toasty.*	**£10.40** FHM/SAO FLY/WRW NYW
BOSCHENDAL CABERNET SAUVIGNON RESERVE 2001, BOSCHENDAL Paarl – *Displaying signs of evolution, this rich, balanced Cabernet has currant leaf and black sloe flavours.*	**£10.70** SAO/EDC
EAGLEVLEI CABERNET SAUVIGNON 2001, EAGLEVLEI Stellenbosch – *Cedar and lead pencil shavings rise from the Bordeaux-style nose. Liqueur de cassis palate.*	**£10.70** TNG

FAIRVIEW CALDERA 2003, WINES OF CHARLES BACK **SWARTLAND** – *Crunchy cranberries peppered with poivre.* *Plums, prunes, and blackberries. Layered and long.*	**£10.90** CCS/FLY LIB
DIEMERSFONTEIN CARPE DIEM SHIRAZ 2003, MARIE **KNIGHT - THIERRYS WESTERN CAPE** – *Dark tobacco,* *leather, and spice nose. Blackcurrant juice flavours. Balanced,* *with a long, clear finish.*	**£11.00** WTS
HORSE MOUNTAIN MICHELE 2004, HORSE MOUNTAIN **PAARL** – *Fresh red and black cherry flavours. Pencil lead, herbs,* *chocolate, and vanilla scents.*	**£11.00** SAO
SPICE ROUTE PINOTAGE 2003, WINES OF CHARLES **BACK SWARTLAND** – *Round, robust, and structured, with* *broad flavours and aromas of redcurrants, strawberries,* *and blackberries. Tarry.*	**£11.00** SAO
WARWICK THREE CAPE LADIES 2002, WARWICK **ESTATE STELLENBOSCH** – *Deepest cassis, chocolate, charred* *cedar, and tar aromas and flavours. Layered and very long.*	**£11.30** SAO/TPE FLY/WDI HAC
BELLINGHAM MAVERICK SYRAH 2003, BELLINGHAM **COASTAL** – *Smoke, blueberries, and hints of peach on the nose.* *Approachable, young, fresh Victoria plum flavours.*	**£12.00** WST
SAXENBURG SHIRAZ SELECT 2001, SAXENBURG **WINES STELLENBOSCH** – *Opaque purple-black. Spicebox,* *grilled meats, raisins, and bonfire perfumes the nose.* *Full-bodied, structured plum palate.*	**£12.50** POR/DEF
FRANS MALAN RESERVE 2001, SIMONSIG **STELLENBOSCH** – *The Malan brothers have produced another* *winner. Chocolatey and filled with fruit, its dark cherry flavours* *supported by smoky tannins.*	**£13.00** SAO/CRI BBO
GLEN CARLOU SYRAH 2003, GLEN CARLOU **PAARL** – *Toast, blackcurrants, prunes, and blueberries* *perfume the nose. Bright soft summer pudding flavours.*	**£13.00** SAO
GLEN CARLOU SYRAH 2004, GLEN CARLOU **PAARL** – *Vibrant blueberries and cream bouquet. Tangy,* *chunky, and full, with good balance and a long satiny finish.*	**£13.00** SAO

NATURE IN CONCERT PINOT NOIR 2003, DANIE DE WET **Breede River Valley** – *Toasty oak and satin cherry fruit on the palate. Scents of vanilla, autumn leaves, and apple on the nose.*	**£13.00** RSS
WARWICK TRILOGY 2002, WARWICK ESTATE **Stellenbosch** – *Deeply coloured, with a soft, minty bouquet. Firm oak. Tarry, yet delicate.*	**£13.20** SAO/TPE FLY/WDI HAC/DEF
REDHILL PINOTAGE 2003, SIMONSIG **Stellenbosch** – *Dark fruit and herbal aromas with a smoky nose, gamey palate with redcurrants and black pepper on the finish.*	**£13.30** CRI/BBO
CREDO CABERNET SAUVIGNON 2003, OMNIA WINES **Stellenbosch** – *Fresh, youthful, and thrusting, its bright hedgerow flavours buoyed by plenty of oak.*	**£14.00** OMN
RAATS CABERNET FRANC 2003, RAATS FAMILY WINES **Stellenbosch** – *Dark cherries and plums cascade over the robust palate. Hints of creosote add depth to the velvety fruit.*	**£14.00** ORB/DEF
BELLINGHAM SPITZ MERLOT 2002, BELLINGHAM WINES **Coastal** – *Sloes and marjoram scent the nose. The palate has plenty of black fruit and cedary tannins.*	**£15.00** WST
KUMALA JOURNEYS END SHIRAZ 2003, JOURNEYS END SHIRAZ **Western Cape** – *Chocolate and red fruit are prominent in this chewy wine. Elegant, with good flavour and colour.*	**£15.00** WST
RIJK'S PRIVATE CELLAR CABERNET SAUVIGNON 2001, RIJK'S PRIVATE CELLAR **Tulbagh** – *Mint, Christmas cake, and blackcurrant nose. The palate has sloe and damson flavours and a lasting finish.*	**£15.00** CHN
MERINDOL 2002, SIMONSIG **Stellenbosch** – *Dutch cocoa, herbs, and perfumed flowers entwine with redcurrants, prunes, and bluish plums on the sleek palate.*	**£15.20** SAO/CRI BBO
FAIRVIEW JAKKALSFONTEIN SHIRAZ 2002, WINES OF CHARLES BACK **Swartland** – *Deeply intense nose. The palate brims with concentrated meaty red fruit. Sweet oak lends ripe tannins.*	**£15.90** CCS/FLY LIB

FAIRVIEW SOLITUDE SHIRAZ 2002, WINES OF CHARLES BACK PAARL – *A unique nose of blueberry cream and oatmeal, mingled with a pepper-gamey flavour. The length is long and lasting.*	**£15.90** CCS/BEN FLY/LIB
JORDAN COBBLERS HILL 2002, JORDAN ESTATE STELLENBOSCH – *Soft and elegant, with ripe cherry fruit and balanced tannins. Succulent and delicious.*	**£16.80** FHM/NEC SAO/FLY WRW
GRAHAM BECK THE RIDGE SYRAH 2001, GRAHAM BECK WINES ROBERTSON – *Star-bright purple. Dense, atttractive cassis, violet, pepper, and earth nose. Cherry and creosote palate. Intense and ageworthy.*	**£17.00** CCS/FLY
VEENWOUDEN MERLOT 2002, VEENWOUDEN PAARL – *Deeply coloured, with upfront hedgerow fruit flavours, woody notes, and a smooth texture.*	**£17.50** SCK/CCS FLA/NYW P&S
GALPIN PEAK PINOT NOIR 2003, BOUCHARD FINLAYSON WALKER BAY – *Bright ruby red. The nose is gamey, with sweet prune and plum fruit – shades of mature St-Emilion!*	**£17.90** WIDELY AVAILABLE
STEYTLER PINOTAGE 2002, KAAPZICHT ESTATE STELLENBOSCH – *Rich and very fleshy, with earthy notes, hints of cinnamon, and faint whiffs of bacon. Lavish cherry flavours.*	**£19.50** SAO/SCK CCS/NYW
STEYTLER VISION 2002, KAAPZICHT ESTATE STELLENBOSCH – *Rubber and smoke appear on the nose. The palate is crammed with small dark berry flavours.*	**£19.50** SAO/SCK CCS/NYW
ESTATE WINE 2001, RUST EN VERDE STELLENBOSCH – *Warm, soft, and characterful, with lots of blackberries, cassis, and a hint of beetroot.*	**£21.20** NEC/SAO SCK/CCS FLA
SYNERGY RESERVE 2002, BEYERSKLOOF STELLENBOSCH – *Bonfire scents mingle with glossy coal notes on the nose. Flavours of rich redcurrants, chocolate, and dark plums.*	**£22.50** RSS/VLW
VERGELEGEN PRESTIGE RED 2001, VERGELEGEN STELLENBOSCH – *Fresh cigar box aromas. Very ripe, big, and full, with warming roast coffee bean flavours.*	**£24.20** FHM/SAO WPR/TOS HAC/P&S

SEAL OF APPROVAL
SOUTH AFRICAN RED

☆ ASDA SOUTH AFRICAN PINOTAGE 2004, WESTERN CAPE WESTERN CAPE – *Smoky bacon, bonfire, and strawberry elements.*	**£3.50** ASD
☆ ASHGROVE CINSAULT RUBY CABERNET 2004, BOVLEI REGIONAL BLEND – *Pepper, soot, and ripe strawberry characteristics.*	**£3.80** MYL/BGN
☆ VINTNERS COLLECTION SHIRAZ PINOTAGE 2003, CONSTELLATION WESTERN CAPE – *Bonfire scents mingle with ripe black fruit flavours.*	**£3.80** LCC

SILVER
SOUTH AFRICAN SPARKLING

☆ GRAHAM BECK BRUT NV, GRAHAM BECK WINES ROBERTSON – *Yeasty aromas, persistent mousse and an appealing golden colour. Flavours of lemons and grapefruit mingle with hazelnuts and biscuits.*	**£9.50** SAO/FLY P&S

BRONZE
SOUTH AFRICAN SPARKLING

☆ PONGRACZ NV, DISTELL WESTERN CAPE – *Cranberries, talcum powder, red honeysuckle, cherry pie, and lime cordial wend their way from this ripe wine.*	**£8.70** SAO/DTE PFC

GOLD
SOUTH AFRICAN SWEET

★ T NOBLE LATE HARVEST 2001, KEN FORRESTER STELLENBOSCH – *Orange zest, sultanas, and honey scent the nose. Delicate botrytis and lusciously sweet lemon marmalade.*	**£9.00** WTS

S I L V E R
SOUTH AFRICAN SWEET

PAUL CLUVER NOBLE LATE HARVEST 2003, PAUL CLUVER **Elgin** – *Clear, deep quince, blossom, lemon, almond, and honeycomb characteristics. Very long, its intense personality offering up something completely different.*	**£10.60** FHM/NEC SAO/DEF

B R O N Z E
SOUTH AFRICAN SWEET

☆ BOWENS FOLLY NOBLE LATE HARVEST 2001, ROBERTSON COOPERATIVE **Robertson** – *Full of yellow apple, green plum, and starfruit flavours, this wine is bright, intense, and very attractive.*	**£4.20** MCT
☆ JOOSTENBERG CHENIN BLANC NOBLE LATE HARVEST 2004, JOOSTENBERG WINES **Paarl** – *Rich lime marmalade with a great balance between sweetness and acidity. Delicious.*	**£5.00** CCS
☆ NEDERBURG NOBLE LATE HARVEST 2004, DISTELL **Western Cape** – *A youthful nose with honeyed aromas. Flavours of satsumas. High acidity. Refreshing and light.*	**£5.60** HBJ/DTE
☆ ROBERTSON WINERY ALMOND GROVE NOBLE LATE HARVEST 2003, ROBERTSON WINERY **Robertson** – *Very sweet orange and passion fruit flavours are off-set with bitter lemon and grapefruit notes and good acidity.*	**£6.00** CHN
NOBILE LATE HARVEST 2004, DIEU DONNÉ VINEYARDS **Paarl** – *A luscious wine with a honeyed quality. Elegant and balanced, with a refreshing lime zest finish.*	**£9.00** PAT
SLANGHOEK NOBLE LATE HARVEST 2003, SLANGHOEK **Breede Rver Valley** – *Interesting honey and green tea flavours. A fresh, mid-weight wine, with a long finish.*	**£9.00** ASD
JORDAN MELLIFERA BOTRYTIS 2003, JORDAN ESTATE **Stellenbosch** – *A citrus and kerosene style with medium weight and notes of orange blossom and honey on the finish.*	**£9.40** FLY/WRW NYW

LORD **N**EETHLING **W**EISSER RIESLING NOBLE LATE HARVEST 2004, NEETHLINGSHOF **S**TELLENBOSCH – *Concentrated, layered, and very sweet, its luxuriant tangerine and pineapple flavours riven by fresh acidity.*	£14.90
	FHM/HBJ

SEAL OF APPROVAL
SOUTH AFRICAN SWEET

☆ CO-OP CAPE SWEET SURRENDER 2003, BERGSIG ESTATE **B**REEDE **R**IVER **V**ALLEY – *Fresh mandarin orange and honey flavours.*	£5.00
	CWS

GOLD **MEDALS HAVE SCORED** the equivalent of at least 18.5/20 (or 95/100) and are exceptional. Silver has scored over 17/20 (or 90/100), bronze over 15.5/20 (or 85/100), and seals of approval over 14/20 (or 80/100).
☆ particularly good value
★ truly great value

FOR **STOCKIST CODES** turn to page 317. For regularly updated information about stockists and the International Wine Challenge, visit **wineint.com**. For a full glossary of wine terms and a complete free wine course, visit **robertjoseph-onwine.com**

S P A I N

In Britain, Spanish wine unfortunately tends to be associated with cheap and cheerful red and white on offer in holiday resorts. with encouragement from well-heeled American wine drinkers, however, Spain's winemakers have recently raised their game. Today, the top wines of regions like Ribera del Duero, Toro, and Priorat can, like the most ambitious efforts of Italy, command higher prices than most Bordeaux. There are still plenty of bargains to be found – as the 200 or so wines listed below demonstrate. While exploring the reds, whites, and sparkling wines, take time to try some of the sherries – arguably the most underrated and most food-friendly wines in the world.

B R O N Z E
CATALONIA + NORTHEAST WHITE

VIÑA ESMERELDA 2004, MIGUEL TORRES Catalonia – *Juicy yellow apples, elderflowers, and hints of pea pod scent and flavour this balanced, refreshing, light-bodied wine.*	£6.10 WIDELY AVAILABLE

T R O P H Y
CATALONIA + NORTHEAST RED

LES ONES 2002, BODEGAS DE CAL GRAU Priorat – *Complex ripe blueberries, plumcake, and clove spice scents. Succulent fruit married to sweet French oak.*	£18.50

S I L V E R
CATALONIA + NORTHEAST RED

☆ ARTESANO 2004, TERRE A VERRE Catalonia – *The nose has attractive liquorice notes leading to a well-defined palate with black pepper flavours and crunchy cherry notes.*	£5.00 THI

LA PLANELLA 2003, JOAN D'ANGUERA CATALONIA – *Good concentrated palate with distinctive terroir notes and liquroice and herbaceous fruit. A reasonably classy wine.*	**£10.00** L&S/VLW
SYRAH COLECCIÓN 2000, ALBET I NOYA CATALONIA – *Strong and robust, with an aromatic nose that displays a mineral character. The palate is spicy and round.*	**£12.00** VRT
JOAN GINÉ GINÉ 2001, BUIL & GINÉ PRIORAT – *Earthy, spicy nose and palate, with scented black fruit notes. Sweet chocolate and spice notes on the finish.*	**£15.00** CCS
COMA VELLA PRIORAT 2002, JOSE VELO-REGO CATALONIA – *Big and rich, with chocolate, mulberries, plums, and vanilla. Harmonious and firm, with rich sweet oak and spice.*	**£16.00** WTS
MORLANDA VI DE GUARDA 2001, FREIXENET SA PRIORAT – *A complex palate of red and black fruit, an attractive chocolate cake note all balanced with fine tannins and acidity.*	**£20.00** BIB
SCALA DEI CARTOIXA 2001, SCALA DEI CATALONIA – *Named after the first Spanish Karthäuser monastery. Strawberries, blueberries, cracked pepper, thyme, and hot stone.*	**£20.00** CON

B R O N Z E
CATALONIA + NORTHEAST RED

RAMON ROQUETA TINTO CRIANZA 2001, BODEGAS ROQUETA CATALONIA – *An inviting nose of smoky black fruits, with a mouthful of spice and leather that lingers on the palate.*	**£7.20** LAI
TERRASOLA SYRAH 2003, JEAN LEON SL CATALONIA – *A generous spicy Spanish red with supple fruit. The ideal accompaniment to chorizo and other piquante delicacies.*	**£7.50** FLY
CLOS DELS CODOLS 2001, TERRES DE CODOLS I LICORELLA, S.L MONTSANT – *Ripe, mature, and characterful, this flavourful blend has strawberry, white pepper, and raspberry flavours and scents.*	**£8.00** MDN

RENÉ BARBIER CABERNET SAUVIGNON LARGA MACERACIÓN 1999, RENÉ BARBIER CATALONIA – *Rich and developed, with a complex raisin and black fruit nose. Mature, yet bright.*	£9.00 FXT
CHATELDON RESERVA CABERNET SAUVIGNON 2000, BODEGAS PINORD CATALONIA – *Garnet red, with a ripe gamey nose and a deep, firm, long palate. Admirably complex.*	£10.00 CCS
LEGITIM DE MULLER 2000, DE MULLER CATALONIA – *Fresh redcurrant flavours are underpinned by a network of spicewood tannins. Sultry scents of pepper and chocolate.*	£10.80 L&S
LES TERRASSES 2002, ALVARO PALACIOS CATALONIA – *Sweet, inky, juicy raspberry fruit flavours. High extract, dry tannins, and a medium-long finish.*	£14.80 C&B
MAS LA PLANA 1999, MIGUEL TORRES CATALONIA – *Some age is evident in the brick-red colour and on the nose. Ripe, with peppery spice. Very fine.*	£20.00 FHM/A&A POR/JEF FLY/ICL
EL BUGADER 2001, JOAN D'ANGUERA CATALONIA – *Bright, deeply coloured, and full of redcurrants and blackberries. Textured, layered, and mature.*	£22.30 NYW
GRAN CLAUSTRO TINTO DE CASTILLO PERELADA 2001, CAVAS DEL CASTILLO DE PERELADA AMPURDÁN COSTA BRAVA – *Ripe toasty fruit, vanilla essence, glowing ruby red cherries, and a long, elegant finish.*	£32.50 FLY

SEAL OF APPROVAL
CATALONIA + NORTHEAST RED

☆ RENÉ BARBIER TINTO 2003, RENÉ BARBIER CATALONIA – *Little hedgerow sloe fruit flavours.*	£4.00 WIM

B R O N Z E
CATALONIA + NORTHEAST SPARKLING

☆ CO-OP CAVA ROSADO BRUT NV, MARQUES DE MONISTROL Catalonia – *Silky strawberry fruit, hedgerow sloes, and little white flowers grace the nose and palate of this refreshing Cava rosé.*	£5.00
	CWS
☆ MHV CAVA NV, COVIDES Catalonia – *Fresh pear juice, loam, and sweet flower perfume. Foamy citrus fruit palate with the merest hint of clove bud spice.*	£5.40
	BNK
☆ CRISTAL CAVA NV, CASTELLBLANCH Ampurdán Costa Brava – *New-mown hay, wildflowers, crushed leaves, and pear drops. This is pleasing Cava with a fine, frothy mousse.*	£5.60
	TOS/RAV
CODORNÍU JAUME NV, CODORNÍU Catalonia – *Tight-knit, layered, and fine, with acacia, spicebox, and tobacco and bags of white stone fruit.*	£20.00
	MCT

S E A L O F A P P R O V A L
CATALONIA + NORTHEAST SPARKLING

☆ ASDA MAS MIRALDA CAVA NV, CODORNÍU Catalonia – *Pears, flowers, and powdered minerals.*	£3.70
	ASD
☆ CASITO CAVA BRUT NV, BODEGAS UNIDAS Catalonia – *Creamy mousse, floral hints, and apple flavours.*	£5.00
	WRT
☆ ASDA EXTRA SPECIAL MAS MIRALDA VINTAGE CAVA 2002, CODORNÍU Catalonia – *Focused, rich, and integrated. Soft and round.*	£5.90
	ASD
☆ CAVA CRISTALINO BRUT 2004, JAUME SERRA Catalonia – *Fruity, round, and medium-weight. Floral.*	£6.00
	MWW

☆ CAVA MAS TAULER BRUT ARTESANO NV, MONT MARCAL **Catalonia** – *Hints of loam deepen the white peach flavours.*	£6.00
	VGN

☆ MARQUÉS DE MONISTROL SELECCIÓN ESPECIALE ROSÉ NV, UNITED WINERIES **Catalonia** – *Redcurrant flavours permeate nose and palate.*	£6.40
	A&A/UWO

☆ PERE VENTURA BRUT TRESOR NV, PERE VENTURA **Catalonia** – *Sliced crisp apples and powdery mayflowers.*	£7.00
	WAV

☆ CORDON NEGRO BRUT 2001, FREIXENET **Catalonia** – *Soft, harmonious, well-crafted white fruit flavours.*	£7.20
	BGN/TOS MWW/NTD WOC

TROPHY
RIOJA + NORTH-CENTRAL RED

SECASTILLA SOMONTANO 2003, VIÑAS DEL VERO **Aragón** – *Ripe, concentrated blackberry fruit laced with sweet oak. Dark bramble fruits, rhubarb, roasted spices, and freshly ground coffee.*	£.00
	NOT AVAILABLE IN THE UK

GOLD
RIOJA + NORTH-CENTRAL RED

☆ LAS RAMAS CAMPO DE BORJA OLD VINES GARNACHA 2003, BODEGAS ARAGONESAS **Aragón** – *The warm, mouthcoating palate has intense raspberry and blackcurrant flavours, fresh acidity, and light tannins.*	£5.00
	VGN
☆ MONTECILLO CRIANZA 2001, BODEGAS MONTECILLO **Rioja** – *Aromas of blueberry and vanilla. Spicy with rich berry fruit, supple tannins, and well-integrated toasty oak.*	£7.00
	HBJ
RESERVA DE LA FAMILIA 1999, BODEGAS LUIS CAÑAS **Rioja** – *Supple redcurrant and Madagascar vanilla nose. Refined ripe fruit and well-judged toasty oak.*	£13.50
	TNG/OCM CCS

SILVER
RIOJA + NORTH-CENTRAL RED

REY DON GARCIA 2002, BODEGAS RUCONIA Rioja – *Vanilla beans, toast, and strawberry fruit flavours and scents. The palate is structured, pure, firm, and modern.*	£8.00 LEA
VINA CANA RIOJA RESERVA 1999, GONZALEZ BYASS Rioja – *Deep raspberry fruit, soft vanilla, and a generous fistful of spice. An intense wine with good concentration and weight.*	£8.00 SMF
BARON DE LEY RESERVA 2000, BODEGAS BARON DE LEY Rioja – *Notes of the farmyard scent the nose. Soft, round hedgerow fruits, notes of leather and spice radiate from the palate.*	£9.70 CEB/FLY THS
COTO DE IMAZ GRAN RESERVA 1995, EL COTO DE RIOJA Rioja – *Warm, rich vanilla pod aromas and red cherry flavours. Clear, dark ruby-garnet colour. Elegant, vibrant, and well-constructed.*	£13.90 ESL/EDC
REMELLURI RESERVA 2000, GRANJA NTRA SRA DE REMELLURI Rioja – *Characterful and balanced, this is a structured wine with rich summer fruits, supported by a framework of taut tannins.*	£14.00 ALL
VALENCISO RESERVA 2001, COMPANIA BODEGUERA DE VALENCISO Rioja – *Juicy black cherries and currants spill from the palate, which has generous toasty overtones and a silky texture.*	£14.00 DCT
CILLAR DE SILOS CRIANZA 2003, CILLAR DE SILOS Basque country – *Dark, youthful, powerful cherry fruit flavours are laced with scents of lavender and wild thyme. Deep tobacco leaf tannins.*	£16.00 TNG
GRAN ALBIÑA 2001, BODEGAS RIOJANAS Rioja – *Spicy, peppery aromas complement the palate of sweetly ripe, evolved baked plum tart flavours. Complex and concentrated.*	£20.00 PBA
MARQUES DE LA CONCORDIA HACIENDA DE SUSAR 2001, UNITED WINERIES Rioja – *Medium-bodied, ripe, and plump, this beauty has pretty plum and redcurrant flavours cascading across the palate.*	£20.00 UWO

AMAREN RESERVA 1999, BODEGAS LUIS CAÑAS	£22.00
Rioja – *Highly coloured. Intense, very ripe black fruit aromas. Fresh acidity and coconut milk flavours. Persistent.*	TNG/OCM CCS

B R O N Z E
RIOJA + NORTH-CENTRAL RED

☆ ASDA RIOJA CLASICO NV, VIÑEDOS DE ALDEANUEVA **Rioja** – *Fresh strawberries, leather, spices, toast, and vanilla. This is an approachable Rioja with plenty of charm.*	£4.20 ASD
☆ CAMPANEO MERLOT 2004, BODEGAS ARAGONESES **Aragón** – *Juicy blackberry jam fruit flavours. Fine, dense tannic structure. Restrained fruitcake overtones.*	£5.00 BGL
☆ ESPIRAL OLD VINE GARNACHA 2004, SAN GREGORIO - NORREL ROBERTSON MW **Aragón** – *A rustic, cheering wine with robust flavours of stewed plums and oriental spices, leading to a clean, warm finish.*	£5.00 WAV
☆ GRAN DON DARIAS 1999, BODEGAS VICTORIANAS **Rioja** – *Silky, harmonious, and attractive. Red stone fruit flavours and tobacco leaf scents.*	£5.00 PLB
☆ GUIA REAL RIOJA TINTO 2003, CARLOS SERRES **Rioja** – *Raspberry fruit, notes of vanilla, and hints of tobacco smoke. The palate is fresh, balanced, and clear.*	£5.00 MDN
PRECIOSO NV, VINEDOS DE ALDEANUEVA **Rioja** – *White pepper, redcurrants, and raspberries flavour this Rioja. Clear, medium-bodied, and liberally laced with toasty notes.*	£5.30 FLY/PLB
PALACIO DE SADA 2003, BODEGA DE BAJA MONTAÑA **Navarre** – *Cherry preserves, wild thyme, and pepper flavour this youthful, medium-bodied wine. Complex, with the texture of satin.*	£5.70 VTS/THS
BORSAO SELECCIÓN 2004, BODEGAS BORSAO **Aragón** – *A fleshy, jammy redcurrant nose with good balance and well-delineated fine tannins on the palate.*	£5.80 FLY/LEA

MARQUÉS DE LA CONCORDIA TEMPRANILLO 2003, MARQUÉS DE LA CONCORDIA RIOJA – *Smooth Morello cherry fruit flavours are dotted with flecks of vanilla. Textured, juicy, and structured. Aromatic.*	£6.00 A&A/UWO
MONTE ARMANTES SHIRAZ GARNACHA 2003, SAN GREGORIO - NORREL ROBERTSON MW ARAGÓN – *A beautifully scented and inky nose and a big, sweet fruit palate. Good structure.*	£6.00 WAV
RESERVA CARINENA 2000, MARQUÉS DE BALLESTAR ARAGÓN – *Fabulous red berry flavours. Medium-bodied, mouthcoating, and peppery. Scents of smoke.*	£6.00 MWW
VEGA DEL RAYO VENDIMIA SELECCIONADA 2003, BODEGAS CARLOS SERRES RIOJA – *Fresh raspberries, spicy oak, leather, blackberries, leaves, cigars, pepper, coffee, and chocolate.*	£6.00 MDN
VIÑA LUR SELECCIÓN 2002, VIÑA PATERNA RIOJA – *Firm red cherry and sloe flavours. Balanced, firm, and smoothly-textured. Tobacco leaf tannins.*	£6.00 WSO
RIOJA CRIANZA TINTO 2003, MARQUÉS DE MUDELA RIOJA – *Buttressed by strong cedar bark tannins, the sun-warmed strawberry fruit is ripe, juicy, and sprinkled with vanilla beans.*	£6.10 MCT
SEÑORIO DE SARRIA VINEDO NO 9 2002, BODEGA DE SARRIA NAVARRE – *Blackcurrant and menthol nose. Silky palate of ripe fruit with good balance and length.*	£6.50 MDN/DEF
PAGOS DE TAHOLA 2003, BODEGAS LARCHAGO RIOJA – *A bowl of fresh berries doused in cream, with an earthy undertone. Likely to please the Rioja fan.*	£6.80 LAI
EXCELSUS 2002, BODEGAS VIÑA HERMINIA RIOJA – *Fresh redcurrants, asphalt, espresso, cigar smoke, and black cherries flavour this chocolatey, seductive wine.*	£7.00 ODD
GUIA REAL VENDIMIA SELECCIONADA RIOJA 2003, CARLOS SERRES RIOJA – *Fine, fresh red and black berry flavours are dotted with spice and leather. Medium-bodied, ripe, and bright.*	£7.00 MDN

PAPA LUNA 2004, SAN GREGORIO – NORREL ROBERTSON MW ARAGÓN – *An intense old-vine feel on the nose. The palate is mineral, savoury, and thickly tannic, and definitely needs some ageing.*	£7.00 WAV
RADCLIFFES RIOJA CRIANZA 2002, RADCLIFFES RIOJA – *Flavours of cherry compôte, bittersweet chocolate, and vanilla beans. Scents of flowers, undergrowth, and freshly made toast.*	£7.00 THS
INURRIETA SUR 2003, BODEGA INURRIETA NAVARRE – *A very petty blueberry, vanilla, and flower nose and palate with fine balance and attractive mineral notes.*	£7.20 EDC/ADN
RIOJA CRIANZA RESERVA 2000, MARQUÉS DE MUDELA RIOJA – *Heaps of black and red berries spill from the balanced, medium-bodied palate. Refreshing, toasty, focused, classic Rioja.*	£7.20 MCT
INURRIETA NORTE 2003, BODEGAS INURRIETA NAVARRE – *This wine has appealing stewed plum aromas and flavours. Ripe and ready for drinking this holiday season.*	£7.50 CEB
CAMPO VIEJO RESERVA 1999, BODEGAS JUAN ALCORTA RIOJA – *Berry aromas and firm tannic structure. Fine depth and complexity. Displays balance and maturity on the finish.*	£8.00 TOS/JSM NTD
CARTA DE ORO RESERVA 2001, BERBERANA RIOJA – *Cigar smoke, vanilla, fresh raspberries, and blueberries pour from the nose and palate of this balanced wine.*	£8.00 UWO/JSM
CASA DE COMENDADOR RESERVA 2000, LAGUNILLA RIOJA – *Pepper, chocolate, charcoal, and savoury red cherry flavours. Intense and deeply coloured, this wine is displaying signs of evolution.*	£8.00 UWO
VEGA DEL RAYO RESERVA 1998, BODEGAS CARLOS SERRES RIOJA – *Black cherries, espresso, and floral perfume. This mature wine is bright garnet red, medium-bodied, and softly textured.*	£8.00 MDN
SUMMA AARES RESERVA 1999, BODEGAS OLARRA RIOJA – *Deep, complex, and layered, with fresh black cherry flavours, tobacco, and pine needle aromas.*	£8.20 RAV

BERONIA RESERVA 2000, BODEGAS BERONIA Rioja – *Strawberries, blackberries, leather, flowers, and spices scent the nose. The palate has black cherry and tobacco flavours.*	**£8.30** GBL/WDI HAC
RESERVA DON JACOBO 1998, BODEGAS CORRAL Rioja – *Firm and structured. Bright blackberry juice flavours are underpinned by integrated tannins. Hints of spicebox.*	**£8.70** MCT
COTO DE IMAZ RESERVA 2000, EL COTO DE RIOJA Rioja – *Aromas of hot blackberry pie and vanilla ice cream. Berry compôte and ripe fruit flavours with oaky vanilla.*	**£9.80** ESL/EDC P&S/VLW
ALTOS DE INURRIETA 2001, BODEGA INURRIETA Navarre – *Mature and earthy, its richly fruited cherry and raspberry palate big, ripe, and toasty.*	**£10.00** MOR
CASTRAVIEJO RESERVA 1999, BODEGA PASTOR DIAZ Rioja – *Powerful, harmonious black cherry flavours intermingle with sweet toast and hints of tar on nose and palate.*	**£10.00** THI
MARQUÉS DE LA CONCORDIA RESERVA 1999, MARQUÉS DE LA CONCORDIA Rioja – *Full-bodied, bright, and packed with elegant, lifted scents of toast and flowers and flavours of ripe strawberries.*	**£10.00** UWO
MARQUÉS DE VITORIA ORIGINAL 2003, BODEGAS MARQUÉS DE VITORIA Rioja – *This fresh, flavourful Rioja has mouthwatering red stone fruit flavour, smooth texture, and fine cedary aromas.*	**£10.00** PLB
GARCIA BURGOS VENDIMIA SELECCIONADA 2003, BODEGAS GARCIA BURGOS Navarre – *Textured red stone fruit flavours. Mouthcoating and moreish. A wine to enjoy with meats and cheeses.*	**£10.20** HPF
LUIS CAÑAS RESERVA 1998, BODEGAS LUIS CAÑAS Rioja – *Round, stylish, evolved, and harmonious, this Rioja displays chocolate covered cherry and roast herbs.*	**£10.80** TNG/OCM CCS
BODEGAS PRIMICIA RESERVA 2001, BODEGAS PRIMICIA Rioja – *A mature wine with savoury notes, mocha raspberry, and black cherry with warm spice and leather flavours.*	**£11.20** LAI

RIOJA GRAN RESERVA 1978, MARQUÉS DE MUDELA **RIOJA** – *Very mature, with savoury grilled meat aromas and flavours of ripe strawberries and cigars. Silky, harmonious, and long.*	**£12.30** MCT
CAMPO VIEJO GRAN RESERVA 1998, BODEGAS JUAN ALCORTA **RIOJA** – *Smoky oak dominates nose and palate. Fresh mulberry and raspberry fruit sits alongside spicy wood.*	**£13.00** JSM/THS
VIÑA ARDANZA RIOJA RESERVA 1998, LA RIOJA ALTA **RIOJA** – *Blackberries, blueberries, anise, smoke, vanilla, and charcoal. A brooding wine, mature, integrated, and long.*	**£14.80** WIDELY AVAILABLE
COTO REAL RESERVA 2000, EL COTO DE RIOJA,S.A. **RIOJA** – *A well-balanced, pleasing marriage of French oak and a mature plummy palate. Some complexity and weight.*	**£15.00** YOB
EL MESON GRAN RESERVA 1995, BODEGAS EL MESON **RIOJA** – *Sweet vanilla pod scents lace the palate of cherries. Mature, integrated, and softly textured.*	**£15.00** SKW
FINCA MONASTARIO 2002, BARON DE LEY **RIOJA** – *Intense blackberries, smoke, and leather. On the palate, chewy tannins add structure to the ripe supple fruit flavours.*	**£15.50** CEB/FLY THS
FINCA VALPIEDRA RESERVA 1999, BODEGA FINCA VALPIEDRA **RIOJA** – *Deep pockets of plum and blueberry fruit. Accents of fennel, liquorice, and saddle leather. Toasty and long.*	**£16.00** LAI
RESERVA SELECCIÓN ESPECIAL 2000, BODEGAS MUGA **RIOJA** – *Sweet vanilla beans, coconut, fresh raspberries, graphite, and bitter chocolate on nose and palate.*	**£16.10** MWW/ICL WRW
MARQUÉS DE RISCAL GRAN RESERVA 1996, MARQUÉS DE RISCAL **RIOJA** – *At the peak of its maturity, this masterful wine has rich, layered cherry and roast nut characteristics.*	**£21.30** ESL/A&A MWW/P& S
AUTOR RESERVA ESPECIAL 1998, BODEGAS FAUSTINO **RIOJA** – *Complex, layered, and long. Cigar leaves, saddles, roast plums, dark chocolate, graphite, sweet vanilla, and undergrowth.*	**£21.50** HOF

| EL BELISARIO 2002, AGRICOLA LA BASTIDA Rioja – *Fresh undulating cherry and cream flavours underpinned by firm tea leaf tannins. Structured and long.* | £23.50 HPF |

SEAL OF APPROVAL
RIOJA + NORTH-CENTRAL RED

| ☆ DON DARIAS 1999, BODEGAS VICTORIANAS Rioja – *Toast, summer fruit flavours, and leafy notes.* | £3.60 TOS/PLB JSM |

SILVER
RIOJA + NORTH-CENTRAL ROSÉ

| ☆ BESTUÉ ROSADO 2004, BODEGAS OTTO BESTUÉ **Aragón** – *Fragrant raspberry fruit liberally sprinkled with spice and fennel. Soft summer fruit pudding flavours on the palate.* | £7.00 GRT |

BRONZE
RIOJA + NORTH-CENTRAL ROSÉ

| FORTIUS ROSADO SELECCIÓN CABERNET SAUVIGNON 2004, BODEGAS VALCARLOS **Navarre** – *An attack of fresh, dry strawberry fruit assails the senses. Very firm tannins sustain the finish.* | £6.00 TNG |

SILVER
RIBERA DEL DUERO + WEST WHITE

| MARTÍN CÓDAX ALBARIÑO 2004, BODEGAS MARTÍN CÓDAX **Galicia** – *Clean citrus fruit nose. Bursting with tropical fruit flavours. Refined, with a mid-weight body and a lingering finish.* | £8.00 ICL |
| ALBARIÑO VALMIÑOR 2004, ADEGAS VALMIÑOR **Galicia** – *Clean fresh pineapple aroma. Pronounced vanilla ice cream and grilled pineapple flavours. Classic Albariño.* | £11.40 FLA/ENO |

PAZO DE SEÑORANS ALBARIÑO 2004, PAZO DE SENORAÑS GALICIA – *A clean, fragrant nose with pretty elderflower notes, a mere hint of acidity and a gentle apple finish.*	**£11.50** WIDELY AVAILABLE

BRONZE
RIBERA DEL DUERO + WEST WHITE

MONTE ALINA 2004, ALVAREZ Y DIEZ CASTILLA Y LEÓN – *Aromatic elderflowers and grapefruit on the nose are matched with citrus acidity herbal white fruit flavours.*	**£6.50** TNG
MANTEL BLANCO SAUVIGNON BLANC 2004, ALVAREZ Y DIEZ CASTILLA Y LEÓN – *Fresh zingy gooseberry and peach fruit on the nose and palate. Just dry, and very attractive.*	**£7.00** TNG
MANTEL BLANCO VERDEJO SAUVIGNON BLANC 2004, ALVAREZ Y DIEZ CASTILLA Y LEÓN – *An aromatic nose with fresh, pure herbaceous aromas. The palate is mid-weight with crisp integrated fruit.*	**£7.00** TNG/FLY
ORIGIN VERDEJO 2004, BODEGAS VAL DE VID CASTILLA Y LEÓN – *Aromatic, grassy, and attractive, with a tart lemon note on the delicate palate offset by elderflower sweetness.*	**£7.00** THS
ERMITA VERACRUZ 2004, BODEGAS VERACRUZ CASTILLA Y LEÓN – *Predominantly herbaceous with zesty, zippy intensity on the nose and palate. Good crispness. A fine thirst-quencher.*	**£8.20** TNG/OCM NYW

TROPHY
RIBERA DEL DUERO + WEST RED

SELECCIÓN ESPECIAL 2001, ABADÍA RETUERTA CASTILLA Y LEÓN – *Complex blackberry, smoke, and spice aromas. The palate is rich and unctuous with lush black fruit and sweet oak.*	**£.00** NOT AVAILABLE IN THE UK
☆ PETALOS DEL BIERZO 2003, DESCENDIENTES DE J. PALACIOS CASTILLA Y LEÓN – *Scented with blackcurrants, toast, and flecks of vanilla. Delicious touches of mint leaves and rich earthy strawberry fruit.*	**£10.00** C&B

GOLD
RIBERA DEL DUERO + WEST RED

TEOFILO REYES 2001, BODEGAS REYES **Castilla y León** – *Aromas of leather, damson, and smoke. Layers of lush dark fruit, supple tannins, and finely judged oak.*	**£16.20** POR/L&S WRW/VLW
PAGO DE LOS CAPELLANES RESERVA 2001, PAGO DE LOS CAPELLANES **Castilla y León** – *Complex leathery wine with damson, blueberry, and allspice aromas. The palate shows intense fruit married to sweet oak.*	**£27.80** MDN/RSV FLA/ICL NYW

SILVER
RIBERA DEL DUERO + WEST RED

CILLAR DE SILOS CRIANZA 2002, CILLAR DE SILOS **Castilla y León** – *Tight-knit, young, and fresh, with firm structure. The medium-bodied raspberry fruit is sustained by very firm tannins.*	**£16.00** TNG
GRAN COLEGIATA CAMPUS 2001, BODEGAS FARIÑA **Castilla y León** – *Powerful meaty nose with strawberry notes and sweet new oak. Firm structure and concentrated fruit. Excellent length.*	**£16.00** DCT
DURIUS MAGISTER 2002, UNITED WINERIES **Castilla y León** – *Opaque, with mint, earth, and chocolate aromas and a palate of elegant, concentrated, soft, high-toned strawberry fruit.*	**£18.50** UWO/TOS

BRONZE
RIBERA DEL DUERO + WEST RED

1860 VINO DE LA TIERRA DE CASTILLA Y LEÓN TEMPRANILLO 2002, MARQUÉS DE RISCAL **Castilla y León** – *Bright, mouthwatering, and integrated, this Castilla y León beauty has fresh red berry flavours.*	**£6.00** MWW
VEGA DE CASTILLA 2003, SENORIO DE CASTILLA **Castilla y León** – *Crushed red cherry juice flavours. Bright, medium-bodied, and spicy. Integrated tannins.*	**£6.00** PLB

ALTOS DE TAMARON JOVEN 2003, BODEGAS PAGOS DEL REY CASTILLA Y LEÓN – *Currants with toasty vanilla oak. Rounded and well-balanced. Attractive hints of coconut and spice.*	**£6.20** JSM/THS
VIÑA ALBALI GRAN RESERVA 1998, FELIX SOLIS CASTILLA Y LEÓN – *Cocoa powder, vanilla pods, strawberries, and soot. This textured, evolved beauty is balanced and long.*	**£6.70** BGN/JSM THS
ALDIS TINTO 2003, VIÑA MAMBRILLA CASTILLA Y LEÓN – *Youthful fruity aromas. Strawberry and vanilla cream palate with velvety tannins that linger on the tongue.*	**£6.80** MCT
PINNA FIDELIS ROBLE 2003, BODEGA PINNA FIDELIS CASTILLA Y LEÓN – *Boot polish and strawberries mingle with plums and coconut. Ripe, full, and robust.*	**£7.00** THI
TORRES DE ANGUIX CRIANZA 2001, TORRES DE ANGUIX CASTILLA Y LEÓN – *Made from organically farmed grapes. Savoury red plum flavours are enhanced by a smooth, toasty texture. Evolving.*	**£7.50** PNW
FINCA SOBREÑO RESERVA 2000, BODEGAS SOBREÑO CASTILLA Y LEÓN – *Mature liquroice and leather aromas. The palate has lovely structure with bittersweet extraction and firm tannins.*	**£9.00** PLB
GRAN COLEGIATA FRENCH OAK CRIANZA 1999, BODEGAS FARIÑA CASTILLA Y LEÓN – *For its age this wine has exceptional flesh. Loads of sweet oak. Broad and opulent palate with powerful spice.*	**£9.00** DCT
BRIGANTIA, PRIETO PICUDO 2002, GALICIANO CASTILLA Y LEÓN – *Soft toasty oak and bramble jelly nose. A good acid backbone brings structure to ample, creamy, raspberry flavours.*	**£9.10** HPF
RIBERAL CRIANZA 2001, BODEGAS FRUTOS VILLAR CASTILLA Y LEÓN – *A clean firm nose with some age. Softness and charm with a sweet chocolate flavour on the finish.*	**£10.20** POR/L&S VLW
VALDUBÓN CRIANZA 2002, BODEGAS VALDUBÓN CASTILLA Y LEÓN – *A deep red, evolved, and meaty nose with good acidity, firm tannins, a medium body, and satisfying long finish.*	**£11.30** FLY

LEGARIS RESERVA 2000, LEGARIS CASTILLA Y LEÓN – *Bright summer fruit nose and palate. Grilled meat essence. Long finish.*	**£15.00** WIM
PARCELA EL PICON 1999, PAGO DE LOS CAPELLANES CASTILLA Y LEÓN – *Game, mulling spice, smoke, and raspberries scent and flavour this wine. Complex, balanced, and evolved.*	**£15.00** MDN
ASTER RESERVA 2001, LA RIOJA ALTA SA CASTILLA Y LEÓN – *An earthy, meaty wine with lots of extraction and a savoury character. This calls out for roast lamb.*	**£17.50** L&S/VLW
CILLAR DE SILOS TORRESILO 2001, CILLAR DE SILOS CASTILLA Y LEÓN – *Black cherry juice oozes from this polished wine. Mature, textured, and wrapped in cedary tannins.*	**£29.00** TNG
D'ANGUIX TORRES DE ANGUIX 2001, TORRES DE ANGUIX CASTILLA Y LEÓN – *Brooding blackberry fruit flavours. Cedary tannins. A sophisticated wine with power and finesse.*	**£30.00** PNW

SEAL OF APPROVAL
SOUTH + THE ISLANDS WHITE

☆ **ALTEZA VIURA 2004, VINIBERIA** CASTILLA-LA MANCHA – *Fresh straw scents mix with stone fruit flavours.*	**£4.00** EHL
☆ **SANTERRA DRY MUSCAT 2004, BODEGAS MURVIEDRO** VALENCIA – *Fresh orange and spice scents and flavours.*	**£4.00** MRN

SILVER
SOUTH + THE ISLANDS RED

★ **BERBERANA DRAGON 2003, UNITED WINERIES** CASTILLA-LA MANCHA – *Fresh wood, inviting cherry fruit, and a textured mouthfeel. Very ripe, with notes of earth and smoke for depth.*	**£4.10** BGN/UWO MWW/JSM

☆ **MARQUÉS DE ROJAS 2004, BODEGAS PIQUERAS** Castilla-La Mancha – *A clean, fresh, cheerful cherry fruit nose. Very good, ripe fruit on the palate with a spicy, peppery lift.*	£5.50 AVB
☆ **FINCA ANTIGUA MERLOT 2003, FINCA ANTIGUA** Castilla-La Mancha – *Lifted menthol and tobacco notes. The palate sings with camphor, plenty of toast, and rich, deep cassis.*	£6.30 JNW
DOMINIO DE MALPICA 2001, OSBORNE SELECCIÓN Castilla-La Mancha – *Dark brick-red, with a brilliant fresh mint nose. The youthful palate is packed with red and black currant fruit.*	£8.20 HAE
ALTOS DE LUZON MONASTRELL TEMPRANILLO CABERNET 2003, FINCA LUZON Murcia – *Cedar and blackberry fruit nose. The palate has vibrant berry fruits, concentrated flavours, and good tannic grip.*	£10.00 WST
CASTAÑO COLECCIÓN 2003, BODEGAS CASTAÑO Murcia – *Stewed fruit, spice, and rich mouthfilling blackberries and cedar. Long powerful finish. Needs more time to fully display its charms.*	£10.00 LIB

BRONZE
SOUTH + THE ISLANDS RED

☆ **SANTERRA MONASTRELL 2004, BODEGAS MURVIEDRO** Valencia – *A crisp and cheerful Monastrell with redcurrant and blackcurrant flavours. A well-made, lushy fruited wine.*	£4.50 BUC
☆ **LA PAZ TEMPRANILLO 2003, VINIBERIA** Castilla-La Mancha – *Black cherries, orange peel, leather, liquorice, and spicebox flavours and aromas spin from this full, flavourful wine.*	£5.00 JSM
☆ **MAD DOGS & ENGLISHMEN 2004, BODEGAS DE MURCIA** Murcia – *An easy-drinking wine with ripe young cherry flavours. Spicy flavours and firm tannins. Long finish.*	£5.00 GYW
☆ **MAXIMO SYRAH CABERNET 2003, BODEGAS MAXIMO** Castilla-La Mancha – *A sleek and approachable palate differentiates this Cabernet. The body is medium-full, well-balanced, and elegant.*	£5.00 SKW

ASH TREE SHIRAZ MONASTRELL 2001, FREIXENET CASTILLA-LA MANCHA – *Lovely deep, smoky, forest fruits on the nose. Smooth and inviting, well-aged wine.*	£5.30 BGN/BNK TOS
LA TRIGAL TEMPRANILLO OAK AGED 2003, VIÑOS Y BODEGAS CASTILLA-LA MANCHA – *Bright, ripe, and smoky. This red stone fruit and pomegranate flavoured wine is ideal for cassoulet.*	£5.40 LAI
FINCA RESERVA DE LA FAMILIA 2003, BODEGAS MUÑOZ CASTILLA-LA MANCHA – *Freshly picked blackberries with a touch of mint, round softness on the palate, and hints of savoury sausage.*	£6.70 LAI
CASA DEL VALLE HACIENDA 2002, CASA DEL VALLE CASTILLA-LA MANCHA – *Soft vanilla oak nose. The palate is ripe and round, with a long finish and insistent dusty tannins.*	£12.00 HOH
CLAVIS 2002, FINCA ANTIGUA CASTILLA-LA MANCHA – *Toasty, taut, and dark, with blackcurrant and damson fruit flavour and a long spicy finish.*	£45.00 BWC

SEAL OF APPROVAL
SOUTH + THE ISLANDS RED

☆ CO-OP TEMPRANILLO OAK AGED NV, FELIX SOLIS CASTILLA-LA MANCHA – *Round cherry flavours. Scents of vanilla.*	£3.70 CWS
☆ ALTEZA TEMPRANILLO 2004, VINIBERIA CASTILLA-LA MANCHA – *Cherry syrup, kirsch, and fresh toast aromas.*	£4.00 EHL
☆ VIÑA DECANA RESERVA 1999, COVINAS VALENCIA – *Cassis, cherries, and hints of undergrowth.*	£4.00 ALD

SEAL OF APPROVAL
SOUTH + THE ISLANDS ROSÉ

☆ VIÑA DECANA ROSADO 2004, COVINAS Valencia – *Fresh strawberry flavours mingle with herbal hints.*	£3.00 ALD

SEAL OF APPROVAL
SOUTH + THE ISLANDS SWEET

☆ ESTRELLA BLANCO DE MOSCATEL 2004, BODEGAS MURVIEDRO Valencia – *Fresh honey, tangerine, and rose elements.*	£3.50 MRN
☆ CASTILLO DE BETERA MOSCATEL 2003, CHERUBINO Valencia – *Scented and sweet. Fresh orange flavours.*	£4.00 PLB

TROPHY
SOUTH + THE ISLANDS FORTIFIED

★ MANZANILLA LA GITANA NV, BODEGAS HIDALGO LA GITANA Jerez – *A fresh nose of citrus and yeast. Light yet intense with refreshing acidity and a salty tang.*	£6.00 WPR/POR MWW/JNW JSM/VLW
MOSCATEL AMBROSIA NV, SANCHEZ ROMATE HERMANOS Andalucia – *Dark notes of prunes, raisins, clove, and treacle. Powerfully sweet candyfloss, tar, golden syrup, fruitcake, and molasses flavours.*	£10.00 EDV
LUSTAU EMPERATRIZ EUGENIA VERY RARE OLOROSO NV, EMILIO LUSTAU Andalucia – *Raisin, fig, and burnt orange aromas. The amber palate is balanced and unctuous with dried fruit intensity and good freshness.*	£18.00 FLY

GOLD
SOUTH + THE ISLANDS FORTIFIED

☆ **TIO PEPE NV, GONZALEZ BYASS** Andalucia – *Complex flor yeast aromas. Impeccably balanced with citrus fruit and rich yeast depth. Intense, long, and tangy.*	**£8.40** WIDELY AVAILABLE
☆ **LUSTAU SOLERA RESERVA RARE AMONTILLADO ESCUADRILLA NV, EMILIO LUSTAU** Andalucia – *Intense raisined fruit and impeccable structure. The finish shows real pedigree with excellent balance and persistence.*	**£9.00** LUS
☆ **LUSTAU ALMACENISTA MANZANILLA PASADA DE SANLUCAR JURADO NV, EMILIO LUSTAU** Andalucia – *A fresh nose of citrus, yeast, and sea salt. The palate is wonderfully clean with firm acidity.*	**£9.10** ESL/LUS RAV/FLY
☆ **LUSTAU SOLERA RESERVA PUERTO FINO NV, EMILIO LUSTAU** Andalucia – *Complex lemon, roast nut, and orchard blossom aromas. Wet earth, herbs, and flor with citrus and green apple flavours.*	**£9.10** WIDELY AVAILABLE
☆ **LUSTAU SOLERA RESERVA DON NUÑO NV, EMILIO LUSTAU** Andalucia – *Intense nose of milk chocolate, walnuts and toffee. The palate is packed with ultra-sweet, golden apples, minerals, and yeast.*	**£10.20** WIDELY AVAILABLE
☆ **LUSTAU ALMACENISTA MANZANILLA OLOROSO JURADO NV, EMILIO LUSTAU** Andalucia – *The nose is fresh and complex with notes of seaweed, salt, citrus, and yeast. The palate is intense with nutty depth.*	**£10.50** GON
☆ **LUSTAU ALMACENISTA AMONTILLADO DEL PUERTO OBREGON NV, EMILIO LUSTAU** Andalucia – *Complex aromas of figs, baked earth, and cinnamon spice. The palate is deeply smoky and nutty with great concentration.*	**£11.00** ESL/LUS FLY/HAC NYW
☆ **APOSTOLES NV, GONZALEZ BYASS** Andalucia – *Delicate and aristocratic, with caramel, toffee, and bruised apple aromas. A long, delicious palate of cashews and dried fruits.*	**£12.60** POR/JSM VLW
☆ **LUSTAU SOLERA RESERVA AMONTILLADO DON RAFAEL NV, EMILIO LUSTAU** Andalucia – *Intense fig, raisin, and nut aromas. The palate is perfectly balanced with concentrated dried fruits and fresh acidity.*	**£14.00** LUS

☆ LUSTAU AÑADA 1989 RICH OLOROSO 1989, EMILIO LUSTAU **A**NDALUCIA – *Rich notes of caramel, molasses, and orange peel. The palate is deep and complex with amazing balance and intensity.*	**£15.00** LUS

SILVER
SOUTH + THE ISLANDS FORTIFIED

★ WAITROSE SOLERA JEREZANA FINO DEL PUERTO SHERRY NV, WAITROSE **A**NDALUCIA – *Attractive notes of truffle and mushroom on a nose of intense toasted Brazil nuts, flor, and sultry apple fruit.*	**£5.30** WTS
☆ STICKY PUDDING WINE NV, BARBADILLO **A**NDALUCIA – *Pale chestnut brown. Sweet Granny Smith apple and soft plump raisin flavours. Fresh acidity. Elegant and balanced.*	**£6.60** JSM
☆ SOLERA 1847 NV, GONZALEZ BYASS **A**NDALUCIA – *Medium-sweet, with caramel, red apples, toffee, orange peel, and nuts. A soft acidic tang lifts palate.*	**£9.00** WTS
☆ AMONTILLADO NPU , SANCHEZ ROMATE HERMANOS **A**NDALUCIA – *NPU is obtained from Fino, and lacks the powerful influence of flor. Smoke and honey notes and mandarin oranges.*	**£9.50** POR
☆ LUSTAU ALMACENISTA MANZANILLA AMONTILLADO JURADO NV, EMILIO LUSTAU **A**NDALUCIA – *Nutty and light, with a seaside tang and brisk, invigorating acidity. The amber liquid is complex and full.*	**£9.50** LUS/FLY WRK/HAC GON/NYW
☆ ALMACENISTA OLOROSO DE JEREZ ZAMORANO NV, EMILIO LUSTAU **A**NDALUCIA – *Rich, inviting fig, pistachio, cocoa, and guava aromas. Long, complex, and absolutely thrilling.*	**£9.80** LUS/FLY GON/NYW
☆ SOLERA RESERVA MANZANILLA PAPIRUSA NV, EMILIO LUSTAU **A**NDALUCIA – *Pure, sophisticated, elegant, and light, this has a smoky edge, nutty notes, zesty acidity, and a fine finish.*	**£9.80** WIDELY AVAILABLE
☆ LUSTAU SOLERA RESERVA LOS ARCOS DRY AMONTILLADO NV, EMILIO LUSTAU **A**NDALUCIA – *A fresh attack of Sicilian lemons saturates the dry palate. Delicate yeast, flower, and nut overtones. Fresh and elegant.*	**£10.00** WIDELY AVAILABLE

☆ SOLERA RESERVA PALO CORTADO PENINSULA NV, EMILIO LUSTAU **ANDALUCIA** – *Complex, salty, and complex, with honey-drizzled hazelnuts and roast almonds on the long, light-bodied palate.*	£10.00
	LAI
LUSTAU SOLERA RESERVA CAPATAZ ANDRES NV, EMILIO LUSTAU **ANDALUCIA** – *Juicy tropical fruit complements the dense, mature palate of sweet roasted apple, and raisin flavour.*	£10.10
	LUS/CCS FLY/WRK WRW/DEF
AMONTILLADO DEL DUQUE NV, GONZALEZ BYASS **ANDALUCIA** – *Pronounced caramel and white chocolate aromas scent the nose. The palate is nutty, smooth, and delicately herbal.*	£12.60
	POR/JSM VLW
FERNANDO DE CASTILLA ANTIQUE AMONTILLADO NV, FERNANDO DE CASTILLA **ANDALUCIA** – *Cinder, toffee, and orange peel aromas. Nutty and spicy, with elegant burnt sugar and floral elements.*	£18.70
	V&C/MDN NYW
CUCO OLOROSO SECO SHERRY NV, BODEGAS BARBADILLO **ANDALUCIA** – *Pleasantly oxidative, with almond and sea breeze aromas. Crisp and nutty, with an inviting salt and vinegar crisps character.*	£20.00
	JEF

BRONZE
SOUTH + THE ISLANDS FORTIFIED

☆ GRAN CAPATAZ AMONTILLADO SHERRY NV, BODEGAS BARBADILLO **ANDALUCIA** – *Light amber. Delicate nuts, candied citrus, sweet toffee, and citrus fruit. Straddles the line between sweet and dry.*	£4.50
	MHV
☆ GRAN CAPATAZ FINO SHERRY NV, BODEGAS BARBADILLO **ANDALUCIA** – *Fresh and crisp. Delicate hints of bonfire smoke, white peach, orange peel, and lemon. Dry and woody.*	£4.50
	MHV
☆ CABRERA MANZANILLA NV, GONZALES BYASS **ANDALUCIA** – *Crisp lemons, a tang of sea air, and whiffs of chalky minerals delight the taster. Dry, nutty, and long.*	£4.70
	POR/WRK
☆ CABRERA MEDIUM DRY AMONTILLADO NV, GONZALEZ BYASS **ANDALUCIA** – *This is nutty, amber-hued Amontillado with clear acidity and fresh citrus flavours. Balanced, mouthwatering, and very well made.*	£4.70
	POR/WRK

☆ SOLERA JEREZANA DRY AMONTILLADO SHERRY NV, WAITROSE **ANDALUCIA** – *Pleasing roast cashew, toffee, and tangy lemon scents. The deep burnished gold palate is fresh and balanced.*	£6.50 WTS
☆ SOLERA JEREZANA PALO CORTADO SHERRY NV, WAITROSE **ANDALUCIA** – *Lifted, long, warm, and spicy, with vivid candied grapefruit, honey, nuts, and minerals on nose and palate.*	£6.50 WTS
☆ THE WINE SOCIETY'S AMONTILLADO MARIBEL NV, SANCHEZ ROMATE HERMANOS **ANDALUCIA** – *Caramel colour, with sweet pecan nuts, grilled lemons, hazelnuts, and honey aromas and flavours. Complex and delicious.*	£7.00 WSO
☆ FINO QUINTA NV, BODEGAS OSBORNE **ANDALUCIA** – *Fine walnuts and green apple fruit blend effortlessly with delicate floral scents. The palate is dry, long, and intense.*	£7.50 HBJ
LA INA NV, ALLIED DOMECQ **ANDALUCIA** – *Lemon rind and green apple flavours. Fresh acidity. Sprinkled with aromas of roast nuts.*	£8.60 ESL/JSM
SIERRA MORENA DORADO 2004, GOMEZ NEVADO **ANDALUCIA** – *Nutty and dry, this organically produced sherry has dry, tangy citrus, and flor flavour.*	£9.00 VER
SOLERA RESERVA FINO BALBAINA NV, EMILIO LUSTAU **ANDALUCIA** – *Fresh yet rich, with delicate roast hazelnut, chalk, aristocratic pear fruit, and deep flor notes. Very refined.*	£9.00 LUS
LA GITANA MANZANILLA NV, HIJOS DE RAINERA PEREZ MARIN **ANDALUCIA** – *Pale and bone dry, with roast nuts, fresh lemons, and flor. Why attempt to resist Joaquín Turina's gypsy girl?*	£9.10 TNI
ALMACENISTA AMONTILLADO DE JEREZ FLORIDO NV, EMILIO LUSTAU **ANDALUCIA** – *Toasted nuts, burnt sugar, and perfumed lemons. The palate has vivid acidity and a firm mineral backbone.*	£9.20 LUS/RAV FLY/NYW
ALMACENISTA FINO DEL PUERTO CUESTA NV, EMILIO LUSTAU **ANDALUCIA** – *Delicate, with a light lemon-yellow hue, citrus flavours, and a tang of sea air. Perfect chilled with olives and almonds.*	£9.50 LUS

SOLERA RESERVA RICH OLD OLOROSO NV, EMILIO LUSTAU Andalucia – *Deep molasses, honey, golden syrup, and roast lemon flavours and aromas. This is dense, exciting Oloroso.*	**£10.00** LUS
THE WINE SOCIETY'S EXHIBITION VIEJO OLOROSO DULCE NV, SANCHEZ ROMATE HERMANOS Andalucia – *Intensely complex. Layer upon layer of pecans, toffee, caramel and coffee swirl from the nose.*	**£10.00** WSO
ALMACENISTA PALO CORTADO VIDES NV, EMILIO LUSTAU Andalucia – *Ochre hue. Deep flavours of citrus, raisins, orange zest, and chalky minerals. Silky smooth and mouthcoating.*	**£11.00** ESL/LUS CCS/FLY GON/NYW
NOÉ NV, GONZALEZ BYASS Andalucia – *Not seduced by the toffee flavours and white chocolate aromas? You could always pour this nectar over ice cream.*	**£12.10** POR/TOS JSM/VLW
SOLERA RESERVA PEDRO XIMÉNEZ SAN EMILIO NV, EMILIO LUSTAU Andalucia – *Bittersweet chocolate, satsumas, apricots, and roast nuts fill the mouth and nose. Dry, with an impression of sweetness.*	**£12.10** WIDELY AVAILABLE
LUSTAU EAST INDIA NV, EMILIO LUSTAU Andalucia – *Lavish chewy caramel, toffee, espresso, roast nut, and lemon marmalade flavours. A backbone of fresh acidity supports the whole.*	**£12.50** WIDELY AVAILABLE
MATUSALEM NV, GONZALEZ BYASS Andalucia – *Chestnut reddish-brown. Deep aromas and flavours of fruitcake, orange rind, ripe figs, Medjool dates, and treacle.*	**£12.60** POR/JSM VLW
SOLERA RESERVA EMILIN NV, EMILIO LUSTAU Andalucia – *Fresh orange rind, tangerine, marmalade, and apricot. Richly sweet, tinged by fresh acidity, and finely balanced.*	**£12.60** CCS/LUS BEN/FLY NYW
LA CILLA PEDRO XIMÉNEZ SHERRY NV, BODEGAS BARBADILLO Andalucia – *Thick, dark and unctuously textured, with burnt caramel notes and walnut skin tannins. Delicious, luscious, and long.*	**£16.00** JEF
SAN RAFAEL OLOROSO DULCE SHERRY NV, BODEGAS BARBADILLO Andalucia – *Delicate yet rich, this Oloroso has chewy caramel, toffee, plump satsuma, and roast lemon flavours. Fine, fresh acidity.*	**£16.00** JEF

ANTIQUE PEDRO XIMÉNEZ NV, FERNANDO DE CASTILLA **A**NDALUCIA – *What could be richer? Plump raisin, Havana rum, melted chocolate, and yeast rise on nose and palate.*	£18.10 V&C/MDN ICL
MOSCATEL LAS CRUCES NV, EMILIO LUSTAU **A**NDALUCIA – *Aromas of honey, tangerines, ripe peach, and spicebox. Delicate yet rich, with fine mouthwatering acidity.*	£27.30 LUS/FLY NYW

SEAL OF APPROVAL
SOUTH + THE ISLANDS FORTIFIED

☆ SOMERFIELD AMONTILLADO SHERRY N/V, GONZALEZ BYASS **A**NDALUCIA – *Roast nuts and bruised apples.*	£4.00 SMF
☆ SOMERFIELD FINO SHERRY N/V, GONZALEZ BYASS **A**NDALUCIA – *Dry, nutty, and refreshing. Minerally.*	£4.50 SMF
☆ CABRERA FINE PALE CREAM NV, GONZALEZ BYASS **A**NDALUCIA – *White apples and white chocolate.*	£4.70 POR/WRK
☆ CABRERA FULL RICH CREAM NV, GONZALEZ BYASS **A**NDALUCIA – *Sweetly rich, nutty and long.*	£4.70 POR/WRK
☆ TESCO FINEST FINO SHERRY NV, TESCO **A**NDALUCIA – *Dry, crisp and fresh. Appley.*	£5.00 TOS
☆ TESCO FINEST MANZANILLA SHERRY NV, TESCO **A**NDALUCIA – *Crisp yellow apple and sea breeze character.*	£5.00 TOS
☆ TESCO FINEST OLOROSO SHERRY NV, TESCO **A**NDALUCIA – *Sweet chocolate and caramel flavours.*	£5.00 TOS

☆ WAITROSE AMONTILLADO SHERRY NV, WAITROSE	£5.00
ANDALUCIA – *Lemony. Yeast and nut scents.*	WTS

STOCKISTS

3DW	3D Wines	01205 820745
A&A	A&A Wines	01483 274666
ABY	Anthony Byrne Wine Agencies	01487 814 555
AD1	Allied Domecq Wine UK	020 8323 8196
ADE	Adel (UK) Ltd	0208 994 3960
ADN	Adnams Wine Merchants	01502 727222
AFI	Alfie Fiandaca Ltd	0208 752 1222
ALD	Aldi Stores Ltd	01827 710 871
ALL	Alliance Wines	01505 506060
ALZ	Allez Vins!	01926 811969
AMP	Amps Fine Wines	01832 273 502
ARF	Arrowfield Wines	01625 827 550
ASD	Asda Stores Ltd	0113 241 9172
AST	Astley Vineyards	01299 822907
ATC	Atlantico UK Ltd	020 8649 7444
ATM	Astrum Wine Cellars	020 8870 5252
AUC	The Australian Wine Club	020 8843 8450
AUS	Australian Wineries LLP	01780 755 810
AVB	Averys of Bristol	01275 811100
AVD	Australian Vineyards Direct Ltd	02072598520
AWO	Australian Wines OnLine	01772 422996
AWS	Albion Wine Shippers	0207 242 0873
BAB	Bablake Wines Ltd	02476 228272
BBL	Bat & Bottle Wine Merchants	0845 1084407
BBO	Barrels & Bottles	0114 255 6611
BBR	Berry Bros & Rudd	0870 900 4300
BBS	Barton Brownsdon & Sadler Ltd	01424 870565
BBV	Breaky Bottom Vineyard	01273 476 427

BCF	Bon Couer Fine Wine	0207 622 5244
BEN	Bennetts Fine Wines	01386 840392
BGL	Bottle Green Ltd	0113 205 4521
BGN	Budgens Stores Limited	020 8422 9511
BLC	Balance Wines Ltd	01225 335588
BLS	Balls Brothers of London	0207 739 1642
BNA	Bona Wines	01666 505911
BNK	Bottleneck (Broadstairs)	01843 861095
BRA	G. Bravo & Son Ltd	020 7836 4693
BRB	Brown Brothers (Europe) Ltd	01628 776446
BRF	Brown-Forman Wines International	020 7478 1300
BRZ	Barrel Booze Ltd	01582 457799
BTH	Booths Supermarkets	01772 251701
BUC	Buckingham Vintners International	01753 521336
BUK	Beams UK Ltd	01322 297 400
BWC	Berkmann Wine Cellars	0207 609 4711
BWL	Bibendum Wine Ltd	020 7449 4120
C&B	Corney & Barrow	0207 265 2400
C&D	C&D Wines Ltd	0208 778 1711
CAB	Cabot Cellars	01582 406 464
CAK	Castel UK	020 8879 3514
CAR	CA Rookes Wine Merchants & Shippers	01789 297777
CAX	Pernod Ricard UK Ltd	020 8538 4000
CBC	City Beverage Co Ltd	0207 729 2111
CCH	Champagne and Chateaux	020 7498 4488
CCS	Cooden Cellars	01323-649663
CEB	Croque-en-Bouche	01684 565612
CEL	The Cellar Door	01256 770397
CHN	Charles Hawkins	01572 823030
CMB	Colombier Vins Fins	01283 552 552

CNL	Connolly's	0121 236 9269
CNT	Constellation Wines	01372 473 000
COE	Coe of Ilford (Coe Vintners)	0208 551 4966
CON	Codorníu UK Ltd	01892 500 250
CPR	Capricorn Wines	0161 908 1360
CPW	Christopher Piper Wines Ltd	01404 814139
CRI	Chalié, Richards & Co Ltd	01403 250500
CST	County Stores (Somerset) Ltd	01823 272235
CTC	Cambridge Wine Warehouse	01954 719090
CTL	Continental Wine & Food Ltd	01484 538333
CVV	Camel Valley Vineyard	01208 77959
CWL	Charles Wells	01234 272766
CWS	Co-operative Group (CWS Ltd)	0161 834 1212
CYT	Concha y Toro	01865 338013
D&D	D&D Wines International Ltd	01565 650952
D&F	D & F Wine Shippers Ltd	0208 838 4399
DAR	d'Arenberg Wines	0207 449 4035
DBO	Boyar International Ltd	0207 537 3707
DBS	Denbies Wine Estate	01306 876616
DBY	D. Byrne & Co	01200 423152
DCT	Decanter Wines Limited	01372-376127
DDL	Dordogne Direct Limited	01285 750607
DEF	deFINE Food & Wine	01606 882 101
DGO	Diageo	020 7927 5200
DOU	Dourthe UK	0207 720 6611
DTE	Distell Europe Limited	020 8898 4158
E&J	Ernest & Julio Gallo Winery	01895 813444
ECA	Edward Cavendish & Sons Ltd	01293 874110
EDC	Edencroft	01270 629975
EHL	Ehrmanns Ltd	0207 418 1800

ELV	El Vino Company Ltd	0207 353 5384
ENG	English Wines Group Plc	01580 763033
ENO	Enotria Winecellars Ltd	0208 961 4411
EOR	Ellis of Richmond Ltd	0208 744 5550
ESL	Edward Sheldon Ltd	01608 661409
EUW	Eurowines	0208 747 2107
EWC	English Wine Centre	01323 870164
FCA	Fraser Crameri Assoc	01580 200 304
FDB	First Drinks Brands Ltd	02380 312000
FEE	Free Run Wines Ltd	01672 540 990
FEN	Fenwick Ltd	0191 232 5100
FHM	Fareham Wine Cellars	01329 822733
FLA	Flagship Wines	01727 841968
FLY	Flying Corkscrew	01442 412 311
FRW	Fraser Williamson Fine Wines	01580 200 304
FTH	Forth Wines Ltd	01577 866001
FUL	Fuller Smith & Turner	0208 996 2000
FWI	Fine Wines of Italy	01962 713 134
FWM	Fields Wine Merchants	0207 589 5753
FXT	Freixenet (DWS) Ltd	01344 758 500
G2W	Grape-2-Wine	01531 660599
GAL	Galtres Fine Wines Ltd	01904 763333
GBA	Georges Barbier of London	0208 852 5801
GON	Gauntleys of Nottingham	0115 911 0555
GRT	Great Western Wine Company Ltd	01225 322800
GSL	Gerrard Seel Ltd	01925 819695
GYW	Guy Anderson Wines	01935 817 617
H&H	H&H Bancroft	0870 444 1700
HAC	Hailsham Cellars	01323 441212
HAE	Halewood International Ltd	0151 481 5697

HAM	Hamer Wine	020 8549 9119
HAR	Harrods Wine Shop	0207 225 5662
HBJ	Hayman, Barwell Jones Ltd	01473 232322
HBY	Hall & Bramley	0151 525 8283
HDS	Hedley Wright Wine Merchants	01279 465 818
HGT	Harrogate Fine Wine Company	01423 522 270
HMA	Hatch Mansfield Agencies Ltd	01344 871 800
HOE	Herbie of Edinburgh	0131 332 9858
HOF	House of Fraser	020 7963 2000
HOH	Hallgarten Wines Ltd	01582 722538
HOT	House of Townend	01482 326891
HPF	Hispanic Fine Wines	0207 7202400
HPW	Hop Pocket Wine Co	01531 640592
HTW	H T White and Company Ltd	01323 720161
HVN	Harvey Nichols	0207 235 5000
HWL	HWCG Wine Growers	01279 873500
ICL	Italian Continental Stores Ltd	01628 770110
J&B	Justerini & Brooks	0207 208 2507
JAR	John Armit Wines	020 7908 0600
JBF	Julian Baker Fine Wines	01206 262 358
JEF	John E Fells & Sons	01442 870900
JNV	Jackson Nugent Vintners	020 8947 9722
JNW	James Nicholson Wine Merchant	02844 830091
JSM	Sainsbury Supermarkets Ltd	0207 695 6000
KJW	Kendall Jackson Europe Ltd	0208 747 2840
KWI	Kwik Save Stores Ltd	01745 887111
L&S	Laymont & Shaw Ltd	01872 270 545
L&T	Lane & Tatham	01380 720123
LAI	Laithwaites	0118 903 0903
LAY	Laytons Wine Merchant Ltd	0207 288 8888

LCC	Landmark Cash & Carry	01908 255 300
LEA	Lea & Sandeman	0207 244 0522
LIB	Liberty Wines	0207 720 5350
LOL	Louis Latour Ltd	0207 409 7276
LUS	Emilio Lustau Almacenista Club	01225 833 330
M&M	Italian Wine Service	01235 813815
M&S	Marks & Spencer Plc	020 7268 3825
MAC	Makro UK	0161 786 2256
MCD	Marne & Champagne Ltd	020 7499 0070
MCT	Matthew Clark	01275 891400
MDN	Meridian Wines	0161 908 1300
MHU	Moët Hennessy UK Ltd	0207 235 9411
MHV	Booker Cash & Carry	01933 371363
MKV	McKinley Vintners	0207 928 7300
MON	Mondial Wine Ltd	020 8335 3455
MOR	Moreno Wine Importers	020 8960 7161
MRN	Morrison Supermarkets	01924 875234
MSW	Midland Wine and Spirits Ltd	01159 580 533
MTC	Manningtree Wine Cellar	01206 395095
MWW	Majestic Wine Warehouses Ltd	01923 298200
MYL	Myliko International (Wines) Ltd	0161 736 9500
MZC	Mentzendorff & Co Ltd	0207 840 3600
NDJ	ND John Wine Merchants	01792 363284
NEC	Nectarous Wines	01242 224466
NFW	Nidderdale Fine Wines	01423 711703
NTD	Nisa Today's	01724 282 028
NTT	Netto	0845 600 0200
NYW	Noel Young Wines	01223 566 744
NZH	The New Zealand House of Wine	01428 648 930
OCM	The Original Wine Company	0115 9654261

ODD	Oddbins	0208 944 4400
ORB	Orbital Wines Ltd	020 7802 5415
OWA	Orca Wine Agencies	08700 500 593
OWL	OW Loeb & Co Ltd	0207 234 0385
OZW	Oz Wines	0845 450 1261
P&S	Philglas & Swiggot	0207 924 4494
PAN	Palandri Wines (Europe) Ltd	0208 878 1459
PAT	Patriarche Père et Fils Ltd	0207 381 4016
PBA	Paul Boutinot Agencies Ltd	0161 908 1370
PFC	Percy Fox & Co	01279.756200
PIM	Pimlico Dozen	0207 834 3647
PLB	PLB Wines	01342 318282
PLE	Peter Lehmann Wines (Europe) Ltd	01227 731353
PNW	Peninsular Wines Ltd	01872 273978
POR	Portland Wine Company (Manchester)	0161 928 0357
PPW	Portugalia Wines	020 8997 4400
PRG	Paragon Vintners Ltd	0207 887 1800
PTN	Thomas Panton Wine Merchants Ltd	01666 503088
RAV	Ravensbourne Wine	020 8692 9655
RBC	Richard Banks & Co	01225 310 125
RDS	Reid Wines	01761 452645
REY	Raymond Reynolds Ltd	01663 742 230
ROD	Rodney Densem Wines Ltd	01270 212200
ROG	Roger Harris Wines	01603 880171
RSN	Richard Speirs Wines	01483 537605
RSS	Raisin Social Ltd	0208 686 8500
RSV	Reserve	0161 438 0101
RUK	Ruinart UK Ltd	0207 416 0592
RVE	Ridgeview Wine Estate	01444 258039
RWA	Richmond Wine Agencies	01892 668552

RWD	Richards Walford	01780 460 451
RWM	Roberson Wine Merchants	0207 371 2121
SAF	Safeway Stores Plc	020 8848 8744
SAO	SA Wines Online	0845 456 2365
SCK	Seckford Wines Ltd	01206 231 254
SEL	Selfridges Ltd	020 7318 3730
SFW	Strathardle Fine Wines	01389 830643
SGL	Stevens Garnier Ltd	01865 263300
SHR	Sharpham Partnership Ltd	01803 732203
SKB	Shakab Ltd	020 7431 8716
SKW	Stokes Fine Wines Ltd	0208 944 5979
SMC	Sommeliers Choice Ltd	020 8689 9643
SMF	Somerfield Stores Ltd	0117 935 9359
SOH	Soho Wine Supply	020 7636 8490
SOM	Sommelier Wine Co	01481 721677
SPR	Spar (UK) Ltd	0208 426 3700
STG	Tony Stebbings	01372 468571
STH	Stephar (UK) Ltd	01493 650069
SWG	SWIG	08000 272 272
SWP	Southcorp Wines Pty Ltd	0208 917 4600
SWS	Stratford's Wine Agencies	01628 810606
TAN	Tanners Wines Ltd	01743 234500
TCW	T C Wines	0151 931 3390
TGP	The Wine Group Ltd	012484 774777
THI	Thierry's Wine Services	01794 507100
THS	Thresher	01707 387 200
TNG	The Naked Grape	0845 226 2550
TNI	The Nobody Inn	01647 252394
TOS	Tesco Stores Ltd	01992 632222
TPE	Terry Platt Wine Merchant Ltd	01492 874 099

TRO	Trout Wines	01264 781472
TSS	Tate-Smith Ltd	01653 693 196
TWK	The Wine Keller Ltd	01628 620 143
TWL	Try Wines Limited	01635 529136
TWM	The Wineman Ltd	01635 203 050
TYR	Tyrrell's Vineyards	01252 812116
UNS	Unwins Wine Group	01322 272711
UWO	United Wineries UK Office	020 7393 2829
V&C	Valvona & Crolla	0131 556 6066
VDO	Val D'Orbieu Wines Ltd	0207 736 3350
VER	Vinceremos Wines	0113 244 0002
VGN	Virgin Wines Online Ltd	0870 164 9593
VIN	Vinum	0208 847 4699
VKB	Vickbar Limited	020 7490 1000
VLW	Villeneuve Wines	01721 722500
VNO	Vinoceros (UK) Ltd	01209 314 711
VRS	Veritaus & Co Ltd	0870 770 4112
VRT	Vintage Roots	0118 976 1999
VTS	Vinites UK	0207 924 4974
WAV	Waverley Group	01738 472 000
WAW	Waterloo Wine Co	0207 403 7967
WBN	Wine Barn Ltd	01962 774102
WDI	Wine Direct Ltd	08450 661122
WDS	Wine Discoveries	01435 883728
WEP	Welshpool Wine Company	01938 553243
WFB	Beringer Blass Wine Estates Ltd	0208 843 8411
WIM	Wimbledon Wine Cellars	020 8540 9979
WOC	Whitesides of Clitheroe	01200 422 281
WOW	Wines of Westhorpe	01709 584 863
WPR	Wine Press	01228 515646

WRI	Wrightson and Company	01325 374134
WRK	Wine Raks	01224 311460
WRT	Winerite Ltd	0113 283 7649
WRW	The Wright Wine Company	01756 700886
WSG	Siegel Wine Agencies Ltd	01256 701101
WSO	The Wine Society Ltd	01438 741177
WST	Western Wines Ltd	01952 235 700
WTS	Waitrose	0800 188 884
WWT	Whitebridge Wines	01785 817 229
WXC	Winery Exchange	01722 417 409
WZD	Winez Ltd	020 7841 6500
YOB	Cockburn & Campbell	0208 875 7007

ACKNOWLEDGEMENTS

The production of a guide like this within the few months that separate the International Wine Challenge tastings and publication in time for Christmas is inevitably a team effort. I would like to give special thanks to a number of people without whom this book would not exist.

First, there is the team led by Chris Ashton, Ashika Cobham, and Will Fuller who, with the help of Julie Campbell, brilliantly handled the terrifying logistics involved in running the International Wine Challenge. Next, there are the 410 top tasters, headed by my co-chairmen Charles Metcalfe and Derek Smedley MW, who not only decided the awards, but also penned the thousands of tasting notes from which the descriptions in this book were culled. Then there were the scribes – Richard Ross and Mary Willmann who did that culling, and Hilary Lumsden and Juanne Branquinho at Mitchell Beazley who turned it all into a book. Finally, there was the crucial input of the team at Wine International – Catharine Lowe, Tina Gellie, Sam Caporn, Dawn Cran, Anne Smith, Jane Parkinson, Tony Loynes, and Colin Bailey-Wood.

WINE ONLINE

robertjoseph-onwine.com. If this Guide has whetted your appetite for more information on wine, you will find plenty on offer at robertjoseph-onwine.com, includng a free interactive wine school where you can develop your vinous skills, links to, and recommendations of, wine producers, merchants, restaurants, and bars; and an online forum where you can exchange opinions with likeminded wine drinkers.

wineint.com. For more information about the International Wine Challenge, regular news, feature, competitions, events and recommendations, visit wineint.com, *Wine International* magazine's dedicated website.